D1082625

Irish Women Dramatists

Irish Studies

James MacKillop, *Series Editor*

Irish Women
Dramatists
1908–2001

ဆု ရွ

Edited by

Eileen Kearney and Charlotte Headrick,

with Kathleen Quinn contributing to the Introduction

Syracuse University Press

First Edition 2014
14 15 16 17 18 19   6 5 4 3 2 1

∞ The paper used in this publication meets the minimum requirements of the
American National Standard for Information Sciences—Permanence of Paper for
Printed Library Materials, ANSI Z39.48-1992.

For a listing of books published and distributed by Syracuse University Press,
visit www.SyracuseUniversityPress.syr.edu.

ISBN: 978-0-8156-3375-4 (paper)   978-0-8156-5292-2 (e-book)

Library of Congress Cataloging-in-Publication Data
Irish women dramatists : 1908–2001 / co-edited by Eileen Kearney and Charlotte
Headrick, with Kathleen Quinn contributing to the introduction. — First edition.
     pages cm. — (Irish studies)
     ISBN 978-0-8156-3375-4 (pbk. : alk. paper) — ISBN 978-0-8156-5292-2 (ebook) 1. English
drama—Irish authors.   2. English drama—Women authors.   3. Ireland—In literature.
I. Kearney, Eileen, editor.   II. Headrick, Charlotte J., editor.
     PR8865.7.W65I75 2014
     822'.909928709415—dc23   2014030675

Manufactured in the United States of America

To my venerable, inspiring teachers, Rosalind Picôt, R.S.M., and Professors Warren J. MacIsaac, George Wickes, and Grant McKernie, who taught me fiercely how to learn.
Eileen Kearney

In memory of Professor Richard Marius, who inspired me to love history, to Professor Thomas Cooke, who taught me so much about good directing, and to my family, Nancy, Bailey, and Fletcher Burkhardt.
Charlotte Headrick

And to all of our emigrant Irish ancestors, who made that long night's journey into day.

Contents

Acknowledgments

஭ This book is the result of years of musing, research, and interviews with many generous, cooperative, and patient Irish playwrights, poets, directors, artists, and academics. They have become our treasured Irish friends, and we look forward to buying drinks for all of them "someday in Fiddler's Green."

First and foremost, we are indebted to Dr. Kathleen Quinn, who began discussions with Eileen Kearney and who contributed immeasurably to the early stages of this book; without her extensive knowledge, research, writing, and curiosity, *Irish Women Dramatists* would not have been born.

We are appreciative of the enthusiastic support and trust of the editorial staff at Syracuse University Press, especially Glenn Wright, Annelise Finegan, Kay Steinmetz, and Jennika Baines. We are particularly grateful to our persistent, encouraging mentor, Jim MacKillop, who has had faith in this project since its beginning. *Go raibh maith agat*!

Our debt to the American Conference for Irish Studies, especially members of the Western region, cannot be measured. This wonderful international group of Irish Studies academics continues to feed our souls and encourage scholarly research.

We thank three faculty members of University College Dublin: Professor Anthony Roche for his generous guidance through the years, Professor Christopher Murray for his aid and expertise, and Cathy Leeney, whose *Seen and Heard: Six New Plays by Irish Women* (2001) began what we hope will become a tradition: the published acknowledgment of Irish women playwrights.

For financial support, Eileen Kearney is grateful to the Center for the Study of Women in Society at the University of Oregon and to Pomona College, Claremont, California, for its early support of this project while she was on its faculty. Charlotte Headrick thanks the Oregon State University Center for Humanities, as well as the Oregon State University Theatre, where she continues to teach and direct.

We honor the memory of poet Sean Dunne, who opened doors for Eileen Kearney's research in Ireland; Jack Deevy, for generously allowing access to Teresa Deevy's papers; and Professor Bill Potts, our beloved American Conference for Irish Studies colleague and muse.

We extend our thanks to Emily Janoch, a former Peace Corps volunteer now with CARE International, for her help in the Xhosa translation and to Jacqueline Deevy for her generosity with the Deevy estate.

Eileen Kearney would like to thank her family and friends, whose support has spanned the long life of this volume: her generous husband, Dan Koetting; her parents, Mary Rowan Kearney and John Gordon Kearney; her siblings, Helen, Lori, Joni, Neal, Tim, Nora, Kevin, and Chris; Annora Kelledy Koetting; and her friends Judy Murphy, Cynthia Splatt, Ed Siegler, Drs. Lyla and Mike Houglum, Mary Bettencourt, Linda Lu, Dr. Stephanie Jenal, Linda Van Doren, Martha Heppard, MD, and Peter Eberhardt.

Charlotte Headrick extends special thanks to Dr. Helen Lojek, Dr. Audrey Eyler, and Dr. Claudia Harris.

This book would certainly not be possible without the impeccably detailed copyediting of Mary Petrusewicz and the quiet generosity of our editorial angels, Brwyn Downing and Olivia Lewis. We thank them all for their incomparable assistance; their "silent voices" have brought this book to fruition.

Last, but certainly not least, we are forever grateful to the pioneering Irish women playwrights Lady Augusta Gregory, Teresa Deevy, Anne Le Marquand Hartigan, Dolores Walshe, Patricia Burke Brogan, Jennifer Johnston, and Nicola McCartney, whose work appears in this anthology. There are so many more whose plays could not be included here, but we highly encourage the publication of subsequent anthologies. The time has come.

Credits and Performance Rights

Eclipsed by Patricia Burke Brogan was previously published by WordsontheStreet Publishing (Galway, Ireland, 2008) and is reproduced with permission.

The plays reprinted in this book may be subject to a royalty for professional, amateur, and educational use. Performance rights for all material protected under copyright law may be obtained from the following:

The King of Spain's Daughter by Teresa Deevy: Ms. Jacqueline Deevy, 12 Rockmount Grove, Rockmount, Kilrush Rd, Ennis, Co. Clare, EIRE, Republic of Ireland.

Eclipsed by Patricia Burke Brogan: Patricia Burke Brogan, "Inisfail," 42 College Road, Galway City, Galway, Republic of Ireland.

Twinkletoes by Jennifer Johnston: David Higham Associates Ltd., 5-8 Lower John Street, Golden Square, London W1R 4HA, England. dha@davidhigham.co.uk.

I Do Like to Be Beside the Seaside by Anne LeMarquand Hartigan: Anne LeMarquand Hartigan, 17 Northbrook Road, Ranelagh, Dublin 6, Ireland.

Heritage by Nicola McCartney: United Agents, 12-26 Lexington Street, London W1F 0LE, United Kingdom.

The Stranded Hours Between by Dolores Walsh: Caroline de Wolfe at Felix de Wolfe in London. caroline@felixdewolfe.com.

IRISH WOMEN DRAMATISTS

Introduction

Occupied Country

Listen:

We are speaking your language
We are wearing your names
Fathers   husbands
We are living your laws
We are your subjects?
Just listen

Our voices are lighter
Must we speak louder
Must we shout?
Our tongues have been tied
Cleft to our palate
Have been cut out
Listen

We are learning our language
Foreign to our ears
We are sounding out
We are on an adventure
There is no turning back
Listen

We have begun to speak
Slipping out of our skins

> We change colours　don't
> Turn away　Look
> Open your eyes it is not
> So dangerous.
>
> You love us like the Church
> Or a zoo animal
> In captivity . . .
> 　　　—Anne Le Marquand Hartigan,
> 　　　　excerpt from unpublished poem

๛ Women have always spoken within domestic spheres. Their voices have nurtured children, preserved culture, and encouraged families. And women have even spoken in more public voices: in fiction and in poetry. But now women are weaving their tales under the stage lights, the most public artistic and literary arena of all. They are learning their own dramatic language; with newfound voices, they are saying, "Listen to us; look at our view of life." This anthology provides a forum for those voices, for that perspective.

As a public and outward act, drama demands interaction among the play, players, and audience; it is inherently an act of socialization. Its ritualistic form requires relevancy to human experience, thus encouraging a communal response to life. Other art forms may portray our outer realities, but drama preeminently shows our struggle to relate to the world around us. As Northrop Frye reminds us, Ireland, with its culture still rooted in the past, is one of the few places an art form as communal as drama is still possible.

Since drama is communal, it is curious that women dramatists have been largely ignored. Such neglect is a loss to performers and other theatre practitioners, to audiences, and to students of the drama, for, as Hélène Cixous articulates, the voice of woman differs from that of man: "Her language does not contain, it carries; it does not hold back, it makes possible."[1] In her introduction to *Making a Spectacle*, Lynda Hart suggests one reason for this omission: "As a form, the drama is more public and social than the other literary arts. The woman playwright's voice reaches a community of spectators in a highly public place that has historically been regarded as a highly subversive, politicized environment. The theatre is the sphere most removed from domesticity, thus the woman who ventures to be heard in this space takes a greater risk than the woman poet or novelist, but it may also offer her greater potential for effecting social change."[2]

Hart's emphasis on the social impact of drama helps us understand one reason women have been marginalized in the theatre. Another reason is economic: converting a script to a dramatic production involves paying for a theatre, performers, a director, sets, lighting, and marketing. Generally, women lack the necessary financial resources. (Many male playwrights do too, of course, but financial backers have traditionally been more willing to take the risk of backing plays written by men.)

Both these reasons—the political power of drama and the financial resources necessary to stage a production—solidify what we have discovered. As Katie Donovan notes, there are more women playwrights now than ever, but they are still ignored by mainstream theatres: "It seems that there is still a fair way to go for women playwrights, whose fiction-writing sisters have long since caught up with their male peers."[3]

"Languaged people," says a character in Lady Gregory's *The Wrens*, "can turn history to their own hand."[4] Yet unless this history is understood, its mistakes will continue. Let us begin, then, by exploring drama in Ireland—mainstream drama as well as the drama on the fringe, where most women playwrights have dwelled.

Background

Unlike most Western cultures, Ireland did not have a native dramatic tradition. Douglas Hyde believed that the development of the romance was a substitute for drama and that the Ossianic poems might have been originally performed rather than merely acted, but Ireland's rich oral tradition probably fulfilled its need for drama. And since Ireland was rural rather than urban, an indigenous drama never developed.

Drama actually began in Ireland with the coming of the Normans. When drama did arrive, it was meant for the ruling class, the Ascendancy. It is certain that the native population had little or no part in the miracle or morality plays that were staged in Dublin and traveled to other towns in medieval times. Writing of the medieval theatre in Dublin, Christopher Fitz-Simon reports, "When vernacular dialogue was introduced into Irish theatrical performances, it was in English, which the vast proportion of the population outside Dublin would have been unable to understand. This underlies the completely foreign nature of the theatre at this period."[5] During the great flowering of Elizabethan drama, the Irish were fighting for their lives outside the Pale. After the first theatre was opened in Dublin in 1637, theatre remained for nearly two centuries within the control of a resident ruling class.[6]

From the Ascendancy, however, "came the long line of dramatists which gave to the world Irish dramatists rather than Irish drama."[7] These prolific playwrights included William Congreve, George Farquhar, Richard Steele, Oliver Goldsmith, Richard Brinsley Sheridan, Dion Boucicault, Oscar Wilde, George Bernard Shaw, and Samuel Beckett—an impressive list by any standard.

Irish Literary Revival

Previous scholars have thoroughly covered the beginnings of the Irish Literary Theatre and, subsequently, the Abbey Theatre, so it will only be briefly discussed here. After the historic 1897 meeting of W. B. Yeats, Lady Gregory, and Edward Martyn, the Irish Literary Theatre was born. In *Our Irish Theatre*, Lady Gregory recounts their plan: "We propose to have performed in Dublin, in the spring of every year certain Celtic and Irish plays, which whatever be their degree of excellence will be written with a high ambition, and so to build up a Celtic and Irish school of dramatic literature. . . . We will show that Ireland is not the home of buffoonery and of easy sentiment, but the home of an ancient idealism."[8]

The founders of this group wanted to give a dramatic voice to Ireland. As Yeats wrote in *Beltaine*, they would "attempt to do in Dublin something of what has been done in London and Paris. . . . [Its] writers will appeal to that limited public which gives understanding, and not to that unlimited public which gives wealth."[9] The short-lived Irish Literary Theatre (1899–1901) laid the foundation for a national theatre with its plays: Yeats's *The Countess Cathleen*, Martyn's *The Heather Field* and *Maeve*, Alice

Milligan's *The Last Feast of the Fianna*, George Moore and Martyn's *The Bending of the Bough*, Moore and Yeats's *Diarmuid and Grania*, and Douglas Hyde's *Casadh an tSugáin* (*The Twisting of the Rope*). In all but Hyde's play, the performers were English and the directing was poor, but many positive traits emerged. For one thing, this experiment promoted Irish themes on stage: Milligan's play (the first "Celtic Twilight" drama) and Hyde's (the first professionally produced Irish-language drama) opened doors previously closed. And, of course, these plays, along with Yeats's poetic gifts and Gregory's talents and dedication, furnished the impetus for a national theatre.

The Fay brothers, W. G. and Frank J., who had formed a company of Irish actors, also provided an impetus. In 1902, their Irish National Dramatic Society produced A. E.'s *Deirdre* and two plays written by Yeats and Lady Gregory: *Cathleen ni Houlihan* and *The Pot of Broth*. The Fays occasionally collaborated with the nationalist women's organization, Inginidhe na hÉireann (Daughters of Erin), a group that presented, on its own, such plays as Milligan's *The Harp That Once* (1901) and Hyde's *An Naomh ar Iarraid* (1903). In 1903, the Fays joined Yeats to establish the Irish National Theatre Society, with Yeats as president. That year saw Lady Gregory's *Twenty-Five* and J. M. Synge's first play, *In the Shadow of the Glen*.

Although plays by Synge, Yeats, and Gregory dominated the theatre in Dublin in the early years of the century, other fine new playwrights—James Cousins, Padraic Colum, Seumas MacManus, and Lennox Robinson, to name a few—emerged. In 1904, when Annie Horniman, an Englishwoman, presented the National Theatre Society with its own building, soon known as the Abbey Theatre, their permanence was secured. Not surprising, perhaps, is the stimulus this dramatic society gave to both professional and amateur groups. In 1902, Bulmer Hobson and Lewis Purcell (David Parkhill) founded the Ulster Literary Theatre, in 1908 the Cork Dramatic Society was born, and in 1914 the Irish Theatre appeared. Many plays also emerged from the numerous amateur groups that flourished during this period. For instance, the Kilkenny Dramatic Club produced Milligan's *The Daughters of Donagh* (1904); the National Players, Miss L. McManus's *O'Donnell's Cross* (1907); the Independent Theatre Company, Eva Gore-Booth's *Unseen Kings* (1912); the Countess of Roden's Company,

Mary Costello's *A Bad Quarter of an Hour* (1913); the Little Theatre, Dorothy Macardle's *Asthara* (1918); and Ira Allen's Company, Sheila Walsh's *The Mother* (1918). These amateur groups presented dramas by both men and women, but then, as now, most plays written by women did not appear in the mainstream theatre. Although some plays written by women were produced in major theatres—Dorothy Macardle's *Ann Kavanagh* (1922), for one—generally the voices of women playwrights were not heard.

Lady Gregory was, of course, the exception. Although she was already fifty when her first play was produced, she wrote over thirty-five more plays, not counting her translations and adaptations. Aside from her prolific writing, she was a collector of folklore, director of the Abbey, and vociferous supporter of many young writers, including Sean O'Casey and Synge, whose unfinished *Deirdre of the Sorrows* she helped complete after his death.

Certainly John Millington Synge deserves special attention in any study of Irish drama. Like Lady Gregory, he developed his own dialect, one filled with the poetry of the earth. Like Yeats, he used a mythic basis for several plays, but Synge's myth transcended the medieval sagas, as in the rhythmic power of *Riders to the Sea*. His dramatic voice was neither male nor female; the country occupied by his imagination was universal.

Sean O'Casey, another great playwright to emerge during this period, has often been credited—particularly in terms of his Dublin trilogy—for advocating the causes of women and other victims of social injustice. In his plays, he certainly exhibits great sympathy for his female characters, but even Juno, O'Casey's strongest woman character, reacts rather than acts. Her forceful words belie her powerlessness. Such a portrayal, however, may be descriptive rather than proscriptive.

Several types of plays emerged during the years of the Revival: heroic, poetic, peasant, and realistic. Each worked to break from the stereotypical buffoon of the stage Irishman, and the dramatic movement succeeded in destroying this clichéd character. From the poetic power of Yeats's Cuchulain cycle to the sheer romp through Lady Gregory's comedies, a wide range of plays—and characters—appeared. Although none of Synge's successors in depicting peasant life matched his poetic language, many realistically portrayed rural Ireland; Padraic Colum, George Fitzmaurice, and Thomas C. Murray each wrote powerful peasant plays.

Alongside these plays, a nationalist drama flourished. Yeats's *Cathleen ni Houlihan* had such an impact on the audience that, years later, he wondered if it had caused the 1916 Rising, a rebellion that has been described as "a movement led by myth-possessed men who willingly perish into images."[10] Many of these "myth-possessed" men and women wrote plays. Thomas MacDonagh, executed in 1916, describes a rebellion of the future in *When the Dawn Is Come* (1908). Terence MacSwiney, who died on a hunger strike in 1920, shows rebels as carrying on a noble tradition that reaches back to the time of Fionn mac Cumhail in *The Last Warriors of Coole* (1910). Padraic Pearse, executed in 1916, demonstrates how much a single rebel can accomplish in *The Singer* (1915). Constance Markievicz, whose 1916 death sentence was commuted, stresses the importance of fidelity to the nationalist cause in *The Invincible Mother* (1925).

Although generalizations seldom work, one cannot help but notice that the voices in nationalist plays differ between the male and female dramatists. Yeats's *Cathleen ni Houlihan*, as well as the plays of MacSwiney, Pearse, and MacDonagh, all point to action and fighting on a community or national level. Markievicz's play, along with Maud Gonne MacBride's *Dawn* (1904) and Lady Gregory's *The Gaol Gate* (1906) and *The Rising of the Moon* (1907), focuses more on the personal level, on the connections between those involved. Only O'Casey bridges this gap, for he shows the personal consequences of large-scale activities.

To understand this distinction between male and female voices, one merely has to examine plays written on similar themes. Yeats's *Cathleen ni Houlihan*, for instance, focuses on a Mother Ireland figure calling young men to leave their homes and families in order to follow her down the road to heroism. Conversely, MacBride's *Dawn* portrays Mother Ireland as the head—and heart—of a family; although she has the same goal as Yeats's character, she strives to meet it from within the confines of her own home. A similar variation appears in MacSwiney's and Milligan's plays about Fionn mac Cumhaill. MacSwiney's play centers on Fionn as a messiah, ready to lead his people to victory or, perhaps, to death. Milligan, however, depicts Fionn, at his own hearth, as an aging warrior whose physical strength has diminished but who retains all his nobility.

During the early years of the twentieth century, women dramatists appeared—and disappeared—rapidly. In Ireland, the following plays were produced in an eleven-year span: Mary E. L. Butler's *Kittie* (1902); O'Brien Butler and Nora Cheeson's *The Sea Swan* (1903); Susan Varian's *Tenement Troubles* (1904); Winifred M. Letts's *The Eyes of the Blind* (1907); Nora Fitzpatrick and Casimir Markievicz's *Home Sweet Home* (1908); Winifred Letts's *The Challenge* (1909); Kathleen Fitzpatrick's *Expiation* and Mary Costello's *The Coming of Aideen* and *The Gods at Play* (1910); Johanna Redmond's *Falsely True, Honor's Choice, The Best of a Bad Bargain*, and *Pro Patria*, Molly F. Scott's *Charity*, and Jane Barlow's *A Bunch of Lavender* (1911); Johanna Redmond's *Leap Year*, Norah Fitzpatrick's *The Dangerous Age*, and Miss M. F. Scott's *Family Rights* (1912); Gertrude Robins's *The Home-Coming*, S[uzanne] R. Day and G. D. Cummins's *Broken Faith*, Florence Eaton's *Playing with Fire*, S. R. Day's *Toilers*, Mrs. Bart Kennedy's *My Lord*, and Alice Maye Finny's *A Local Demon* (1913).[11] The questions raised by such a list are important to this study. What happened to these women? Did they stop writing plays or did they have trouble getting their other plays produced? Did they try to write about women's experience in a male voice, thus diminishing their potency? Or did the male-dominated power structure of the theatres find women's voices too difficult to interpret? We will probably never know. But, certainly, these minor playwrights enriched the Irish theatrical scene in the early years of the Revival.

The Status Of Irish Women

As a backdrop to the years spanned in this anthology, it is important to have at least a basic, albeit abbreviated, understanding of the sociopolitical climate that suppressed Irish women for much of the twentieth century. Each of the playwrights included herein had to go against the grain in some way in order to become seen and heard, the focal grain here being the limited rights of women in the early twentieth century through the late 1970s, when the winds of change blew with hurricane speed. Two of these plays come from the early period and the Irish Free State era, but most of them were penned after the blossoming 1970s. Here then is what shaped these playwrights' collective mindset.

In the wake of the Victorian era, in which repressive patriarchal attitudes abounded, women remained quite fashionably uninvolved politically. Old habits die hard, and the expansion of women's rights on this unsceptered isle was a slow if steady uphill battle.

The opening decades of the twentieth century were full of movement and creativity in Ireland. Although they rarely received as much public recognition as their male counterparts, women did make a substantial contribution to the Irish Renaissance. It was an exciting time to be a woman, but a frustrating time to be an Irish woman seeking artistic recognition. Regardless of this pervasive, quiet rumble of feminist enlightenment, it was difficult for women artists to gain admission to the inner circle of the Dublin theatre scene, and in particular that of the famed Abbey Theatre. From all appearances, Irish women of all creeds and backgrounds were making significant statements on aspects of Irish life—except, as the historian Margaret MacCurtain emphasizes, politics, from which Irish women were excluded.[12]

To begin with, when Lady Gregory's *The Workhouse Ward* premiered in 1908, Irish women still could not vote; this did not change until ten years later, when in 1918 Irish women did gain the vote, but only those over the age of thirty. Four years later, when the Irish Free State (1922–1937)[13] was established by treaty, a resurgence of spirit spread throughout Ireland. It was during this period that Teresa Deevy's plays were performed at the Abbey Theatre.

Although in the eyes of the predominantly male Sinn Fein government the women of post-Treaty Ireland may have come a long way compared with their predecessors, they still had a long way to go in attaining even a semblance of equal rights with their male counterparts. One need only look at the legislative patterns of the day to realize that, as the historian Margaret Ward points out, President Eamon de Valera, and hence a good portion of Ireland, believed adamantly that "a woman's place was in the home."[14] MacCurtain reflects on how the majority of Irish women view the two decades after the 1921 Treaty as crucial to their experience of being female in Ireland: "Self-determination was to come tardily, but it was to come surprisingly to the older woman as well as to the young, to the widow as well as to the married woman, to the woman in paid employment as well as to the woman working at home. And the debate was to be about equality of opportunity."[15] The prolific novelist and occasional dramatist Maeve Binchy adds that "life for women since 1922 should have been joyful and optimistic, but too often it was blighted by the fear of raising a head too high over a parapet: a woman who called attention to herself was a woman who would not win."[16]

One might connect the Irish woman's lack of political power to her very limited opportunities in education. This in turn perpetuated her poor self-image and encouraged her to consider little other than getting married and bearing generally a large number of children. Lack of education of course limited her employment opportunities, which in turn limited any monetary earning power she might have. The obvious absence of the Irish woman's voice in education, employment, marital rights, and family planning completes the circle and brings the focus back to her overall lack of political power.

In 1932 the Irish government proposed to legally bar the recruitment of married women to the civil service (many of whom were national teachers) or their retention after marriage. Originally imposed in public service, the restriction soon spread throughout private companies. This most inexcusable practice forced Irish women to resign from work upon marriage. The Irish state essentially offered women a choice between work and marriage. Far removed from the sexist line of reasoning prevalent in some modern societies, a free-thinking Irish woman would not view marriage as a vehicle whereby she would no longer have to work, but rather as a barrier to continuing work or even to seeking employment. The marriage bar ensured that the majority of working women were young, and it deprived the Irish female image of the important elements of authority and maturity. Employers tended to view women as poor investments, not good long-term prospects, and their promotional policies regarding women were deplorable. The bar was also extremely detrimental to single women, as it virtually destroyed their promotional prospects. There was also a general lack of career orientation in Irish women. Many women did not seriously consider a career, tending instead to view employment as a stop-gap between school and marriage. Parents, peer groups, and the educational system strongly reinforced this orientation. The marriage bar was not strongly challenged until 1972, with the publication of the Report of the Commission on the Status of Women.[17] The marriage bar was removed from the civil service on July 31, 1973, and was not officially declared illegal until the Employment Equality Act of 1977.[18]

Post-Treaty Irish women, therefore, retreated into a secondary role defined within the framework of marriage and family life: women were assigned a home-based, full-time role as housewives, whose talents and energies were devoted to looking after husband and children.[19]

The psychologist Patricia Redlich points out that in the 1937 constitution, the priorities given to home-oriented duties is very much in line with the Church's view that a woman's role in life is fulfilled as a mother and a homemaker.[20] The Church's dominant influence can be seen here in this encouragement and conditioning to conform to a very rigid role behavior.

Although several women made rather feeble attempts to debate the issues presented in the 1937 constitution, most of the issues concerning all of the above legislation were not challenged by feminist voices until the 1950s, and they were soft voices at that. Maurice Manning claims that it was not until 1969 with the arrival of Mary Robinson in the Senate that a woman of parliamentary stature appeared.[21]

Since those early decades, much has been challenged and much has been changed. But the fact remains that in the period of the 1920s and 1930s, Irish women were characterized by reticence, abstinence, and diffidence as far as parliamentary matters were concerned, and by a sense of knowing their place in a male-dominated political world.[22] Regardless of changes made in the field of education for women in Ireland, there still existed in the 1970s Irish educational system the reinforcement of traditional role conditioning whereby the woman is home centered and the man is employment centered. Until this time, the Irish state's laws and social provisions remained repressive of liberty in the two areas of sex and work. The fact that contraception was outlawed, that working women accepted ridiculously low wages, and that married women were taxed at a higher rate than men, all had the result that in these two areas, women paid a higher price for less.[23]

In reference to the 1972 Report of the Commission on the Status of Women, then Senator Mary Robinson observed, "By the time the average girl leaves school she sees her future life in terms of a relatively short period of gainful employment followed by marriage and responsibility for looking after the home and caring for children."[24]

The Report of the Commission on the Status of Women was the first official documentation of the position of women in Ireland. It raised many issues that were profound and complex, difficult and embarrassing, highlighting women's status in the economic, legal, social, educational, and political spheres in Ireland. It also exposed injustices and inequities experienced by women across the whole range of societal life. McCarthy concludes, "It emerged that all significant areas of living were permeated by practices and attitudes that reflect negative views and perceptions of women."[25]

In spite of progressive changes brought about over several decades, therefore, traditional demands were still made on the Irish woman and the traditional role assigned to her remained: she was to serve and maintain the needs of other members of the family and ensure that they were free to carry out their own tasks. As a result, Irish women were most often resigned to accepting unhappy conditions and unhappy relationships. Over the years, they adopted the philosophy that for the sake of the family they would put up with anything.

This complacency has changed with lightning speed, of course, in recent decades in Ireland, although owing to the Catholic stronghold, it was still impossible to obtain a divorce until 1995 with the passing of the Divorce Referendum, which finally lifted the ban on divorce in Ireland.

In contrasting the "different country" in which Maeve Binchy grew up in the 1940s and 1950s with Ireland today, the author reflects on how women's rights have evolved, making "us Irish women realise what a long and triumphant journey we have taken." In her long essay in the *Irish Times*, Binchy recalls how none of her friends' mothers worked, and that a middle-class mother working outside the home was "as unthinkable as a home on Mars." She also points out that young women were told in their homes, at school, in magazines, and in sermons that they should be "quiet and docile and not to appear too bright or questioning." Later in the essay,

Binchy speaks of the "hurricane of change" that has "blown through Ireland," and how she has "stood and watched it blow, taking with it so much of the old, the safe, the sure, and the seriously hypocritical." It is with a real sense of admiration that she cites the changes in Ireland: divorce, civil marriage, a weakening adherence to the Roman Catholic Church, and the acknowledgement and affirmation of second marriages. She reflects that although discrimination against women is now illegal in Ireland, which might be taken for granted in other countries, this was "a very big deal when you consider how recently these Irish women suffered from such an inferiority complex that even the thought of sueing under the anti-discrimination or sexual harassment laws of the 1980s was tantamount to ritual public suicide."[26]

Since half of Ireland's population had been suppressed by the Church and government for so long, is it any wonder it has taken these women decades to find their voices in the language that Le Marquand Hartigan asserts we are all still learning?

After the Revival

During the Irish Literary Revival, some of the finest plays ever written in the English language appeared. Yet it was only a beginning. Although the Revival officially ended when O'Casey left the country in 1926, many playwrights who began during that period continued producing fine work. Several of Yeats's most acclaimed plays came out in the 1930s—*The Words upon the Window-Pane* (1934), *Purgatory* (1939), and the final play of his Cuchulain cycle, *The Death of Cuchulain* (1939, produced in 1945). Lennox Robinson and T. C. Murray continued their creative dramas with such works as *Drama at Inish* (1933) and *Bird's Nest* (1948) for Robinson and *Michaelmas Eve* (1932) for Murray.

Newer dramatists emerged at this time. Kate O'Brien achieved success with *Distinguished Villa* (1926), but soon turned from the stage to novel writing. In 1931, Teresa Deevy and Paul Vincent Carroll jointly won an Abbey play competition. Several of Deevy's plays, including *The King of Spain's Daughter* (1935) and *Katie Roche* (1936), were produced at the Abbey in the 1930s. *Katie Roche* enjoyed a successful revival at the Abbey in 1994. Many of her later plays, though, were written for the radio. One cannot help but wonder if the male-dominated power structure forced these women into leaving the stage. Carroll, however, continued writing for the stage with such renowned works as *Shadow and Substance* (1937), *The White Steed* (1939), and *The Devil Came from Dublin* (1955). Christine Longford achieved some success in 1933 with *Mr. Jiggins of Jigginstown*, as did Mary Manning with *Youth's the Season* (1931) and *Storm over Wicklow* (1933), but Anne Daly's *Leave It to the Doctor* (1959) was severely criticized. Denis Johnston began his prolific playwriting career with many productions at the Abbey and Gate theatres; his most notable plays include *The Old Lady Says "No!"* (1928), *Dreaming Dust* (1940), and *The Scythe and the Sunset* (1958). And Brendan Behan's short but gifted playwriting career produced such works as *The Quare Fellow* (1954) and *The Hostage* (1958). Other new playwrights to appear during these years were Michael J. Molloy (*The King of Friday's Men*, 1948; *The Paddy Pedlar*, 1953), Bryan MacMahon (*Song of the Anvil*, 1960; *The Honey Spike*, 1967), and John B. Keane (*Sive*, 1959; *The Field*, 1965).

Some writers known mainly in other genres also succeeded with their dramas. Frank O'Connor, for instance, took a brief sojourn from fiction to collaborate with Hugh Hunt on *The Invincibles* and *In the Train* (1937). The sensitive depiction of life in the Dublin tenements in Maura Laverty's *Liffey Lane* (1947) is similar in voice, if not in form, to her fiction. Laverty and Mary Manning had three plays each produced at the Gate Theatre. The novelist Edna O'Brien began writing stage plays, which include *A Cheap Bunch of Nice Flowers* (1963), *A Pagan Place* (1972), and *Virginia* (1981). And the novelist M. J. Farrell (Molly Keane) wrote several plays with John Perry, including *Spring Meeting* (1938), *Treasure Hunt* (1949), and *Dazzling Prospect* (1961). Perry collaborated with Elizabeth Bowen in writing her play *Castle Anna* (1948) several years after he transposed her short story "Oh, Madam" into a stage monologue. And Bowen wrote a historical pageant for Kinsale (1965) and a nativity play that was produced in the 1960s at Limerick Cathedral and in 1970 at the Protestant cathedral in Derry.

Contemporary Theatre (1970–1990)

Theatre in Ireland in the 1970s and 1980s was as exciting as it had ever been. The canon of male playwrights is instantly recognizable. Brian Friel, the most renowned playwright at this time, achieved international acclaim with such plays as his earlier *Philadelphia, Here I Come* (1964), *Translations* (1980), and *Dancing at Lughnasa* (1990). Other noted male playwrights included Hugh Leonard (*Da,* 1972; *A Life,* 1979), Frank McGuinness (*Observe the Sons of Ulster Marching towards the Somme,* 1985), Thomas Kilroy (*Talbot's Box,* 1977), and Thomas Murphy (*The Gigli Concert,* 1983). Recent decades in Irish theatre gave rise to several notable dramatists: Declan Hughes (*Love and a Bottle,* 1995), Gary Mitchell (*Tearing the Loom,* 1998; *The Force of Change,* 2000), Conor McPherson (*The Weir,* 1997; *Shining City,* 2003; *The Night Alive,* 2013), and Martin McDonagh (*The Cripple of Inishmaan,* 1996; *The Pillowman,* 2003; *A Behanding in Spokane,* 2010), to name four. Emerging from the undercurrent, however, were the dramatic voices of Irish women.

In his essay "Recent Irish Drama," Christopher Murray appended a list of new Irish plays staged in Ireland from May 1979 through May 1981. Of the sixty-one playwrights included, only six were women.[27] But such trends seemed to be changing, for Irish drama in these decades had a sudden plethora of women playwrights. In 1982, the *Irish Times* and Dublin Theatre Festival co-sponsored a competition for a play by a woman. After examining the almost two hundred entries, the judges concluded that many were better than plays by male authors who had been produced in recent years. Mary Halpin's *Semi-Private* received the award for the best play; Christina Reid's *Tea in a China Cup* was judged a close second. Both plays speak strongly about women's issues in women's voices. Other finalists in the competition were *Boat People* by Alice O'Donoghue, *Cradlesong* by Rita E. Kelly, *No Chips for Johnny* by Una Lynch-Caffrey, *Facade* by Ann O'Musoy, *Country Banking* by Nesta Tuomey, and *Supermarket* by Barbara Walsh.

Ever since this competition, the door to literary and dramatic success seems to have been sprung open for Irish women. The changing status of women in Ireland is reflected in the subject matter of the plays. There are now plays that examine women's place in an ever-changing society, their complicated lives as women, and the tension caused by choices between hearth and career.

Women playwrights today are examining their own status in society as well as the status of other powerless groups. Sheila Flitton's *For Better or for Worse* and Margaret Neylon's *Home from Home* focus on the problems faced by battered wives, Dolores Walshe's *The Sins in Sally Gardens* shows family violence in more general terms, Miriam Gallagher's *Dusty Bluebells* treats women in prison, Geraldine Aron's *The Stanley Parkers* describes the impact of AIDS on a middle-aged homosexual couple, Walshe's *In the Talking Dark* treats the racial tensions in South Africa, Big Telly (an all-women theatre company in Northern Ireland) describes bag ladies in *Onions Make You Cry*, and Christina Reid's *Joyriders* shows the devastating effects of poverty. Anne Le Marquand Hartigan's *I Do Like to Be Beside the Seaside* and Jennifer Johnston's *The Porch* address the problems of the elderly, as does Angela Clarke's *All My Worldly Goods*, while Marie Jones's *The Hamster Wheel*, Reid's *Tea in a China Cup*, and Ena May's *She's Your Mother, Too, You Know* concentrate more on caregivers for the elderly and infirm. Set in a hospital gynecological ward, Mary Halpin's *Semi-Private* focuses on the biological as well as the societal problems unique to women, and Miriam Gallagher's *Labels* shows problems within the male-dominated medical profession. Geraldine Aron's *The Donahue Sisters* is a chilling account of what happens when the powerless take power.

Writers from Northern Ireland often show the impact of the current political unrest. Reid's *Did You Hear the One About the Irishman . . . ?* uses black humor to underline the devastation, while Jones's *Somewhere over the Balcony* shows how humor can be a tool for survival; both plays are nonsectarian. Anne Devlin's *Ourselves Alone* presents female bonding as an alternative to male violence in Northern Ireland, and Dolores Walshe's *The Stranded Hours Between* suggests a similar alternative for South Africa. Jennifer Johnston's *Christine* and *Mustn't Forget High Noon* portray a couple destroyed by the turmoil in the North.

Women writing in all parts of the country focus on problems of families or couples failing to communicate: Ena May's *Out of the Beehive*, Anne Le Marquand Hartigan's *Strings*, Carolyn Swift's *The Civilised Way of Doing Things*, Harriet O'Carroll's *The Image of Her Mother*, and Dolores Walshe's *A Country in Our Heads*.

During this time period, women were also dramatizing actual events. Anne Le Marquand Hartigan's *La Corbière* sympathetically describes a group of prostitutes who drowned; Miriam Gallagher's *The Ring of Mount de Balison* focuses on eight hundred years of Ranelagh history; Chara-banc's *Lay up Your Ends* describes the 1911 strike in the Belfast linen mills; and Maeve Binchy's *Deeply Regretted By* shows the impact of bigamy on the "second" family. In *Lady G*, Carolyn Swift presents the many facets of Lady Gregory as a woman rather than just as a supporter of Yeats, Synge, and O'Casey. Another biographical play, Maureen Charlton's *Berlioz and the Girl from Ennis*, describes the stormy relationship between the com-poser Berlioz and Harriet Smithson, his Irish wife.

Women playwrights are dramatizing mythic events as well. In *Women in Arms*, Mary Elizabeth Burke-Kennedy portrays such powerful mythic figures as Maeve and Deirdre. Mary Halpin's *Shady Ladies* juxtaposes mythic and historic women with an actress of today, and Miriam Galla-gher focuses on legend in *The Sealwoman and the Fisher: A Play for Dancers*.

Women are using a variety of techniques to illustrate their themes. *Ullaloo*, one of Marina Carr's earliest plays, is an almost-absurdist drama somewhat reminiscent of Beckett, yet innovative rather than derivative; its surrealistic approach is not unlike that of Miriam Gallagher's *Omelettes*. Burke-Kennedy uses the story-theatre technique in *Women in Arms*, and many use the monologue format to voice their concerns. Johnston's *Christine* and *Mustn't Forget High Noon*, for instance, are two extended monologues.

One possible reason for the upsurge in women writing plays—and in women's plays being produced—can be found in the vibrant new theatre groups that have arisen in Ireland; many of these groups were founded (or co-founded) by women who yearned to have their voices heard in the theatre: Lynne Parker, Rough Magic; Garry Hynes, Druid; Mary Eliza-beth Burke-Kennedy, Storytellers' Theatre Company and, with Deirdre O'Connell, Focus; Jill Holmes and Zoe Seaton, Big Telly; Brenda Winter, Replay; Emelie Fitzgibbon, Graffiti; and Brenda Winter, Marie Jones, Elea-nor Methven, and Carol Moore (also known as Carol Scanlan), Charabanc.

Charabanc contributed drama that is particularly energetic and excit-ing. Founded by five actresses in 1983 because of their frustration over the lack of roles for women, the company achieved remarkable success in translating political struggles, past and present, to the stage, where their gift for satire and black comedy shone.[28] Founding member Carol Moore once reflected that Charabanc's working process completely tossed aside both dominating male prerogatives and the traditional power structure of most theatres. Since its first production, *Lay up Your Ends*, through *Oul' Delf and False Teeth, Now You're Talkin', Gold in the Streets, The Girls in the Big Picture, Somewhere over the Balcony, Weddin's, Wee'ins and Wakes*, and *The Hamster Wheel*, it concentrated on problems that affect Catholics and Protestants alike—violence, poverty, discrimination, division, and women's issues. *The Blind Fiddler of Glenadauch*, however, differs somewhat with its focus on the Catholic community's loss of an identifiable cultural tradition. Charabanc's triumphant tours in Northern Ireland, the Republic of Ireland, England, Scotland, Russia, Lithuania, and the United States brought their talents, perspectives, and issues before the world. The troupe flourished until it disbanded in 1995. Their plays brought women's voices to the fore.

Contemporary Theatre: 1991–Present

The 1990s saw numerous talented dramatists reach the forefront of Irish theatre. Eileen Kearney recalls a conversation in the mid-1980s with Christopher Fitz-Simon, former literary head of the Abbey Theatre. Marina Carr was just starting to be known. He said, "I guarantee we will all hear more of this young woman. You will hear of her again." And, of course, we have. Carr, along with Marie Jones, are two shining stars of present-day Irish theatre. Both have won wide acclaim and awards for their work. Carr is one of the few women to have an ongoing relationship with the Abbey. Since the late 1980s her work has been produced there. *Ullaloo* (1991), *The Mai* (1994), *Portia Coughlan* (1996), *By the Bog of Cats* (1998), and *On Raftery's Hill* (2000) have been produced in Dublin and then found their way to other venues such as the Royal Court Theatre,[29] which saw the London premiere of *On Raftery's Hill* in the summer of 2000. In the fall of 2001, Carr's reworking of the Medea myth, *By the Bog of Cats*, had its American premiere at the San Jose Repertory Theatre in California, with Holly Hunter in the leading role. Hunter reprised this role in London's West End in 2004 and 2005. Productions of *The Mai* have occurred all over the United States. Carr also wrote *Meat and Salt* (2003), a play for young audiences that was produced at Dublin's Peacock Theatre. *Ariel*, a reworking of Euripides's *Iphigenia at Aulis,* dates from 2002, and *Woman and Scarecrow* premiered at the Royal Court Theatre in 2006.

Marie Jones left Charabanc in the early 1990s and worked for a time with the Belfast-based DubbelJoint Theatre Company. Charabanc disbanded in 1995, having been the most successful touring company in the history of Ireland. Jones's post-Charabanc plays include a one-man show, *A Night in November* (1994), that has played internationally, *Ruby* (2000), *Weddin's, Wee'ins, and Wakes* (1989, 2001),[30] *Women on the Verge of HRT* (1995), and her wildly successful *Stones in His Pockets* (1996).[31] First produced at Belfast's Lyric Theatre in 1999 under the direction of Ian McElhinney, it went on to London's West End and later to Broadway in 2001, garnering many awards along the way: the Laurence Olivier Award for best comedy, the *Irish Times*/ESB Award for best play, a special judges' award from the Belfast Arts Awards, the John Hewitt Award, and three nominations for Broadway's 2001 Tony Awards.

Although the names of Marina Carr and Marie Jones might be the most recognizable in the litany of Irish women playwrights today, these two women are not alone. Anne Devlin continues to write and her plays continue to hold the stage. In 1994, *After Easter* was produced at The Other Place in Stratford-upon-Avon by the Royal Shakespeare Company and later transferred to the Barbican in London in 1995. Belfast's Lyric Theatre also produced the play, and, along with Devlin's still popular *Ourselves Alone* (1985), it has had several productions in the United States.

Christina Reid's plays were published as a collection by Methuen in 1997 under the title *Christina Reid, Plays I.* The collection includes *The Belle of the Belfast City* (1989) and *Clowns* (1996), a sequel to *Joyriders* (1986). In 2000 the National Theatre in London produced *King of the Castle,* which is a play for young people and was commissioned by British Telecom. Theatre-in-Education (TIE) groups all over the United Kingdom participated in this project and two groups brought productions of the play to the National.

In the 1990s the award-winning Rough Magic Theatre Company conducted a playwriting competition for women writers, out of which came three successful productions: Gina Moxley's *Danti-Dan* (1995), Pom Boyd's *Down onto Blue* (1994), and the poet Paula Meehan's *Mrs. Sweeney* (1997). *Danti-Dan,* which deals with the cruelty of adolescent children, transferred to London's Hampstead Theatre after its initial Dublin production. Both Boyd and Moxley have continued to write for the theatre. After her first play *Mrs. Sweeney*, Meehan continued to work in the theatrical medium and wrote *Cell* (1999), which she based on her work with prisoners. Boyd penned *Boomtown* in 1999, Moxley's *Tea Set* appeared in 2000, and in 2003 the Abbey produced Meehan's *The Wolf of Winter*. In 1999, Rough Magic published *Rough Magic: First Plays*, which was the first Irish drama anthology of its size to have an equal number of plays by Irish men and women (three each),[32] including plays by Boyd, Moxley, and Meehan. Gemma O'Connor's one-woman show *SigNora Joyce* (1991), which examines the life of Nora Barnacle Joyce, played in London. In 2002 Mary Elizabeth Burke-Kennedy's *Women in Arms* was revived in Ireland. Emma Donoghue, a scholar, novelist, and playwright, received praise for *I Know My Own Heart* (1993) and *Ladies and Gentlemen* (1996), both of which are based on historical records, reclaiming often-suppressed lesbian histories. She adapted her own volume *Kissing the Witch* for the stage, and San Francisco's Magic Theatre produced it in 2000.

In 1992 in Galway, the playwright, poet, and painter Patricia Burke Brogan saw the first production of her play *Eclipsed*, which examines the scandal of the Magdalene Laundries. It later won a Fringe First at the Edinburgh Festival. Brogan's next play, *Stained Glass at Samhain*, opened in Galway at the Town Hall Theatre in 2002, as did her newest play, *Requiem of Love*, in 2005.

Michelle Read's *Romantic Friction* (1997) opened in Dublin, won a Fringe First in 1998, and later was featured in the Irish Theatre Festival at the Actor's Centre in London in the summer of 1999. Her plays *Romantic Friction, The Lost Letters of a Victorian Lady* (1996), and *The Other Side* (2003) all reflect the zaniness of Read's background as a stand-up comedienne.

Jennifer Johnston's *Desert Lullaby* was produced by the Lyric Theatre in 1996, followed by a subsequent production in New York. Her monologue *Twinkletoes* was produced in Dublin at Bewleys in 1993 with the actress Carol Moore, a founding member of Charabanc, in the role of Karen. The production was directed by Caroline Fitzgerald.

Like Dolores Walshe, Elizabeth Kuti has expanded the boundaries of what an Irish playwright writes. Born of a Hungarian father and a British mother, Kuti studied at Dublin's Trinity University, where she composed the last two acts of Frances Sheridan's unfinished play *A Trip to Bath* (1765), now retitled *The Whisperers (1999)*.[33] Her play *Treehouses* (2000) received Honorable Mention for the Susan Smith Blackburn Prize.[34]

In the spring of 2000, the Kennedy Center in Washington, DC, held an Irish play festival and invited Rough Magic's production of Stewart Parker's *Pentecost*. Rough Magic's founding member Lynne Parker directed her uncle's play in a highly acclaimed production that toured in Dublin as well as in London's Donmar Warehouse, a major fringe venue.

Also invited to the Kennedy Center was Galway's Druid Theatre production of Marina Carr's *On Raftery's Hill*. This co-production of the Druid Theatre and the Royal Court Theatre was directed by Garry Hynes, the founding member and artistic director of the Druid Theatre, who later served as artistic director of the Abbey. Although she had written two plays years earlier, *The Pursuit of Pleasure* (1977) and *Island Protected by a Bridge of Glass* (1980), Hynes, like Lynne Parker, is most noted for her directing. In 1998 Hynes became the first woman in history to win the Tony Award for best director for her Broadway production of Martin McDonough's *The Beauty Queen of Leenane*.

What is most amazing about the Kennedy Center event is the convergence of energy and talent, showcasing some of Ireland's most accomplished women in theatre. The actual festival highlighted the work of Ireland's two most famous directors, Parker and Hynes. Acting in Parker's *Pentecost* were Eleanor Methven and Carol Moore, two of the founding members of Charabanc, who thereby continued the troupe's legacy. At this same time, another founding member, Marie Jones, was enjoying the early success of her play *Stones in His Pocket*, which was to win a myriad of awards. Brenda Winter also continued her work with Replay Theatre. Thus, when the scholar and Irish theatre historian Claudia Harris wrote in 1997 that "Charabanc changed the face of Irish Theatre,"[35] her words were prophetic.

In 2000 the *Irish Times* Theatre Award for best production went to *Convictions*, a collection of short plays addressing issues about the Crumlin Road Prison. Nicola McCartney and Marie Jones were two of the seven dramatists commissioned to write these dramatic works. This award-winning multiauthored theatre event was staged in the Crumlin Road Courthouse in Belfast. Each play was site specific and each dramatist was given a specific room in the prison in which to base her or his play.

At the time of this writing, the sheer volume of Irish women's innovative theatrical voices is energizing. Emma Donoghue and Elizabeth Kuti continue to contribute new plays to the constantly expanding canon. In addition to some of the better-known dramatists discussed, there are a number of other women playwrights on the cutting edge of current Irish drama: Nicola McCartney, *The Millies* (2002) and *All Legendary Obstacles* (2003), produced by the Abbey Theatre; Hilary Fannin, *Mackerel Sky* (1997), *Sleeping Around* (2002, in collaboration with Abi Morgan, Mark Ravenhill, and Stephen Greenhor), and *Doldrum Bay* (2003); Emelie FitzGibbon, *Meal Ticket* (1989) and *The Changeling* (1998), both Theatre for Young Audiences vehicles; Rita Ann Higgins, *Face Licker Come Home* (1991) and *Down All the Roundabouts (or No-one is Entitled to a View)*(1999); Siofra Campbell, *Couch* (2000); Claire Dowling, *The Marlboro Man* (1994); Ioanna Anderson, *Words of Advice for Young People* (2004); Oonagh Kearney, *Calling Hilary* (1998) and *Urban Angels* (2001); Deirdre Kinahan, *Be Carna: Women of the Flesh* (1999), *Attaboy, Mr. Synge!* (2002), *Rum and Raisin* (with Alice Barry, 2003), and *These Halcyon Days* (2112); Alice Barry, *Pam Ella* [one-act] (2002) and *Rum and Raisin* (with Deirdre Kinahan, 2003); Lisa McGee, *Girls and Dolls* (2007); and Carmel Winters, *B for Baby* (2011).

In the first decade of the twenty-first century, a number of exciting and award-winning women dramatists have emerged, including Lucy Caldwell, Morna Regan, Ursula Rani Sarma, and Abbie Spallen. Belfast native Lucy Caldwell won the 2006 George Devine Award and the 2007 Susan Smith Blackburn Award for *Leaves*, which had productions at both the Druid Theatre and the Royal Court Theatre. Abbie Spallen also hails from Belfast and has won wide praise for *Pumpgirl* (2006), which has had multiple productions. Morna Regan's *Midden* (2001) earned her the European Playwright Award. Ursula Rani Sarma, who is of Irish-Indian descent, has penned several plays, including *Blue* (2000), *Gift* (2001), *The Spider Man* (2006), and *The Magic Tree* (2008).

Every day we witness the emergence of young, dynamic Irish women playwrights. One would hope that these young dramatists are having an easier time being produced and published than their predecessors. A brief excursion into the Abbey Theatre archives reveals how few women playwrights have been produced there over the last century. Sadly, of the exceedingly few plays by women the Abbey has chosen to produce, the majority of these were staged in its smaller venue, the Peacock, rather than on its Main Stage. Even the Druid, under the direction of the Tony Award-winning Garry Hynes, has a lamentable record supporting women playwrights, with the exception of Marina Carr. To cope with the situation, women have formed companies of their own, such as Charabanc, Replay, Storytellers, Gallow Glass, and others. The women of Charabanc led the way in finding women to direct their productions and their influence is still being felt. It is especially important to acknowledge what Lynne Parker and the Rough Magic Theatre Company have accomplished in celebrating drama written by women. From Gina Moxley and Pam Boyd to Paula Meehan, Elizabeth Kuti, and Morna Regan, Parker and Rough Magic have championed women playwrights. Additionally, Parker has encouraged other women directors to produce new productions of plays first championed by Rough Magic.

Women's Voices

In discussing the place of Irish women in playwriting in 2008, Ursula Rani Sarma reflects: "I'm not sure what the place for female playwrights is in Irish theatre at all. People ask 'where are the women playwrights?' But they are there—there are so many of them, I mean, I have a play under commission for the first Irish Theatre Festival taking place in New York later this year, and three out of the five writers commissioned are women. There are women writing, loads of them. They are just not being programmed. But, you know, there's no point in complaining. As an active member of the theatre community, I should challenge that, and maybe I will. I'm certainly interested in staging Irish female writers' work with my own company, Djinn. I mean, I'm not a radical feminist by any means, but I do think the balance should be redressed."[36]

It is a truism in the theatre that it can be relatively easy to find a venue for the premiere of a new drama, but as many dramatists agree, the trick is to find a second and third production of a new play. Some women dramatists have found champions for their work, and those include Marina Carr and Marie Jones. Others are still involved in the struggle. They have strong plays but are still searching for those elusive second, third, even seventh and eighth productions of their plays. As Sarma so aptly points out, "they are there—there are so many of them."

The plays in this volume are representative of the fine dramatic writing by Irish women that exists, and they represent a cross section of that writing. We have selected the plays in the hope that they will not only be read and embraced but will also find new productions.

What the American dramatist Sarah Schulman says of theatre in New York is also applicable to theatre in Ireland. Jonathan Mandell writes in his interview of the playwright, "Ms. Schulman believes that the worst consequence of theater-as-marketing is that there are plenty of good, vibrant plays with authentic characters written by playwrights who are not in the mainstream but are being kept out by the commercial theater establishment. . . . Schulman elaborates, 'In New York City, you can see a bad play by a white man every night of the week. . . . Why are there so few plays by anybody else? It is a profoundly discriminatory system.'"[37]

As Cixous so astutely expressed, women see and experience the world differently than men do, so they write about it differently. The plays anthologized here illustrate the views of women in their own voices, voices that have been silenced by being marginalized. These playwrights have given us works that stretch our imaginations, cover a myriad of themes, and challenge the stereotype of what it means to be Irish.

It has been said that the innovative drama that developed during the Literary Revival was a result of Ireland's lack of a native dramatic tradition. So Yeats, Synge, and the other playwrights, freed from the past, could build their own tradition. Women playwrights, in Ireland and elsewhere, have had few dramatic models for expressing their voices in the past; thus, they too were free to build their own tradition, a tradition crafted through the experiences of women. If Lady Gregory opened the door, Teresa Deevy helped pave the way thereafter, inspiring other Irish women to express themselves through dramatic writing.

In *A Room of One's Own*, Virginia Woolf muses that "masterpieces are not single and solitary births; they are the outcome of many years of thinking in common, of thinking by the body of the people, so that the experience of the mass is behind the single voice."[38] As women's voices continue to spread throughout the theatrical world, the masterpieces will arise. Anne Le Marquand Hartigan reminds us, "We are learning our language. We have begun to speak." This language, these voices, will continue to speak, telling their stories, finding their voices in a medium that is most rightfully their own, enriching and expanding theatre everywhere. Not only do these women belong to Ireland, but they also belong to the world.

May 2014
Eileen Kearney, University of Colorado Denver
Charlotte Headrick, Oregon State University, Corvallis
Kathleen Quinn, Queen's University, Belfast, Northern Ireland

Notes

1. Hélène Cixous, "The Laugh of the Medusa," in *New French Feminisms*, ed. Elaine Marks and Isabelle de Courtivron (Amherst: University of Massachusetts Press, 1980), 249.

2. Lynda Hart, ed., *Making a Spectacle: Feminist Essays on Contemporary Women's Theatre* (Ann Arbor: University of Michigan Press, 1989), 2.

3. Katie Donovan, "A Plethora of Women Playwrights," *Irish Times*, September 18, 1989, 9.

4. Lady Augusta Gregory, *The Wrens*, in *The Image and Other Plays* (New York: G. P. Putnam's Sons, 1922), 230.

5. Christopher Fitz-Simon, *The Irish Theatre* (London: Thames and Hudson, 1983), 10.

6. Michael O hAodha, *Theatre in Ireland* (Oxford: Blackwell, 1974), xii.

7. Andrew E. Malone, *The Irish Drama* (New York: Scribner's, 1929), 13.

8. Lady Augusta Gregory, *Our Irish Theatre: A Chapter of Autobiography* (New York: Putnam's, 1913), 8–9.

9. W. B. Yeats, "Plans and Methods," *Beltaine: The Organ of the Irish Literary Theatre*, no. 1 (May 1899): 6–7.

10. William Irwin Thompson, *The Imagination of an Insurrection: Dublin, Easter 1916* (New York: Harper Colophon Books, 1972), vi.

11. This list is incomplete. It omits plays previously mentioned, plays for which no record has been found, and plays by Lady Gregory and Alice Milligan.

12. Margaret MacCurtain, "Women, the Vote, and Revolution," in *Women in Irish Society: The Historical Dimension*, ed. Margaret MacCurtain and Donncha O Corrain (Dublin: Arlen, 1978), 47.

13. The Irish Free State came to an end in 1937, when the citizens voted by referendum to replace the 1922 constitution. It was succeeded by the entirely sovereign modern state of Ireland.

14. Margaret Ward, "Marginality and Militancy: Cuman na mBan, 1914–1936," in *Ireland: Divided Nation, Divided Class*, ed. Austen Morgan and Bob Purdie (London: Ink Links, 1980), 102.

15. Margaret MacCurtain, "The Historical Image," in *Irish Women: Image and Achievement*, ed. Eilean Ni Chuilleanain (Dublin: Arlen, 1985), 17.

16. Maeve Binchy, "Gone with the Wind of Change," *Irish Times*, September 26, 1998.

17. Mary E. Daly, "Women, Work, and Trade Unionism," in MacCurtain and O Corrain, *Women in Irish Society*, 77.

18. Eunice McCarthy, "Women and Work in Ireland: The Present, and Preparing for the Future," in MacCurtain and O Corrain, *Women in Irish Society*, 104–5.

19. Margaret MacCurtain, "Women, the Vote, and Revolution," in MacCurtain and O Corrain, *Women in Irish Society*, 49.

20. Patricia Redlich, "Women and the Family," in MacCurtain and O Corrain, *Women in Irish Society*, 86.

21. Maurice Manning, "Women in Irish National and Local Politics 1922–77," in MacCurtain and O Corrain, *Women in Irish Society*, 96.

22. Ibid.

23. Eilean Ni Chuilleanain, "Introduction," in Ni Chuilleanain, *Irish Women*, 6.

24. Mary Robinson, "Women and the New Irish State," in MacCurtain and O Corrain, *Women in Irish Society*, 58.

25. Eunice McCarthy, "Women and Work in Ireland: The Present, and Preparing for the Future," in MacCurtain and O Corrain, *Women in Irish Society*, 103.

26. Binchy, "Gone with the Wind of Change."

27. Christopher Murray, "Recent Irish Drama," in *Studies in Anglo-Irish Literature*, ed. Heinz Kosok (Bonn: Herbert Grundmann, 1982), 439–46.

28. Eileen Kearney, "Current Women's Voices in the Irish Theatre: New Dramatic Visions," Contemporary Irish Drama Special Issue, *Colby Quarterly* 27, no. 4 (1991): 230.

29. It should be noted that London's Royal Court Theatre has had an ongoing commitment to recent Irish theatre; witness the plays of Conor McPherson and Dolores Walshe.

30. Marie Jones developed with Charabanc the original one-act of this play in 1989. Jones later developed it into a full-length play of the same title in 2001, which played at the Lyric Theatre in Belfast. Charabanc founding members Carol Moore and Eleanor Methven were also in the 2001 production.

31. An early version of *Stones in His Pockets* was produced in 1996 by the DubbelJoint Theatre Company and directed by Pam Brighton at the Amharclann na Carraige/Theatre on the Rock.

32. Frank McGuinness edited *The Dazzling Dark* in 1996, published by Faber and Faber, which included plays by two men (Jimmy Murphy and Tom MacIntyre) and two women (Gina Moxley and Marina Carr).

33. Frances Sheridan was the mother of famed Irish playwright Richard Brinsley Sheridan and the "grandmother" of all Irish women playwrights.

34. This prize acknowledges outstanding women dramatists writing for the English-speaking theatre. Finalists have included Mary Elizabeth Burke-Kennedy, Jennifer Johnston, Nicola McCartney, Edna O'Brien, and Christina Reid. Anne Devlin won in 1985–1986 for *Ourselves Alone*, as did Marina Carr in 1996–1997 for *Portia Coughlan*.

35. Claudia Harris, "Notes on the Production," American premiere of *Lay up Your Ends*, directed by Charlotte J. Headrick, Oregon State University, Corvallis, OR, April 3–5, 10–12, 1997.

36. Sara Keating, "Back to Her Roots via 'The Magic Tree,'" *Irish Times*, July 1, 2008.

37. Jonathan Mandell, "When She Wrote, the Dross of Her Life Became Gold," *New York Times*, January 20, 2002, Arts and Leisure section, 3.

38. Virginia Woolf, *A Room of One's Own* (New York: Harcourt, Brace, Jovanovich, 1981), 65.

Lady Augusta Gregory
(1852–1932)

 Isabella Augusta Persse was born at Roxborough, County Galway, on March 15, 1852. The twelfth in a family of sixteen children of Protestant landowners, she developed a fiercely independent spirit at an early age, paving the way for her future journey down the theatrically oriented road less traveled.

 While accompanying her invalid brother to the Continent, she met Sir William Gregory, a neighbor from nearby Coole Park. Her 1880 marriage to Gregory—a childless widower and retired governor of Ceylon who was more than thirty years her senior—broadened her horizons in the political, artistic, and social life of Europe. Although they frequently traveled to foreign lands, they divided their time principally between London and Coole. Their only child, William Robert, was born in 1881; his death in World War I was to affect Lady Gregory deeply. Her husband died in 1892, after which she continued to wear mourning clothes the rest of her life.

 In 1896 Lady Gregory was introduced to W. B. Yeats, and the rest is Irish theatre history. With Yeats and Edward Martyn, she founded the Irish Literary Theatre in 1899, which evolved into the Irish National Theatre Society and later became the now legendary Abbey. As a driving force in this dramatic and theatrical renaissance, Lady Gregory's strong influence on Yeats, Synge, and O'Casey is apparent. She devoted most of the last thirty years of her life to tirelessly working in many capacities with the Abbey, including encouraging new playwrights. She herself was a new (if late-blooming) playwright; her first play *Twenty Five* premiered in the Irish National Theatre Society's first season in March 1903, one day before her fifty-first birthday.

Of all the women playwrights in Ireland, Lady Augusta Gregory is the name most widely known and recognized. Much has been written about the now legendary leading figure of the Irish Renaissance who, along with W. B. Yeats, John Synge, Douglas Hyde, George Moore, and others, changed utterly the direction of artistic, literary, and dramatic expression in Ireland. Widespread information about her personal life and her multifaceted roles as playwright, folklorist, essayist, poet, translator, editor, director, fund-raiser, and businesswoman is now readily accessible. Lady Gregory's fame and recognition are simultaneously inspiring and disappointing. Although her legacy serves as a veritable role model for the strong voice of women's influence on and contribution to the Irish theatre scene, the fact that she alone appears in most anthologies as the sole Irish women playwright makes her fame a two-edged sword.

Over the years Lady Gregory wrote five volumes of folktales and folk history, which she compiled from her collected folktales and legends of Galway. She authored forty plays, most of them written in the Kiltartan dialect for which she became famous. Although most of these plays were comedic one-acts, for example, *The Workhouse Ward*, *Spreading the News*, and *Hyacinth Halvey*, some of them are drawn from historical and folkloric sources, for example, *Dervorgilla*. She also translated four of Molière's plays into her Kiltartan dialect. In addition, she co-authored several plays with Yeats, among them *Cathleen ni Houlihan* and *The Pot of Broth*. Other invaluable records of this vibrant period of Irish theatre history are Lady Gregory's autobiographical account of the early Abbey, scrupulously chronicled in *Our Irish Theatre* (1913), and her journals, edited by Lennox Robinson, which were published posthumously in 1947.

The final scripted version of *The Workhouse Ward* has an interesting evolution. During the summer of 1903, Lady Gregory wrote the scenario for *The Poorhouse* for Douglas Hyde to write in Irish. This "scenario" was able to stand on its own as a completed play and all Hyde had to do was translate it into Irish. Several years later, she translated it back into English and changed the title to *The Workhouse Ward*. The one-act comedy premiered at the Abbey Theatre on April 20, 1908.

The Workhouse Ward

CHARACTERS

MIKE MCINERNEY, a pauper.
MICHEAL MISKELL, a pauper.
MRS. DONOHOE, a countrywoman.

SCENE

A ward in Cloon Workhouse.[1] *The two old men in their beds.*

MICHEAL MISKELL. Isn't it a hard case, Mike McInerney, myself and yourself to be left here in the bed, and it the rest day of Saint Colman, and the rest of the ward attending on the Mass.

MIKE MCINERNEY. Is it sitting up by the hearth you are wishful to be, Micheal Miskell, with cold in the shoulders and with speckled shins? Let you rise up so, and you well be able to do it, not like myself that has pains the same as tin-tacks[2] within in my inside.

MICHEAL MISKELL. If you have pains within in your inside there is no one can see it or know of it the way they can see my own knees that are swelled up with the rheumatism, and my hands that are twisted in ridges the same as an old cabbage stalk. It is easy to be talking about soreness and about pains, and they maybe not to be in it at all.

MIKE MCINERNEY. To open me to analyse me you would know what sort of a pain and a soreness I have in my heart and in my chest. But I'm not one like yourself to be cursing and praying and tormenting the time the nuns are at hand, thinking to get a bigger share than myself of nourishment and of the milk.

MICHEAL MISKELL. That's the way you do be picking at me and faulting me. I had a share and a good share in my early time, and it's well you know that, and the both of us reared in Skehanagh.

MIKE MCINERNEY. You may say that, indeed, we are both of us reared in Skehanagh. Little wonder you to have good nourishment the time we were both rising, and you bringing away my rabbits out of the snare.

MICHEAL MISKELL. And you didn't bring away my own eels, I suppose, I was after spearing in the Turlough? Selling them to the nuns in the convent you did, and letting on they to be your own. For you were always a cheater and a schemer, grabbing every earthly thing for your own profit.

MIKE MCINERNEY. And you were no grabber yourself, I suppose, 'til your land and all you had grabbed wore away from you!

MICHEAL MISKELL. If I lost it itself, it was through the crosses I met with and I going through the world. I never was a rambler and a card player like yourself, Mike McInerney, that ran through all and lavished it unknown to your mother!

MIKE MCINERNEY. Lavished it, is it? And if I did was it you yourself led me to lavish it or some other one? It is on my own floor I would be today and in the face of my family, but for the misfortune I had to be put with a bad next-door neighbour that was yourself. What way did my means go from me is it? Spending on fencing, spending on walls, making up gates, putting up doors, that would keep your hens and your ducks from coming in through starvation on my floor, and every four footed beast you had from preying and trespassing on my oats and my mangolds³ and my little lock of hay!

MICHEAL MISKELL. O to listen to you! And I striving to please you and to be kind to you and to close my ears to the abuse you would be calling and letting out of your mouth. To trespass on your crops is it? It's little temptation there was for my poor beasts to ask to cross the mering.⁴ My God Almighty! What had you but a little corner of a field!

MIKE MCINERNEY. And what do you say to my garden that your two pigs had destroyed on me the year of the big tree being knocked, and they making gaps in the wall.

MICHEAL MISKELL. Ah, there does be a great deal of gaps knocked in a twelvemonth. Why wouldn't they be knocked by the thunder, the same as the tree, or some storm that came up from the west?

MIKE MCINERNEY. It was the west wind, I suppose, that devoured my green cabbage? And that rooted up my Champion potatoes? And that ate the gooseberries themselves from off the bush?

MICHEAL MISKELL. What are you saying? The two quietest pigs ever I had, no way wicked and well ringed. They were not ten minutes in it. It would be hard for them to eat strawberries in that time, let alone gooseberries that's full of thorns.

MIKE McINERNEY. They were not quiet, but very ravenous pigs you had that time, as active as a fox they were, killing my young ducks. Once they had blood tasted you couldn't stop them.

MICHEAL MISKELL. And what happened myself the fair day of Esserkelly,[5] the time I was passing your door? Two brazened dogs that rushed out and took a piece of me. I never was the better of it or of the start I got, but wasting from then 'til now!

MIKE McINERNEY. Thinking you were a wild beast they did, that had made his escape out of the travelling show, with the red eyes of you and the ugly face of you, and the two crooked legs of you that wouldn't hardly stop a pig in a gap. Sure any dog that had any life in it at all would be roused and stirred seeing the like of you going the road!

MICHEAL MISKELL. I did well taking out a summons against you that time. It is a great wonder you not to have been bound over through your lifetime, but the laws of England is queer.

MIKE McINERNEY. What ailed me that I did not summons yourself after you stealing away the clutch of eggs I had in the barrel, and I away in Ardrahan, searching out a clocking hen.

MICHEAL MISKELL. To steal your eggs is it? Is that what you are saying now? (*Holds up his hands.*) The Lord is in heaven, and Peter and the saints, and yourself that was in Ardrahan that day put a hand on them as soon as myself! Isn't it a bad story for me to be wearing out my days beside you the same as a spancelled[6] goat. Chained I am and tethered I am to a man that is ramsacking his mind for lies!

MIKE McINERNEY. If it is a bad story for you, Micheal Miskell, it is a worse story again for myself. A Miskell to be next and near me through the whole of the four quarters of the year. I never heard there to be any great name on the Miskells as there was on my own race and name.

MICHEAL MISKELL. You didn't, is it? Well, you could hear it if you had but ears to hear it. Go across to Lisheen Crannagh and down to the sea and to Newtown Lynch and the mills of Duras and you'll find a Miskell, and as far as Dublin!

MIKE McINERNEY. What signifies Crannagh and the mills of Duras? Look at all my own generations that are buried at the Seven Churches. And how many generations of the Miskells are buried in it? Answer me that!

MICHEAL MISKELL. I tell you but for the wheat that was to be sowed there would be more side cars and more common cars at my father's funeral (God rest his soul!) than at any funeral ever left your own door. And as to my mother, she was a Cuffe from Claregalway, and it's she had the purer blood!

MIKE McINERNEY. And what do you say to the banshee?[7] Isn't she apt to have knowledge of the ancient race? Was ever she heard to screech or to cry for the Miskells? Or the Cuffes from Claregalway? She was not, but for the six families, the Hyneses, the Foxes, the Faheys, the Dooleys, the McInerneys. It is of the nature of the McInerneys she is I am thinking, crying them the same as a king's children.

MICHEAL MISKELL. It is a pity the banshee not to be crying for yourself at this minute, and giving you a warning to quit your lies and your chat and your arguing and your contrary ways; for there is no one under the rising sun could stand you. I tell you you are not behaving as in the presence of the Lord!

MIKE McINERNEY. Is it wishful for my death you are? Let it come and meet me now and welcome so long as it will part me from yourself! And I say, and I would kiss the book on it, I to have one request only to be granted, and I leaving it in my will, it is what I would request, nine furrows of the field, nine ridges of the hills, nine waves of the ocean to be put between your grave and my own grave the time we will be laid in the ground!

MICHEAL MISKELL. Amen to that! Nine ridges, is it? No, but let the whole ridge of the world separate us 'til the Day of Judgment! I would not be laid anear you at the Seven Churches, I to get Ireland without a divide!

MIKE McINERNEY. And after that again! I'd sooner than ten pound in my hand, I to know that my shadow and my ghost will not be knocking about with your shadow and your ghost, and the both of us wasting our time. I'd sooner be delayed in Purgatory! Now, have you anything to say?

MICHEAL MISKELL. I have everything to say, if I had but the time to say it!

MIKE McINERNEY. (*Sitting up.*) Let me up out of this 'til I'll choke you!

MICHEAL MISKELL. You scolding pauper, you!

MIKE McINERNEY. (*Shaking his fist at him.*) Wait a while!

MICHEAL MISKELL. (*Shaking his fist.*) Wait a while yourself!

Mrs. Donohoe comes in with a parcel. She is a countrywoman with a frilled cap and a shawl. She stands still a minute. The two old men lie down and compose themselves.

MRS. DONOHOE. They bade me come up here by the stair. I never was in this place at all. I don't know am I right. Which now of the two of ye is Mike McInerney?

MIKE McINERNEY. Who is it calling me by my name?

MRS. DONOHOE. Sure amn't I your sister, Honor McInerney that was, that is now Honor Donohoe.

MIKE McINERNEY. So you are, I believe. I didn't know you 'til you pushed anear me. It is time indeed for you to come see me, and I in this place five year or more. Thinking me to be no credit to you, I suppose, among that tribe of the Donohoes. I wonder they to give you leave to come ask am I living yet or dead?

MRS. DONOHOE. Ah, sure, I buried the whole string of them. Himself was the last to go. (*Wipes her eyes.*) The Lord be praised he got a fine natural death. Sure we must go through our crosses. And he got a lovely funeral; it would delight you to hear the priest reading the Mass. My poor John Donohoe! A nice clean man, you couldn't but be fond of him. Very severe on the tobacco he was, but he wouldn't touch the drink.

MIKE McINERNEY. And is it in Curranroe you are living yet?

MRS. DONOHOE. It is so. He left all to myself. But it is a lonesome thing the head of a house to have died!

MIKE McINERNEY. I hope that he has left you a nice way of living?

MRS. DONOHOE. Fair enough, fair enough. A wide lovely house I have; a few acres of grass land . . . The grass does be very sweet that grows among the stones. And as to the sea, there is something from it every day of the year, a handful of periwinkles[8] to make kitchen, or cockles[9] maybe. There is many a thing in the sea is not decent, but cockles is fit to put before the Lord!

MIKE MCINERNEY. You have all that! And you without ere a man in the house?

MRS. DONOHOE. It is what I am thinking, yourself might come and keep me company. It is no credit to me a brother of my own to be in this place at all.

MIKE MCINERNEY. I'll go with you! Let me out of this! It is the name of the McInerneys will be rising on every side!

MRS. DONOHOE. I don't know. I was ignorant of you being kept to the bed.

MIKE MCINERNEY. I am not kept to it, but maybe an odd time when there is a colic rises up within me. My stomach always gets better the time there is a change in the moon. I'd like well to draw anear you. My heavy blessing on you, Honor Donohoe, for the hand you have held out to me this day.

MRS. DONOHOE. Sure you could be keeping the fire in, and stirring the pot with the bit of Indian meal for the hens, and milking the goat and taking the tacklings[10] off the donkey at the door; and maybe putting out the cabbage plants in their time. For when the old man died the garden died.

MIKE MCINERNEY. I could to be sure, and be cutting the potatoes for seed. What luck could there be in a place and a man not to be in it? Is that now a suit of clothes you have brought with you?

MRS. DONOHOE. It is so, the way you will be tasty coming in among the neighbours at Curranroe.

MIKE MCINERNEY. My joy you are! It is well you earned me! Let me up out of this! (*He sits up and spreads out the clothes and tries on coat.*) That now is a good frieze[11] coat . . . and a hat in the fashion . . . (*He puts on hat.*)

MICHEAL MISKELL. (*Alarmed.*) And is it going out of this you are, Mike McInerny?

MIKE MCINERNEY. Don't you hear I am going? To Curranroe I am going. Going am I to a place where I will get every good thing!

MICHEAL MISKELL. And is it to leave me her after you you will?

MIKE MCINERNEY. (*In a rising chant.*) Every good thing! The goat and the kid are there, the sheep and the lamb are there, the cow does be running and she coming to be milked! Ploughing and seed sowing, blossom at Christmas time, the cuckoo speaking through the dark days of the year! Ah, what are you talking about? Wheat high in hedges, no talk about the rent! Salmon in the rivers as plenty as turf! Spending and getting and nothing scarce! Sport and pleasure, and music on the strings! Age will go from me and I will be young again. Geese and turkeys for the hundreds and drink for the whole world!

MICHEAL MISKELL. Ah, Mike, is it truth you are saying, you to go from me and to leave me with rude people and with townspeople, and with people of every parish in the union, and they having no respect for me or no wish for me at all!

MIKE MCINERNEY. Whist now and I'll leave you . . . my pipe (*Hands it over.*) and I'll engage it is Honor Donohoe won't refuse to be sending you a few ounces of tobacco an odd time, and neighbours coming to the fair in November or in the month of May.

MICHEAL MISKELL. Ah, what signifies tobacco? All that I am craving is the talk. There to be no one at all to say out to whatever thought might be rising in my innate mind! To be lying here and no conversible person in it would be the abomination of misery!

MIKE MCINERNEY. Look now, Honor . . . It is what I often heard said, two to be better than one . . . Sure if you had an old trouser was full of holes . . . or a skirt . . . wouldn't you put another in under it that might be as tattered as itself, and the two of them together would make some sort of a decent show?

MRS. DONOHOE. Ah, what are you saying? There is not holes in that suit I brought you now, but as sound it is as the day I spun it for himself.

MIKE MCINERNEY. It is what I am thinking, Honor . . . I do be weak an odd time . . . any load I would carry, it preys upon my side . . . and this man does be weak an odd time with the swelling in his knees . . . but the two of us together it's not likely it is at the one time we would fail. Bring the both of us with you, Honor, and the height of the castle of luck on you, and the both of us together will make one good hardy man!

MRS. DONOHOE. I'd like my job! Is it queer in the head you are grown asking me to bring in a stranger off the road?

MICHEAL MISKELL. I am not, ma'am, but an old neighbour I am. If I had forecasted this asking I would have asked it myself. Micheal Miskell I am, that was in the next house to you in Skehanagh!

MRS. DONOHOE. For pity's sake! Micheal Miskell is it? That's worse again. Yourself and Mike that never left fighting and scolding and attacking one another! Sparring at one another like two young pups you were, and threatening one another after like two grown dogs!

MIKE MCINERNEY. All the quarrelling was ever in the place it was myself did it. Sure his anger rises fast and goes away like the wind. Bring him out with myself now, Honor Donohoe, and God bless you.

MRS. DONOHOE. Well, then, I will not bring him out, and I will not bring yourself out, and you not to learn better sense. Are you making yourself ready to come?

MIKE MCINERNEY. I am thinking, maybe . . . it is a mean thing for a man that is shivering into seventy years to go changing from place to place.

MRS. DONOHOE. Well, take your luck or leave it. All I asked was to save you from the hurt and the harm of the year.

MIKE MCINERNEY. Bring the both of us with you or I will not stir out of this.

MRS. DONOHOE. Give me back my fine suit so (*Begins gathering up the clothes.*), 'til I'll go look for a man of my own!

MIKE MCINERNEY. Let you do so, as you are so unnatural and so disobliging, and look for some man of your own, God help him! For I will not go with you at all!

MRS. DONOHOE. It is too much time I lost with you, and dark night waiting to overtake me on the road. Let the two of you stop together, and the back of my hand to you. It is I will leave you there the same as God left the Jews!

She goes out. The old men lie down and are silent for a moment.

MICHEAL MISKELL. Maybe the house is not so wide as what she says.

MIKE MCINERNEY. Why wouldn't it be wide?

MICHEAL MISKELL. Ah, there does be a good deal of middling poor houses down by the sea.

MIKE MCINERNEY. What would you know about wide houses? Whatever sort of a house you had yourself it was too wide for the provision you had into it.

MICHEAL MISKELL. Whatever provision I had in my house it was wholesome provision and natural provision. Herself and her periwinkles! Periwinkles is a hungry sort of food.

MIKE MCINERNEY. Stop your impudence and your chat or it will be the worse for you. I'd bear with my own father and mother as long as any man would, but if they'd vex me I would give them the length of a rope as soon as another!

MICHEAL MISKELL. I would never ask at all to go eating periwinkles.

MIKE MCINERNEY. (*Sitting up.*) Have you anyone to fight me?

MICHEAL MISKELL. (*Whimpering.*) I have not, only the Lord!

MIKE MCINERNEY. Let you leave putting insults on me so, and death picking at you!

MICHEAL MISKELL. Sure I am saying nothing at all to displease you. It is why I wouldn't go eating periwinkles, I'm in dread I might swallow the pin.

MIKE MCINERNEY. Who in the world wide is asking you to eat them? You're as tricky as a fish in the full tide!

MICHEAL MISKELL. Tricky is it! Oh, my curse and the curse of the four and twenty men upon you!

MIKE MCINERNEY. That the worm may chew you from skin to marrow bone! (*Seizes his pillow.*)

MICHEAL MISKELL. (*Seizing his own pillow.*) I'll leave my death on you, you scheming vagabone!

MIKE MCINERNEY. By cripes! I'll pull out your pin feathers! (*Throwing pillow.*)

MICHEAL MISKELL. (*Throwing pillow.*) You tyrant! You big bully you!

MIKE McINERNEY. (*Throwing pillow and seizing mug.*) Take this so, you stobbing[12] ruffian you!

They throw all within their reach at one another, mugs, prayer books, pipes, etc.

THE END

Notes

1. workhouse: Poorhouse; a house established for the unemployed poor of a parish.

2. tin-tacks: Short metal nails.

3. mangolds (also called mangel): A variety of beet with a large root, cultivated as feed for livestock.

4. mering: Boundary.

5. Esserkelly: A town in the west of Ireland that has a fair. Legend has it that the banshee stops and wails at Esserkelly castle with a red petticoat about her head.

6. spancelled: Tied up, fettered.

7. banshee (Irish: bean sidhe): A woman of the fairies; commonly refers to a supernatural being who wails under the windows of a house where someone is about to die.

8. periwinkles (also called winkle): A small herbivorous shore-dwelling mollusk with a spiral shell.

9. cockles: An edible, burrowing bivalve mollusk with a spiral shell.

10. tacklings: Devices such as ropes, hooks, etc. for lifting heavy objects.

11. frieze: Coarse woolen cloth.

12. stobbing: Ignorant.

Teresa Deevy
(1894–1963)

     When the Abbey Theatre rejected Sean O'Casey's *The Silver Tassie* in 1928, the first chapter of Ireland's national subsidized theatre closed. In the decade that followed, however, new playwrights surfaced in a quiet spirit of artistic rebellion. The most significant dramatist of the 1930s was Teresa Deevy, a remarkable woman who holds a place second only to Lady Gregory in the gallery of Irish women dramatists.

Deevy wrote twenty-five plays, six of which were produced at the Abbey between 1930 and 1936. Often called "the Irish Chekhov" because of her subject matter and style, she was considered an experimental playwright by her contemporary critics.[1] She was noted for her vivid characterizations and her finely individualized dialogue. The latter accomplishment is quite impressive in light of the fact that she was totally deaf.

The youngest of thirteen children, Teresa Deevy was born in Waterford on January 19, 1894. Her father, Edward Deevy, died when she was only three, and her mother, Mary Feehan Deevy, was a deeply religious woman who passed on her staunch Catholic beliefs to her children. Deevy received her early schooling at the Ursuline Convent in Waterford. Shortly after entering University College Dublin in 1913, she developed Meniere's disease, a condition that causes loss of hearing. She transferred to University College Cork, and by the time she graduated she was completely deaf.

After moving to London to study lipreading, Deevy began to frequent the theatre. She attended as many productions as possible, always trying to read the script beforehand. She was especially impressed by Chekhov and Shaw, and the influences of the former later surfaced in her own plays. She returned to Ireland in 1919, determined to devote all her energy to playwriting and to find a theatre that would showcase her talents.

Deevy's first one-act plays, *Reserved Ground* and *After To-Morrow*, were rejected by the Abbey Theatre, but Lennox Robinson, a member of the reading committee, encouraged her to continue. In 1930, the Abbey produced her three-act play *Reapers*, which presents Irish middle-class life in a provincial town. The following year, the Abbey opened Deevy's next play, *A Disciple* (originally titled *In Search of Valour*), which introduced what the poet Sean Dunne identifies as the typical Deevy theme: "the contradiction between desire and the impossibility of fulfillment."[2] *Temporal Powers*, which deals with poverty in an unsentimental yet moving way, opened at the Abbey in 1932 and won a joint prize with Paul Vincent Carroll's *Things That Are Caesar's*. Her next one-act play, *The King of Spain's Daughter*, opened at the Abbey in 1935. Its flighty protagonist, Annie Kinsella, is the literary precursor of Deevy's most well-known character, Katie Roche.

The 1936 season saw two of Deevy's full-length plays staged: *Katie Roche* and *The Wild Goose*. Of all Deevy's plays, *Katie Roche* has received the widest critical acclaim from both literary and production standpoints. It is a study of a vibrant, fiercely independent young woman who allows her romantic passions to rule her heart, while her social conditioning rules her head. Hailed by Dublin critics, the play was revived at the Abbey in 1938, 1949, 1953, and 1975. After the Abbey rejected *Wife to James Whelan* in 1942, Deevy turned to writing for radio; the Abbey's Experimental Theatre, now known as the Peacock Theatre, did, however, produce *Light Falling* in 1948.

During Deevy's last few years, her writing amounted to little. She tried to write a ballet, *Possession*, which was based on the Irish legend of the *Táin*,[3] and she began—but never completed—a play about Thomas Francis Meagher. She also wrote some children's stories and co-authored a children's book called *Lisheen*.[4] Teresa Deevy died on January 19, 1963. Her obituary notices were laudatory; one, for example, called her "a major

Irish playwright" and asserted that "the Irish theatre had suffered a heavy loss by her death."[5]

The King of Spain's Daughter was published five times: first in New York's *Theatre Arts* in June 1935; next in *The Dublin Magazine* 11, no. 1, in 1936; again in *Three Plays* by Teresa Deevy (Macmillan) in 1939; then in *"The King of Spain's Daughter" and Other One-Act Plays* by Teresa Deevy (Dublin, New Frontiers Press) in 1947; and most recently in *Selected Plays of Irish Playwright Teresa Deevy, 1894–1963*, edited by Eibhear Walshe (Edwin Mellen Press) in 2003. This last volume republishes the three plays in the 1939 collection (*Katie Roche, The King of Spain's Daughter*, and *The Wild Goose*) and also publishes for the first time Deevy's compelling radio drama, *Supreme Dominion*.

The King of Spain's Daughter opened at the Abbey on April 29, 1935. Although Lennox Robinson had directed every Deevy play up until this point, this production was directed by Fred Johnson, an Abbey actor who had appeared in *Reapers*. The production starred Ria Mooney as Annie Kinsella and featured Ann Clery, J. Winter, John Stephenson, and the up-and-coming young actor Cyril Cusack. *The King of Spain's Daughter* shared the bill with a revival of *Wrack*, a full-length peasant drama by the Donegal naturalist Peadar O'Donnell, which Robinson had directed during the 1932 season.[6] The Abbey revived *The King of Spain's Daughter* on July 27, 1936, featuring much of the same cast. The play was also successfully televised in London by the BBC in the pioneering days of prewar television.[7] Its American premiere was directed by Charlotte Headrick at Oregon State University in 2013 and toured to Corvallis's Majestic Theatre in 2014.

Deevy's unpublished plays include *Light Falling, One Look and What It Led To, In the Cellar of My Friend, Dignity, Within a Marble City, Polinka, The Finding of the Ball, Holiday House, Reapers, Going Beyond Alma's Glory, Mac-Conglinne, A Minute's Wait, After Tomorrow, Possession, Concerning Meagher, or How Did He Die* and *Reserved Ground*. In 1995, *The Irish University Review* was the first to publish Deevy's three-act play *Wife to James Whelan*; it was directed by Jonathan Bank in 2010 at the Mint Theatre in New York, and was published again in 2011 in *Teresa Deevy Reclaimed*, vol. 1, edited by John Harrington, Christopher Morash, and Jonathan Bank.

The King of Spain's Daughter

CHARACTERS

PETER KINSELLA, a labourer.
JIM HARRIS, a labourer.
MRS. MARKS, a neighbour.
ANNIE KINSELLA, Peter's daughter.
RODDY MANN, a loafer.

SCENE

An open space on a grassy road. At each side are road barriers with notices, "No Traffic" and "Road Closed." At the back an old dilapidated wall; a small door in the centre of the wall stands open and fields can be seen beyond. County Council workers have been employed here. Two coats, a thermos flask, an old sack, and a man's hat and stick have been left on a pile of stones near one of the barriers. Peter Kinsella, a heavily built man of fifty, comes through the doorway. He carries a pickax; his overalls and boots are covered with a fine dust. He stands in the centre, looks away to the left, shading his eyes, then to right. Jim Harris comes on, whistling. He is twenty-four, wears a cap and dusty overalls. He leaves his spade against the wall, goes to the barrier at the right side, leans on it, looking away to the right.

TIME

The action of the play takes place on a grassy road in Ireland during the dinner hour of a day in April.

ACT I

JIM. Great work at the weddin' below. Miss What's-her-name getting married. The women were gathered at the wharf an hour and a half before time for send-off. (*Laughs. Peter nods without interest.*) Right well it looked from above, with the white launch, an' the flags flyin' an' the sun on the water. Brave and gay at the start, however 'twill go. (*He takes his thermos flask.*) Come on, man. With the noise of the sirens I didn't hear the whistle, an' I kept workin' five minutes too long. Wasn't that a terrible thing to have happen to me?

PETER. She's late with my dinner.

JIM. (*Dismayed.*) What! Didn't she come here at all?

PETER. She did not. Late—the second time in the week.

JIM. 'Tis on account of that weddin'. She'll be up by now. They don't feel
time or weather when they're waitin' for a bride.

PETER. I'll make her feel something . . . her father without his dinner.

JIM. (*Looking to the right.*) Is it at the wharf she is? Or the far side of the river
watchin' the start?

PETER. Do I, or anyone, ever know where Annie'd be? Only sisters you
have, but they'd give you more thought than that daughter of mine.
Oh, she'll be sorry yet.

JIM. It is because of the day; the women can think of nothin' else; they're
all the same. Molly and Dot were up at the dawn—would it be a fine
day! You'd think they were guests invited. They know her by eyesight
so they'll go stand in the crowd and see how she'll look.

PETER. If I knew where to get Annie.

JIM. Annie'll be here now. They're scatterin' away off the wharf, though I
can't pick her out.

PETER. And how would you? More than likely she's off with Roddy
Mann. Philanderin' with the like of him—that's all she's fit for—or
with any boy she can lay hold of.

JIM. If she goes on a bit aself[8] 'tis because she must; she's made that way,
she can't help it.

PETER. I'll make her help it! You're in no great hurry to have her.

JIM. (*Flings round on him.*) You know that I am!

PETER. Why don't you marry her so? And stop her goin' on? You're in no
hurry.

JIM. I want that, and you know it. How can I force the girl?

PETER. Ay, how indeed? (*Laughs contemptuously.*) Aw, you're very young.

*Peter goes to the door, stands there looking out across the fields. Jim sits down
on the stones and begins his dinner. Mrs. Marks, a big woman of fifty-five or so,
wearing a shawl and with a basket on her arm, comes to the barrier at the right.
She pushes the barrier a little aside and comes on.*

MRS. MARKS. Can I pass this way? 'Twould be a short cut.

JIM. Are you a motor car, ma'am? (*Looks her up and down.*) You are not, 'tis two legs are under you. You can, and welcome.

MRS. MARKS. I thought you had sense in your head, Jim Harris. (*Puts down her basket, resting it against a large stone.*) There's a terrible weight in that basket, there is.

JIM. That was a great send-off they gave the bridal pair.

MRS. MARKS. It was so. I wasn't on the wharf on account of my bad knee, but I seen from above, an' I met some of them now. I'm glad she had it fine, the poor young thing.

JIM. What "poor" is on her? Isn't it the day of her life?

MRS. MARKS. You could never tell that. It might. They say he wanted the money. They say it was signed and settled before ever he seen her. Well, she'll have her red carpet and all her fine show for her poor heart to feed on. That's the way.

PETER. (*Coming from the door.*) Fine day, ma'am.

MRS. MARKS. It is indeed, thanks be to God. 'Tis a day of the earth and the sky.

JIM. With the whole month of April floatin' around.

MRS. MARKS. Annie was tellin' me the bride looked like a queen.

PETER. Did you see Annie? She didn't bring me my dinner.

MRS. MARKS. Oh, look at that now! A shame and a sin! She's off across the field with that Roddy Mann.

JIM. (*Jumps up.*) I'll go call her.

PETER. Stop where you are! (*Peter strides off.*)

JIM. (*To Mrs. Marks.*) You had a right to keep that to yourself.

MRS. MARKS. To leave her father without his bit! An' she romancin' around!

JIM. He'll have her life.

MRS. MARKS. She earns what she gets. Why don't she settle down? She's a bold wild thing.

JIM. He treats her cruel; it don't do her any good.

MRS. MARKS. And what would do her good? That Annie Kinsella will be romancin' all her life with whoever she can.

JIM. The way he treats her—it only drives her on worse.

MRS. MARKS. You're too soft-hearted, Jimmy Harris. But I have a great
wish for you, for the sake of your mother, God rest her soul. You'd be
better to give Annie up.

JIM. Give up me life, is it?

MRS. MARKS. You have two good sisters, can't you settle with them, or
get a sensible girl. I'm telling you now, that one, her head is full of folly
and her heart is full of wile. She'd do you no good.

JIM. You have a lot of old talk. (*Silence. Then distant cheering.*) They're not
done with it yet.

MRS. MARKS. I was thinking of my marriage day when I was looking at
them two. It is a thought would sadden anyone.

JIM. How is that, Mrs. Marks?

MRS. MARKS. That's how it is; the truth is the best to be told in the end.

JIM. Haven't you Bill and Mary, and the little place? You didn't fare bad.

MRS. MARKS. Bad. What have bad or good to do with it? That is outside
of the question. For twenty years you're thinking of that day, an' for
thirty years you're lookin' back at it. After that you don't mind—you
haven't the feelin'—exceptin' maybe an odd day, like today. (*She takes
her basket. They hear someone coming. Mrs. Marks puts down her basket
again, and waits, expectant.*) Annie . . . and you may be sure she's not
alone.

*Annie Kinsella is seen in the doorway. She is about twenty. She wears a dark
shawl, a red dress, black shoes and stockings—all very neat. Her hair is bright
gold. With her is Roddy Mann, a big lounging figure, cap pulled low over his eyes.*

ANNIE. Now, Roddy, don't come any farther. (*Low tone. Mrs. Marks listens;
Jim moves a little farther from the doorway.*) Give me the tin.

Roddy hands a tin to her.

RODDY. What did you promise?

ANNIE. (*Low, eager.*) Wait first 'till I tell you how she looked.

RODDY. You have told me already; you have talked of nothin' else.

ANNIE. She was like what you'd dream. I think I never seen anything
so grand. She was like a livin' flame passin' down by us. She was

dressed in flamin' red from top to toe, and . . . (*Puts her hand to her breast.*) Here she had a diamond clasp.

RODDY. And there you have your heart. Now give us a kiss. What did you promise? Leave down the tin.

Annie puts the tin on the ground, slips her hands up about his neck and gives him a long kiss.

ANNIE. That will do now.

RODDY. You have my heart scalded.

He moves off. Annie takes up the tin, wipes her mouth on her sleeve, very thoroughly, turns to wave to Roddy. Comes in.

ANNIE. Jimmy, it was like heaven. She looked that lovely. The launch was all white, and the deck covered with flowers. They had a red carpet . . .

JIM. You're late with his dinner.

ANNIE. Late! (*Alarmed.*) The whistle didn't go!

JIM. Ten minutes apast one.

ANNIE. He'll have my life!

MRS. MARKS. An' small balme to him so! Without a bit or a sup! A man wants his dinner. He's gone down to find you.

JIM. Why couldn't you come?

ANNIE. What misfortune came over me? I am at a loss for a word. What will I do now?

MRS. MARKS. Take it down to him, run.

ANNIE. He'd kill me, he'd kill me dead. I think I'll stop here till he'll come.

JIM. Here he is now.

All look toward the doorway.

MRS. MARKS. (*Turns to Jim.*) Don't be drawn into it, you. 'Twould be a mistake. Keep your eyes on the ground; 'tis the safest place. You won't see what's happening, and you won't lose your head.

PETER. (*Coming in.*) Is she there? (*He sees Annie.*) Ah-h!

ANNIE. (*Nervous, almost perky.*) I'm a bit late with the dinner; 'tis because of the weddin' I didn't hear the whistle: I didn't know it had gone one.

Annie leaves his dinner tin on the ground, not too near him, and moves away.

PETER. Hand me that tin.

Annie hands it, keeping as far as possible from him. Peter, taking the tin, hits out at her. Annie dodges and partly escapes, but cries out; Jim springs forward; Mrs. Marks catches Jim by the arm.

MRS. MARKS. 'Tis a terrible misfortune for any man to take the least iota interest in a girl like that!

This flow stops them all.

JIM. (*After a silence.*) What do you want here, Mrs. Marks?
MRS. MARKS. I wouldn't be in it at all but for the sake of your mother, 'tis well she's in the grave.
PETER. (*To Annie.*) Go down there, you . . . (*Gestures toward the barrier at the left.*) . . . And rake up the few stones I have agen the wall.

Annie hesitates, looks at her father, at Jim, at Mrs. Marks.

PETER. Do you hear what I'm saying?
ANNIE. I don't mind what'll happen; I can take care of myself.

Goes off, left, with a backward look at Jim. Jim would follow her but for Peter's forbidding look. Peter goes over to where the coats have been left on the stones. Takes his stick from under the coats.

JIM. This is the best sheltered place for takin' your dinner. You can have the sack on top of them stones.
PETER. Mind yer business.
MRS. MARKS. Steady now, keep steady. Don't let us have anything happen!
JIM. (*To Peter.*) You have your dinner now, can't you leave her alone?
PETER. Do she belong to you? (*Pause.*) Do she? When she do you can talk.

Peter goes.

MRS. MARKS. Supposin' you were to get a blow instead of herself—what good would that be? It might do you a grievous harm! Great cheer to see her standin' upright if yourself was lyin' low! I wouldn't stir up the embers in a man like that. (*Jim walks away from her.*) Now I'll tell you this—though I know you won't listen—if you were a man at all you'd make her marry you.

JIM. An' how can I do that?

MRS. MARKS. Ah, you're too soft-hearted for any woman. 'Tis the hard man wins, and right he should. (*Confidential now.*) Annie Kinsella— when I met her down there—was tellin' me how grand the bride looked. "She was dressed," said she, "in shimmerin' green from head to foot."

JIM. What's wrong with that?

MRS. MARKS. Didn't you hear her now to Roddy Mann, "She was dressed in flamin' red from top to toe."

JIM. So she did.

MRS. MARKS. That's the count she puts on the truth! I'm only tellin' you now so's you'll harden your heart! Whatever'll come easy is what she'll say. Now—for the sake of your mother—if you marry that girl, don't believe one word she'll tell you. That's the only way you'll have peace of mind! (*A cry. Jim starts forward; Mrs. Marks catches his arm.*) Be a man now! Be a man, and don't get yourself hurt!

JIM. Keep out of my way!

Jim tries to push her aside. Annie, a little dishevelled, frightened, and with her shawl trailing, runs on. She runs to the barrier at the right side, leans against it, and moans, nursing her shoulder.

MRS. MARKS. (*To Jim.*) Now strengthen your heart, quiet your mind. Don't do yourself harm on anyone's account. We get what we merit, and God is good. (*Pause.*) I'll leave ye now. (*Takes her basket, does not notice that she has left a small parcel on the stone, moves off. Near the barrier she stops again, looks back at Jim.*) Don't be moved to any foolish compassion. The hard man wins.

Mrs. Marks goes. Jim comes a little forward, sits down on an old plank, his back to Annie; takes a small notebook from his pocket, turns the pages; glances over his shoulder in Annie's direction, slips the notebook into his pocket again; waits for

*Annie to come to him. After a moment she brushes aside her tears, comes over and
sits down close beside him.*

ANNIE. It was a grand sight, Jim, it was like heaven.

JIM. (*Catches her wrist.*) He hurt you then, did he do you any harm?

ANNIE. Ah, leave that now! Let us leave that behind us . . . the band was
    playing, and the flags were grand . . .

JIM. 'Tis a shame you'd madden him. He'll harm you some day, and all
    your own fault. You won't have any life left. An' what can I do?

ANNIE. Didn't you see the launch at all?

JIM. I saw well from above.

ANNIE. You should have been on the wharf. The cheering an' the music,
    an' all the sun on the river, an' everyone happy . . .

JIM. We'd all be happy if you'd have sense.

ANNIE. She looked lovely passin' along, her hand restin' in his, and her
    body swayin' beside him down the path. The arms of the two fami-
    lies were painted on the launch, the sun was shinin' on it; everything
    was white or burnin' red, but she was dressed in pale, pale gold and
    (*Hands to her breast.*) two red flowers were crushed agen her here.

JIM. (*Springs up.*) What lies are you tellin'? I saw her myself: she was
    dressed in grey; she had no flowers.

ANNIE. (*Gentle, bewildered.*) Jimmy, what's wrong with you?

JIM. She was dressed in grey. Tell the truth!

ANNIE. It was in pale gold I saw her.

JIM. (*Furious.*) And in shimmerin' green, an' in flamin' red, an' in milk
    white when it will suit you!

Silence.

ANNIE. (*Gets up slowly.*) You are a pack of blind owls—all the lot of you!
    I saw what I saw!

She turns from him.

JIM. But why won't you tell the truth, an' it just as easy?

ANNIE. Stop your fool talk! The truth! Burstin' in where you don't know.
    Oh, if I could have love!

JIM. Will you leave talkin' of love when I'm tired of askin' you'd come to the priest with me! Are we to be married ever? Are we?

ANNIE. (*Quietly.*) Whisht,[9] Jimmy, whisht.

Annie looks off away to the right, in the direction of the river.

JIM. Are we? I must know.

ANNIE. (*To herself.*)

Then the wet windin' roads,

Brown bogs and black water,

And my thoughts on white ships

And the King of Spain's daughter.

JIM. I'm sick of that thing! Who's the King of Spain's daughter?

ANNIE. Myself.

JIM. Yourself . . . (*A laugh.*) And the bride beyond!

ANNIE. It is myself I seen in her—sailin' out into the sun, and to adventure.

JIM. Are you going to marry me? Make up your mind.

They hear a sound as of someone coming.

ANNIE. What's that? (*Frightened.*) Is he coming? Jim, he says he'll make me sign on for the factory.

JIM. The factory? In the town beyond? (*She nods.*) That you couldn't stand before?

ANNIE. I was there six months; it would be five years this time.

JIM. Five years! You couldn't do that!

ANNIE. They're only takin' them will be bound for five years. I couldn't face it. (*Falters.*) Every mornin' walkin' the road, every evenin' draggin' back so tired. He has the card, he says he'll come make me sign it now.

JIM. It was a pity you didn't bring his dinner in time!

ANNIE. It was a great misfortune for me. I am at a loss to explain it.

JIM. And I think he knew that Roddy was with you.

ANNIE. It is that decided him.

JIM. Why do you go with Roddy, and Jack?

ANNIE. It is very unfortunate that I do . . . I would face any life—no matter what—before I'd go back to that place.

JIM. Did you kiss Roddy Mann again today?

ANNIE. (*Injured.*) And who else was there for me to kiss?

JIM. When I left you last night, did you go back to Jack Bolger?

ANNIE. Last night . . . no, I don't think I did, last night.

JIM. (*Furious.*) We're all the wan! You have no heart.

ANNIE. So must I go to the factory? Won't you marry me now?

JIM. Annie! Won't I, is it? You know well . . . (*Overjoyed, but checks himself.*) Will you come with me tonight and we'll tell the priest?

ANNIE. Is it stand beside you an' you sayin' that? (*Insulted.*) The ground would open under me! Go tell him yourself, let you.

JIM. Would you go back on me then?

ANNIE. I would not.

JIM. You would not? You've changed your mind often.

ANNIE. I'll be in the chapel the day he'll name.

JIM. You will? And come with me then?

ANNIE. What else is there for me?

JIM. Annie! (*Checks himself.*) I'll tell them to look out for a place so they can get a room in the town.

ANNIE. Tell who?

JIM. Molly and Dot. 'Tis I have the house: they knew they'd have to go.

ANNIE. Well, then, they needn't. Let them stop where they are. What would I do without a woman to talk to?

JIM. I want you to myself.

ANNIE. I never heard the like! A good "man" he'd make to begin by turnin' his two sisters on the road! And they after mindin' the place since his mother died.

JIM. Will you go back on me so?

ANNIE. Leave Molly and Dot stay where they are.

JIM. I will not.

ANNIE. What great harm would they do?

JIM. They'd be in it—spoilin' the world.

ANNIE. Spoilin' the world! I think you're crazy.

JIM. When we shut the house door I'll have no one in it but you and me.

ANNIE. (*After a moment.*) I think I'll stop with my father.

JIM. And go to the factory?

ANNIE. Maybe I wouldn't do either, but run away.

JIM. He'd go after you: he'd have you crippled.

ANNIE. I haven't signed yet. I might get on the soft side of him yet if I'd promise . . .

JIM. What promise would you keep? (*Silence.*) I have twenty pounds saved.

ANNIE. Where did you get that?

Not greatly interested. Jim takes out his notebook, opens it.

JIM. Four years ago you said I had no money. I have the house now, and besides what I earn I put by two shillin's every week.

ANNIE. Two shillin's . . . you did! Every week . . . since that time long ago?

JIM. (*Turning the pages of his notebook.*) A hundred shillings . . . that was five pounds the first year . . . and another five then . . . and another . . . and this is the fourth . . .

ANNIE. (*Awed.*) You kept it up all along?

JIM. Did you think I'd fall tired?

ANNIE. Let me see. I didn't know you were doin' that. (*Takes the notebook, turns the pages. Silence. Then*) Oh, 'tis smudged and dirty. Why couldn't you keep it clean?

Angered. Throws the book from her. Silence.

JIM. Two hundred weeks, and that's all you'd care. (*Walks away.*)

ANNIE. What would you do with it?

JIM. (*Coming a little way back to her.*) It would set us up . . . to buy a few things. I'd have to give the priest some. Then whatever you'd like for the house, and yourself, so's we could settle down right.

ANNIE. Settle down. (*A knell[10] to her.*) I dunno could I ever get into service in a place in London?

JIM. (*In fury.*) If your father heard you were at the crossroad last night—or if the priest heard tell of it—dancin' on the board, an' restin' in the ditch with your cheek agen mine and your body pressed to me.

ANNIE. It is only in the dark I could do it—for when I'd see the kind you are . . .

JIM. (*Catches her.*) What's wrong with me now?

ANNIE. (*Holding back.*) Is it *me* to go near you—me?

JIM. (*Crushing her to him.*) What's wrong with me?

ANNIE. Jimmy! He's coming! Let go, let me go!

PETER. (*Coming on.*) So that's what you're at! (*Annie tries to escape. Jim holds her.*) Stop there, stop there the two of you! (*To Jim.*) You can let her go now. (*Jim releases Annie. She stands motionless.*) Was she teasin' you?

JIM. She was.

PETER. Tauntin' you like?

JIM. She was.

PETER. I know . . . leadin' you on?

JIM. That's it.

PETER. Well, me fine lady, we'll put a stop to your fun. You can do some work now. Stay where you are! Stay there the two of you. (*Goes to where the coats have been left, takes a card and a pencil from his coat pocket. Comes over to Annie.*) Write your name there. (*Annie looks at Jim, he avoids her look.*) Do you hear what I say? Write your name. We'll have no more cajolin'.

Annie writes her name on the card. Peter, taking back the card, hits at her. Jim knocks aside Peter's blow, they face each other angrily.)

JIM. Can't you leave her alone!

PETER. Standin' up for her now, but you have no right! No more than to be kissin' her like you were. She don't want you. You can go your road. (*Wheels round to Annie.*) Will you marry him now, or go to the factory? Five years there, or your life with him?

JIM. I'm not askin' you, Annie, I wouldn't, . . . that way.

PETER. He's backin' out now.

ANNIE. (*To Jim.*) I might as well have you. (*Low.*) Who would I ever meet would be fit for me? Where would I ever find a way out of here?

PETER. Have ye settled it so?

JIM. We have.

PETER. You'll take her like that?

JIM. I will.

PETER. Well, I'll keep the card, fearin' she'd change. (*Puts the card in his pocket. Goes off.*)

ANNIE. (*Softly.*) You have me ruined. It is all over now. You can go settle with the priest.

JIM. You won't ever regret it. You won't.

But she turns away.

ANNIE. Go on after him now.

Jim hesitates, goes. Annie moves over to the barrier, looks off away to the right. Mrs. Marks comes to the barrier at the left side, shades her eyes, looking on the ground for her parcel.

MRS. MARKS. Well, look where I left it. (*Comes on, takes the parcel she had forgotten.*) Well and indeed! My head will never spare my heels! Searchin' high and low. (*Sees Jim's notebook on the ground.*) What is that there?

ANNIE. That belongs to Jim Harris. (*Takes the book.*) Jim Harris and myself are getting married very soon.

MRS. MARKS. What! Is he going to marry you in face of all! Well, well, you might talk your head off, or you might spare your breath—it don't make any difference!

ANNIE. Maybe I won't mind it as much as I think.

MRS. MARKS. Be a good wife to him now. Don't give him the bad time you gave your poor father. Often I felt for that poor man when he wouldn't know where you'd be. (*More kindly.*) You have no wish for it? (*Annie shakes her head.*) And there's many a girl would be boundin' with joy. Is there any other you'd liefer[11] have? (*Annie shakes her head.*) Well now, well, you'll be all right. A good sensible boy. And you'll have a nice little place. Mind you keep it well, that'll give you somethin' to do. You won't feel the days slippin'. (*Annie moves restlessly away from her.*) Well, well, if you could get to care for him that would be a blessin' from God. It might come to you later. Sometimes it do, and more times it don't. It might come with the child.

ANNIE. I dread that.

MRS. MARKS. What's that you said? Fie on you then! Did you think you needn't suffer like the rest of the world? Did you think you were put here to walk plain and easy through the gates of heaven?

ANNIE. I dread it . . . dread it.

MRS. MARKS. Would you ask to get in on what others would suffer?

ANNIE. (*To herself.*) I couldn't bear I'd be no more than any other wife. (*Distant cheering is heard; Annie listens, looks away toward the river; flashes.*) It won't be all they'll say of me: "She married Jimmy Harris."

MRS. MARKS. And what better could they say? You have a right to be grateful. Oh, you're a wild creature!

But Annie is not listening; she has opened Jim's notebook, studies it.

ANNIE. (*Turning the pages.*) June . . . July . . . October . . . November . . . December . . .

MRS. MARKS. Poor Jimmy Harris . . . I hope he's doin' a wise thing.

ANNIE. February, March, April . . . June, July, August . . . October—and I was black out with him then—November, December, April, June, August . . .

MRS. MARKS. A good, sensible boy.

ANNIE. Boy! (*She laughs exultantly.*) I think he is a man might cut your throat!

MRS. MARKS. God save us all!

ANNIE. He put by two shillin's every week for two hundred weeks. I think he is a man that—supposin' he was jealous—might cut your throat.

Quiet, exultant, she goes.

MRS. MARKS. The Lord preserve us! That she'd find joy in such a thought!

THE END

Notes

1. Tomas MacAnna, Abbey Theatre director, in a personal interview with Eileen Kearney, August 24, 1984.

2. Sean Dunne, "Rediscovering Teresa Deevy," *Cork Examiner*, March 20, 1984, 10.

3. A copy of this ballet remains in Deevy's estate papers in "Landscape," her Waterford home.

4. Dunne, "Rediscovering Teresa Deevy," 10.

5. Ibid.

6. Lennox Robinson, *Ireland's Abbey Theatre: A History, 1899–1951* (London: Sidgwick, 1951), 148.

7. Denis Johnston, Abbey Theatre program notes for the revival of *Katie Roche*, June 2, 1975.

8. aself: Herself.

9. whisht: Be quiet!

10. knell: The mournful sound of a bell rung slowly for a death or funeral, signifying the end of something (i.e., her free spirit).

11. liefer: Rather.

Anne Le Marquand Hartigan
(1937–)

🔊 Anne Le Marquand Hartigan, a remarkably versatile playwright, poet, and painter, was born in 1937 in England of an Irish mother and a father from the Channel Island of Jersey. She grew up in Reading, where she was schooled and attended university, studying fine art (painting). In 1962 she moved to Ireland, where she lived outside Drogheda on her family farm; there she and her husband raised their six children. She now lives in Dublin.

Because of her wide range of integrated talents, Hartigan comes to her art forms from several diverse avenues. Having acted in several university productions, she demonstrates a keen sense of the theatrical side of script writing. She is a visually oriented poet, and this orientation transfers to her plays. As a painter, she has exhibited in Britain and Ireland, winning awards for *Batik*.

Although her short stories and essays have been published in magazines and in anthologies such as *Territories of the Voice* (later published as *A Green and Mortal Sound*) and *Irish Spirit*, Hartigan is more widely known for her award-winning poetry, which appears in anthologies in the United States, Ireland, and Germany and has been translated into German and Russian. Her poetry volumes include *Long Tongue* (1982); *Return Single* (1986); *Now is a Moveable Feast* (1991), which has been successfully performed on stage and on the radio several times; *Immortal Sins* (1993); and *Nourishment* (2005). She has also published *Clearing the Space: A Why of Writing* (1996), a personal meditation on writing and creativity. Her volume of poetry and prose, *To Keep the Light Burning* (2008), was written to help to those experiencing loss and grief from the death of loved ones. Her most recent volume of poetry, *Unsweet Dreams*, was published in 2011.

Hartigan has written several noteworthy plays, all of which have been produced. Patrick Mason directed a workshop production of her one-act play *Strings* for the Galway Arts Festival in University College Galway's theatre in 1981. Her full-length play *Beds*, an innovative promenade theatre piece, ran for seven performances in the Damer Theatre in the 1982 Dublin Theatre Festival under the direction of Robert Gordon. Cathy Leeney directed *La Corbière*, which ran for two weeks in the Dublin Theatre Festival in October 1989 at the Project Theatre. This play started life as a poem written in response to the tale of the fate of French prostitutes who were shipwrecked at Corbière Lighthouse during World War II. Hartigan reworked the poem as a one-act play for a cast of six. One of its more recent stagings was a production in Beirut. In 2006, *La Corbière* was produced in Washington, DC, by Solas Nua Theatre Company. It was published in 2001 in *Seen and Heard: Six New Plays by Irish Women*, edited by Cathy Leeney.

Hartigan's *Jersey Lilies* (1996) is a trilogy of one-act plays inspired by events surrounding the Nazi occupation in wartime Jersey. It includes *La Corbière*, *Le Crapaud* (The Toad), and *Les Yeux* (The Eyes). It premiered in 1996 at the Samuel Beckett Theatre in Dublin, performed by the playwright Anne Hartigan and the actor-director Robert Gordon. Her most recent full-length play, *The Secret Game* (1995), won the Mobil Prize for Irish playwrights in 1995 and had a 2003 reading produced by Scott Morfee at the Soho Playhouse in New York. It was never published until recently in 2014. *In Other Worlds* (2003), Hartigan's most recent play, was commissioned for a festival of plays by European writers. This short one-act play was performed on three continents in 2003: in Ohio, United States; the Edinburgh Fringe Festival in Scotland; and in Otago, New Zealand (directed by Florence Hartigan).

I Do Like to Be Beside the Seaside[1] (1984), Hartigan's first full-length play, was first produced as a rehearsed staged reading in June 1984 at the Abbey Theatre in Dublin. The production was directed by Christopher Fitz-Simon, former literary manager of the Abbey.

I Do Like to Be Beside the Seaside

The action takes place in the interior of The Retreat, an old people's home on the seafront of an east coast town and on a cliff top nearby. The country is Ireland.

CHARACTERS

The Residents:
MISS EVANS
MR. MULCAHY
MRS. MORGAN
MRS. EVA MURPHY
MR. FRANCIS BUTLER

The Staff:
MRS. PRICE, Matron
TESSIE, Housemaid
MAURA, Housemaid

The Others:
MARGIE, Eva's daughter
PAUL, Margie's husband
PATSY, Maura's boyfriend

ACT 1
SCENE 1

The set should have the feeling of void. The occupants seem to float in their own world. This world is timeless. The few objects in the void/room are starkly real in an unreal world; a modern metal tea trolley, the large TV set, a crucifix, the fire. The few things are the only reality for most of the old people in the room. The cast is dressed in shades of grey, up to some white on Eva's clothes. She might have a little subdued colour as well, down to black. The two maids, Tessie and Maura, have white aprons. One or two of the chairs are occupied by dummies of elderly people. The front stage is the window towards the sea in a sitting room in an old people's home. There is the sound of rain lashing on the windowpanes and the sound of the sea breaking on the seashore outside. Apron stage. Time is immaterial . . .

The stage is dark. Lights up slowly on Bridget Evans. She stands front right. She is wiping a small hole in the condensation on the window, so as to peer out. She supports herself with her other hand on her walker. She carries a handbag that is looped on the rail of her walker. The lights now rise on the whole stage to show Mr. Mulcahy in his chair left front and Eva, who sits at the chess table reading her book. She is in a wheelchair.

Miss Bridget Evans. Cold. (*She peers out through the little space she has cleared in the window.*) It's so cold. (*Silence. She begins to turn very slowly with her walker. She stops to consider.*) Maybe today I could get to the fire before her? (*She completes her turn.*) I would like to sit by the fire. (*Pause. She shuffles. She can only move very, very slowly.*) A real fire is so nice. (*Shuffle.*)

Mr. Mulcahy is hunched in a chair wrapped in a rug. He stares out the window towards the sea. Pays no attention to anything going on around him. You might wonder if he is conscious of where he is. He lives in his thoughts.

Mr. Mulcahy. It's cold. (*Clatter of cups heard.*) It's cold today.

Tessie and Maura are arranging cups and saucers on the trolley. They pour tea and take it to the old people who wait in various parts of the room. Tessie takes a cup of tea to Mr. Mulcahy.

Tessie. How are you today, Mr. Mulcahy?

She expects no answer. He accepts the tea but does not look at her or answer. He holds the cup on his knees but does not drink from it. Tessie returns to the trolley. Spot on Tessie and Maura at the trolley.

Tessie. (*Bored.*) Jesus. (*Maura is regarding her nails. Tessie sighs.*) Jesus, it's always the same. (*Maura is regarding her stockings.*) Always the same bloody thing. (*Maura is regarding her shoes.*) I'm going, I'm getting out of this bloody dump. (*Maura is back to her nails again.*)

Maura. Do you like the colour of my nails? (*Holding her hand at arm's length. Tessie doesn't bother to look.*) It's not so bad . . .

Tessie. (*Interrupting.*) I'm fed up. I'm handing in my notice.

Maura. You keep saying that. (*She wiggles an ankle.*) But you never do it.

TESSIE. I'm pissed off with old people.

MAURA. (*Interrupting.*) Do you think my ankles have swelled?

TESSIE. (*Paying no attention.*) This time is different. Mick's after offering me a job.

MAURA. (*Jeering slightly.*) What? Mick at the shop? I wouldn't work for that old feller. (*Stops looking at her ankles.*) They say they swell at this time of the month. Before "your friend,"[2] you know. Mick's an old bastard.

TESSIE. It'd be more gas[3] than this dump.

MAURA. He'd never stamp your cards.[4]

TESSIE. He would mine. He fancies me.

MAURA. Janey Mac, he fancies everyone. He's the one they say forgot he had a fag[5] in his mouth when he tried to kiss Mary Byrne after a dance. And he's ancient. About forty.

TESSIE. Oh, you can talk. I think you fancy some of the old crabs here.

MAURA. No I don't. I just like them. They're like old babies. Mr. Butler's gorgeous.

TESSIE. I think he's mad. Wait till I tell you what he was doing the other morning. There, in the garden, going like the clatters in that wheel-chair of his, round and round the gold fish pond. And that one, Mrs. Murphy, egging him on and counting the rounds he'd done. They're soft in the head if you ask me.

MAURA. They have great craic[6] together.

TESSIE. And he's as pleased as punch that he'd done eleven! (*Pause.*) Told me I should get myself out of here. What did I want to be stuck with the likes of them? Go off and see the world, he says. What's a nice girl like you doing in a place like this, he says. He can say that again. And he says he'll give me something. Some old picture he has up in his room. Says it's worth a few bob.

MAURA. Would you believe that? (*Pause.*) Anyway, I'm going out with Patsy.

TESSIE. (*A bit jealous and surprised.*) Him! (*Pause.*) Janey, you'd better watch it. He was going out with Rose Callaghan and she's just gone to England in a hurry.[7]

MAURA. So what?

TESSIE. You know what. Everybody's saying in the village . . .

MAURA. They're always saying something in the village. (*Silence. Pushes back cuticles of her nails.*) You know what? (*Giggles.*) Matron told me to wear a bra.

TESSIE. Oh, she's just jealous. If she let hers out they'd drop to her knees.

MAURA. Ah, stop it, Tess. She's not so bad. (*Maura is now looking at the nails on other hand.*)

TESSIE. Janey, it's always the same bloody thing. (*Silence.*)

MAURA. (*Holding out her hand to admire the nail polish.*) Do you like the colour? (*Tessie pays no attention.*) Ah, it's not so bad.

TESSIE. Jesus.

Lights up to include Mr. Mulcahy and Eva, who sit at the chess table.

MR. MULCAHY. It's cold. (*Whining. He fidgets with his rug. Now trying to tuck it in. Now untucking it. Continues to gaze out the window.*)

Enter Matron. She crosses to the front and makes some adjustment to the curtain.

MATRON. How are we, Miss Evans? (*She doesn't wait for an answer.*) Mr. Mulcahy, I see you're fine . . . fine. (*Mr. Mulcahy takes no notice. She goes upstage and smiles and nods at the other occupants. She straightens a cushion that does not need attention.*) Ah, Mrs . . . (*She is looking at Mrs. Eva Murphy.*) Dreadful day . . . just dreadful. (*She turns to the trolley and inspects it with an eagle eye.*) Now, girls, have you everything? Get more scones, Tessie. You need more scones. Right.

Matron exits. Tessie and Maura exchange glances. Tessie exits to get more scones and returns.

TESSIE. (*Muttering.*) The old bat! (*The two girls continue to serve tea.*)

MR. MULCAHY. (*Grumbling. Whining. Complaining.*) It's cold today. (*He shuffles his knees together and takes a sip of tea.*) Rotten tea. Ghastly. (*Pause.*) She never could make a good cup of tea. (*Pause.*) An idiot woman, my dear sister. She'd insist on making tea by the drawing-room fire. Insist. With all her little gadgets. Patty in the kitchen could make a great cup. A grand cup. That wasn't good enough. Oh, no, no. My sister said servants just didn't understand about tea. She had to do it herself. With her la-di-da tea kettle and tea caddy. (*Pause.*) She'd ring the bell. (*Mimics.*) "You can bring up the tea things now, Patty," she'd say. Such a stupid fuss to make a bad cup of tea. God almighty. Made a bloody ceremony out of it. (*Pause.*) All women are whores.

MISS EVANS. Maybe I will sit by the TV. (*Pause.*) It's not so far to the chair by the TV. (*She shuffles towards the TV.*) I would like to get to the fire before her. A fire is so nice. Nice to sit by the fire. (*Pause.*) No, it's much nearer to the chair by the TV.

(*Silence.*)

MR. MULCAHY. (*He has put down his cup and slowly rubs his knees . . . Sings to the tune of "Any Old Iron."*)
Any old bones
Any old bones
That's what I've got, old bones.
Old rag and bone man . . .
Aching and aching.
My own background music, a golden aching oldie. (*Sings to "Where Did You Get That Hat?"*)
Where did you get that ache?
Where did you get that pain . . . ?

Silence.

MISS EVANS. But I'd prefer the fire. I'd much prefer to sit by the fire. That would be nice. (*Silence.*) Everyone feels better by the fire.

MR. MULCAHY. She was there. She was there in the background. Whispering. Her, with her china tea. (*Mimics.*) "The servants just don't appreciate the subtleties, so I have to do it all myself." (*He sighs.*) Her dear little sensitive sighs. Her talking and talking—she never stopped talking. Changing everything with her fiddly white fingers. Pling. Changing everything, interfering, so I couldn't do anything, couldn't go anywhere, couldn't go . . . (*Comes back to reality. His fingers have been twisting and twining the mohair rug.*) But, I'm not going anywhere. I'm sitting in this chair, a rug of mohair around my knees. (*Peers over at his knees.*) Those knees. (*He almost laughs.*) Don't seem mine, so cold and a long way away. (*Pause.*) Did she give me this rug? Just like her to choose mohair. Long fussy stuff. Interfering. (*Mimics.*) "Dickey, Dickey, the horses were on the lawn again last night. They make those dreadful holes with their hooves. I've asked you, again and again, to see to the fences. It's not much to ask. It's only a small thing to ask. You could see to that at least . . . Surely you could manage that . . . a little thing like that."

MISS EVANS. (*Silence.*) Matron thinks I'm managing very well with this walker. "You're managing very well, Miss Evans," she says, "very well."

MR. MULCAHY. I could never get away. She'd always find me out. (*Pause.*) Even as a child she knew. Knew all my special places. Interfering. (*Pause.*) Except once. Once in the trees! She never found me there. I beat her that time! Up in the chestnut tree!

Silence.

MISS EVANS. I used to find twigs for the fire under the trees. Lying on the grass under the trees. The rooks dropped them, building their nests. I felt sorry for them when they'd gone to so much trouble getting them up there. But it was handy for me. (*She shuffles on.*) Very handy. (*Pause.*) Sometimes I would collect them along the back hedge. Not in the wood. Mother said not to go in the wood. You never know what would be in a wood, Mother said.

Silence.

MR. MULCAHY. (*Staring at the crucifix that hangs on the wall.*) You there! You didn't dare to try old age, did you? Old age. (*Scathing.*) What do you know about it, Jesus Christ? Nothing. You popped it young, in your prime, a bloody hero. (*Pause.*) Died for us. Died for us? I didn't want you to die for me. I never asked you to die for me. You just go along and die for someone else. Not for me, thank you very much. How *dare* you die for me! (*Pause.*) I don't want your bloody death hanging round my neck. (*Silence.*) I had to look at your bleeding picture. She made me. "Sweet Jesus died for you," she'd say, "for your sins. Your wicked sins made sweet Jesus die for you. Jesus died on the cross for your sins." (*Pause.*) Blackmail. Your death hasn't done me any good. Hasn't done anyone any good. Opening the gates of heaven with your blood. Funny, funny. There are no gates. No, no, no. No heaven to shut or open. None at all. Eternal closing time. (*Silence.*) The stupid boy left the gates open; that's why the horses were all over the lawn. That's why, woman, that's why. (*Pause.*) It's not the fences . . . I know it's not the fences . . . "Your Blessed Mother in heaven weeps when you do that . . . she weeps for your sins against her dearly beloved son." A dearly beloved son. (*Pause.*) All women are whores!

Silence.

MISS EVANS. I liked to lay the fire with little sticks. Small dry sticks. I would collect them along the back hedge, not in the wood. Mother said not to go in the wood. You never knew what would be in a wood, Mother said. (*She shuffles on.*) I was good at laying fires, she said. "Leave the fire to Bridget." Mother knew I was good at fires. (*Pause.*) I really liked to lay the fires. I'd like to lay a fire again. I liked clearing the ashes, that soft scraping sound when you put the shovel under the ash. (*Pause.*) That is a beautiful sound. One of my favourite sounds. (*She shuffles on.*)

Mrs. Morgan enters. She is bossy and nosey. She carries a handbag. She sits in the seat by the fire, which she considers her own. She is spry and active. She controls the TV without any consideration for others. She is an impatient woman.

MRS. MORGAN. Bring me my tea, girl! My two scones! (*Maura brings her tea and scones, which she feels with a bony finger.*) Hard! Stale! Take it away! (*Maura takes it away.*) Disgraceful! (*Tessie replaces the rejected scones, and Mrs. Morgan tests them.*) Better. But not much.

Maura goes out for fresh tea. Mr. Francis Butler comes in and parks his wheelchair opposite Mrs. Eva Murphy at the chess table.

EVA. Francis. (*Pause. Spot only on them. Quietly.*) Tell me what happened. (*Very quietly.*) Please?
FRANCIS. (*With exhaustion and depression.*) There's nothing to tell you. Nothing at all.

EVA. My God. (*He begins to arrange the chess pieces.*) Really nothing. No reply, no answer, nothing?

FRANCIS. No. None.

EVA. But your cousin. What about your cousin? Did your solicitor contact your cousin?

FRANCIS. Can't be traced . . .

EVA. But the cousin who met your eldest boy, Robin, a year ago, remember? How about that cousin?

FRANCIS. Moved. Can't be found.

EVA. But . . .

FRANCIS. Nothing. Stupid of me to hope.

EVA. There must be other ways of contacting them.

FRANCIS. The American continent is vast. If you lose contact, where do you start?

EVA. Did he try the Embassy?

FRANCIS. Yes, yes.

EVA. What about the police?

FRANCIS. That too. Even that. I could see I exasperated the poor man. He really tried. He's tried everything.

EVA. There must be some way . . .

FRANCIS. There's nothing left to be done. There he was, trying not to say I told you so. He's a decent man, my solicitor. He pointed out that he had warned me, advised me not to make over everything to them. To keep the house at least. That there could be problems. I just didn't want my boys to be tied like I had been. Stupid. Downright stupid. I can't blame my solicitor; he did everything to dissuade me. I'm just a bloody stupid fool.

EVA. I like fools.

FRANCIS. That proves you're an even bigger one!

EVA. Thanks!

FRANCIS. I just never dreamed I'd live this long. All those medics shook their dandruff over me years ago: "You might make it to forty in a warm climate," they said. "Move to a warm climate," they said. But how could I? Couldn't. No work for me there. And Joan, Joan couldn't stand the heat. It would have killed her. She was extremely sensitive to heat.

EVA. I forget what you were like at forty.

FRANCIS. None of my family lived long.

EVA. How could I remember what you were like at forty? I hadn't met you at forty!

FRANCIS. They all snuffed it early.

EVA. You were smashing at sixty.

FRANCIS. Mind you, most of them drank themselves under the sod. The best way to go.

EVA. So that means . . . you won't be able . . . that you've nothing?

FRANCIS. Was it Oscar Wilde who said that making mistakes enabled you to notice it when you made the same mistake again? (*Looks at Eva.*)

EVA. (*Looking away from Francis.*) So you won't be staying on here?

FRANCIS. (*Quietly.*) No. I won't be staying on here.

EVA. Will you have to leave soon?

FRANCIS. Yes.

EVA. A matter of weeks?

FRANCIS. About that. In about a week.

EVA. Oh.

FRANCIS. I'm sorry, Eva. What a mess! (*Pause.*) But we are prepared, aren't we?

EVA. Yes. (*Silence. She arranges some chess pieces.*) We are ready. Some people never manage to be ready.

FRANCIS. (*Looking at Eva.*) Oh, then. On with our game.

EVA. (*Looking at Francis.*) On with our game. Let our game begin! (*They start to play chess.*)

Enter Margie and Paul with the Matron, back left—between Margie and Paul. Paul is carrying a paper bag.

MARGIE. We are glad to have caught you . . .

Matron looks at Margie.

PAUL. We wanted a word . . .

Matron looks at Paul.

MATRON. (*Looks out front.*) How can I help you?
MARGIE. We need to discuss . . .

Matron looks at Margie.

PAUL. . . . our concern for Mrs. Murphy . . .

Matron looks at Paul.

MARGIE. My mother is difficult . . .

Matron looks at Margie.

PAUL. My mother-in-law is . . . an individual.

Matron looks at Paul.

MARGIE. Considering her age . . .

Matron looks at Margie, etc.

MATRON. Mrs. Murphy is no trouble, enjoys life most days . . .
MARGIE. You know our change of plans . . .
PAUL. Now we've moved nearer . . .
MARGIE. She needs us, her family . . .
PAUL. We can do more for her . . .
MARGIE. I understand her little ways . . .
MATRON. She's quite independent . . .
MARGIE. But she's weakening, weakening the doctor says . . .
PAUL. Now that she's confined to her chair . . .
MATRON. She's contented here.
MARGIE. Of course, Mrs. Price, you look after her so well! We have always
    had complete confidence in you. Complete. But we have to consider
    many things, Paul and I. It has not been easy making the journeys
    here. That's why, when Paul's job allowed it, we moved nearer. And
    now she isn't mobile. Can't drive anymore. We find that the expenses
    are mounting. We feel . . . we know . . . she'd be better close to us.
PAUL. Things are not easy, no . . . not at all easy.

MARGIE. Quite frankly, Matron, the expenses . . . well . . . things don't get cheaper, do they? (*Pause.*) But the main thing is mother's comfort. What's best for her is the main thing. I feel sure she'll really be happier closer to me. I'm her nearest and dearest. I'm her only child, you know.

MATRON. Naturally, like yourself, I wish only the best for Mrs. Murphy. But she is contented here. Has good friends. They can mean a lot when one is getting on. I hope you have carefully considered how great a responsibility you are taking on. I have a fully trained staff. I ensure all my patients are under constant but unobtrusive observation. On your own this could become a heavy burden. Day and night, every day of the week. But I do know, too, that she is devoted to you and speaks of you and your husband very often. She would hate to cause you any trouble. But moving the elderly is most distressing for them. Must be considered carefully.

MARGIE. Dear Mrs. Price, you've understood so well. Mother is an easily influenced person. She can behave very unpredictably, you know. She gave Paul and I some headaches in the past. Oh dear, got up some mad schemes. Putting her little bit of money into some theatre group. Managed to put a stop to that, moving her here. Thank God we've discovered you and this lovely home of yours. Took her away from temptation. Sometimes I think I'm the mother and she's the child.

PAUL. Margie means she feels she has to protect Mother from herself . . .

MATRON. I don't honestly see that she's in any great danger here. We are very experienced with the elderly and Mrs. Murphy enjoys company, it's very good for her. Knowing her as I do, she'll agree to your plans even if they are not what she wants. I only hope they are what she wants. I would be grateful, however, if you would be good enough to let me know if and when she is going. I have people on my waiting list to be considered.

MARGIE. We have to face facts. It is going to be impossible for her to stay.

PAUL. It's sad. But my wife is right.

MARGIE. Dr. Collins agrees. He sees my point of view.

PAUL. He's a very good man. My mother-in-law has great confidence in him.

MARGIE. So you understand, Matron, we will be moving her soon. There are strong influences here you may not be aware of. I have all the plans made. I'll speak to you again, after my little chat with Mother.

MATRON. You will do as you think best, of course. But I do suggest that you don't rush things. The elderly have their own little ways. But I must say, I have never noticed your mother unduly influenced by anyone. She's quite a character. Enjoys life. She won't make difficulties for you. I'm certain of that.

PAUL. Thank you, Matron. You are very helpful. My wife is a great organiser. Full of plans. She's very understanding. A woman who understands.

MRS. MORGAN. Matron! My bowels.

MATRON. I have already spoken to the night nurse. She has your laxative, she will see you this evening at bedtime.

The light fades. Exit Matron. Margie and Paul cross to Eva and Francis as the light comes up on the chess table.

MARGIE. Mother!

EVA. (*Warmly.*) Darling!

Margie gives her mother her cheek, on each side of her face.

MARGIE. (*With no great show of friendship.*) Good afternoon, Mr. Butler.

FRANCIS. Good afternoon, Margery. Paul, good to see you. How are you?

Paul and Francis shake hands.

PAUL. I'm grand. Grand.

MARGIE. Well, Mother, let's have a look at you. (*Francis is engrossed in the chess pieces.*) Oh, dear, I think we look a bit peaky. Don't you think that Mother looks a bit peaky, Paul? Just a tiny little bit tired? (*Eva's eyes drift back to the chess table in order not to show her annoyance.*)

PAUL. Well, er . . . I don't think . . .

MARGIE. (*Interrupting.*) Oh yes, she does. She looks peaky. We'll have to do something about that, shan't we, Paul? All last winter I worried. Only Paul knows how I worried. You, over here, so far away from us. Your family.

EVA. I hate you to worry, dear . . .

MARGIE. And now, here we are again, winter nearly upon us. We must do something, Paul. We can't leave Mother alone and unhappy so far away from her nearest and dearest . . .

PAUL. But it's different now, Margie, now that we've moved. We are nearer . . . she's very concerned for you, Mother.

Francis looks up from the chessboard at Eva.

MARGIE. We can't leave Mother out here alone, can we, Paul?

EVA. I'm not here alone . . .

PAUL. We would just like to be sure you're well . . . well cared for . . .

EVA. Why don't you both sit down, dear? Bring those chairs up, will you, Paul? (*Paul brings two chairs and they sit facing front, between Francis and Eva.*) Thank you, Paul. That's lovely. It's lovely to see you both. And how good of you to come in this terrible weather. You really shouldn't have bothered. I told you on the phone, I'm right as rain. (*Francis winces and looks to the heavens.*)

PAUL. (*To Francis.*) How are you keeping, Mr. Butler?

FRANCIS. Well, for an old dinosaur, I'm not doing too badly.

MARGIE. No, Mother, it is not alright. You can't imagine the time we had coming, the roads . . .

PAUL. Oh, they aren't so very bad. Just the rain, and a little flooding.

MARGIE. It's too isolated here. Too near the sea. Too wild, altogether. You need to live inland at your time of life. Away from the winds . . . where it's sheltered. You'd be so much better off living with me and Paul. (*Pause.*) Or next door (*Stress.*) With the nuns.

Francis raises eyes to heaven, then contemplates chess, listening.

EVA. (*Softly, but firmly.*) But I like it here. I like the sea and the winds . . . I like . . . (*She looks Francis in the eyes.*) I like the company.

Francis and Eva smile at each other. Margie shifts with irritation, and Paul looks uneasy.

PAUL. You're a great nature lover. We know that. A romantic. But one has to be practical, face facts.

Eva and Francis resume their chess.

MARGIE. (*In a low voice to Paul.*) I don't know how she can bear it here. Look at that old man in the window. (*She indicates Mr. Mulcahy.*) Never says a word. Gaga, if you ask me. He dribbles. (*To Eva.*) No, Mother, I know you so well. I know just how you're feeling. How you're putting a good face on it. How much you miss us, and being so far from the chapel.

Francis nonchalantly lights a cigar. Eva makes a swift move with her queen and takes Francis's bishop.

EVA. That settles the clergy! (*She leans back, chuckling.*)

FRANCIS. Good Lord, I missed that. (*Amazed.*) You've taken my bloody bishop!

MARGIE. (*Annoyed.*) Mother, please be serious.

EVA. (*Eva is serious.*) I'm sorry, dear. We chess players get carried away. (*She smiles.*) Forgive me.

MARGIE. I do understand you, Mother. You make the best of everything. "Look on the bright side," as Daddy used to say. But now we've moved and things can be different . . . Better. Now you have a choice: to live with me and Paul, or next door with the nuns. It's grand to have daily mass on my doorstep! I'd be so close to keep an eye on things for you. You could do just as you please, and it would be far less expensive. Far . . . (*Silence.*)

EVA. I do just as I please here.

Francis puts a hand on his knight. Eva is all attention.

MARGIE. A family is so different. A real home. Where you belong . . . mine and Paul's home.

EVA. But the stairs . . .

MARGIE. Oh, the stairs would be no bother. Remember the little room downstairs at the back? You don't realize how busy we've been! You don't know what Paul and I have been up to. We thought this all out when we bought the house. Well, we've done it up. Paul's done it all himself. I chose the wallpaper. I chose little violets as I know you love flowers. It looks really pretty. You'll love it. All on the ground floor so you'll manage. It's small, but cozy. Really cozy, now that we've done it up.

EVA. You don't mean pokey, dear? (*Quietly.*) There's no view.

MARGIE. (*Not deterred.*) But, you'll have a lovely view of the rock garden from the sitting room. (*Pause.*)

PAUL. I can take you for drives . . .

MARGIE. Of course, if you prefer the nuns, I understand. I quite understand. I won't feel hurt. (*Pause.*) It's a perfect place . . . Such a good staff. Some of the girls here are not quite . . . are a bit . . . rough. (*Looking at Maura and Tessie with disapproval.*) Not Matron's fault, of course. Out here in the wilds, what could you expect? Barbarians. (*She looks to Francis for approval, but he is absorbed in the chess pieces. She whispers to Eva.*) Is he getting deafer? Or going a little . . . you know?

EVA. (*Whispering.*) Oh, yes, he's much deafer. And you're right, his mind wanders a little now and then . . . says very odd things, too.

Eva avoids catching Francis' eye. He gives her a pinch under the table. She jumps. Margie is oblivious to this.

MARGIE. See what I mean, Mother? This place is just not suitable. Not the sort of people you're used to mixing with. Very mixed company, indeed. I've discussed it with Dr. Collins many times, and now he agrees with me that, as you are now mostly confined to your chair, you need extra care. Family care . . .

EVA. (*Interrupting, slightly desperately.*) But I am cared for, I'm *happy* here.

MARGIE. Of course, of course you are, dear. But you'll be so much happier close to your own family. Near Paul and me. Won't she, Paul?

PAUL. It's your happiness we are considering.

MARGIE. We are thinking of you.

PAUL. And I brought you something. (*Produces bottle of brandy, gives it to Eva.*) I think you enjoy a drop of this brandy. I got it from the duty-free[8] the other day. Hope you enjoy it. Share it with your friends. It won't do you any harm to have a drop now and again. Warms the cockles. Eh, Mr. Butler?

EVA. Oh, thank you, Paul . . .

MARGIE. I think it would be a great help to you, Mother, getting to sleep
at night. Get Matron to put a little in your hot milk. Brandy is great in
hot milk. With sugar. Plenty of sugar. Help you to drop off.

EVA. How very thoughtful of you, Paul, very kind indeed. Thank you so
much.

MARGIE. That bottle should last you ages. It's very good in hot milk—
helps you to relax. We all need to relax.

EVA. I wouldn't dream of ruining a cognac as good as this in hot milk,
Margie. But Francis and I will share a glass together after supper. Or
shall we have some now, lace our cups of tea?

MARGIE. Mother!

FRANCIS. Not a bad idea. Might be good for our game.

EVA. Would be good for our game, but later. We'll enjoy it another time.

MARGIE. It's important to relax. When you live with us, Mother, you'll
learn how to relax.

*Silence. Lights on all cast. Miss Evans has arrived at the chair near the TV, she
sits. She is resigned to the loss of the chair by the fire. Mr. Mulcahy starts to hum
and then sing, "I Do Like to Be Beside the Seaside." Mrs. Morgan, irritated by
Mr. Mulcahy's singing, hops up, strides over to shake him by the shoulder in a
dictatorial manner, speaking loudly and slowly into his ear.*

MRS. MORGAN. Mr. Mulcahy, will you please be quiet! This is a drawing room. Have you no consideration for others? We wish to watch
television, and we keep it low so as not to disturb others. I ask you to
stop. For the sake of everyone. (*Turns.*) Such a vulgar tune. (*Returns to
her seat.*)

*Mr. Mulcahy shows no sign of having heard anything, but he stops singing. Miss
Evans slowly takes knitting out of her bag and attempts to knit with badly stiff-
ened fingers. Mrs. Morgan hops up and down, changing the TV programme without any consideration for Miss Evans, who makes feeble gestures in an attempt to
stop her, but she is helpless against Mrs. Morgan, of whom she is a little afraid.
Maura and Tessie return with fresh tea and scones.*
Matron enters on another tour of inspection.

MATRON. Right! That tea's a bit strong, girls; put in more hot water. Ah, good afternoon, Mrs. Morgan. All's well? (*Mrs. Morgan grunts.*) The Pope is on the telly tonight, I believe. We must all watch His Holiness.

Tessie carries the teapot over to Mr. Mulcahy.

TESSIE. (*Loudly.*) Would you like a little more tea, Mr. Mulcahy? This is lovely and hot. (*Mr. Mulcahy makes no reply, but she fills his cup all the same. She returns to the trolley and speaks to Maura.*) What bloody weather. It's lashing.

Tessie and Maura exit.

MR. MULCAHY. My feet are cold. I can't remember . . . what was it like to have warm feet? (*He peers over his knees to look at his feet.*) There they are, my feet, away down there. They make me laugh. (*He laughs.*) You try this. This oldness. Come on, tell me. What's the good of it? Where does it get me? (*Considers.*) She won't be able to see me when I'm dead. At least she can't interfere with *that*. (*Chuckles.*) She would have enjoyed that. That's one place she can't interfere with. She'd have loved to be there with her busybodies. "He makes a lovely corpse," they'd say. Damn idiots. What's lovely about an empty skin, falling jaw, no smile? No love. What's that? Love? She put a stop to that. (*Silence.*) All women are whores.

MISS EVANS. You have to watch a fire when you first light it. Oh yes, you have to watch it. Mother would say to me, "You watch the fire, Bridget. Watch the fire." Sometimes I would put the poker in and hold the middle up because it could collapse and fall in the middle and that would spoil it. (*Shakes her head in sad disapproval.*) But when it went well, the little flames would peep out round the coal. (*This makes her happy.*) That was nice. That was so nice. (*She knits painfully, slowly.*)

MR. MULCAHY. Fires of hell. "Remember the fires of hell," she'd say. If you do that, you'll burn in the fires of hell . . .

MISS EVANS. Flick, they would go, flick with their hot tongues . . .

MR. MULCAHY. Christ, you're meant to know about love? Never taught me a damn thing. (*Chuckles.*) I bet you're tickled pink she loved you. "Sweet Jesus, take me," she'd pray. "Sweet Jesus, take me," over and over again. (*Pause.*) You took your time over it. (*Pause.*) Don't think you were all that keen to have her. She was a very ardent lover of yours, you know. Oh, to have seen her face when she found out there wasn't any heaven!

Silence.

MISS EVANS. Then I'd pop a little piece of coal on the flame. Right on the top! (*She giggles.*) Right on the flame tip. "Feed the flame," Mother would say, "feed the flame."

Mrs. Morgan grunts. She heaves herself out of the chair and thrusts forward to the TV and changes the programme.

MRS. MORGAN. Time for the news!

MISS EVANS. Oh . . . er . . . I liked . . . (*Puts forward a nervous hand in protest. Mrs. Morgan takes no notice and returns to her chair.*)

MRS. MORGAN. We should all take an interest in current affairs. Keep ourselves informed. Up to date.

MR. MULCAHY. Cold. You were sensible in one thing, Christ—choosing a warm country. (*Pause.*) Was it cold on the cross? (*Pause.*) A naked body dying in pain for our devotion? A body twisting in torture for us to pray to? For children to say their night prayers before? "Say your prayers," she said. "Ask God to keep you pure. Sweet dreams, darling, sweet dreams . . ." A white naked body, smeared with blood. (*Pause.*) A beautiful young man's naked body. (*Pause.*) Dead.

MISS EVANS. Cheerful! It makes you feel cheerful. Happy. You can always feel happy when you sit by a fire. When I sit by a fire, it's like home. There is so much to watch when you sit by a fire.

MR. MULCAHY. Did you want to be God? (*Pause.*) Did they crucify you? Or did they make it up as a good story? You're the hero. Noble and in glory. Easy. (*Pause.*) Can you see the good without the bad? (*Silence.*) To know there is light, you need the dark. You need the devil, Mr. Christ. (*Chuckles.*) Your best friend.

MISS EVANS. So comfy. Warm and comfy to sit by. A warm fire is a good friend. Good to sit with. No need to chat. No need at all.

MARGIE. (*Standing up briskly.*) Well, Mother, we must be off. The cats will be famished. They know when it's six o'clock. When you think about what I've said, Mother, you'll see it's all for the best. Only the best is good enough for you, Mother. (*She kisses Eva. Eva puts her arms around her to embrace her warmly, as if to keep her longer.*)

EVA. I know, darling. You're very good. I understand. Be careful going home now, won't you? Take good care.

MARGIE. Goodness, Mother, it's not like you to fuss. You know what a good driver Paul is. Never goes over forty. It's all those terrible speed merchants that cause the accidents. So . . . we'll see you soon because I'm getting on with the new plans. Bye-bye, Mother. God bless. (*Turns to Francis.*) Goodbye, Mr. Butler. I'm glad to see you're keeping so well.

FRANCIS. Thank you. Yes, I am. Safe journey.

PAUL. (*Kissing his mother-in-law.*) Goodbye, Mother. Mind yourself.

EVA. Oh, I do, I do.

Margie and Paul start to exit.

EVA. Margie . . .

MARGIE. Yes, Mother?

EVA. I just wondered . . . (*Pause.*) Now that you have this more convenient house, will you . . . I wondered if you planned . . . Oh, never mind. Some other . . . time. (*Looks down at the chess game.*) Off you go, dear. I don't want to make you late.

FRANCIS. You mustn't keep the cats waiting . . .

EVA. And Margie, remember, I understand, I won't make things difficult for you. I won't.

MARGIE. (*Gives a little smile and wave from the doorway.*) Bye-bye. See you soon.

Eva waves and blows a kiss. Paul and Margie exit. Francis and Eva concentrate on their chess game.

EVA. (*Very quietly.*) You know what I was going to ask her?

FRANCIS. I do. (*Pause.*) They will. I'm certain they will have a family. But later. Sometime later.

MRS. MORGAN. Mr. Mulcahy! There you go again, disturbing the peace! Would you kindly desist? Have some consideration for the rest of us, who never interfere with anyone.

Mr. Mulcahy stops singing. Mrs. Morgan changes the programme on the TV, and again Miss Evans is helpless with her protests.

MISS EVANS. Er . . . I would like . . . I do like . . . Oh, leave the warthogs! I have never before seen a warthog. Very educational. It's very interesting learning about wild animals . . . mother *never ever* saw a warthog!

MRS. MORGAN. (*Grunts.*) Dirty beasts!

Miss Evans resigns herself to the new programme. Mrs. Morgan drifts to sleep and snores occasionally. Mr. Mulcahy picks up his teacup and holds it in his lap.

MR. MULCAHY. Brandy! Give me brandy. Here's to the grape. (*Raises the teacup a little.*) The juice of the grape. That is a good friend. Reliable. Never let me down. Never. Gave me the last drop of your golden blood. (*Pause. He tries a sip of tea.*) Cold.

Tessie and Maura come back. Tessie takes Mr. Mulcahy's cup. They stand at each end of the trolley. Eva has her queen raised. Mr. Mulcahy angrily stares at the window. The rain and wind lash the panes. Still. The lights fade.

ACT 2
SCENE 1

A cliff-top near The Retreat. Just below the summit. In contrast to the void in Act 1, this scene is light, space, air, life, growth. Colours are green, blue, yellow, white . . . the colours of spring. Sound of breakers far below. Larks sing. The edge of the cliff is backstage.

FRANCIS. (*Enters in his wheelchair. He is very tired, but excited. He is dexterous with the chair. He calls over his shoulder to Eva, offstage. He is puffed.⁹*) How are you doing? Can you manage? (*He turns to await Eva's approach.*) The ground is level here; we can rest for a while. Are you alright, love?

EVA. (*Sounds puffed.*) Of course I'm alright. I'm doing fine.

FRANCIS. Take it easy. No need to hurry. Are you sure you can manage?

EVA. (*Arriving slowly, with great effort.*) I'm sure. Hurry? Don't make me laugh. I haven't any puff left.

FRANCIS. (*Leaning back in his chair.*) You're a great girl. Well done. What a climb! I'm exhausted.

EVA. Rubbish. Speak for yourself. You sound like an old man.

FRANCIS. I am an old man. About two hundred at the moment.

EVA. Oh, how you've deceived a girl like me. I never go out with old men!

FRANCIS. There's always a first time.

EVA. It's the first time we've been up here. (*She leans back in her chair and closes her eyes.*) How far have we got? Is it very much further?

FRANCIS. (*Sits up/looks around.*) Not bad. Not bad at all. I think it's only one small steep bit, and we'll be there. Well done, us. (*He sits back.*) It's just great to be out, and the day, perfect. Away from all them down there. Right away.

EVA. (*Opens her eyes.*) My God, it's beautiful. Coming up, I couldn't look at anything except the path in front of my wheels. We've nearly made it. I think we might make it. (*Leans back laughing.*) Great. Great.

FRANCIS. (*Worried.*) Eva, have you got the bottle?

EVA. Will you ever stop fussing? Of course I've got the bottle. I'd never forget that. Do you need a drop now? Would it help?

FRANCIS. No, no. We'll wait 'til we get to the top. As we planned.

Silence.

EVA. (*Chuckles tiredly.*) My dear daughter. If she could see me now. Whizzing up mountains with her bottle of brandy!

FRANCIS. Not exactly whizzing . . .

EVA. As if I'd waste cognac in hot milk.

FRANCIS. It might be quite nice, you know.

EVA. It's a really good brandy, though. They appreciate our tastes, even if they don't approve . . .

FRANCIS. I'll try it when I'm old, when I'm about three hundred. In the hot milk, I mean.

EVA. Three hundred is a great age to start something new.

FRANCIS. If Margie could see you now, she'd say, "There goes Mother, up to her old tricks again. Thought she'd grown out of them." Has a Puritan streak, your daughter. Where did you get her from?

EVA. I don't know. I really don't know. Her father wasn't a Puritan. Bill was a bit stiff, reserved, shy. But not Puritan. (*Pause.*) Funny, when I think of him, I can never clearly see his face. The rest of him I can remember. The way he stood, always leaning back as if he was going to fall over. Unsteady on his feet. But his face drifts away when I try to catch it with my memory. (*Pause.*)

FRANCIS. Joan's face I can see sharply. Even though it's such a long time since she . . . but there was nothing shy about Joan, was there? Nothing.

EVA. Does my daughter understand me at all? Perhaps I'm just blind to her? Don't help her enough. I'd love to be able to reach her, but she seems to sail further and further away. Do you think if she had a child, she might loosen, relax? I'd hoped she'd have a child. But she's obsessed with the neatness of her house, her garden, her Paul. Was that because I was such a sloppy housekeeper? Still, there's a funny side: Margie doesn't approve of you. Did you notice Paul trying to stick up for you? Saying how nice it must be to be near, as we were such old friends. And Margie bristling and changing the subject.

FRANCIS. I noticed. That's why I had the coughing fit—to hide my laughter. Should get out my false beard.

EVA. Do you think they guess *how* old and *how* friendly?

FRANCIS. I'd really prefer a gorilla suit. Would you fancy me in a gorilla suit?

EVA. Don't know if you'd look that different. And Matron would put you out at once. She can't abide animals.

FRANCIS. Hey, that's not nice. Gorillas are gentle, lovable people. Often misunderstood.

EVA. You in a gorilla suit would not be the same thing at all.

FRANCIS. I think it would liven the place up no end.

Thoughtful pause.

EVA. I wish I could make things right with Margie. I want her to be happy, not to interfere with her life. She seems almost . . . to hound me. To hound us.

FRANCIS. Rather like being a child again. "Now darling, you'd have a lovely time staying with Auntie Mary and playing with your cousins."

You know she makes you eat baked beans, puts you to bed at six, and your cousins are shits. But you have to go. Can do nothing. (*Pause.*) Perhaps . . .

EVA. We should push on. (*With slight restlessness.*)

FRANCIS. Push is the word. Are you feeling up to it?

EVA. (*Ruffled.*) Of course I'm up to it. (*With more assurance.*) I'm always up to it.

FRANCIS. Yes, you're always up to it. (*Silence.*)

EVA. We've got this far. I wasn't sure we'd get as far as this. (*Pause.*) Down there seems a long way off . . .

FRANCIS. Another world. (*Pause.*) It doesn't exist. (*Silence.*)

EVA. Do we exist? (*Silence.*)

FRANCIS. If we get to the top, we will see the view.

EVA. I do hope we can see the view when we reach the top.

FRANCIS. We should be able to see as far as the islands. From the map, I'm sure we should see the islands.

(*Silence.*)

EVA. You and your views. We'll see it. Haven't we always, you and I? Remember the mountain? Our first one. You worrying about the rain . . .

FRANCIS. I wanted you to see it at its best.

EVA. Fretting, in case the mists came and swallowed the view.

FRANCIS. That place has always been important to me. Special. So remote. High. (*Pause.*) The world laid out before one. (*Quietly.*) We should have been able to live together there.

Silence.

EVA. I saw a Yeats[10] painting when I was young called *A Present of Islands*. That was the present you gave me that day, despite the rain, a present of islands.

FRANCIS. Not a bad title for a painting. But you can have Jack Yeats. No form. Must have form.

EVA. (*Laughing.*) Female form, you mean.

FRANCIS. (*Warming to his subject.*) Yes, yes, lots of lovely ladies. Painters have a duty to paint naked ladies. What do they do now? Rubbish. Ugh. I hate it.

EVA. Matron doesn't think much of your poster.

FRANCIS. What poster? It's classical. What's she got to complain of? It's my room.

EVA. It's not the Botticelli[11] she minds. It's the other one. She came to me the other day and said the woman who cleans your room objected. She had been fussed before about the Botticelli and complained to Mrs. Price. But she managed to persuade her that it was "Art." But the other one—the girl in sox and a hat and nothing else—she didn't think it was "Art." (*Francis tries to interrupt, but Eva goes on.*) Matron said to me, "My dear Mrs. Murphy, you seem, er, to have influence on our Mr. Butler. Could you please ask him to put that, er, that picture inside the door of his wardrobe?

FRANCIS. Inside my wardrobe?

EVA. Yes, then she said you could look at it when you wanted and not disturb the staff.

FRANCIS. (*Very mock-indignant.*) Disturb the staff! Damn it. If I stuck up a great randy Bacchus,[12] it might disturb the staff. They are all middle-aged women, for God's sake. Disturbed. By the bottom of a young girl. Bloody hell!

EVA. Well, I said I had no idea what you had in your room, but you were rather an eccentric old fellow. But I'd do my best . . .

FRANCIS. (*Interrupting.*) You'd do your best! Eccentric. Me? Wait till I get you . . .

He begins to chase her in his wheelchair. She tries to wheel away, but she is tired. She laughs and protests.

EVA. Francis, Francis. Stop it. You can't . . . my chair isn't as fast as yours. It's not fair . . . stop it . . . you can't . . .

FRANCIS. (*Not stopping.*) Ha ha. I'm the wheelchair wizard, and I've got you in my power. Now squeal for mercy, lady. Squeal. (*He has charged into her after a chase and leans out to grab her.*)

EVA. (*Trying to avoid him and distract his attention.*) Francis, Francis, you daft idiot. You'll break the bottle.

FRANCIS. (*Stops, suddenly worried.*) Good Lord. The bottle. Is it safe?

EVA. (*Out of danger, having distracted his attention.*) You're underestimating me if you think your larking around would let me break a bottle of booze.

FRANCIS. Cheat. Rotten cheat. I'd have had you across my knee in a flash.

EVA. (*Laughing and rueful.*) You needn't tell me. I know you. My mother warned me not to go out with wheelchairs like you! Rake!

FRANCIS. Rake? Me? I'm your honest garden fork. Your reliable spade. Your friendly neighborhood ever-ready wheelbarrow. Wheel me anywhere. I carry anything. Wheel me away; feel free . . . I'm a simple soul . . .

EVA. "Who lightly draws his breath . . ."

FRANCIS. True, true, always sweetness and light. And I'm steady. Never put a spoke in anywhere . . .

EVA. Francis . . .

FRANCIS. (*Quietly.*) Well, only if asked, invited. By someone nice. Someone nice. Someone special.

They look warmly at each other. Then Eva breaks away to continue teasing.

EVA. No, no, no. You're not such a goody-goody. Remember the Southerbys' party?

FRANCIS. (*Playing innocent.*) What?

EVA. Oh, you know. That cup of coffee. It was such a stiff party. Boring. You just tipped it down Samantha Southerby's back!

FRANCIS. Did I? I didn't. It was the dress. That dress. It was red crepe-dechine to a chauvinist pig. How could I resist? That plunging backline. A weak, impressionable man like me. I succumbed, I yielded. Well . . . at least it was cold. The coffee, I mean.

EVA. (*Laughing.*) It livened up a very dead party. (*Pause. Quietly.*) Do you know it's the small things, the silly things that count. Not the big occasions. Not birth. Life. (*Pause.*) Death.

FRANCIS. Once you've done the first, the rest are inevitable.

EVA. Boring. (*Pause.*) Even love. Is love a bit boring too?

FRANCIS. Sacrilege. Sacrilege! (*Pause.*)

EVA. I don't think I know what love is. Lived as long as this, and I don't know. (*Pause.*) Did my parents know? Will Margie know?

FRANCIS. Our time is so short . . .

EVA. Perhaps knowing has nothing to do with it?

FRANCIS. Just a small spit of time . . .

EVA. I would have liked to have felt close to my daughter. Last time in her home, she was worried when I leant on her new cushions. And I think she washes the lavatory after me. I'm not at ease with her. I'm not even myself. So little time together, and we waste it.

FRANCIS. Nothing else to do with time but waste it. Best times of my life were wasted. Lazy, hedonistic times. With you, my idiot. And if it's one of your small things, getting to the top of this cliff to see the view, perhaps we should . . .

EVA. It is what I mean. Time is getting on. Maybe we should . . .

FRANCIS. Move . . . on?

EVA. It is proving quite a big thing to get to the top of this mountain. I know it's only a cliff, but it feels like a mountain.

FRANCIS. There's no need. We don't have to. It's only our game. You can always say "pax."[13]

EVA. We need to see the view, across the sea to the islands, to be part of a large landscape. Like the peaceful view from your house, your home.

FRANCIS. Home. (*Sighs.*) Where is that? Gone. Everything gone. Flies away. All that time we spend on our homes. Painting them. Knocking down and building up. Putting in cupboards. Carefully restoring with respect for the past. For those who went before us. Lived their lives in that place. Left something of themselves there. Deep in the stones. They're gone. Then we're gone. Finished. In comes the next man, who cries, "What bloody fool did this job? Old-fashioned crap. Out. Sweep it all away." And there goes your little life's work. Your cosseted shrubs in the garden, swallowed by a dinosaur digger. Muuuncch! (*Makes a large munching sound and moves his hands and arms as if he were a huge digger.*)

EVA. You shouldn't hurry in a garden. I discovered that working in your garden, Fran, when I tried to get things done. I have never seen a gardener hurry. They always go steady wheelbarrow pace. That is the pace of the earth. So then I slowed down. Made, forced, myself to go slow. To look at things. Not to worry if I hadn't tidied up this, weeded that. The garden told me the pace to go. Slowly, slowly, sliding like a snail in my wheelchair. Wheelbarrow pace. Your home and garden was a good place to be, Fran. So what if it was transient? It was good.

FRANCIS. Of course it was good. You and I always had fun. (*Pause.*) But it's pointless imagining your children will like anything of yours. My home, with its history, in the family for generations. Felt I had added in a small way to their work. It was really satisfying to see a tree I had planted twenty years ago, established. A mass of shrubs slowly take form, to play a part in a landscape. It helped me to stand under those great trees. I found my true proportions there. That's why we need mountains, you and I. We can feel our real size.

EVA. It is restful. To be the right size. (*Silence.*)

FRANCIS. But the future? Forget it. My two boys, somewhere in America. Haven't heard from them for, my God, must be three years . . . and the house . . . I don't dare to think of it. (*With anger.*) Maybe pulled down to make way for one of those estates[14] with houses barely a foot apart. They might have left one or two of the larger trees, don't you think? Perhaps I should be pleased that so many homes can be on my small spot of land. But the land . . . Is the land pleased?

EVA. (*Concerned for his distress, changes the subject.*) Should we move on . . . ?

FRANCIS. It's time to move on . . .

EVA. We can't keep . . .

FRANCIS. Putting it off. We're a little afraid . . .

EVA. Afraid we haven't the strength. It is time to make a move. We should move on.

FRANCIS. (*Quietly.*) We keep putting it off because we are afraid.

EVA. Are you scared, Francis, that we won't manage to play our game to the end?

FRANCIS. Yes, no, I don't know. We do want to do it, don't we? You wouldn't rather turn back now?

EVA. (*Looking at him. Pausing.*) I think we should . . . go on. It's the best thing to do, go on.

FRANCIS. Yes. On we go.

EVA. I do want to be up there when the sun is shining. I must have the sun shining when we are up there.

FRANCIS. Take heed there, sun. Listen to the lady. Forward. To the breach. What's stopping us? Let us fly. We are invincible. (*Quips à la Groucho Marx.*) If we can make it. (*Adds.*) Of course we can make it! (*Quips.*) Think of the reward at the top. (*They move in their wheelchairs slowly towards the summit.*) Don't rush it now. Take it slowly. Careful, careful, there is a stone there. Mind.

EVA. I'm fine. Don't worry. My chariot is in prime condition. Unlike its driver. I could be flipping around Brand's Hatch.[15]

FRANCIS. How I wish I had my Sunbeam[16] now!

EVA. A fat lot of use it would be to us here.

FRANCIS. What a car! Couldn't she go?

EVA. You were the worst driver I ever met. The very worst.

FRANCIS. Remember going flat out down the back road?

EVA. Dangerous. Fast and dangerous. A drive with you would leave me trembling.

FRANCIS. It was a beautiful car.

EVA. When it went.

They struggle to the top of the cliff. They are overjoyed. Exhausted. Elated. High. They gaze out to sea.

FRANCIS. Eva! Eva! We're here. This is the summit.

EVA. We're at the top.

FRANCIS. We've done it . . .

EVA. We've made it . . .

FRANCIS. I wasn't sure . . .

EVA. I didn't know if . . .

FRANCIS. All the old fools down there will never believe it.

EVA. No one would ever believe we could do it, but we have, Fran. We have, we have.

FRANCIS. God Almighty, we have. (*They embrace. Eva laughs but is near tears.*)

EVA. Fran!

FRANCIS. Eva!

EVA. The view! We *can* see the islands.

Silence. They park their chairs close together to look out to sea.

FRANCIS. We needed this.

EVA. We both need this.

FRANCIS. A world laid out in front of us.

EVA. A new world. (*Looking up.*) Now, come on, sun. (*Silence.*)

FRANCIS. (*Very quietly indeed. Very lightly.*) It is as if we were threads in an Indian carpet. Too involved to see the base pattern. But now, here, as we look down on the sea, out towards the islands, up to the clouds, we . . .

EVA . . . are two small incidentals.

FRANCIS. Dropped stitches. (*They both laugh.*)

EVA. No, two threads who weave from different corners, then meet, and a new pattern grows . . .

FRANCIS. Some of it slightly irregular . . .

EVA. But good colours . . .

FRANCIS. Rich. (*Silence.*) I feel . . . rested.

EVA. Complete. (*Silence.*)

FRANCIS. Eva, the bottle. The bottle. We have a lot to celebrate. Come on, Eva, out with it.

EVA. Hold on. Hold your horses. I had to store it safely for the journey, with someone like you around. (*She rummages in her rugs and brings out the bottle of brandy triumphantly.*) Voilà! (*At the same moment, Francis produces a bottle of red wine and holds it aloft.*)

FRANCIS. Snap!

EVA. You devil! Wine! Where did you get that? Oh, good, good.

FRANCIS. We've always celebrated with wine.

EVA. All those times together, when we were young things in our fifties. Those times in Italy . . .

FRANCIS. In France. Spain. All those chateaux we explored. Remember: Rambures, Pierefond.

EVA. It was so good. Fun.

FRANCIS. This must be the best celebration of all . . .

EVA. Oh, have you got the corkscrew?

FRANCIS. Never fear, I have. Just one second and I'll have the cork out. (*Pulls the cork.*) There. To us, my love. To us. (*He hands her the bottle with a flourish.*) Madam, would you like to try . . . ?

Eva takes the first swig. Laughs. Passes back the bottle to Francis. He drinks. They both laugh.

EVA. Francis, I want to get out of this chair and sit on the grass. I must have the feel of grass. Let's sit on the grass and drink wine.

FRANCIS. Your wish is my command, lady. Just wait a moment and I'll give you my hand. (*He gets slowly out of his chair and takes the bottle from Eva.*) I'll put these down safely first . . . now, Madam, would you like my arm? (*They help each other, laughing.*)

EVA. Thank you, thank you. (*They sit side by side on the grass, looking out to sea. Eva holds the bottle aloft before taking the next swig.*) To us. And our wheelchairs and all who push in them! This is lovely.

FRANCIS. This is . . . life.

They lie down together on the grass, drinking now and then. Enter front stage from the same entrance as Eva and Francis, Patsy, running. He is an active and agile youth of nineteen. He is followed by Maura. He calls back to her.

PATSY. We're nearly there. Nearly at the top. It's great! Smashing! Come on, girl. What's keeping you?

MAURA. (*Off stage right.*) Oh me heel. I think I broke me heel.

PATSY. Take yer shoes off. You'd be better off; they're not made for walking.

MAURA. (*Enters following Patsy, holding in her hand one high-heeled shoe.*) I think it's broken. I hope it's not broken.

PATSY. Isn't it great? We'll soon be at the top. Come here to me, girl. (*Patsy turns around and looks everywhere then throws himself on the ground. He rolls over, grabs Maura's legs, and pulls her down on top of him.*)

MAURA. (*She squeals in protest; she's hot and in a bad temper.*) Will you leave off, Patsy Dwyer? Give over. (*She rolls away from him.*) Stop messing. (*She examines her shoe.*)

PATSY. (*Good temperedly.*) Here, give it to me. Let's have a look.

She hands him the shoe.

MAURA. They're me new shoes. Cost a fortune.

PATSY. It's nothing. Bottom of the heel a little loose. Not made for the country, though. Leave 'em off. Take your stockings off, too. Get the sun on your legs.

He puts his hand on her leg, appreciatively.)

MAURA. (*Pushes it off crossly, still absorbed in her shoe.*) Ah, Jesus, those scratches. They're ruined on me. The stones on the path made scratches. Oh, Janey.

PATSY. They're tiny. Sure no one but yourself would notice. (*Moves closer to her.*) Cheer up! It's lovely to be here with you.

He turns her to him and kisses her. She resists, begins to enjoy it, then pushes him off.

MAURA. Go away out of that. (*She looks around.*) It's very high up.

PATSY. Have you never been up here before?

MAURA. Never.

PATSY. We must go on to the very top. There's a grand view.

MAURA. (*Unenthusiastic.*) I dunno. I'm tired. My feet hurt.

PATSY. It's those silly shoes.

MAURA. They're not silly. Do you always take girls up here?

PATSY. (*Grinning.*) If they'll come.

MAURA. (*Offended.*) Oh, I see.

PATSY. No, you don't. You don't see at all. (*He jumps up and begins to pick some small pink flowers.*)

MAURA. What are those?

PATSY. Sea pinks. They're for you. (*He crouches down with a spring and presents them to her.*)

MAURA. (*Without enthusiasm.*) Oh thanks. (*She doesn't know what to do with them.*)

PATSY. Will we climb on?

MAURA. Ah no, well . . . come here.

They kiss. His hand wanders to her breast as they lie down together, but then Maura lies on a sharp stone.

MAURA. Oh my God, I'm crucified! (*She pulls up her skirt to look at her thigh.*) I was lying on a bloody boulder. I'm bruised and my tights are destroyed.

PATSY. (*Laughing.*) I told you to take them off. (*Bends to kiss her bruise.*) Kiss it. Better? (*Maura pushes him away again.*) Look. I'll climb on a bit to see where we've got to, right? Back in a sec.

Patsy springs off before she can protest, going part of the route Eva and Francis went. Maura sits up, arms around her knees. She is still in a pet.[17] It is getting cold.

PATSY. (*Coming down again.*) Hey, we're not too far from the top.

MAURA. (*Interrupting.*) I'm perished.

PATSY. (*Continuing.*) You'll never guess what I saw. I think two of them old jobs from your home are up there.

MAURA. They're never! They'd never get up there, any of 'em. They can hardly put one foot in front of the other. I'm frozen with cold.

PATSY. Here. Have me jacket. (*He takes off his jacket and puts it around her shoulders. Their mouths meet, and they cuddle.*)

PATSY. You're lovely, Maura. Lovely.

Silence.

MAURA. Jesus Christ, I'm bit! Something's eating me! (*She shakes her skirt and rubs her legs.*)

PATSY. (*Sympathetic.*) Show us. (*He looks at the ground to see what's the cause of the trouble. Then both begin to laugh.*) Oh, it's ants. Oh they can bite like the devil. (*Maura hops around, trying to brush them off, getting crosser and crosser, while Patsy rolls on the ground, roaring with laughter at her antics.*) Oh, you're lovely, Maura . . .

MAURA. (*Pulling off her tights.*) They've got inside my tights! The little bastards.

PATSY. You're so funny . . . oh, the ants . . .

MAURA. (*Raging.*) I've had enough of this bloody mountain. I'll be late for work, Patsy Dwyer, and I'm bit to death, and all you can do is roar laughing. I'm going. (*She runs off the same path as they entered, carrying her shoes.*) I'm off.

Patsy can't stop laughing but picks himself up.

PATSY. Hey Maura, wait . . . wait. (*He picks up the abandoned sea pinks.*) Hey Maura, wait. (*He runs after her.*)

The sounds of their running and his calling fade away. At the summit, Eva and Francis exchange bottles so when one is swigging wine, the other is slugging brandy. They climb back into their wheelchairs.

FRANCIS. Do you think Tessie has wheeled in the tea trolley by now? Just think: We're missing those bloody scones. (*They exchange bottles.*) They'll just think we've gone down the strand. They won't worry yet. (*They swig and exchange bottles.*)

EVA. (*Spilling some down her jersey.*) Oh dear, I'm spilling some. What a waste. Matron would say, "Really now, Mrs. Murphy, messing up our lovely new jumper, are we? Tut, tut. What would your daughter say if she found you in this state? Dear, dear. You are a naughty girl. You do give us a headache. We'll have to find you a clean one, shan't we? (*They exchange bottles and swig.*) My God, she bores the pants off me.

FRANCIS. Knickers. (*Has a slurp.*)

EVA. Watch your language, my man. (*They exchange bottles and slurp.*)

FRANCIS. I prefer the word "knickers." Sounds evocative. (*Exchange bottles.*) Jollier.

EVA. Sounds like school, brown wool and scratchy, to me. (*Sarcastic.*) So romantic . . .

FRANCIS. Women have no soul. No imagination. White legs flying over the hockey pitch. A glimpse of brown knickers . . . ah . . .

EVA. (*Flatly.*) And eager beaver Miss Thomson, whistle to lips, eyes sparkling. (*Mock melodramatic.*) "Come on, teams! Oh come on, teams!" My heart pounds with excitement at the memory. (They are getting pleasantly high.) Give me the bottle, you greedy man!

FRANCIS. Nearly finished. (*Regretfully.*) Should have bought two. But this is good.

EVA. Here's to all our times together. On mountains, in trains.

FRANCIS. In pubs . . .

EVA. In kitchens, in the rain . . .

FRANCIS. In cars . . .

EVA. Dancing . . .

FRANCIS. Eating . . .

EVA. Drinking . . .

FRANCIS. In bed . . .

EVA. Everywhere. (*Looks up. Pause.*) The sun is coming out. I knew it would. Now we will see the whole view. Just look, Fran. It's as clear as clear.

Silence. They are absorbed by the view. Lark's song.

FRANCIS. Time is getting on. (*They drink. Silence.*)

EVA. It is always doing that. (*Silence.*)

FRANCIS. You would think it would have thought of other ways to go by now. (*Drinks.*)

EVA. Go backwards, or sideways? (*Pause.*)

FRANCIS. Which would you choose? (*Drinks.*)

EVA. Sideways. (*Drinks.*)

FRANCIS. So would I. Here's to sideways. (*They continue drinking. Pause.*) I wonder what we would find there . . .

EVA. Well, I'd find you there, for starters.

FRANCIS. Oh, so you would. And I'd find you there, too, so (*Pause.*) that's alright. (*Quietly. Drinks.*) You look pale, Eva. Are you alright?

EVA. Yes I am. But it's you that looks pale. I expect it is all this drink.

FRANCIS. Maybe it's time to go on . . . finish our game.

EVA. I want to leave while the sun is still shining . . .

FRANCIS. We'd better get on . . . (*Pause.*)

EVA. You're right. We'd better . . . (*Pause.*) Fran, you cheat. You've drunk nearly all the brandy. (*She takes another large mouthful of brandy.*)

FRANCIS. Well, you know me. (*Drinks.*) Very unreliable. A slippery customer. Mrs. Morgan is always whispering "whisser-whisser-whisser" to Miss Evans, and I know she's saying, "Watch that Mr. Butler; he's very unreliable. He'll sit on your evening paper, he'll snore during the news . . ."

EVA. I'm a bit dizzy. I don't feel quite so . . .

FRANCIS. Do you want to call it off? It's only our game, you know. There's always tomorrow.

EVA. There isn't always tomorrow. No. (*She drinks, laughs, and passes the bottle to Francis.*) Just enough for your last slurp for the road.

FRANCIS. To us, and sideways.

EVA. To sideways, and us. (*Francis drinks.*)

FRANCIS. Ready?

EVA. Yes.

FRANCIS. Ready?

EVA. Yes.

FRANCIS. How are your brakes?

EVA. (*Laughs.*) Never had any of those.

FRANCIS. And your spare wheel?

EVA. Only spare tyres.

FRANCIS. Fool.

EVA. Fool. (*They embrace.*)

FRANCIS. Onwards! Five, four, three, two, one . . . go!

They spin their chairs around towards the sea. They wheel swiftly over the cliff edge, holding hands and throwing the empty bottles into the air.

FRANCIS. Together.

FRANCIS AND EVA. Wheeeeeee eeeeee eeeeee eeeee!

Silence. Sound of distant breakers below. Gulls cry. Bright sun. Lark's song. Lights fade. NB: Three possible ways to stage Francis and Eva going over the cliff. (1) Lights higher and turn on audience and dazzle them. (2) Eva and Francis stand and jump, leaving wheelchairs empty; this would entail a minor change in the text in the next scene. (3) Clouds in the scene—sloping stage—dips behind.

(INTERVAL)

ACT 2

SCENE 2

Scene, same as in Act 1. (Colours: grey to white.) Time: later in the same afternoon as Act 2, Scene 1. No wheelchairs by the chess table, but the chess pieces are still in place. Trolley as before, but Maura is absent. Miss Evans is front right, as before. Looking out the window. She turns towards the room.

MISS EVANS. Maybe today I could get to the fire before her.

TESSIE. (*To herself.*) God almighty, where's Maura gone? (*She arranges cups on the trolley.*) She'll be kill't. The old faggot will ate her.

MISS EVANS. I'd like to try for the fire, not the TV. (*She shuffles a few little steps.*) I can't stop her with the TV. (*Pause.*) It would be nice to sit by the fire.

TESSIE. (*Nearly knocking something off the trolley.*) Ooops.

Enter Matron, front right. She passes Miss Evans with an automatic smile.

MATRON. Good afternoon, Miss Evans. (*Miss Evans trembles on her walker. She does this when anyone passes.*) Mr. Mulcahy, I see we're well. (*Matron's path exactly follows that in Act 1. The actions are the same.*) All correct here, Tessie?

TESSIE. Yes, Missus.

MATRON. Where is Maura?

TESSIE. She's gone to get a clean apron, Missus. (*Matron shows displeasure at her use of "Missus."*) She'll be here in a minute.

MATRON. I've told you before, Tessie, many times. Do not use the term "Missus" on its own. Never do that. I'm *Mrs. Price* or Matron. I have a correct title; Matron. Kindly address me as Matron.

TESSIE. Sorry, Matron, Matron. (*Matron exits. Tessie raises her eyes to the heavens. Mimics:*) "Matron, Matron."

MISS EVANS. It would be nice to sit by the fire. (*Pause.*) I always liked a fire.

TESSIE. (*To herself.*) I'll bring in the tea. (*She leaves.*)

MISS EVANS. I always liked a fire. A real fire. I liked laying it. Roll the paper up, not too tight. No, no, not too tight. It must hold the air, make nice spongy balls. Roll the paper up. (*Chuckle.*) I'd read bits and feel sorry I missed them, and it did seem a pity to burn that nice girl's face . . .

Tessie reenters, carrying a large pot of tea. She slips past Miss Evans, who shuffles on with even more determination, but this makes no difference to her progress.

MISS EVANS. As I'm a bit early, perhaps today I could get to the fire before her. It's better to try for the fire, not the TV.

Tessie pours tea.

MR. MULCAHY. She didn't know everything. There were some things she didn't know. She couldn't poke her nose in everywhere. (*Fidgets with his rug.*)

TESSIE. (*To herself.*) Where the fuck are you, Maura? Leaving me with this lot. Would you ever hurry up?

MISS EVANS. I would arrange the sticks very carefully. The little ones first; they catch well. Criss-cross I would go. With two big bits of coal to hold them up at the sides, the paper all rolled into fat balls in the middle. Mother used to say, "Hurry up, Bridget. We'll die of the cold." Mother used to say, "Hurry up."

Miss Evans shuffles. Mrs. Morgan enters.

MRS. MORGAN. Who turned the television off, I wonder? (*She peers around and turns on the TV. She sits in the TV chair. She slyly notes Miss Evans's progress. She knows that her seat by the fire is not yet threatened. Tessie brings her tea.*)

MR. MULCAHY. "Dickie, Dickie," she'd say, "bring me this. Bring me that." Sometimes I pretended not to hear. (*Pause.*) Let her moan. (*Pauses and chuckles.*) She never knew. (*Pause.*) She never knew what hit her. (*Silence.*) I did.

MISS EVANS. One step. (*Shuffles.*) Two steps. Matron says I'm really improving. "You *are* improving," she says . . .

TESSIE. (*Brings a cup of tea to Mr. Mulcahy.*) A nice cup of tea for you, Mr. Mulcahy? (*He makes no sign. She puts the cup in his hands and returns to the trolley.*)

Enter Maura. She is pale and distraught.

TESSIE. At last! Janey, where have you been?

MAURA. (*Adjusting her apron and fussing about her appearance. She is trembling.*) Oh lay off, will you? I'm alright.

TESSIE. (*Fed up and snappy.*) So yer alright, are yer? Of course yer alright. Thanks very much. Bloody help, I'm sure. (*Maura runs to the window and gazes out.*) What's up with you?

MAURA. I saw something.

TESSIE. You what? (*She follows Maura to the window.*)

MAURA. I saw something queer.

MISS EVANS. If I get down early, maybe I'll get to the fire. A bright fire. (*Pause.*) Sometimes it goes out. (*Shakes her head at this sad possibility.*)

TESSIE. (*To Maura.*) Tell us.

Maura turns away and goes back to the trolley.

MAURA. Maybe I didn't see anything.

TESSIE. Make up yer mind.

MAURA. I couldn't have seen it . . .

TESSIE. Janey, come on, tell us.

MAURA. I seen . . . a vision.

TESSIE. Ah, will you fuck off?

MAURA. Must have been that . . . or I'm going daft or something.

TESSIE. Will you ever tell us, for God's sake?

MAURA. (*Looks at her shoe. She is nearly in tears.*) My effing shoe . . . banjaxed[18] . . . it's all scratched. I wish I never went.

TESSIE. (*Trying to hush Maura up.*) Are you going bananas? Would you ever stop and get on with the tea? You're making a show of us.

Tessie takes scones to an impatient Mrs. Morgan. Returns to trolley. Mrs. Morgan is trying to overhear.

MAURA. (*Looking at Tessie.*) Don't you believe me?

TESSIE. I do not. Did you see the Blessed Virgin standing in a bikini, waving her rosary at you? Saying, "Here's your life belt. Shall I throw it to you?"

MAURA. Shut up, Tess, will you?

TESSIE. (*Putting an arm around Maura.*) Well, tell us, for God's sake.

MAURA. (*Quietly.*) I saw them drop from the sky. (*Silence.*)

TESSIE. Out of the sky?

MAURA. The two of them. They held hands, and they were laughing.

TESSIE. Who, Maura, who?

MAURA. Like flying, but they were falling . . .

TESSIE. What are you on about?

MAURA. The chairs were flying, too . . .

TESSIE. (*Losing patience, sarcastic.*) Did they have wings? Did you have a trumpet?

MAURA. What can I do about my shoe? My brand-new shoe . . .

TESSIE. (*Cross.*) Ah, shut up and do the tea.

They serve tea. Maura, as if mesmerised, looks often towards the window.

MISS EVANS. If I had fir cones, it was grand. Fir cones catch well. Such a lovely shape, it seemed a pity to burn them. But they do catch so well. Then the small bits of coal all over the top. All over the top. (*Pause.*) I was pleased when I did it with one match. That pleased me. That was nice. (*Pause. Shuffle.*) It would be nice to sit by the fire. (*Continues shuffling.*)

(*Mrs. Morgan moves to the chair by the fire with her cup of tea.*)

MR. MULCAHY. She won't have that satisfaction. (*Pause.*) She will never see me a corpse. I saw to that. (*Pause.*) She can't interfere with that. I've won. Won that little game. I could stare at her lying there . . . and I could walk away, and she couldn't stop me . . .

Matron enters and crosses to trolley. She shows signs of agitation which she transfers into her annoyance with Maura.

MATRON. Ah, so you're here at last, Maura.

MAURA. I'm sorry, Matron . . .

MATRON. I expect my staff to be punctual. How can I run this establishment efficiently if I can't rely on my staff? You are much too slip-shod. It will not happen again. (*Notices Maura is trembling.*) What's up with you, girl? (*Mrs. Morgan is all ears.*) Are you unwell?

MAURA. It's nothing. I'm fine.

TESSIE. She's okay, Matron, she's just had a bit of a turn.

MATRON. Pull yourself together, Maura. Perhaps you had better come to my office, girl. You are upsetting the patients. Carry on, Miss Evans. There's nothing to worry about.

Exit Matron with Maura.

MRS. MORGAN. (*Loudly.*) Listen to this: "A conference of five hundred experts called in Spain to discuss the finding of a million-year-old human skull has been cancelled after the discovery that it is probably a *donkey's.*" Experts! Huh!

MISS EVANS. "Don't play with fire," Mother would say. "Don't play with fire." There was a big dirty coal glove[19] to use, but I preferred to use my fingers. It was easier to pop the coal on with my fingers. "Feed the flame," Mother would say, "feed the flame." (*Shuffle.*) I didn't like the coal glove. Made my hands awkward, so sometimes I'd drop the coal in the wrong place, and the sticks would break under the weight. Oh, dear, I didn't like that to happen! (*Pause. Shuffle.*) The coal glove was a present, so we had to use it. (*Pause.*) It was a present from Aunt Lily. She made it herself. (*Pause.*) Aunt Lily would come and drink tea and say, "I'm glad to see you're getting such good wear out of the coal glove."

A white-faced Margie, followed by a horror-struck Paul, barges into the room, followed by Matron, who is trying to divert them into her office. Maura follows. Their entrance makes no impression on Miss Evans or Mr. Mulcahy. Mrs. Morgan, who is engrossed in racing on the TV, gradually begins to think something is up and strains to overhear. Maura joins Tessie. Margie and Paul stand in front of the chess table. Matron is still trying to hustle them away so no one overhears.

MARGIE. Oh my God, what I've heard . . .

MATRON. (*Very flustered.*) Oh, dear Mrs. . . . . I'm so distressed. I'm . . . please, could you come somewhere private?

MARGIE. (*Pause.*) It can't be true.

MATRON. Please come to my office.

PAUL. Oh, it mustn't be true . . . what we've just heard.

MATRON. It would be quieter there . . .

MARGIE. I don't believe such a thing could have happened.

PAUL. Dear God, how could it . . .

MARGIE. Possibly have happened?

PAUL. It's unbelievable.

MARGIE. (*To Matron.*) It's not true.

MATRON. Oh my dear, I'm afraid you will have to be strong.

PAUL. Oh Margie, it's true.

MATRON. If you'd just let me take you . . .

MARGIE. (*Angry.*) She shouldn't have been let . . .

Mrs. Morgan is staring.

PAUL. Not on her own.

MARGIE. Needed more supervision. She was not responsible.

MRS. MORGAN. Shh! I am trying to watch this programme.

MATRON. I must insist that you come to my office. I must consider the other guests.

MARGIE. (*Not listening to Matron.*) Mother was getting quite muddled. Anyone could see her mind was wandering.

PAUL. No, she knew what she was doing.

MARGIE. I saw the signs. She was getting senile.

MATRON. Such a thing to happen. Please would you come . . .

MARGIE. And that *man.* (*Glares.*) That man was positively dangerous!

PAUL. Not that bad . . .

MARGIE. He was very bad for Mother, quite upset her. A very bad influence, affected her mind.

PAUL. No, no, not really. He was quite . . .

MARGIE. I know my mother. She was easily led.

PAUL. I never thought that . . .

MARGIE. Oh, the things that will be said . . . She should have been with me. Or with the nuns. She was obstinate. Difficult. Would not be helped. I tried and I tried. Did all that I could. I did everything . . .

PAUL. You did everything that you should and more.

MARGIE. She was not properly supervised. To take such risks . . . (*To Matron.*) How dare you let them up there!

PAUL. She knew about risk.

MATRON. You're distraught. You're distressed . . . I'll help you call, I can . . .

Margie weeps. Maura and Tessie bring her a chair and a cup of tea. Margie sits and leans on a supportive Paul. Matron tries to comfort both, more or less giving up on trying to get them out of the room.

MARGIE. Help? How dare you say you'll help! My mother was your responsibility. Oh, how right I was to want to remove her! I'll never forgive myself. You, you . . .

PAUL. Sit down, Margie. We'll manage. We'll be alright.

MRS. MORGAN. (*Keeping her eyes on the TV.*) I think it's disgraceful, visitors causing such a disturbance at tea-time. Tea should be peaceful.

TESSIE. Have a cup of tea. It'll warm you up. Sugar is good for you when you've had a shock.

MARGIE. I don't believe it . . . It's not my fault.

MAURA. I told you it's true . . . It's my fault.

MATRON. Please come to my study. It would be much more private.

PAUL. Margie, let's go somewhere private . . .

MATRON. Mr. Daly, please persuade your wife to come somewhere private. This is unsettling my patients. We all need peace and quiet.

MAURA. It was the truth I saw. I told you.

MATRON. (*Quietly.*) Who was on duty? Why weren't they missed?

MAURA. I wish it was a dream. I wish I could wake up into a dream, but there's only what's real.

MATRON. I am responsible. I could be closed.

TESSIE. (*To Margie.*) You'll feel better with tea inside you.

MARGIE. Oh, not tea. No tea. No more tea. I don't need anything. I need . . . (*Pause.*) I need my mother. (*Pause.*) I need . . .

TESSIE. Your husband is with you.

MARGIE. My mother . . .

PAUL. Margie, I'm with you . . .

MARGIE. Where is she? I want to see her. Mother?

PAUL. We'll manage. We're together, Margie. We'll manage.

MARGIE. Mother. (*Silence.*) I need . . .

MISS EVANS. "Look at your dirty hands," Mother would say, when I used my fingers and not the coal glove. "I can't put up with dirty hands." Aunt Lily gave Mother a present of plants. She would check with her finger to feel if Mother had watered them. Mother didn't know she did that. But I saw Aunt Lily do it. I saw her.

Silence.

MR. MULCAHY. There's no sweet Jesus waiting for you. I told her. I told her that as she was dying. She couldn't speak. But she heard. Her eyes watching me. There's no sweet Jesus waiting for you. No one. Nothing. You're just going to rot in your grave. Turn into dung. No eternal fuck with your sweet Jesus.

MISS EVANS. I would like to get to the fireside today. Oh, that would be so very nice. If I can get there before *her*. (*Pause.*) To sit by the fire. I would like a fire to sit by me. Fires talk. The flames make that fluttering noise, fire talk. I like to listen to fire talk. Sometimes when Mother was out, I would pull a stick out of the fire and wave it against the fire back. It looked like ribbons if I waved it quickly. Like a rainbow. Very pretty. I liked that.

Margie stands up and moves towards the window. Paul and Matron, on either side, support her. Margie moves slowly, as if drawn to look out to the cliff where the tragedy happened. Maura follows. They stand in a frightened huddle. Mrs. Morgan joins the group looking out and up towards the cliff top. Tessie holds a picture in her arms, across her chest. She stands behind the group that is front stage. Matron steps a few steps away from the group. She looks to Mr. Mulcahy. He does not look at her. She looks away and then looks with the others at the cliff top.

MAURA. (*Whispering.*) They fell from the sky. From the cliff . . . from the mountain . . . over there, out there.

They all look up and out.

TESSIE. Out there. Up there.

As they stand still, looking out, they have a sculptured quality. Miss Evans has arrived at the seat by the fire. She sits. She is completely content and utterly unaware of the tragedy. A smile of contentment spreads over her face. She looks into the fire.

MISS EVANS. I like to sit by the fire. "I always liked a fire," (*Pause.*) Mother said.

Mr. Mulcahy stares blankly out the window. He sings "I Do Like to Be Beside the Seaside," for the first time without interruption. The rest remain motionless.

Light remains on Miss Evans and Mr. Mulcahy. The other group becomes a silhouette. Sound of wind and lashing rain on the windowpanes.

The lights fade.

THE END

Notes

1. A popular English music-hall song written and composed by John A. Glover-Kind in 1907. Its refrain goes: Oh! I do like to be beside the seaside/ I do like to be beside the sea!/ I do like to stroll upon the Prom, Prom, Prom!/ Where the brass bands play:/ "Tiddely-om-pom-pom!"/ So just let me be beside the seaside/ I'll be beside myself with glee/ And there's lots of girls beside, I should like to be beside/ Beside the seaside!/ Beside the sea!

2. your friend: Menstruation.

3. gas: Fun.

4. stamp your cards: Provide unemployment insurance.

5. fag: Cigarette.

6. craic: Irish for good times, great fun.

7. gone to England in a hurry: Since abortion is illegal in the Republic of Ireland, women often travel to England to terminate pregnancies.

8. duty-free: A shop usually located at airports or on a ferry where goods are sold without the customary excise taxes.

9. puffed: Winded; out of breath.

10. Yeats: Jack Butler Yeats (1871–1957), landscape painter and brother of the poet William Butler Yeats.

11. Botticelli: Sandro Botticelli (1444–1510), Italian painter.

12. Bacchus: The Greek god of wine.

13. pax: Latin word for "peace." When used by children playing games, it means "I give up."

14. estates: New housing developments.

15. Brand's Hatch: A London area famous for car racing.

16. Sunbeam: A sports car.

17. in a pet: Irritable.

18. banjaxed: Ruined.

19. coal glove: Large mitten used for handling coal.

Dolores Walshe

(1949–)

🔊 Dolores Walshe is a Dubliner, born and raised in the Liberties. She earned a BA from University College-Dublin in English Literature, History, Ethics, and Politics, and later received a Higher Diploma in Education from Trinity College. Although she has traveled extensively in Europe, the United States, and Africa and has lived and worked in Dublin, Belfast, New York, San Francisco, Amsterdam, and South Africa, she continues to live in Ireland.

Walshe began writing poetry and short stories in 1986 and achieved remarkable success. Her stories have been broadcast on Irish National Broadcasting and by the BBC (British Broadcasting Corporation). In 1987 she had a story short-listed for the Hennessy Literary Award, won a story competition in the *Sunday Tribune*, and was awarded a place on the annual National Writers' Workshop sponsored by the Irish Arts Council. In 1988 she won first prize in the RTÉ (Radio Telefís Éireann) Radio 1 Poetry competition. In 1990 she received a grant from the Irish Arts Council and her story "Mael Dún of Africa" won the Bloomsday Award. Her short-story collection *Moonmad* appeared in 1994. In 2009, she won the RTÉ Radio 1 Francis MacManus Short Story competition. In 2010 she won both the Fiction Slam Award at the Listowel Writers' Week and the Fish International Short Story Award. She was short-listed for the William Trevor/Elizabeth Bowen International Short Story Award in 2012, and most recently she was awarded an Arts Council Bursary in Literature in 2014. She has also published two novels, *Where the Trees Weep* (1992) and *Fragile We Are* (1998).

Walshe's achievements as a dramatist are equally notable. Her first play, *In the Talking Dark*[1], won the O. Z. Whitehead/Society of Irish Playwrights/PEN Playwriting Literary Award in 1987. In 1989 it placed in the top five of almost two thousand international entries in the Mobil Playwriting Competition in conjunction with the Royal Exchange Theatre in Manchester, England, and it was the only play—other than the winning play—that the Royal Exchange decided to stage. Directed by Braham Murray, it ran at the Royal Exchange from April 13 through May 6, 1989. Her other plays include *A Country in Our Heads* (1991), *The Sins in Sally Gardens* (1990), and *Seeing an Angel in Hades* (1991). *A Country in Our Heads*, set in California, was produced in the Dublin Theatre Festival in 1991.

Among Walshe's many awards, she is the recipient of a grant from the Irish Film Board. She won the RTÉ P. J. O'Connor Play Award in 2012, and was short-listed for it in 2014 for her radio play *Stoning Daisy*. She was nominated for the Stewart Parker Trust Award, and has had play readings at the Mephisto Theatre in Galway (2012) and at The New Theatre's Festival of New Writing in Dublin (2013). Over the years her plays have been produced at Andrew's Lane Theatre, the Dublin Theatre Festival, and the Royal Exchange Theatre in Manchester.

Walshe's long-standing interest in South Africa provides the setting for her plays *In the Talking Dark* (1987) and *The Stranded Hours Between* (1989) and for her 1992 novel *Where the Trees Weep*. In April 1990, her poetry was read at the Mandela Concert in London to mark Nelson Mandela's visit. Her poems appeared in a televised documentary commissioned by the International Defence and Aid Fund for Southern Africa, and they were read in Stockholm and at Dublin's Gaiety Theatre to honor Mandela's visit to Ireland. In *The Stranded Hours Between*, which won a joint first prize in the 1989 O. Z. Whitehead competition, Walshe deals with major political issues—apartheid and violence—in a family setting. It is published here for the first time.

The Stranded Hours Between

CHARACTERS

ISEULT VAN LELYVELD, a white woman, late thirties.
STOFFEL VAN LELYVELD, Iseult's husband, white, early forties.

mKULIE (nomKululeko mJolo), a black woman, early thirties.
ANDRIES DE WIT, a white man, late forties.

SCENE

Stage left is a rondawel[2] with imitation wattle and daub walls and a thatched coni-
cal roof. The front curved aspect is open, with the suggestion of a main door and
a window to the left of the door. We are looking into one half of the interior of the
rondawel, which is well furnished and appears to have every convenience. On the
left, a straight dividing wall cuts the hut in two. It contains two doors which lead
to other bedrooms. To the right is the kitchen area, centre is a large double bed with
nightstands and lamps, and to the left a shower curtain is pulled around a bathtub
and toilet beyond. Furnishings as appropriate. The floor area is tiled and adorned
with African handwoven rugs with bright designs. The walls are decorated with
African memorabilia: spears, shields, masks, batiks, etc. Mixing oddly with this,
there is every evidence of modernity. Stage right is a flagged patio area, gauzed
in, furnished with table, chairs, sun canopy, and a braai.[3] A path leads from it to
the door of the hut, and from it around the right side of the hut. In front of the
hut and to the left leading offstage there is savanna[4] grass and a suggestion of low
mopane[5] bushveld.[6]

LOCATION

A small, exclusive holiday village located in the southwestern block of Kruger
National Park, South Africa.

SOUND EFFECTS

As appropriate in a vast expanse of big game country: shrilling crickets, animal
and bird noises.

TIME

Present day.

ACT 1
SCENE 1

An African drum beats in a muted tone. Sound fades as the lights come up. Stoffel
stands before patio area, suitcase at his feet, staring out through gauze. The light

is softening towards sunset. Iseult is flitting about indoors, opening cupboards, wardrobes, running her hands over the furnishings.

STOFFEL. (*Removes gauze. Whistles at view, quietly.*) A beauty. (*Loosens tie, sighs.*) Ja, a real beauty. This is the life, eh? (*Places portable typewriter on table, picks up note and brochure.*)

ISEULT. (*Still flitting, calls.*) Stoffel? Stoffel! Come and look; it's heaven, really. Quite the loveliest bungalow . . .

STOFFEL. It's a hut, a rondawel. Make an effort, will you? (*Reads note aloud.*) Kruger National Park bids you welcome. We hope your stay will prove most enjoyable. (*Snorts.*) He hopes I'll give the place a good write-up! (*Continues reading.*) He says he'll drop by about six. (*Glances at his watch.*) C'mon. If we're quick, we can get dinner over before he arrives. (*Reads.*) Senior ranger for the southwestern block.

ISEULT. Who?

STOFFEL. Name's (*Reads.*) de . . . Wit, ja, that's it. (*Calls.*) Anything to drink?

ISEULT. (*Rushes to fridge, opens it.*) Champagne. (*Takes out bottle, stares at it.*) Imagine! They must think we're . . . important.

STOFFEL. Beer?

ISEULT. Mm, yes. And food, tons of it. D'you think all this is meant for us? Stoffel, come and see!

STOFFEL. (*Examining barbeque grill.*) Meat?

ISEULT. Looks like half a cow all wrapped up in neat packages. But it's frozen. Poor beast.

STOFFEL. Microwave?

ISEULT. (*Looks.*) Yes, yes, there's one on top of . . . I don't know . . . a dishwasher? Or a dryer, maybe. One thing's certain: we don't have one back in the flat. Come and see!

STOFFEL. I saw some charcoal round the back. Sooner we get this braai lit . . . put some chops in the microwave, will you?

ISEULT. Oh, don't forget my little case from the car!

STOFFEL. Y'want me to carry your case?

ISEULT. (*Half laughs.*) Oh, come on, Stoffel.

STOFFEL. To stand accused of treading on your feminist toes?

ISEULT. Only my big toes are feminist; the rest of me thinks they went too far.

STOFFEL. Funny how convenient that excuse is every time you need a man to fetch and carry.

He goes round back of hut. Iseult puts meat in microwave, rushes out, carries in suitcase, places it on bed, opens it, begins to unpack.

ISEULT. (*Stops and looks about, happily.*) Oh, Mama, if you could . . . be here! (*Continues unpacking. Stoffel returns with small case, charcoal.*) Stoffel? That you?

STOFFEL. (*Examines himself.*) Well, if it isn't, I'm doing a hell of a good job imitating myself. Why, who else were you expecting?

ISEULT. (*Nervous laugh.*) Oh, I don't know. A lion, maybe. (*She joins him on the patio.*)

STOFFEL. (*Preparing barbeque. As he speaks, Iseult picks up brochure, peruses it.*) Don't worry, fence round this place's electrified.

ISEULT. (*Perusing brochure.*) Almost 20,000 square kilometers of big game country, 137 species of mammal, 114 of reptile, 450 of . . . (*Shudders, tosses brochure on table as she speaks.*) What a menagerie! (*Pause.*) And us. One sample of . . . frantica sapiens flapping round this little (*Shivers.*) ghost town.

STOFFEL. You couldn't wait to get here. Stop behaving like a woman.

ISEULT. (*Laughs.*) I'd have to have a sex change.

STOFFEL. I think I prefer you as you are. (*Kisses her.*)

ISEULT. It's nice, seeing you . . . y'know, back to your old self. Oh, I'm glad we're here!

STOFFEL. Glad's nothing to what I am. (*Teases.*) Four wrong turns! I was beginning to think we'd end up in Zimbabwe.

ISEULT. You know I always get confused when I have to look at the map upside down.

STOFFEL. Wonder if that's what Columbus said when he thought he'd found India?

ISEULT. You kept turning, I kept turning, after a while (*Sways, rolls eyes, indicating dizziness.*) the cheapest way I ever got drunk. (*They laugh, pause.*) We've six whole days before you have to be back in the office. Oh, it'll be good. I just know it will! (*Pause.*) Ever since we moved to Pretoria . . . I'm beginning to wonder if the new job was a good idea.

STOFFEL. C'mon, Isul! The biggest, most respected newspaper in the country! Never in my wildest dreams did I . . . I thought I'd have to spend the rest of my life working for that two-bit provincial rag. And the money, the car, the perks, how can you say that? We couldn't wait to get out of that piddling town!

ISEULT. Yes, but at least we didn't have a machine gun under the bed when we lived on your Papa's farm. The only rifle you kept was for killing pests.

STOFFEL. (*Enters hut, searches kitchen for meat tongs, returns to patio.*) It's not a machine g . . . !

ISEULT. None of it's good for Hennie. A flat's no place for a boy his age . . .

STOFFEL. Look, the flat's just the start. Later on, we'll be able to afford . . .

ISEULT. That fence is broken. Near the place where the shopping centre's going to be. You think we'll be safe?

STOFFEL. What? On the way in? Why didn't you say?

ISEULT. I did . . .

STOFFEL. D'you think they'd consider it an emergency? Maybe I should call them on that radio in the kitchen, what? (*Hesitates.*) Still, I don't want to look a fool. (*Glances at his watch.*) That ranger'd better turn up. I don't exactly relish the prospect of a night in this place with the fence. (*Pause.*) Vandals, probably. And poachers. Park's had a lot of those bastards lately. Well, I've plenty of ammo. Anyone comes snooping's liable to have his head blown off.

ISEULT. Don't talk like that. You never used to! (*Pause.*) Don't y'think we should cook indoors? Smell of meat might draw . . .

STOFFEL. Where're the braai chops? This thing's nearly hot enough.

ISEULT. After all, we're living with (*Stares out at the bush.*) the lions. (*Takes small case, goes indoors.*)

STOFFEL. You're not exactly a lion's idea of cordon bleu, not when there's enough antelope out there to feed thousands of them. Start the salad, will you? (*Iseult takes meat from microwave, goes outside, hands it to him, stares at view.*)

STOFFEL. It's still wrapped! (*Laughs.*) Christ, Isul! What menu were you planning, beef in a succulent batter of plastic?

ISEULT. (*Picks up brochure again. Peruses it.*) Wildebeest, elephant, crocodile (*Lips move as she continues to peruse silently. Pause.*) impala, my God, more than 160,000 . . . and the lions. (*Pause.*) We might be alone in the world. Just us . . . and them. (*Stares out into bush. Pause. Shivers.*) Those mountains . . . not exactly the blue ridged ones of Dakota, are they? Not that I've seen Dakota. Still, I have a, a picture . . . in my head . . . of how they look, how they should be. (*Staring into distance.*) Not like that, all . . . congested . . . the gun-metal blue of the wildebeest about them. (*Pause.*) Brutish, isn't it?

STOFFEL. The stuff'll taste of plastic. I know it will. (*Laughs.*) One of these days you'll poison us. (*Pause.*) Brutish?

ISEULT. Brute-making.

STOFFEL. That's not how we say it.

ISEULT. I'm doing the best I can. It doesn't feel . . . comfortable, speaking Afrikaans. I haven't used it since . . . not for a long time. I don't feel . . . real.

STOFFEL. If you'd your way, you'd have me apologising for being an Afrikaner! We've been speaking English for years, just to please you. Isn't it time you did something for me? Look, with this new position, we get to meet a lot of big bugs; there'll be champagne and oyster suppers, cocktail parties. This thing is Afrikaner owned. I don't want my wife looking like a fish out of water. It's not as if you can't, Isul; you spoke Afrikaans with your father 'til the day he died.

ISEULT. Yes, well, I had to, didn't I? (*Pause.*) Y'know, when he was gone, when Rachel came back to help us . . . (*Spreads arms wide, indicates with her right hand.*) Mama speaking English . . . (*Indicates with her left hand.*) Rachel speaking (*With click.*) Xhosa, me in the middle, (*Pause.*) like the filling in a warm sandwich. (*Small laugh.*) My mother tongues. (*Slight pause.*) Afrikaans makes me feel . . . undressed.

STOFFEL. You could make an effort, for my sake. There's a chance for me, Isul, I can be something bigger than a small-town hack reporting on crop yields and soil erosion. (*Pause.*) You'd want to've been at my end of the phone when you rang the other day, that ferret-faced editor, ears twitching the moment he realised you were English speaking. (*Pause.*) Just as well that didn't come out when I was still at the interview stage, yes, sir! Of course, I told him immediately that your father was an Afrikaner. (*Pause.*) This is my big chance, Isul. Ja, I'll agree, some of us can be a bit . . . gummed up. But these're nice people . . . educated . . . they have nice children; they come from nice homes. (*Pause.*) Rich homes. And if they accept you as one of them, why, we've got it made! This big do next week—you could show them how fluently you speak. I don't want them thinking my wife's a, a, foreigner. (*Pause.*) It'd be better if you said nothing about . . . the blacks.

ISEULT. So, I'm to . . . make sounds without making waves, is that it?

STOFFEL. All I'm asking is a little consideration! (*Pause.*) I didn't say any-thing about your father . . . people get funny ideas . . . (*Pause.*) Of course, most of them'd share his views about the Bantus, deep down. Still, they'd never let it be seen, they're too civilised. (*Pause.*) There's no need to tell them you can speak Xhosa—what'd be the point? No sense in giving them fuel. It's a cut-throat business, Isul; in the time I've been there, I've seen things . . . (*Pause, nervous.*) Careers carved up clean as fillet soon's someone decides he's not going to censor an incident in one of the townships. (*Pause.*) That's how I got the job in the first place: one of those men, seems he objected to the new regulations. (*Pause.*) Sometimes I feel like I'm walking on raw meat. (*Pause.*) Ach maan, I don't want to think about it. (*Pause.*) Unless . . . you *could* say you studied tribal languages at university. Ja, that's an idea!

ISEULT. Just think, if we'd never gone to Pretoria, if we'd stayed on the farm, I'd've grown old . . . without ever coming to know you.

STOFFEL. You're talking double Dutch!

ISEULT. Yes, well, a . . . mismatched pottery of words. D'you blame me not wanting to speak it?

STOFFEL. It's a beautiful language, stop trying to . . .

ISEULT. It's been . . . bastardised!

STOFFEL. Christ! (*Slight pause.*) When Hennie got his school report, to think a son of mine can't score a bull's eye in his own language! If you hadn't spoken English to him all the time!

ISEULT. He was my son too, until you began showing him how to use that gun. "A son of mine" . . . you make it sound like he's part of some . . . battalion in your head. Thank goodness he isn't; hard enough losing the one child I have, without . . .

STOFFEL. Silly! He's getting older; he's growing away.

ISEULT. Yes. He's growing more like you every day.

STOFFEL. Nice state of affairs when a mother's jealous of her own . . .

ISEULT. I'm not jealous, Stoffel. I, I'm . . . afraid . . . I never used to be afraid on the farm.

STOFFEL. If you took your pills like the doctor told you, you wouldn't feel . . .

ISEULT. Yes, well, that's just the trouble, isn't it? I wouldn't feel. (*Pause.*) I wouldn't feel any (*Her arm sweeps to encompass the view.*) of this . . . brute-making.

STOFFEL. Stop saying that! (*Indicates view.*) I'll be able to write a terrific article: splendid isolation, vast expanses of savanna and bush, great herds of eland[7] roaming in freedom—head's buzzing already.

ISEULT. And the lions.

STOFFEL. There're people all around us. Next rest camp's only 20 kilometers down the road. Booked solid, de Wit said.

ISEULT. But not this place. (*Rubs her bare arms.*) It's not the same, is it? No holiday spirit if you can't see other people, the church, supermarket, the swimming pool . . . all . . . quiet. Like coming on the *Marie Celeste*.[8] (*Pause.*) Like having a zoo backwards—we're the ones on the inside. Being . . . watched.

STOFFEL. It's costing us nothing. The sweets of the trade. All I've got to do is give it a good write-up before the official opening. You'd better make the most of it. It'll be a long time before my salary'll run to this.

ISEULT. What'd we do if a lion came to stare at us through the fence?

STOFFEL. We could erect a sign saying "Please don't feed *on* the animals." (*They laugh.*)

ISEULT. Climb that tree, I suppose.

STOFFEL. Lions can climb. They're good swimmers, too. Man, now that'd make some story, what! "Couple has narrow escape in wildlife sanctuary. Chased by marauding lions." Liven up my article no end.

ISEULT. That'd be dishonest. (*Shivers.*) I hope. (*Goes indoors.*)

STOFFEL. Bring out the salad, will you, and the champagne. We haven't had a proper celebration yet. (*Iseult begins preparing salad. Stoffel follows her in, continues talking as he moves to and fro between kitchen and patio, carrying plates, glass, champagne, etc., to table.*) 386 kilometers—it was a hell of a drive. I'm bloody starving.

ISEULT. It was worth it, to get out of Pretoria.

STOFFEL. (*Standing outside, freezes as she gasps.*) What, what?

ISEULT. A fly, real ugly . . .

STOFFEL. I wish you wouldn't do that! (*Relaxes, continues setting table. Stops.*) Where'd I leave the gun? Did you take it out of the boot?

ISEULT. Come and swat it, Stoffel; it might be a tsetse.

STOFFEL. Don't worry, they've been eradicated. Whole area's been sprayed. Leave it; it'll fly out. (*Moves to braai.*) This stuff's ready. C'mon. (*Serves meat onto plates, brings to table, begins opening champagne. Iseult opens overnight case, takes out cutlery.*)

ISEULT. (*Appears with salad, cutlery.*) If it pops, it'll sound like a gun. Might bring one of the rangers. We could ask him about the fence.

STOFFEL. Wonder what voltage it is? Can't be too high, or the animals'd . . . if someone's anxious enough to break in, it's hardly likely to stop them, is it? But the gun sure as hell will. I'd better get it. (*Stops.*) Our own cutlery? This place isn't burglar proof, Isul.

ISEULT. I thought maybe we'd meet somebody, have dinner. It'd look nice, having Mama's silver.

STOFFEL. There'll be no one here but us. This is a private camp. That means it's got to be booked *en bloc*. Think of the cost! The rich'll be here this time next week, people like Oppenheimer and du Plessis. Of course, they won't dine here, they'll use the dapper little restaurant beside the gym. And they'll go home, leaving that kudu in the freezer, having paid for every rib. Crazy, huh? That cow could keep us going for half a year. (*Pause. Indicates silver.*) You can put it away after dinner. Only one's going to be here is Papa.

ISEULT. Yes, well, it's not liable to impress him, is it? He'd be happier eating off a tin plate. It's our first real holiday. Why'd you have to invite him?

STOFFEL. Look, he won't be here for a few days. And we're better off having him here where nobody'll see him. He's been threatening to come to Pretoria for. Wait for it! (*Champagne pops.*) Aaah, that's the style! (*Pours, lifts his glass.*) To my new job! And lots more of this! (*Clinks glasses, gulps, pours again. They begin to eat.*)

ISEULT. That old bat next door was very impressed. Of course, I didn't tell her we weren't paying.

STOFFEL. Good! Bloody knobkerrie![9] Should stick in her gullet, at least 'til she sees the write-up in the travel supplement.

ISEULT. (*Looks toward hut.*) Like a little . . . laager,[10] isn't it? This whole place might be a, an onion . . . built in layers around us . . . borders, fences, walls. Then in the middle where the eye should be, you find it's not really an eye after all, it's a . . . little sticky smear of yellow, all bunched up . . . like fear.

STOFFEL. No sense in not protecting ourselves. (*Pause.*) Y'might've put some in the salad.

ISEULT. What?

STOFFEL. Onion! (*They laugh.*) That's better. (*Pause.*)

ISEULT. Yes, it's splendid, (*Looks around.*) isn't it, really? Very authentic, I imagine. Wish Hennie were here. He'd love it.

STOFFEL. But not Papa? Huh?

ISEULT. You can't expect me to feel overjoyed at the prospect of having your father. He's got . . . terrible habits. He . . . he picks his nose. I've . . .

STOFFEL. (*Half choking.*) For God's sake, I'm trying to eat! Christ, you'll never let me forget what I've come from. Well, you don't exactly spring from . . . sanity!

ISEULT. (*Rises.*) That's a terrible thing to say! Terrible! *Pause.*

STOFFEL. Look, I'm sorry, I meant to say "royalty." (*Arms about her.*) Isul? A slip of the tongue, that's all.

ISEULT. You should be the one to see that doctor. Instead you made me go, because I was getting on your nerves. I, I'm taking those pills . . . by proxy.

STOFFEL. (*Leads her to sit, then sits himself.*) I've been so used to speaking English, the words just got mixed up. C'mon. Finish your dinner. Isul? (*He reaches to touch her; she jerks away.*)

ISEULT. Yes, well, at least Mama had certain standards. No matter how little we had, it was always . . . well done. The soup spoon always pointed away from you . . .

STOFFEL. For all your wealth, all you managed to claw back from that house, when your parents died, was the silver! I was even the one to do that for you; I got it out of hock! (*Slight pause.*) My father may be an ignorant pig farmer, but at least he can manage to meet his debts. (*Pause.*)

ISEULT. Hennie would enjoy this, don't you think?

STOFFEL. He's with all his friends, he'd rather be with them.

ISEULT. I wish you hadn't sent him. If it's supposed to be an adventure camp, why do they have to learn all about guns?

STOFFEL. What d'you expect when the army are running it? And it's not costing us a cent!

ISEULT. But he's only thirteen. He should be listening to pop music and . . .

STOFFEL. We'd've stuck out like a sore thumb if we hadn't let him go. And that captain's right: more he learns about handling a rifle, the better. The kaffirs[11] aren't lying down any more.

ISEULT. Don't use that word. I hate it!

STOFFEL. The way that white family in Moreleta Park was killed . . . butchers! I'm telling you, Isul, you don't know the half of it! (*Begins tapping table.*) That township's only a stone's throw away from us.

ISEULT. I hope they make him keep the safety catch on when he's not using . . .

STOFFEL. You ought to read the papers, keep abreast of the situation. I bring home a free copy every day and you never look at it. (*Accusing.*) How come we're speaking English again? You've slipped us into it, haven't you? C'mon. (*Raps table.*) Afrikaans.

ISEULT. (*Clearing away. Following exchanges as she moves in and out.*) What do I want to read the papers for? It . . . addles me.

STOFFEL. (*Calls.*) Put the coffee on, will you?

ISEULT. Reading between the lines every day, watching it all grow there (*Pause.*) in the white spaces. It makes my eyes . . . skid.

STOFFEL. You're being deliberately obtuse.

ISEULT. No, I'm not. I know what's happening. I've always known (*Pause, bitter.*) thanks to Papa.

STOFFEL. Then don't just ignore it; join the Civil Defence with me!

ISEULT. You're getting like him, Stoffel. That ugly thing under the bed is just the beginning of it.

STOFFEL. Just because I keep a gun doesn't mean I'm one of those who'd wipe his family off the face of the earth because he's afraid of the Bantus! I'm just . . . vigilant, is all.

ISEULT. (*Outside. Sharply, staring towards bush.*) What's that?

STOFFEL. (*Rises in defensive crouch.*) What? (*Pause. Both stare and listen.*)

ISEULT. I heard something, like a twig . . . cracking.

STOFFEL. Well, there's nothing now. (*Moves to side of hut.*) I'll get the gun. (*Pause.*) And twigs . . . snap. Hah! See how rusty you are! (*Exits.*)

ISEULT. This one cracked. D'you suppose it was a lion? Lions never get . . . drunk. (*Pause. Next word drawn out, sharp.*) Crack. (*Pause.*) I heard it in you, Mama, that night, cracking, cracking, as his finger curled round the trigger. I knew then it was true, that we would die there, linked together, without my ever knowing what it was that cracked. Then the click. Crack. Click. (*Faster.*) No bullets. Empty cartridge. Papa swaying. Eyes-rolling-legs-buckling-vomit-spilling-into-the-frayed-potholes-of-the-carpet-you-laughing-me-laughing-gripping-hands, laughing-and-laughing-you-crying, crying and crying, a . . . reservoir of tears. I drowned, Mama . . . I drowned in your tears. And now he's . . . making me speak it . . . (*Shivers, low.*) He's bringing it back.

STOFFEL. (*As he returns, rifle in hand, box of ammunition.*) I should show you how to use this.

ISEULT. (*With distaste.*) No thanks. (*Goes indoors to make coffee as Stoffel loads magazine into rifle.*) Oh, there's no milk, I'm afraid. Or butter, there's no butter, either. No, wait, there's (*Lifts out plastic container, reads.*) banana syllabub.[12] Would you like some dessert?

STOFFEL. I thought you said there was everything!

ISEULT. Syllabub. Beautiful . . . delicate . . . don't you think?

STOFFEL. (*Glances at his watch.*) Christ, you might've said so earlier.

ISEULT. (*Coaxing.*) We can have it black, for once, can't we?

STOFFEL. You know I hate it black. And what about breakfast? No, I'll go now.

ISEULT. I'll come with you. I'll just get a sweater.

STOFFEL. (*Moving towards side of hut.*) No, you stay, that ranger should be here any time now. You tell him about that fence. Get him to do something about it before dark.

ISEULT. But Stoffel, wait. (*Makes to follow him, notices some cutlery still on table, picks it up, and rushes inside with it as Stoffel leaves, the following words called over his shoulder.*)

STOFFEL. Let him know how worried you are, make a real meal out of it. Women are better at these things.

Iseult comes out quickly with key in her hand to lock the door. Hears engine starting up and driving off. Sags. Looks about her, shivers, hurries to the table, picks up the coffeepot and the gun. Withdraws to the hut. Turns on radio. It crackles. She twists dial. It continues to crackle. She switches it off. Begins washing dishes. When she's finished, she goes to sit on bed, knits. The room slowly darkens. She switches on lamplight, picks up newspaper, flips through it, stops a moment perusing something, throws it aside, picks up book, peruses it. A muted roar sounds far off. She clutches the book.

ISEULT. (*Half whispers.*) Stoffel, Stoffel, what's keeping you?

Lights down on hut.

SCENE 2

Moonlight. Animal sounds: a baboon barking, etc. Bushveld area before the hut. The hut is in darkness. To the right, the table and chairs have been pushed back and draped. Before them, a black tangle of acacia thorns are just discernible. The bushes rustle, move a little, indicating that someone is present. mKulie's voice lamenting in Xhosa (with clicks where they occur in certain words.)

mKULIE. Emmenore![13] Eligama luncuthu kodwa xabelikwaza liba liquazi! Ndilahlekile, Vusi, ndilahlekile! (*Voice breaking with grief.*) Luthona na usindiso? Amothemba. (*Car noise. mKulie's voice arrested on next word. Harsh sobs stifled as bushes rustle, then still.*) Opheli![14]

Moonlight on bushveld fades, comes up on hut at same time as interior of hut is lit softly by bedside light. Iseult, tense, stands at window as Stoffel comes around side of hut, hurrying.

STOFFEL. Isul? (*Knocks.*) Snel![15]

ISEULT. (*Rushing to open door.*) Where were you? I was worried sick! (*He is sweating, breathless.*) Are you hurt? What is it?

STOFFEL. A drink, get me a drink! (*Goes to sit on bed.*) You and your bloody milk!

ISEULT. Me? (*Pours drink, takes it to him. Tired voice.*) Now what've I done?

STOFFEL. Did he show up, that ranger? (*Iseult shakes her head.*) Y'mean the fence is still . . . ? (*Gulps drink.*) I'm driving down the track towards the tarred road, I round a bend, and there's this leopard right smack in front of me. I swerve to avoid it and hit a rock. The tyre bursts like a clap from a gun. You want to've seen him: he exploded like a limpet mine,[16] cleared the track in one gigantic leap. Maan, those legs, I never saw such power!

ISEULT. A . . . a leopard? Y'mean we could be driving along and . . . ? In that flimsy car!

STOFFEL. I had to wait ages, just to be sure he wasn't coming back. I never changed a tyre so fast in all my life. By then, it was dark. I wasn't supposed to be outside the camp, so I turned and headed back, and that's when I saw him. Isul, pour me another, will you? (*Goes to check door, picks gun up.*)

ISEULT. Saw what? What?

STOFFEL. Somebody's out there, Isul, some dark bastard up to no good. Came out of the night like a thing possessed. Tore across the road right under my nose, big bovine eyes flaring like a demon. Christ, I almost had a heart attack. Well, if he comes anywhere near us . . . (*Cocks gun.*)

ISEULT. (*Relaxes.*) Oh. I thought you meant another animal.

STOFFEL. (*Harsh laugh.*) Is there a worse kind of animal? Give me a leopard any day.

ISEULT. You sound like a real Boer![17]

STOFFEL. If you'd told me earlier about the milk . . .

ISEULT. (*Sighs.*) Don't you ever get tired of blaming me? (*Picks up knitting.*) What's happening to us, Stoffel? You're . . . solidifying . . . right in front of me. I, I can't do anything to stop it. (*Pause. Holds out knitting, examining it.*) It's for Hennie. Don't you think the pattern's very . . . jagged, like . . . teeth gnawing at his chest when he wears it? (*Pause.*) It's quite put me off finishing it. (*Throws it on the bed.*)

STOFFEL. (*Cradling gun, peering out window as he finishes drink.*) Suppose I'll get some mileage out of that leopard for the article. (*Pause.*) Nothing out there. (*Places the gun on floor beside bed, goes to pour drinks, brings one to Iseult.*)

ISEULT. No thanks.

STOFFEL. (*Pause. Gently.*) Look, I'm sorry, okay? It's been a long day.

ISEULT. Every day's the same for you, Stoffel. "Long and arduous," that's what you've said ever since we moved to the city.

STOFFEL. C'mere. (*He pulls her from bed, into his arms.*) Let's not fight, huh? We're here to enjoy ourselves, aren't we? Let's start all over again.

ISEULT. The way we spend it . . . the days divorced, the nights married. (*Muted roar, quite faint. She starts, looks towards door.*)

STOFFEL. (*Kissing her ear.*) An animal somewhere out in the bush. My little mouse frightened? (*Growls in her ear.*)

ISEULT. Stop it, you know I hate it when you . . . (*As he kisses her, muted cry, very faint. Iseult tenses.*) There! Didn't you hear it? It sounded like a . . . like a scream.

STOFFEL. Good. Maybe that kaffir and the leopard've crossed paths. One less to worry about.

ISEULT. Stoffel, if you don't stop saying things like that, I'll . . .

He kisses her again, pushing her onto bed, falling with her. His arm reaches to switch out light.

SCENE 3

The patio. Andries de Wit is seated at table. He is wearing a ranger's uniform. Iseult is standing, pouring coffee.

ISEULT. He's gone to find you, actually. I'm sorry, we've no milk.

ANDRIES. There was none in the fridge? My apologies.

ISEULT. Oh, everything else is lovely, Mijnheer . . . de Wit, you said?

ANDRIES. Please. I have asked you twice now to call me Andries. (*Takes proffered cup.*) And you spent a comfortable night? (*He admires her openly.*)

ISEULT. Yes, yes, fine. You're quite sure you don't mind speaking it?

ANDRIES. No, indeed. When my wife was alive, we spoke it all the time. Her parents were English. I'm glad, too, reminds me of . . . happy times. And we get a large number of holidaymakers from abroad, does me good to practice. You'll correct me if I have mistakes?

ISEULT. And blacks? It's open to all races now, isn't it?

ANDRIES. (*Embarrassed.*) Well, in theory . . . I've nothing personal against them, you understand? If it were left to me . . . but the fact of the matter is . . .

ISEULT. You're always booked up?

ANDRIES. (*Relieved.*) Yes, it's a very popular place. It's advisable to book a year in advance. (*Indicates.*) This'll be the sixteenth camp. Our most luxurious.

ISEULT. Sugar? We always bring our own cutlery. Stoffel has a thing about it, I'm afraid. He says if he doesn't eat off silver, the food tastes positively crude. (*Slight pause.*) Noisy, though, isn't it? At night, I mean. Takes a bit of getting used to.

ANDRIES. There's more noise in the city. Give me the open air any day.

ISEULT. Aren't you afraid of all those animals? I thought I heard a scream last night.

ANDRIES. A scream? Could have been a wild dog. They can sound very plaintive. Let's hope it wasn't another refugee.

ISEULT. We were rather hoping you'd come. The fence . . .

ANDRIES. Yes, my apologies. I always make it my business to welcome people personally, but we had a spot of trouble . . .

ISEULT. Refugee?

ANDRIES. (*Surprised.*) You know about it?

ISEULT. What?

ANDRIES. The refugees, we caught two of them last evening; that's why I didn't call. By the time I had things sorted out, it was dark. We've had a lot of trouble with them lately, I'm afraid.

ISEULT. In this place? (*Shocked.*) You can't be serious!

ANDRIES. On the contrary. They're trying to get to Gazankulu, the home-land. There's a mission there. We caught about a dozen last month, travelling in groups of twos and threes. They'd lost as many again to the lions. I hope your husband won't mention that in his article. We've had enough publicity about it already.

ISEULT. Lions? You mean they . . . they . . . ?

ANDRIES. Naturally, I've every sympathy for these people, I'm sure they've good reason to run. But our ecosystem? (*He leans forward, earnest.*) The fact of the matter is, gives us nothing but headache. Soon's a lion becomes man eating, we end up having to cull the antelopes, restore the natural balance.

ISEULT. Good God!

ANDRIES. Haven't you read about it? Of course, they won't bother you; they're too afraid of being handed over to the police. You needn't worry yourself on that score. You're quite safe here.

ISEULT. Safe?

ANDRIES. I promise, I shall make it my personal business . . . whist! (*Indicates need for silence. She stiffens, peering with him towards the bush.*)

ISEULT. (*Terrified.*) What is it?

ANDRIES. A honeybadger. (*He draws her by the arm.*) If you move this way a bit . . . (*Points, awed tone.*) The prince of the veld, it's not often you'll spot him.

ISEULT. (*Relieved.*) That little thing?

ANDRIES. (*Warm tone.*) You won't meet a more fearless little commando in the whole of the bush—10 kilograms of muscle, bone, tooth and claw. He can bring down a young antelope while you blink. But his favourite dish is honey. There should be . . . yes! (*Moves her closer as he indicates.*) You see that little bird on the branch? It's a honeyguide. Soon as it takes off, the badger'll follow. There, you see? Must be a beehive round here someplace. The honeyguide'll lead him straight to it, join in the feast when he smashes the nest.

ISEULT. Doesn't he get stung?

ANDRIES. Skin's thick as hide.

ISEULT. What an odd . . . alliance. Beautiful, really.

ANDRIES. (*Looking at her.*) Very.

ISEULT. (*Half laugh.*) I'll never feel the same about Winnie the Pooh.

ANDRIES. He only takes what he needs to survive. He's never aggressive, unless he's attacked. Then he'll fight to the bitter end.

ISEULT. He could teach Stoffel a thing or two. (*Pause.*) Twelve, you say? Last month? (*Shivers.*) Poor things! What happens to the ones you catch?

ANDRIES. Well, they're deported . . .

ISEULT. But if they're desperate enough to run into a big game park, they must be running from something dreadful!

ANDRIES. Yes, well, it'd be more than my job's worth if I didn't hand them over to the police.

ISEULT. Oh somebody should do something!

ANDRIES. It's . . . not that I don't . . . feel for them. I do, I assure you! I used to be a policeman, a long time ago. (*Bitter laugh. Pause.*) I was going to be the best, medals for bravery, outstanding heroism . . . (*Snorts.*) There wasn't a more tender cub! (*Pause.*) Inside a week, when I'd look in the mirror, my eyes were dead. If I hadn't left when I did, I'd've ended up on the other side of the desk in the truth room. (*Pause.*) I, I never . . . hurt . . . anybody. I'd like you to know that. (*Pause.*) But I watched. (*Pause.*) For a long time afterwards, everything I looked at was . . . tainted.

ISEULT. (*Stares out into bush.*) Funny place to come.

ANDRIES. At least the savagery here is natural.

ISEULT. Yes. Ours is (*Pause.*) homemade. (*Pause.*) Isn't that the most . . . (*Pause. She looks at him.*) unconscionable?

ANDRIES. Well, I'd best be off. I have a lot of work . . .

ISEULT. Oh, don't go, please? You haven't finished your coffee. Besides, my husband wanted to ask you about the fence. (*Noise.*) Oh, there's his car now.

ANDRIES. The fence?

ISEULT. It's broken.

ANDRIES. Ja? Ah, zo, that's why you're nervous? (*Speaks the following as Stoffel comes around side of hut.*) I will look into it immediately. If you're worried about anything, you must call me. (*Inclines towards her.*) I promise I'll keep a special eye on you.

ISEULT. (*Notices Stoffel carrying cartons of milk, butter.*) Oh, this is Ranger de Wit, the man you spoke to on the phone last week. Stoffel, he says . . .

Andries holds out his hand.

STOFFEL. My wife tell you about the fence? (*Thrusts the milk and butter at Iseult. Shakes hands.*) van Lelyveld.

ANDRIES. My apologies about the milk, sir.

STOFFEL. It's the fence I'm worried about. Up near the cucumber bush . . .

ANDRIES. How bad?

STOFFEL. About 3 meters of it.

ANDRIES. (*Removes radio from his belt as he moves towards side of hut.*) I can't understand: it would have given enough of a shock to any animal that blundered . . . unless there's a fault with the generator. I'll have it investigated immediately.

STOFFEL. Looked to me like the wires'd been snipped. (*Slight pause. The two men regard each other.*) There was a kaffir on the loose last night; I saw him clear as anything.

ISEULT. Maybe it was one of those refugees . . . Stoffel, he says . . .

STOFFEL. Refugees aren't thinking about wire clippers when they're running across the border.

ISEULT. (*To Stoffel.*) You, you know about . . . those people, those poor?

ANDRIES. (*To Stoffel.*) What time was this?

STOFFEL. After dark.

ANDRIES. Travel's restricted to daylight hours. It isn't advisable for you to . . .

STOFFEL. No, you're damn right! You caught them before dark. I called at your station; they filled me in. This was after, I'm telling you!

ANDRIES. I will investigate . . .

STOFFEL. You do that! (*Pause.*)

ANDRIES. (*Inclines towards Iseult, smiling.*) Zo. Thank you for the coffee. It was a pleasure talking with you. (*Curt nod to Stoffel. Exits.*)

ISEULT. (*Calls.*) Do come again. You're welcome to a coffee any time. (*Low.*) You knew, Stoffel, you knew about those refugees. I'd never've come if I'd . . . oh, I can't bear to think of them!

STOFFEL. Bloody jumped-up little . . . (*Lifts spoon. Stares at it, voice acid.*) Ja, I see he merited the best. What were you doing talking in English? You could've sliced his accent with a machete. Christ, it's ridiculous, talking to my fellow countryman in a foreign language! (*Mimics her, simpering.*) Do come again. (*Mimics Andries's voice, bowing.*) It was a great . . . pleasure . . . talking with you. I know his kind of talk, his "special eye!"

ISEULT. My God, what sort of mind! I was just chatting to him . . .

STOFFEL. Don't come the innocent! He was making eyes at you!

ISEULT. What of it! I didn't do anything, did I? Isn't that what's important?

STOFFEL. You were lapping it up!

ISEULT. God, you're sick!

STOFFEL. You're attracted to him. Go on, admit it!

ISEULT. He's an ordinary man, a, a nice man whose wife is dead. He still misses her, you can tell. All he wanted was a chat, a nice, simple . . .

STOFFEL. Oh yes?

ISEULT. (*Points.*) That flower on the bush, it's very nice, but it stays right there, its little stem fixed firmly to the branch. I've no designs on it, you hear me? (*Broken.*) I can't take much more. I'm beginning to feel . . . cornered, only I don't know what for! You know what Hennie called you when you wouldn't let him walk to the shop for an ice-cream last week? A jailor, Stoffel—imagine, your own child! (*Pause.*) We were happy on the farm. We didn't have much, but we were happy. Hennie loved being able to run in the fields. He misses the dog. I miss the dog. (*Begins to cry.*) Ever since you let him clean that gun . . . he spends his time in his room, stroking it the same way he used to stroke the dog! I don't have a son any more: I have a goddamn soldier!

STOFFEL. The streets aren't safe. There are too many blacks out there willing to take a pot shot at us. (*Goes to her, comforts her.*) Don't, don't Isul. I'm sorry. I went to the shop, didn't I? I went in the car and I bought him one. (*Pause. Staring out towards the bush.*) That day in the office, I'd been reading (*Shakes head.*) 'n there was this noise, distant, like the prattle of an automatic . . . when I looked down, I found myself standing there, the coffee cup dancing on the saucer . . . vicious . . . like one of those witchdoctors. Christ, if anybody'd seen! I look at what . . .

goes in the papers; I see what doesn't—things that'd . . . scald your insides. I hear noises in the night. I think maybe I'm dreaming. But I'm awake. Lying in the dark. Listening. (*Pause.*) I hope he fixes that fence.

ISEULT. I want to go home.

STOFFEL. Well, maybe we'd be better off going back.

ISEULT. To the farm.

STOFFEL. You're joking!

ISEULT. You could still write. You could work for the Dagblad again, I'm sure they'd be delighted to have you back. Your Papa'd be glad. He's old. He's only got two boys; it's not enough help.

STOFFEL. Since when's that worried you? You couldn't wait to get away from that damp old house and lead a civilized life!

ISEULT. (*Begins to move about, her actions jittery.*) Yes, well, I didn't think it'd be like this!

STOFFEL. Stop doing that! Did you take your pills?

ISEULT. They put me to sleep! I can't think straight when I . . .

STOFFEL. They keep you calm.

ISEULT. If I take one, will it make you feel better? If I thought that, I'd take the whole bottle; I'd chew the glass . . .

STOFFEL. (*Panicked.*) Stop it!

ISEULT. Even when we're in bed, there's a roughness in you. You don't make love anymore; you make . . . hate! (*Raises her voice.*) I want my husband back!

STOFFEL. Ssh! (*Hugs her.*) Look, I'll make it up to you, I promise. It'll be like it was. (*Kisses her eyes, cheeks, etc.*) You're right. I know I've been . . . but I'll . . . change, you'll see. Best foot forward from now on, huh?

ISEULT. I don't want you to change. I want the old Stoffel.

STOFFEL. Then you shall have him, I swear it. Anything my lady wishes. (*Drops to one knee with a flourish.*) I'm yours to command! (*Pause. Tickles her knees.*) Hey? Hey? Hey?

ISEULT. (*Small laugh.*) Oh, cut it out!

STOFFEL. (*Presses his face into her thighs.*) I've always been yours, Isul. I, I don't know what I'd do without you. (*Pause. Rises.*) Tell you what! We won't even speak Afrikaans if it bothers you so much. (*Slight pause.*) For the rest of today.

ISEULT. (*Laughs.*) The rest of today.

STOFFEL. How's that? (*Nuzzles her neck.*)

ISEULT. (*Teases.*) Maybe I should insist on teaching you Xhosa . . .

STOFFEL. Don't push your luck. (*Grins.*) That old black crone may've had you and your mother over a barrel, but there's no way . . .

ISEULT. Don't call her that! We'd've starved after Papa died if it hadn't been for Rachel.

STOFFEL. (*Teasing.*) You're the only one I know who takes an inch and makes it elastic.

ISEULT. She brought us the washing and the sewing, never asked for a cent above her keep! She'd drag those bundles from the far side of town, where nobody knew us.

STOFFEL. Look, I'm ravenous. How about breakfast?

ISEULT. Mama wouldn't learn it, of course. Must say I quite liked it, all those clicks. Passed the time while we were sewing.

STOFFEL. What d'you fancy? Grape juice, cereal, the works?

ISEULT. Promise me you'll keep that gun away from Hennie? And you'll let him go places like other children?

STOFFEL. I'll be the most easygoing father, even when he leaves a layer of scum round the bath. Now, I could eat an olifant![18] What d'you say to bacon and eggs? You sit there, feet up, admire the view, and later we'll take a drive . . . (*Moves indoors, begins to prepare food.*) I'll make some notes, get that article drafted. I'll even take you shopping if you like. There's a nice crafts shop in the next camp. (*Begins to whistle.*)

ISEULT. (*Low.*) The old Stoffel. (*Pause.*) Is it . . . possible? (*Pause. Presses her palms to her face.*) Yes, yes, it'll come right. (*Pause.*) I know it will. (*Pause.*) Why did you marry him, Mama? (*Pause.*) Was he once . . . different?

SCENE 4

Interior of hut. Night. Outside, all is in near darkness. A shape on the ground near door. It moves intermittently, in a dragging motion that seems to have no sense of direction. Iseult and Stoffel in bed, arms about each other. Stoffel is reading a newspaper. Iseult's head is resting on his chest, eyes closed. Soft light from lamp illuminates bed only.

ISEULT. Wonder how Hennie's doing.

STOFFEL. (*Without taking his eyes from paper, kisses top of her head.*) What's tomorrow? The third day? The assault course, I think. We'll phone him in the morning from the camp at Letaba. View's supposed to be terrific from there.

ISEULT. Hope he's made some friends.

STOFFEL. (*Snorts at something in paper.*) Hey, look at this!

ISEULT. We came to get away, didn't we? (*Yawns.*)

STOFFEL. You should get more exercise. (*Slaps his midriff.*) Look at this! Not an inch of fat.

ISEULT. (*Shudders.*) Don't know how y'had the nerve, getting out of the car in an unprotected area. That sign was enough for me.

STOFFEL. You missed the eland, really beautiful! (*Pause.*) There's an eland on our coat of arms, on the dexter[19] side.

ISEULT. (*Sleepily.*) We haven't got a coat of arms.

STOFFEL. I meant our city.

ISEULT. That's not a coat of arms; it's a . . . a state of mind. (*Raises up a little.*) Did you see that little bird? All tail, three-quarters of him at least. It may be good for flight, but he almost toppled over when he ran.

STOFFEL. Ran? (*Laughs, kisses top of her head.*) Birds don't run.

ISEULT. This one did. He was running away from that lion in the bush. (*Pause.*) That tawny coat might've been a rustle of grass, except for the eyes, lazy with . . . sin. (*Pause.*) I think he forgot how to fly, he was so afraid. (*Pause.*) Poor squirt.

STOFFEL. (*Hugging her.*) You'n your big heart. Just don't start worrying about the insects, will you? There must be a few million species of them around here. (*Sighs.*) Must say I'm satisfied. Got enough for two articles, never mind one, and that's just the western tip of the park. (*Tenses. Listens. As he does so, the shape outside slumps against the door.*)

ISEULT. What is it?

STOFFEL. (*Puts his finger to his lips, pushes her away, climbs out, lifts gun from floor beside bed, listens. He is rigid. Low.*) I heard someone.

ISEULT. (*Kneeling, terrified. Whispers.*) You mean something's out there? What? What'd you hear?

STOFFEL. (*Hoarse whisper.*) We left the bloody shutters open. Put out the light, quickly! (*Begins to move towards door.*)

ISEULT. But we'll be in the dark, you know I . . .

STOFFEL. (*Hoarse with fear.*) Put out the fucking light!

ISEULT. (*Reaches to put out light, her voice a high-pitched squeak as she does so.*) Stoffel, wait for me, please! (*Hut is plunged into darkness [a complete blackout]. Very slight pause. Whisper.*) Stoffel? (*Pause. Louder, voice teetering.*) Stoffel?

STOFFEL. Sssssh! (*Slight pause. Following exchanges whispered.*) Here, by the door! (*A faint silver light begins to permeate the room very slowly from the direction of the window.*)

ISEULT. Can you hear anything now?

STOFFEL. Hush! (*Pause.*) Someone just thumped against the outside wall.

ISEULT. (*Moving from bed towards door, hands outstretched in the near darkness.*) Y'mean it's trying to get in?

STOFFEL. I don't know what's bloody happening! If you'd let me listen . . . (*Following words uttered as Iseult clutches him from behind and he jerks in fright.*) Christ! Don't do that!

ISEULT. D'you suppose it's a lion? What kind of, of thing d'you . . . ?

STOFFEL. Fucking human kind, that's what! D'you think your average lion'd bother with a pair of clippers? The bastard must've been in here all the time, and, now de Wit's had the fence fixed, he can't get out.

ISEULT. Y'mean it's not an animal?

STOFFEL. (*Levelling gun at door.*) He's an animal, all right, and he's in for a bellyful of lead if he doesn't move soon. (*Shouts.*) Hey, you, out there! (*Pause.*) I don't know what your game is, but you'd better clear off! (*Pause.*) There're seven of us here and we're armed to the hilt! (*Leans towards door, cocks rifle.*) Y'hear? That's no joke; that's an AK-47 all ready to blast you into the gravel! (*Pause.*) Y'hear? (*Pause.*) You got to the count of three to clear off! (*Whispers to Iseult.*) Stay here and listen. (*Moves to window, presses his body against wall as he tries to peer out without being seen.*) Can't see him.

ISEULT. (*Ear pressed to wood.*) I can hear breathing. (*Slight pause.*) You're sure it's not an animal?

STOFFEL. (*Still peering.*) Not a fucking thing!

Iseult goes for a chair, carries it to window, climbs up on it.

STOFFEL. Get down, for Christ's sake. You might be shot at! (*Tries to pull her down.*)

ISEULT. Wait! There's a hump by the door, I can see a . . . leg, yes, it is a leg. You were right: it's a person, it is a person!

STOFFEL. Only one?

ISEULT. (*Peers.*) There's no sign of anybody else.

STOFFEL. (*Pulls her down.*) Could be a trick. Could be others hiding in the bush.

ISEULT. That leg, it's so . . . still. (*Pause.*) Like whoever it was . . . was . . . (*Pause.*) It could be one of those refugees. (*Pause. Moves towards door.*) I'm going to open it.

STOFFEL. (*Pulls her back.*) No! (*Moves towards emergency radio in kitchen.*) I'll contact the ranger station. There's bound to be someone on call . . .

ISEULT. And what'll you tell them? To drag one of the rangers out of bed because there's someone lying hurt outside our door and we're afraid to open it?

STOFFEL. (*Stands indecisive, hand over radio.*) I, I . . .

ISEULT. (*Drawing bolt.*) I'm taking a look.

STOFFEL. (*Lunging towards her.*) No!

By the time he reaches her, she's opened the door. As Iseult looks down, he levels the gun at the shape on the ground, then raises it to point outside.

ISEULT. (*Bending down.*) Why, it's a (*Pause.*) woman! (*Bends to touch her.*) She's so cold. There's blood on her arms. Quick, help me get her inside.

STOFFEL. (*Straining to see out.*) Are you crazy? There could be half a dozen more waiting to rush us . . .

ISEULT. Then get out of the way! Step over her and keep guard while I drag her into . . .

STOFFEL. We can't . . .

ISEULT. Stoffel, if you don't move, I'll push you out! There's no way I'm going to leave her lying there! Besides, if she got sealed in behind the fence, it's also possible some animals might've . . . there're enough buildings and bits of bush for things to lurk in. She's bleeding—God knows what she might draw to our door! Will you get out? (*Pushes him. He steps over the body, darting the gun about as he peers. Iseult drags in the limp form. Quickly, he backs inside after them, closes door and bolts it. Together they stand staring downwards. Stoffel goes to lamp, switches it on. mKulie is lying in a crumpled heap on the floor, eyes closed. She is filthy. There are scratches on her arms and legs, dark patches of sweat on her dress.*) Oh, you poor thing, look at you! (*Iseult bends down, taps her face gently.*) Hey there, wake up! You're safe now, safe.

STOFFEL. (*Pause. Standing his distance, watching, the gun still cradled in his arm.*) We should call the station.

ISEULT. At least she's breathing evenly. I think she's fainted.

STOFFEL. (*Moves towards kitchen.*) I'll call and tell them.

ISEULT. At this hour? There isn't a first-aid post for miles. Anyway, the scratches are superficial (*Touches mKulie's arm.*) except for this. She'll need a bandage. (*Pause. She pushes back mKulie's hair.*) Why, she's quite beautiful, really, under all that muck. She's not very black, is she? More the shade of . . . honey. She doesn't look like Rachel, anyhow. Mama used to say Rachel was born in a bucket of tar, that God forgot to take her out before she was soaked to the bone.

STOFFEL. You shouldn't touch her, she might have malaria, or, or . . . some such disease.

ISEULT. We took the antimalaria tablets. Anyway, I don't think it's catchable unless you're bitten. Help me take her to the bathroom, we can get her cleaned up. Maybe some water might revive . . .

STOFFEL. I don't think we should touch her, just leave her where she is.

ISEULT. Stoffel!

STOFFEL. She's . . . she's dirty.

ISEULT. Y'think you'd look any cleaner? She must be half starved. She's lucky she's alive.

STOFFEL. Half starved! With that belly? Well fed, if y'ask me!

ISEULT. (*Touching mKulie's stomach.*) Swelling's too high . . . I think she's pregnant.

STOFFEL. Terrific! All we need now is for her to squat on the (*Points.*) rug and spit out half a dozen little black bastards to join the party.

ISEULT. Stop, stop it! She's flesh and blood!
STOFFEL. Ja?

Pause. They stare at each other.

ISEULT. I'm going to clean her up. Give her something to eat. (*Pause.*) It's
the least we can do. (*Pause.*) She's not going anywhere 'til I find out
why she's here, how she got here. (*Begins to try to lift mKulie.*) Now,
help me get her in the bathroom. (*Strains, drags mKulie a couple of inches.
Stops, defeated. Tries again. Following spoken as she looks at mKulie.*) I'll
keep at it, Stoffel, if it takes all night. (*Pause. She manages to move the
limp body a little more.*) (*Low, pleading.*) Look at her, that's a . . . person.
(*Pause.*) And she's hurt.

*Stoffel looks at them. He hesitates, then places the gun on the bed and moves
across to them. His hands flap reluctantly for a moment before he bends to place
them under mKulie's arms, drawing her into a semi-upright position as he begins
to drag her across the floor. Iseult hurries before them, pulling back the shower
curtain and turning on the water in the bath as Stoffel arrives with his burden.
He props mKulie at the side of the bath and steps back. mKulie begins to stir as
Iseult dampens a cloth.*

STOFFEL. (*Sharply.*) Not that, that's one of ours! (*Reaches for a towel, hands it
to her. Iseult wets a piece of the towel and bends to wipe mKulie's face. mKulie's eyes flicker for a moment, then open. She stares about, eyes widening as
she registers the water filling in the tub.*)
MKULIE. Vusi! Vusi! (*She screams, thrashing wildly to get away from Iseult.
She lunges from the bathroom area, knocking over a small table with Stoffel's
notes before they can think to react.*)
ISEULT. Quick! Catch her before she hurts herself! (*She and Stoffel leap after
her as she blunders dazedly about the room, moaning continuously.*)
MKULIE. Vusi!
STOFFEL. Christ, we'll owe a fortune in damages! (*He catches mKulie. She
screams, thrashing out wildly at him.*)
ISEULT. (*Loud soothing voice as she grasps mKulie's arm.*) It's all right, really!
We're trying to help, can't you understand? Oh, don't, don't, you'll
hurt yourself!

STOFFEL. (*Gasps as he struggles.*) Strong as a bloody ox! (*Falls with the woman, his chest at a right angle to hers as he pins her beneath him on the floor. Her legs kick aimlessly. Finally, she stills.*)

ISEULT. (*Kneeling beside her, her hands cupping mKulie's face, stroking her hair, speaking slowly, each word carefully enunciated.*) It's all right! You're safe here . . . we're not going to hurt you, do you understand? (*Pause.*)

STOFFEL. Ja, try Afrikaans, tell her if she doesn't stop attacking the furniture, I'll break her bloody neck!

mKulie whimpers at his tone.

ISEULT. (*Soothing her.*) Ssh! It's okay. (*Slowly.*) Do you speak Afrikaans? (*Pause.*) Afrikaans? (*Pause. mKulie stares at her.*) Here, let's give her something to eat. At least then she'll realise we mean her no harm. Hold her 'til I find something . . . (*Rises, goes to kitchen, searches.*) Now, I wonder what I should give her?

STOFFEL. For Christ's sake, Isul, don't start making out a menu!

mKULIE. (*Whimpering, struggling.*) Ndiva inxolo enkulu![20]

STOFFEL. (*To Iseult.*) Quick, quick, will you?

Iseult comes with glass of milk and cake, kneels, holds them before mKulie's eyes. mKulie fixes her gaze on the food. Pause. She mutters.

ISEULT. There! I think you can let her go now. (*Stoffel slowly releases her, rises. Iseult proffers the food. mKulie looks at both of them in turn, then back at the food. She sits up slowly, reaches tentatively for the food, takes it, gulps drink, wolfs down cake. Stoffel snorts, moves away, gets a fresh towel, wipes himself vigorously. While mKulie eats, Iseult points to herself, speaking the following.*) I am Iseult. (*Pause. Tapping her chest.*) Iseult. (*Points to Stoffel.*) That's Stoffel, you understand? (*Points to herself.*) Iseult. (*Nods. Pause. Points to Stoffel.*) Stoffel. (*Nods. Pause. Points to mKulie.*) And you? (*Pause.*) You?

STOFFEL. Wasting your breath! (*mKulie darts him a look, looks away quickly, turns back to Iseult.*) I just hope she's not diseased, is all!

mKULIE. (*Very low, to Iseult.*) Shangaan? Changana? (*Slight pause.*) Tsonga! (*Pause with click on next word*) Xhosa?

STOFFEL. (*To Iseult, indicating mKulie's speech.*) What'd I tell you? Gobbledygook!

ISEULT. (*Slowly, tentatively, with click.*) Xhosa?

mKULIE. (*Nodding, low, excited, to Iseult, with click.*) NonKululeko. NonKu-luleko, my name is . . .

ISEULT. (*Slowly, to mKulie. Surprised, with click.*) NomKululeko . . . your . . . name . . . is . . . why (*Click on next word.*) Xhosa! You speak (*Click.*) Xhosa! (*mKulie nods vigorously.*) Imagine! (*Iseult shrieks with delight. mKulie smiles.*)

STOFFEL. (*Looking from mKulie to Iseult.*) What, what?

ISEULT. (*To mKulie, click.*) Xhosa! I can't believe it!

mKULIE. Yes, yes, auntie! My mother was of the (*Click.*) Xhosa tribe! You speak it, auntie? You speak it too? (*Claps her hands. They laugh.*)

STOFFEL. (*To Iseult.*) What's going on? What's she saying?

ISEULT. (*Hands joined. With fervour.*) Rachel, Rachel, bless you!

STOFFEL. (*Roars. mKulie flinches.*) Isul, for Christ's sake, what're you jab-bering about?

ISEULT. (*Turns to him.*) Oh. Stoffel, she speaks (*With click.*) Xhosa. Can you believe it?

STOFFEL. (*Sneers.*) Is that what it is? I thought you were a pair of bloody castanets! What'd she say? Is she alone? Is there anyone else out there? (*He prowls the hut during the following exchanges, eyeing the women suspiciously.*)

ISEULT. (*To mKulie.*) Are you alone? Where've you come from? How'd you get in?

mKULIE. I am alone. (*Shivers.*) Now. (*Pause.*) When first we ran, the mother of my husband was with me. (*Bows head, covering her face. Pause. Speaks through her hands.*) But now . . . now . . . she is . . .

ISEULT. What happened?

mKULIE. She was old. Slow and heavy with her years. (*Half-sob.*) My man, Vusi? He was wrong, wrong! (*Looking out at bush.*) There is no place to hide, no safe place! They can climb the tallest reaches of the baobab.[21] (*Sobbing.*) Their eyes burn up the darkness, making of it a thing of light!

ISEULT. (*Touches mKulie.*) Oh what is it?

mKULIE. She could not run, she could not climb high enough. *Pause.*

ISEULT. Y'mean . . . ? (*Pause.*) Oh my God!

STOFFEL. (*Shocked. Sound of Iseult's voice arrests him.*) What? What? Isul?

ISEULT. (*Staring at mKulie. Low.*) She says her mother was . . . savaged.

STOFFEL. And the rest of them? (*Pause.*) What about the rest of them?

ISEULT. (*Coldly, snapping.*) She's alone!

STOFFEL. (*Slumps.*) Hey, now, that, that's good news. (*Goes, pours drink. Stops suddenly.*) But did she see anyone else out there? Ask her.

ISEULT. (*Gently pushes back mKulie's hair.*) Where've you come from?

mKULIE. (*Drops her hands in her lap.*) Mozambique. We fled across the border when Emmenore came. Oh the name has music, but when they screamed it, the word was blood!

STOFFEL. (*Gulps drink, pours another.*) What does she say?

mKulie looks at him quickly, then back to Iseult.

ISEULT. But didn't you know what you were running into?

mKULIE. It is safer here. Vusi, my man? Once he told me. Safer, he said, with the wild animals. (*Pause.*) The bandits poisoned our well when they burned our huts, they took all the children out into the bush. Vusi and I, all of us, we heard the (*Shakes head violently.*) screams, terrible . . . screams . . . unending. (*Covers her ears.*) Vusi could not bear it. He ran at them, clutching his head, begging them to stop, stop! (*Pause.*) They laughed . . . the Emmenore. (*Pause.*) Laughed. (*Pause.*) They asked him if the children's noise was too big, if it was giving him a head pain. Yes! He said, Yes! It is too big, please please stop it, stop hurting the children! (*Pause.*) That made them smile, all, all of them smiled. (*Pause.*)

STOFFEL. What's she jabbering about? (*The two women ignore him.*)

mKULIE. One of them, a young boy, very black, patted Vusi's shoulder, and his voice, his voice was so . . . soft, like the wind on a leaf. You have asked us so nicely, he said, you are so polite, so polite with all those nice pleases, we are going to do something for you. We are going to stop the noise for you.

STOFFEL. Isul!

mKULIE. Vusi smiled. (*Pause.*) Such a . . . beautiful . . . (*Pause.*) While he was thanking . . . thanking . . . two bandits stepped up behind him. (*Pause. Agonised howl.*) They cut off his ears!

Pause. Iseult is rigid, on her knees, head bowed. She begins to weep silently.

STOFFEL. (*Moves toward her.*) What, what is it?

Iseult rises, still weeping, moves to window without looking at either of them.

mKULIE. Then they held his head down in the river. 'Til . . . 'til . . . (*Pause.*) the water bubbling from the sides of his head . . . his blood . . . painting the river like the sun at evening . . .

STOFFEL. Isul, what? (*Grabs gun from bed, circles mKulie, giving her a wide berth, goes to Iseult.*)

STOFFEL. (*Fearful.*) Are there more of them? Is that it? (*He touches her; she pushes him away. He turns towards mKulie.*) What the fuck've you said?

mKulie shrinks as he aims gun.

ISEULT. Stop, stop it! Put that filthy thing away! (*She lunges at gun.*)

STOFFEL. For Christ's sake, you'll set it off. It's cocked! Okay, okay, I'll put it down, see? (*Moves to kitchen counter, lays gun down.*)

ISEULT. (*Without looking at him.*) They cut off her husband's ears. Then they . . . drowned him. (*Pause. Looks at him.*) I . . . I can't look at her. I, I . . . don't know what to say to her . . .

STOFFEL. Who, did she say who? Were they in the park?

ISEULT. No, they weren't in the goddamn park. All we've got here are animals!

STOFFEL. (*Relieved.*) So there's nobody else out there! (*mKulie begins to retch. Iseult runs to her.*) Come! Come! (*Helps her rise, stumble to the bathroom. Pulls the shower curtain. Long pause. Iseult emerges, alone. Goes to stare out window. Suggestion of dawn. Pause.*)

ISEULT. What they did to her husband . . . (*Pause.*)

STOFFEL. Ja, it's . . . a . . . very unpleasant . . . state of affairs. (*Pause. Iseult stares at him.*)

ISEULT. (*Paces furiously.*) We're backing the Emmenore. We're backing these bandits, calling them resistance fighters because they happen to be on our side . . . well, aren't we? (*Pause. Shouts.*) Goddamn you, answer me!

STOFFEL. Yes! But it's not our fault . . .

ISEULT. Then whose?

STOFFEL. For God's sake, we're not the bloody government!

ISEULT. Then who is? Where'd we get our state of mind from? You tell me, no, really!

STOFFEL. She can't stay here!

Sun continues to rise.

ISEULT. Your fear smells. But hers, it . . . reeks. (*Points.*) She's in there spewing fear . . . it's coming up in great fleshy gobbets . . .

STOFFEL. She's throwing up because you gave her cake! God knows what she ate out there!

ISEULT. Oh, don't blame it on God. Don't blame it on a . . . word! Blame it on the coat of arms hanging in our heads!

STOFFEL. We have to inform the Park authorities!

ISEULT. Between the "G" and the "D" there's a zero, a great big empty space, somebody said that. Who said it, d'you know? Well, it's not true. Between those letters, there's a, a cesspool. It's full of us, us! (*Enjoins hands piously, tone fervent.*) Come, let us bow to God the Laager!

STOFFEL. You're freaky. You know that?

ISEULT. Like my Papa, d'you mean? (*Pause.*) You and he should've applied for a job in the Ministry of War, they'd have lapped you up. There's still time for you, though. And Hennie!

STOFFEL. Christ, what're you . . .

ISEULT. You've robbed my son!

STOFFEL. . . . talking about?

ISEULT. He isn't mine anymore!

STOFFEL. You can't own . . .

ISEULT. No, I can't, because you own him! He's up there (*Taps her forehead.*) on your coat of arms, blazing from the battlements, his eyes hungry with . . . possibilities!

STOFFEL. All I'm doing is protecting us!

ISEULT. Yes, like Papa!

STOFFEL. Don't you liken me to that, that lunatic! (*Pause.*)

ISEULT. (*Covers her eyes.*) I kept them closed. (*Pause.*) But her words made pictures . . . (*Stares out window. Pause.*) Those ears. I keep seeing them, lying there on the sand . . . two little black maps of Africa. (*Pause.*) Somewhere in you, Stoffel, there's a piece . . . a piece that is . . . heart. (*Pause.*)

STOFFEL. We can't! (*Pause.*) She's an illegal alien. We could be arrested for harbouring . . .

ISEULT. When we leave here, we could hide her in the boot, take her to the mission in Gazankulu.

STOFFEL. Not a chance! If we were stopped . . . (*Glances towards bathroom.*) What's keeping her?

ISEULT. Why should we be stopped? We've never protested about anything in our lives, two dum-dums like us. We're a policeman's answer to a baton charge! (*Pause.*) She's afraid to come out. D'you blame her! (*Pause.*)

STOFFEL. We can't do it, Isul . . . they'd eat us alive. I'd lose my job, everything. We'd be ostracized . . . (*Picks up gun, strokes it.*)

ISEULT. Yes, well, I've nothing to lose.

STOFFEL. What about Hennie?

Iseult laughs mirthlessly. Pause.

ISEULT. If she goes, I go. (*Pause. Stoffel snorts. She turns to face him.*) I'll leave you. (*Pause.*)

STOFFEL. (*Paces, gun in hand.*) You wouldn't dare!

ISEULT. Try me!

STOFFEL. You wouldn't have the guts. (*Pause.*) What would you do? Where would you go? You've no money of your own! (*Pause. Smashes fist on counter. Iseult jumps. He roars.*) You're bluffing! (*Pause. Begins knocking things about, searching as he shouts. Iseult becomes rigid, sits, picks up knitting, tries to knit, but the needles tap erratically. She stops, holds the bundle tight to her chest.*) Those fucking pills! Where've you put them? I should've made you take them! (*Pause.*) Leave me! If it weren't for me, you'd be living on welfare. You can't fucking type; you can't even add, for Christ's sake, (*Iseult stares straight ahead, trembling, her body rocking slightly.*) I was the one who reached out and hauled you out of that half-world you were living in after your mother died, wandering about that bloody park like a starved sparrow, your eyes . . . scorched bloody hollows of grief, and you're not much better now. Christ, what possessed me to take more than a passing glance at you? I should've left you sitting there . . . (*Pause. Quietly.*) You can't, you can't mean it. (*Pause.*) You, you can't, Isul! (*Pause.*)

ISEULT. I flushed them down the toilet before we left the flat.

STOFFEL. I can't cope with you!

ISEULT. Yes, what does that mean? You can't cope with me because of the way *you* are!

STOFFEL. D'you've any idea what it's like, living with a haunted woman!

ISEULT. You, you manage me because it's the only way you can avoid having to manage yourself. You use me, bully me, so you can keep on lying to yourself about what you are! (*Pause. Quietly.*) Can't you understand? I've woken up. I can't go back to sleep, not even to, to save us!

STOFFEL. Save us! (*Frightened.*) What kind of silly talk! (*Pause.*) Just because we've had a few rows lately . . . look how it was today! You were . . . happy, weren't you? Just like it always was.

ISEULT. (*Shakes head.*) We said the words. We made all the right . . . gestures. (*Pause.*) Like a prayer resurrected from childhood, stumbled over in the need for belief. (*Pause.*) Sometimes I think . . . in that grey city . . . we buried it too deep. It won't . . . excavate. We don't know how to . . . (*Emphasis.*) be . . . together any more. There's no . . . presence, nothing between us and the words.

STOFFEL. Just because I wanted you to speak Afrikaans . . .

ISEULT. Whatever language we speak, the words won't . . . meet. (*Pause.*) I, I can't live with an armoured tank.

STOFFEL. For Christ's sake, I'm just protecting us!

ISEULT. From what! The blacks? You look in their eyes. What you see isn't their savagery: it's the image of your own, the snivelling brute in your own heart. That's what you're afraid of!

STOFFEL. (*Faces her, jabbing gun repeatedly in the air for emphasis as he speaks.*) Shut up, shut up you crazy . . .

ISEULT. (*Rises.*) Don't you dare point that thing at me! (*Points at door.*) If you're looking to shoot something, go on outside. Maybe you'll find your match in the bush, though I doubt it! (*Pause. They stare at each other. He strides angrily to door, leaves. Outside he hesitates for a moment, looks about, then heads around side of hut. Iseult listens. Goes to window, checks he's not coming back. Sags, trembling, goes to bathroom, knocks gently, voice low.*) You can come out now, really. (*Pause.*) He won't do anything, I'm sure of it. (*Pause.*) At least, not yet. (*Pause.*) You're safe here. (*Pause.*) I'll help you, I promise . . . I'll find a way. (*Pause. Low.*) Rachel?

ACT 2
SCENE 1

Day. The patio. mKulie and Iseult sitting at the table, unravelling Iseult's knitting. mKulie is clean, dressed in a shift frock, a bandage on her arm, her hair tied neatly in a red ribbon. Scratches still in evidence.

ISEULT. He's not that bad, really. (*Pause.*) Just that he's . . . a little nervous. (*Pause.*) Dress fits you rather well.

MKULIE. (*Smooths her dress with reverence.*) Thank you. (*During following exchanges until she rises, mKulie's eyes are constantly drawn to the hut.*)

ISEULT. Oh, you've thanked me enough. (*Pause.*) I never liked it anyway. Sometimes, lately, I've worn it when Stoffel's being, well you know how men can be. (*Pause. Indicates mKulie's dress.*) It flaps, you see. On me, I mean. Sometimes I've stood in it, my eyes closed, my arms spread, hoping the wind'd lift me, that I'd . . . fly away. (*Pause.*) Lately, I've often thought . . . if his mother hadn't died after he was born . . . if she'd knitted her way into his life . . . sometimes at night, the way he twists . . . thrashes . . . I've slept far out, holding on to the edge . . . I'm afraid of . . . being swallowed. Even my dreams are . . . out of kilter . . . there . . . I'm talking nonsense, oh don't mind me! You're here now. Safe. That's all that matters, isn't it? (*Pause.*) When he saw how clean you looked, he was quite . . . impressed. He's quite kind, really, when you look deep enough. He . . . he (*Pause.*) minds me. He (*Pause.*) he's just afraid it'll be him there one day, in your skin, people looking at him as if he doesn't exist. (*Slight pause.*) There're . . . worse than him, much worse. (*Pause.*) Can you remember the words I taught you?

MKULIE. Ja, medem. Ja, baas. (*They smile. Pause.*)

ISEULT. I don't know how you did it. I don't know how you stayed out there . . . (*Shivers. Pause*) I'd've gone . . . mad. (*Pause. Casts on stitches while mKulie continues unraveling.*) When his Papa comes on Wednesday . . . he won't expect much from you. I'm afraid he's got a . . . watchee-do-ee-monkey mind. Still, that's in our favour right now. Just you remember all the words I've taught you.

MKULIE. Ja, medem.

mKulie is staring at the hut. Iseult smiles. Pause. mKulie rises, moves to walk around the perimeter of hut, staring at it. Now and again she feels the wall, steps back to view it more completely. She reaches up, pulls a blade of dried grass from the roof, examines it, sucks it, passes her tongue over and around it in a flicking action. Iseult glances at her periodically.

ISEULT. About the tenth time you've done that.

mKulie begins to laugh, pressing her fingers to her lips to stem the flow of it. Iseult stops, watches her. The laughter lengthens into a drawn-out spasm that suddenly veers towards agonised weeping. She drops to her knees before the hut, head bowed as she covers her face. Iseult jumps up, goes to her, hunkers down.

ISEULT. Don't, oh don't! (*Puts her arms around mKulie's heaving shoulders.*) Oh, please don't! Don't look at it any more! (*They stay thus until mKulie's weeping gradually subsides. Iseult tries to see mKulie's face.*) Shall I get you some coffee? (*mKulie shakes her bowed head.*) You should eat more; you've hardly eaten anything since you arrived. You mustn't worry. Everything'll come right, I promise. Haven't I promised you?

Pause. mKulie raises her head, looks at the hut.

MKULIE. There is no dirt floor. (*Pause.*)
ISEULT. You must think of the baby. (*mKulie touches her stomach, they look at each other. Iseult helps her up, leads her to sit again. Iseult sits. Pause. Iseult begins knitting again.*)
ISEULT. I shall make you something wonderful to wear. (*Pause.*) I was knitting a jumper for my son, but the pattern was . . . terrifying. (*Pause as mKulie picks up wool, begins unraveling.*) I haven't told Stoffel yet. (*Pause. mKulie watches her.*) It's just that the right opportunity hasn't presented itself. (*Pause.*) It took me long enough to persuade him that we'd take you to the mission, but in the end, you saw him, he even let you climb

in the boot. (*Jerks a finger at mKulie.*) It'll be a bit smelly, mind. (*Pause.*) I'll manage it; I'll manage it all. (*Pause.*) I just don't want to spring it on him too suddenly. (*Pause.*) I'm sorry about your name; he simply refuses to wrap his tongue round it. He says his Papa'll ask why he hadn't given you a biblical name. (*Muses.*) Child born of freedom . . . it's beautiful, really; it's a shame to lose it. (*Rhythmic, drawn out, with click.*) nomKululeko. Why, it's even nicer than "syllabub." (*Pause, again rhythmic, drawn out.*) m-Kul-ie.

mKULIE. I do not mind. I am glad to be safe.

ISEULT. It's really rather nice having another woman to talk to. Reminds me of old times. (*Pause.*) When Papa . . . when he was gone, Rachel came back. We hadn't asked her to come; (*Emphasis.*) she just . . . came. We hadn't seen her in two years, not since Papa'd begun spending like it grew on trees. Mama'd had to let her go then. (*Pause.*) Those men Papa used to bring home—thin white faces and mean little eyes . . . all those guns, twin-barrelled, like Papa's. Rachel used to hide upstairs with us. We'd hear them, in the drawing room, bottles clink-ing, voices pummelling the ceiling beneath our feet. Mama used to give the noise a number, force eight, she'd say, on the Richter scale. (*Pause.*) And the smell of their hatred thicker than the soured-apple smell of Papa's breath when we crept down in the half-light to drag him to bed. (*Pause.*) Once, one of them took me on his knee. I was too big for his knee, but he did it anyway. There was scum in the cor-ners of his mouth. (*Pause.*) When he kissed me, some of it stuck to my skin. (*Pause.*) I wanted to cut my lips off! (*Pause.*) Rachel held me while Mama washed my mouth. I bit Mama's finger, not on purpose, I was (*Half-laugh.*) trying to swallow the soap. (*Pause.*) I thought if I didn't, I'd never be clean again. (*Laughs.*) How Rachel scolded me! (*Pause.*) It's funny to hear you speak like her. (*Pause.*) This may sound mad . . . but I feel kind of . . . safe . . . with you here; I don't think about the lions any more. (*Car noise.*) There! My God, how time flies when he's not around. (*They begin gathering the wool as Andries walks around the side of the hut. mKulie leaps up. Pause. Andries stares at mKulie, then looks ques-tioningly at Iseult. Iseult puts a hand to her heart.*) My goodness, you gave us quite a start, creeping up on us like that!

ANDRIES. (*Frowns, still watching mKulie.*) Creeping? Madam, I assure you
. . .

ISEULT. Didn't he, Rachel? (*Nods at mKulie.*)

mKULIE. (*Bows head.*) Ja, medem.

ISEULT. (*Shunting the wool in mKulie's direction, waving her towards the hut.*)
Now, clear up and start on lunch. Baas'll be here soon.

Head down, mKulie collects the wool and withdraws to the hut. Andries' gaze follows her. He turns back to Iseult, eyes questioning. Pause.

ISEULT. She wants to learn how to knit. (*Shudders.*) There're really some
things you're better off not trying to teach these blacks, don't you
agree? Still, she's rather a good cook.

ANDRIES. I didn't know you had . . . your servant with you. She's badly
scratched . . .

ISEULT. Would you like some coffee? (*Calls.*) *Rachel*, Mijnheer de Wit will
have some coffee! (*To Andries.*) You were saying, oh, the scratches, yes,
stupid creature fell into a thorn bush, that one over there in fact . . .
the very first day, imagine! You'd think someone'd murdered her; you
know how they can wail for the least thing! In the end I sent her to bed
and made the breakfast myself. I hate cooking, but (*Shrugs.*) there it is.
(*Pause. Andries goes to stand looking out at the bush, his back to her. Iseult
stands by table watching him. mKulie appears with tray, cups, etc. She darts
a look at Andries's back, then looks questioningly at Iseult as she holds out
tray. Iseult nods vigorously, holding out her hands. Andries turns to watch
them.*)

ISEULT. Ah, coffee! (*mKulie gives her the tray and retires hurriedly. She begins
to prepare salad, noisly chopping vegetables, etc. She is very aware of Andries
outside. Now and again she peeps out the window at him. Outside, Iseult
begins setting cups, pouring, etc.*)

ISEULT. Mijnheer? You'll have milk? I seem to recall we'd none last time
you were here.

ANDRIES. (*Turns. Pause.*) Your memory is foolproof.

ISEULT. Foolproof?

ANDRIES. I mean it's good. (*Pause.*) And what was she doing out in the
bush before breakfast?

ISEULT. (*Spoon poised over sugar.*) I'm afraid I've forgotten how many you take? One, is it? (*He nods. Pause.*) Why, she was . . . worshipping the sun.

ANDRIES. Pardon?

ISEULT. At least, that's what I think. It's very hard to tell with them some-times—they're so superstitious about everything . . . even . . . frogs, did you know? Imagine being afraid of something that croaks! (*Slight pause.*) Yes, a pity about the scratches, rather ruins that lovely skin, the colour of honey, did you notice? (*Pause.*) Do come and have your coffee. You . . . you look . . . tired. Aren't you feeling well? How are all your animals? Y'know I was reading that book in the hut, the one that tells the history of the park? Do sit down, I feel like a midget. (*Andries hesitates, moves to table, sits, drinks. He is very ill-at-ease.*) That ranger at the turn of the century, what was his name? The one who fought the full-grown lion?

ANDRIES. Zo, you mean Wolhuter? Ja, he was a brave man.

ISEULT. D'you think that was bravery or, or . . . desperation? (*Pause. Andries stares at her.*) Oh, how's your honeybadger?

ANDRIES. My . . . ?

ISEULT. (*Teasing.*) Your little pet!

ANDRIES. There's no room for pets here.

ISEULT. Still, you'd help him, wouldn't you?

ANDRIES. Help?

ISEULT. If he were . . . hurt. I mean, he's such a sweet little squirt, really. Your wife must've loved him. He doesn't even harm the bees. All he does is take the honey. It's not even honey that's, that's manufac-tured for, for public consumption. Who cares about that honey? That's honey nobody wants. Even the bees are probably . . . thrilled . . . to get rid of it. (*Pause.*) It's not like that meat processing plant you have up at Skukuza, is it? That place you feed the animals into to produce skins and trophies, all that biltong[22] and bone meal?

ANDRIES. Madam, I . . .

ISEULT. Oh, please, call me Iseult!

ANDRIES. (*Inclines head.*) I can assure you we only cull those species whose population levels increase beyond natural controls. We use dart guns from the helicopters . . . our method is very humane.

ISEULT. Is it? I thought it had more to do with minimising injury. That man in the canning factory told me nobody wants to buy bruised meat. (*Pause. They stare at each other. Softly.*) Poor things. We're all poor things, really. (*Pause.*) Don't y'think? (*Pause.*) Groping our way through the . . . savage . . . sameness, (*Pause.*) the culling . . . and the . . . killing. (*Pause.*) Nothing's ever destroyed, is it? Just . . . repackaged. Bone ash. Phosphate. Fertiliser. (*Pause.*) Y'know, no matter how small it was ground, you could still see bits of teeth. Mama told me that. None of it surprised Rachel until Mama said all those millions of people had been white. Then she simply refused to believe it. She thought Mama was making it up. (*Pause.*) D'you know what I read in the paper? Even the elephants are fleeing Mozambique. Imagine, wild animals preferring captivity! (*Pause.*) Poor blundering Dumbos! (*Pause.*) At least the bees can fly. They haven't been harnessed. They're a bit too tiny for a bullet through the skull. I hope your honeybadger makes the most of it. While it lasts.

Pause.

ANDRIES. No one likes culling. You're not alone, I can assure you . . . (*Iseult rises on hearing sound of car. Leans towards him.*)
ISEULT. Y'know, seeing that honeybadger . . . it's one of the nicest memories I'll . . . take away with me . . . when we leave.

Andries stares at her. Stoffel arrives, stops, tenses as he sees Andries. Iseult goes to him, pecks his cheek.

ISEULT. You're just in time; Rachel almost has lunch ready.
STOFFEL. (*Darts a look at Andries as he speaks.*) Rachel?
ISEULT. I was just telling Mijnheer de Wit . . . Andries . . . how good a cook she is. Stoffel?
STOFFEL. Ja, ja, a . . . good cook. (*Smacks his hands.*) So where's lunch? I could eat a . . . wildebeest. (*Pause.*)
ANDRIES. A little on the tough side; I wouldn't recommend it. (*He laughs. The others echo it awkwardly.*)
ISEULT. (*To Andries.*) Will you . . . join us?

ANDRIES. (*Inclines towards her.*) Thank you, no. (*To Stoffel.*) You asked at the office to see how the census is taken? (*Stoffel nods.*) Unfortunately, you've missed the olifant census . . .

STOFFEL. How many'll be culled?

ANDRIES. About five hundred.

ISEULT. So many!

ANDRIES. (*To Iseult.*) I can assure you . . . (*To Stoffel.*) The buffalo census is still being carried out. If you're free tomorrow afternoon, perhaps I could escort you? (*Glances at Iseult.*) I was also going to invite your wife, but . . .

STOFFEL. (*Relaxes.*) That's decent of you, I . . .

ISEULT. (*Shudders.*) Not me, not my cup of tea. Would you excuse me? I'll just see how lunch is doing.

ANDRIES. (*Glances at his watch.*) And I must be off. (*Looks at Iseult.*) I will say . . . goodbye?

ISEULT. And thank you for . . . fixing the fence.

ANDRIES. (*Looks at her for a moment, glances at Stoffel as he moves towards side of hut.*) Two o'clock at the station tomorrow?

STOFFEL. Ja, that'd be terrific. Thank, thank you.

Andries leaves. They stand looking after him. Iseult is nervous throughout the lunch that follows. They listen 'til the car drives off.

STOFFEL. (*Turning to Iseult.*) What the hell're you playing at now!

ISEULT. He took us by surprise. There wasn't time to hide her.

STOFFEL. Y'mean, he sneaked up . . . ?

ISEULT. We thought it was you, that's all.

STOFFEL. (*Paces.*) Christ, why'd I ever let you talk me into . . . ? (*Stops.*) He knows, doesn't he?

ISEULT. No, no!

STOFFEL. You're lying! (*Pause.*)

ISEULT. I'm not! If he knew, why wouldn't he have said something? Eh? (*Pause. She turns away, tense, twisting her hands as she speaks.*) We've nothing to fear from him.

STOFFEL. Right now he could be headed for the police.

ISEULT. He's not, I tell you!

STOFFEL. And since when is he (*Mimics Iseult.*) "Andries?"

ISEULT. (*Pause. Tiredly.*) You'd better hear what I told him, so you don't put your foot in it tomorrow.

STOFFEL. Later. Get her to bring me a beer, I'm gasping. (*Iseult begins to move indoors. Stoffel roars.*) No! Let *her*! She's supposed to be our servant. Then let her act like one!

ISEULT. (*Hesitates. Pause. She calls out towards hut.*) mKulie?

STOFFEL. Don't call her that!

ISEULT. Could y'please bring Stoffel some beer? I'm afraid he's . . .

STOFFEL. (*Roars.*) Rachel! Beer! (*mKulie comes from hut, a can of beer and a glass in her hand. Stoffel glances at her, looks at Iseult.*) Y'see? (*Pause as mKulie places it before him.*) Tell her to put it on a tray next time.

Iseult moves indoors, mKulie following quickly as he opens can, pours. The women return carrying trays laden with dishes, food. They set it out quickly on the table while Stoffel watches mKulie. mKulie returns indoors. Iseult pours chilled wine. Throughout the following exchanges between Iseult and Stoffel, mKulie sits staring out. Whenever Stoffel raises his voice, her body clenches.

STOFFEL. (*Lifts glass.*) What's this? We never normally have wine at lunchtime.

ISEULT. Oh, I thought you might like it. Must've been very hot out there. So, how'd it go? Did you get as far as Luvuvhu Gorge? (*Pause. Stoffel is eating. Iseult begins to eat.*) Did you make any notes? I could read them out to you this afternoon if you want to type them up. If you like? Or maybe, if you're going out again, I'll come with you? If you want?

STOFFEL. You're sure he didn't cop on? What about her scratches?

ISEULT. I give you my word. He never suspected a thing, honestly! And mKul—Rachel served him just like she was bred to it. He even commented on how well we had her trained, in fact. (*Pause.*) I told him she fell in the thorn bushes. He's a bit of a pain, actually. Did nothing but rabbit on about his animals. I thought you'd never show up! (*Pauses, shudders.*) I'd hate to be stuck with him tomorrow. I didn't want to appear too rude refusing. That's why I thought I'd better invite him to lunch. Thank goodness he refused.

Stoffel relaxes, drinks wine. Pause. They eat.

STOFFEL. Ach, he's not a bad sort. He had that fence seen to promptly.

ISEULT. Y'like the chicken? (*Stoffel grunts.*) Rachel filled it with all sorts of things, nuts, bits of mango, spices, you wouldn't believe. She refused to use a roasting tin, wrapped it all up in two big glossy leaves, said it sealed in all the juices—she's really a first-class cook.

STOFFEL. (*Drinks. Sighs with satisfaction.*) Not bad, I must say. You ought to get the recipe from her. A meal like that'd impress the people at the office, no end.

ISEULT. Mmm . . . wouldn't mind entertaining with someone like her around. It'd be a breeze. (*Pause.*) You'd want to've seen her this morning! Tidying, cleaning, she even insisted on washing your shirts by hand, the expensive ones you got for the office.

STOFFEL. Ja? (*Drinks, grins.*) You could take a leaf out of her book. (*Pause.*)

ISEULT. You could invite what's-his-name for dinner, y'know, that foreign affairs correspondent who likes your work, the one you said had great pull? (*Pause.*) Stoffel, just say . . .

STOFFEL. Don't even think of it!

ISEULT. Imagining's free, isn't it? Doesn't carry any . . . consequences. (*Pause.*) Remember when we lived with your father? How we'd dream of getting off the farm, making a life for ourselves? And it all came true. (*Pause.*) I'm not saying this'll come true . . . I'm just saying, imagine. (*Pause.*) She wouldn't cost us anything except what she eats.

STOFFEL. That, and a prison sentence! (*Pause.*) So what's the hare-brained scheme, huh? We lock her away in the hall cupboard like a black Anna Frank?[23] And what about when she spits out her little brat?

ISEULT. She isn't pregnant.

STOFFEL. Huh?

ISEULT. You were right. She's tubby from eating nothing: only mealie pap.[24]

STOFFEL. How're we going to get her out of here, that's what I'd like to know!

ISEULT. (*Stares.*) But you said . . . we agreed!

STOFFEL. I didn't go to the gorge; I drove up to Phalaborwa Gate. (*Pause.*) It was teeming with police. They're waiting to catch them as they try to sneak out. (*Snorts.*) The ones who make it, is all.

ISEULT. But there're other gates, we can . . . (*Pause as Stoffel looks at her.*) We've never been stopped before. Why should they suddenly decide to suspect us now? All our papers are in order. It'll be so easy, I promise you! Eh? We're white, Stoffel. Paid up members of the NP.[25] You've done your stint in the army. We're nice ordinary citizens; we don't look left or right!

STOFFEL. My, we have been reading the papers, haven't we?

ISEULT. Someday, this would make the kind of story that's liable to be on the front cover of *Time* or *Life*: the day you smuggled a Mozambiquan refugee right under the eyes of the South African police. (*Pause.*) The day you helped a black.

STOFFEL. (*Pause as he stares at her.*) Ja, I could write it from the wilderness . . . Dear Sir, I want to tell you—blank—and when she—blank—and then my wife and I—blank—and—blank—in—blank—when—blank—after—blank—of—blank—so you see—blank—because—blank—I most fervently urge you to publish this letter to make people—blank. Yours faithfully, Stoffel van Lelyveld, Cell 3B, Pretoria Maximum Security Prison. Stamped, signed, and censored by J. H. Vorster, Head of Prisons. (*Pause.*) Notice the way they encourage the prepositions? Harmless little words those, left in to titillate, what? (*Pause.*) Why? Why're you so hell-bent on risking everything we've just managed to build up? You, who've never shown the slightest interest in what's going on in this fucking country!

Pause.

ISEULT. When Rachel came back . . . it was as if she knew about the electricity being cut off, about the house being dark. She brought us candles. Oh, how the shadows danced! And, and the smell of hot dribbles splashing on my skin, then the warmth of it! (*Pause.*) Stoffel?

STOFFEL. There's still time to extricate ourselves . . .

ISEULT. (*Coldly.*) How? What about Andries de Witt?

STOFFEL. I could tell him you're a, a nurse, that she was running a temperature, feverish, I don't know, something like that, that you . . .

ISEULT. He wouldn't believe it!

STOFFEL. . . . wanted her condition to be stable before they shoved her in a truck and drove her all the way back, medical ethics and all that, I'm sure he'd swallow it.

ISEULT. There's a car-hire firm at Phalaborwa airport. I, I'll pawn Mama's silver if I have to! (*Long pause. Gets up, moves about. She is tense. Goes to stare out into the bush.*) Last night I dreamed we were sleeping. A lion walked under our bed, lifted us high on his back. In the thick of the sheets I could feel the purr in his throat as he moved through the bush. (*Pause.*) When you made love to me, I was still sleeping. Suddenly your hands grasped my throat, pressed down hard. I woke up in the dream and found you choking me. Then I woke up from the dream of waking up. For a long time I lay looking at you, hardly believing I'd dreamed such a dream. I kept thinking you'd dreamed it, not I. It wasn't of my making . . . it was an . . . implant. I kept staring at you, the ridge on your forehead, the line of your nose, the little whistle coming through your teeth, and, and (*Turns.*) Stoffel, it was a face I didn't know! A face I'd never known! I kept searching and searching, but I couldn't find you! (*She begins to cry.*)

STOFFEL. (*Stares, runs his fingers through his hair.*) Christ, I can see how your father was . . . you and your mother must've driven him . . . (*Pause.*) Stop it, will you? (*Pause.*) Stop it! (*Pause.*) Isul, please! (*Long pause.*) Okay, okay, I'll do it, but it's the last bloody thing I'll ever do for you! (*Pause.*) And no more wild talk about keeping her! (*Iseult nods her head.*) We'll take her close's we can, dump her at the first likely spot along the border. She'll have to make her own way from there. (*Pause.*) Agreed? (*Iseult nods.*) Now for God's sake let's get out of here!

ISEULT. (*Steps towards him. Stops.*) Yes, yes, I'll just fix my face, tell her we're going.

Iseult hurries inside. mKulie stands. Iseult whispers to her, then heads for the bathroom. mKulie goes outside to clear the table. Stoffel is still drinking. He watches her as she begins to pile dishes. She does not look at him. As she reaches for his plate, he grasps her wrist. She freezes, staring down at the table.

STOFFEL. D'you've any idea the trouble you're causing me? (*Pause. He continues to stare at her. She keeps her face averted.*) I could say anything I liked to you right now and you wouldn't have a clue, would you?

mKULIE. Ja, baas.

STOFFEL. (*Laughs. Stares. Pause. Flings her arm away in disgust as he speaks.*) I'll Ja-baas you! (*Pause. mKulie continues to stack dishes.*) Don't you know you should have a tray? You shouldn't scrape plates in front of the people you serve. They find it . . . obnoxious, all those smears of leftover food. (*Pause.*) So you cooked it specially for me, did you? (*Reaches out, touches her hair. She freezes, but does not draw away. Simultaneously, Iseult comes from bathroom, crosses hut, steps outside, stops dead in her tracks as she sees his hand on mKulie's hair.*)

STOFFEL. (*Jerks his hand away from mKulie as he notices Iseult. Rises.*) I thought I saw a tsetse land on her hair. If, if we're to get her to Gazankulu in one piece, we don't want her coming down with sleeping sickness. You ready at last? (*Looks about.*) Where'd I leave the card key for the gate. You seen it? (*Pause.*) Isul? Wake up, will you?

ISEULT. (*Moves forward.*) Yes, yes, we can't let her . . .

STOFFEL. (*As he spots key.*) Ah! (*Grabs it.*) C'mon, then, before the whole afternoon's wasted. (*Heads for side of hut.*)

ISEULT. (*Low, to mKulie as she follows Stoffel.*) Stay inside and lock the door in case that ranger comes back. We'll talk tonight, when he's asleep. (*Squeezes her arm and smiles.*) And don't worry!

STOFFEL. (*Calls.*) Isul! (*Car starts up.*)

mKULIE. I can go, this makes trouble for you.

ISEULT. Go?

mKULIE. (*Indicates.*) Out in the bush, I can . . .

ISEULT. (*Shocked.*) Are you mad? You'll do no such thing! Everything's all right; we're going to see you safe . . . (*Car horn.*) I'll explain it all later. Now you go in the hut like I said! (*Grips mKulie's arm.*) Promise me! (*mKulie nods.*) That's it. You stay. (*Urgent.*) You must stay. (*Begins moving towards side of hut.*) I'd better go, keep him sweet. (*Exits.*)

mKulie, tense, stands listening until car drives off. She looks around.

mKULIE. (*Whispers.*) Oh, Vusi, Vusi, help me! (*Pause.*) Is it madness to trust this white auntie? (*Pause as she clears dishes, brings them into hut, returns for remainder. She bends to pick up Stoffel's sweater, which is on the flags.*[26] *She holds it with obvious distaste between the tip of her thumb and index finger, then drops it on chair.*) When you died, Vusi, my face . . . rippled in your eyes. (*Pause.*) It's still there . . . Vusi . . . rippling. (*Pause. She stares at sweater.*) This man has bedrock in his blood. (*Pause, stares out into bush.*) Oh, tell me what to do!

SCENE 2

Sunset. Sound of crickets, birds, animals, etc. Iseult and Stoffel sit relaxing at the table on the patio, brandies before them. Iseult is knitting. mKulie is in the hut, washing dishes.

STOFFEL. This is the life, huh? (*Lifts glass.*) Best brandy, black maid in the kitchen. Someday we'll have it all!

ISEULT. (*Glances towards hut.*) I really should help her.

STOFFEL. Someday I might even own (*Indicates newspaper.*) my own. Think of it!

ISEULT. (*Again glancing at hut.*) Once Mama tried to make Rachel sit with us at table, but she wouldn't. (*Pause*) Y'know what Rachel said? She said the division was cut into her bones. (*Pause. Starts to rise.*) I'll just go and see . . .

STOFFEL. Relax, will you, Isul? Even if we had a maid, you'd end up genuflecting.

ISEULT. Yes, well, neither Mama nor I ever wanted . . .

STOFFEL. Least I know how to treat the servants. I thought you'd've learned something from the way Papa works his boys.

ISEULT. When's he coming?

STOFFEL. Day after tomorrow, get her to cook him some fish, he's fond of . . . (*Listens. Car noise. mKulie comes to window to watch.*) Sounds like de Wit's jeep. (*Iseult rises, tense.*) Sit, for God's sake, and try to look relaxed. (*Pause. Andries comes quickly round side of hut. mKulie draws back a little as she sees him.*) Ah, de Wit! (*Lifts brandy bottle.*) You'll join us?

ANDRIES. (*Shakes head.*) I'm glad I haven't interrupted your dinner. We've had a spot of trouble with some poachers up at Punda Maria. Unfortunately one of our holidaymakers decided to take it upon himself to deal with them. Ended up being shot. (*Stoffel rises, Iseult tenses.*) I came to warn (*Looks at Iseult.*) you . . .

STOFFEL. Didn't you get the bastards? You want some help? (*Indicates hut.*) I've got my gun . . .

ANDRIES. The police took care of it. Besides, Punda's several hundred kilometers away. (*Looks at Iseult.*) I didn't want you worrying if you picked it up on the radio. Or if you saw a couple of the boys in blue about the park tomorrow. (*Pause.*) You'll remember to close the shutters tonight?

STOFFEL. The fence! Is it . . . ?

ANDRIES. Fine. Actually, you have the best protection. Most of the other villages are walled. I must be off. A young olifant rambled onto the golf course at Skukuza and refuses to leave. (*Smiles at Iseult.*) From what I hear, he's ruined everybody's game (*Inclines towards her. Nods to Stoffel.*) 'Til tomorrow? (*Leaves quickly.*)

Stoffel makes to call him back, hesitates, takes a couple of steps towards side of hut, hesitates. Pause. Noise of jeep starting up, driving off. mKulie goes back to stacking dishes in cupboards. Stoffel paces.

ISEULT. It was good of him to come.

STOFFEL. (*Stops. Points at her.*) That was a warning, Iseult!

ISEULT. (*Rises.*) But he doesn't know about . . . (*Indicates hut.*)

STOFFEL. (*Pacing again. Sneers.*) The police took care of it! I'd like to believe it! (*Imitates Andrie's voice.*) You'll remember to close the shutters? Hadn't the guts to look me in the eye, the shifty . . . (*Stops. Points at her again.*) He knew, Isul, he knew I'd know he was lying!

ISEULT. (*Bewildered.*) About what? He doesn't know about mKulie, I swear to you!

STOFFEL. (*Pacing.*) I'll bet they haven't got all the bastards. I'll bet that's what it is!

ISEULT. Y'mean the poachers? But he said . . .

STOFFEL. Let's get inside. It'll be dark soon.

ISEULT. I'm sure he wouldn't . . .

She stares at Stoffel as he grabs brandy glasses, bottle. He heads indoors. Stops. Stares at mKulie. She averts her eyes, hanging the last knife on a wall rack. Iseult enters quickly behind him, knitting in hand. Her gaze darts from one to the other. She moves forward between them, rubbing Stoffel's arm.

ISEULT. Oh, look how nice she's left everything! (*She nods, smiling at mKulie. mKulie attempts to smile back as Iseult opens her mouth to say something.*)

STOFFEL. (*Low. Deliberate. Still staring at mKulie.*) If you thank her, I shall slit her throat.

ISEULT. Stoffel!

STOFFEL. That's if she doesn't manage to get me first.

ISEULT. She wouldn't harm a fly!

STOFFEL. No? She'd prove no better than any other murdering savage if I gave her half a chance! (*Jerks his arm towards bedroom door on left.*) Get her out of here!

Trembling, mKulie begins to move before Iseult can speak.

ISEULT. I'm sorry, it's just that he's . . .

STOFFEL. (*To Iseult.*) No more monkey talk!

mKulie hurries into bedroom, closes door. Pause. He walks to kitchen counter, slams down bottle, glasses. Pours himself a brandy, gulps it.

ISEULT. (*Tentative.*) Stoffel?

STOFFEL. Bolt the door, and close those fucking shutters! (*Harsh laugh.*) Decent of him to tell us to batten the hatches, huh? (*Goes to radio, switches it on. It crackles, then stills. Iseult hesitates, watching him. She goes outside, closes shutters. The interior dims as she does so. She returns, bolts door, locks shutters from the inside, steps backwards into the centre of the room, hugging her arms. Goes to switch on bedside lamp, returns to centre of room. Stoffel mutters as he twists the dial on the radio.*) What the hell is up with this thing?

ISEULT. Turn the dial more slowly. It's . . . sensitive. Radios are sensitive things. (*Pause.*) It doesn't like it when we're all penned up.

STOFFEL. Not a fucking bleep. (*He bangs it. Iseult jerks a little as he does so. It crackles, then is silent. He repeats the process. It crackles again. Outside, the light is fading. During the following exchanges, it gradually darkens. He snorts, moves to counter. Pours another drink, gulps it. Stops, stares at Iseult.*) It doesn't like . . . ? What d'you think it is, a bloody household pet?

Stoffel moves to check door and shutters. Iseult looks about for her knitting, finds it, sits, begins to knit. She watches him covertly as he goes to lift gun from floor beside bed. He checks and cocks it, trains it on the wall, continues in a sweeping motion, stopping briefly at the door, the window, and mKulie's room. He sits on the bed, staring at it.

ISEULT. I really think he'd've told us if there was anything to worry about . . .

STOFFEL. Y'know why he skedaddled? He was afraid I'd ask questions, that he'd have the bother of moving us this late in the evening. He's a bloody nerve expecting us to stay here alone. (*Pause.*) If it weren't for (*Points at mKulie's room.*) her, I could've asked him to move us to another camp. We'd be surrounded by people now.

ISEULT. I'm sure you're wrong. I . . .

STOFFEL. (*Groans.*) And the police, they'll be swarming like bluebottles after that murder!

ISEULT. But that's miles away, I'm sure they won't . . .

STOFFEL. Those murdering black bastards. If I . . .

ISEULT. Who says they're black? He never said . . .

STOFFEL. Of course they're black, just (*Indicates mKulie's room.*) like that tar baby . . .

ISEULT. You can't be sure of that!

STOFFEL. They're poachers! Why the hell d'you think they're poaching? It's a lucrative business for anyone who can't afford the shirt on his back. You like to tell me who that is in this country? Huh?

ISEULT. Even some whites are poor . . .

STOFFEL. Ja, the odd few needles in the haystack, like you and your mother! Set that against a whole blighted harvest!

ISEULT. Yes, well, they need to live! They need to eat just like anybody
else! There's enough culling done here to feed an army, never mind
. . .

STOFFEL. Terrific! Talk like that to the police tomorrow, and see where it
gets you! (*Pause. Roars.*) She goes!

ISEULT. (*Screams.*) No! (*Pleading, as he paces.*) Maybe if we just got her outside the gate, past the police . . .

STOFFEL. Even if the police didn't pick her up, you can be sure some
farmer would.

ISEULT. Farmer?

STOFFEL. It's harvest time. They scour the countryside right up to
Gazankulu, looking for illegals to work on their banana plantations.
Promise them a roof over their heads while they work . . .

ISEULT. Why, that's . . .

STOFFEL. Afterwards they hand them over to the police to be deported,
that way they don't have to pay them. Beaten and half-starved. She's
better off going back now!

ISEULT. Whipped. (*Pause.*) Like banana syllabub.

STOFFEL. First thing in the morning. I don't care what explaining I have
to do!

ISEULT. (*Low.*) You promised.

STOFFEL. Christ, I must've been off my head to let you talk me into it!
(*Pause.*) And you can talk all you want about leaving me. You've no
place to go, no money of your own. (*Looks about, finds her handbag,
removes her wallet, credit cards. Holds cards out before her.*) If you're thinking about using these, forget it! (*He snaps them in two.*) You want to
pawn your paltry bit of silver, then start walking! Let's see how far
you'll get in this wilderness! (*Pause.*) I'll take a chance on that fellow
de Wit. I'll go find him first thing in the morning. I'll tell him what a
nutter my wife is . . .

ISEULT. You gave me your word.

STOFFEL. If he were married himself . . . (*Persuasive, as though he's talking
to Andries.*) You know what wives are, when they get a bee in their
bonnet.

ISEULT. Stoffel, please!

STOFFEL. (*Roars.*) No! (*Pause. He goes to pour another drink. His voice is beginning to slur. Paces.*) I'm calling the shots from now on! Just you hope to Christ he hasn't told anyone else!

ISEULT. (*Rises.*) Listen to me, Stoffel. He knows! (*Pause.*) He knows she's here! It's okay, it's fine! He knows, and he hasn't done anything about it. He hasn't turned her in! (*Pause.*) Stoffel? (*Pause.*)

STOFFEL. (*Raises his glass to fling it, hesitates. He is fighting to control himself. Gradually, he achieves it. He walks slowly to counter, places glass down with infinite care. Walks to bed, picks up gun, examines it, speaks as he does so.*) You bitch. (*Pause.*) I knew it the moment he looked at you!

ISEULT. No! Please, listen! When he came this morning? Took us by surprise? He knew. (*Pause.*) But he never said anything. (*Pause.*) When he didn't come back, the relief! I knew we were safe! (*Pause.*) This business tonight, it was just to warn us to keep mKulie out of sight. If the police saw her scratches . . . Stoffel, he's on our side! (*Pause.*)

STOFFEL. (*Still examining gun.*) You sat there, all through lunch . . . knowing at any moment he could've come back, the police in tow . . . knowing . . . and you wouldn't tell me!

ISEULT. I, I didn't want to worry you. I kept hoping it'd be all right. What was the point of upsetting you if nothing came of it? You were worried enough as it was. You were . . .

STOFFEL. You knew if you told me, I'd've run after him and turned her in.

ISEULT. No, it wasn't like that!

STOFFEL. You set that against the risk of my being arrested? Losing you, Hennie, everything I have?

ISEULT. Stoffel, please, I'd've been arrested, too. Why should I . . . ?

STOFFEL. No! (*Pause.*) You knew I'd take the rap, if it came right down to it. (*Pause. Voice low. Bitter half-laugh.*) Y'know what I kept telling myself through all this? If we were caught, if it came to the crunch, I'd get that doctor to say you were ill, that you weren't responsible. I'd've pleaded with them to let you and Hennie go to the farm, stay with Papa, while I . . . (*Pause.*) They've a special way of treating anyone who helps kaffirs. (*Pause.*) All I wanted, Isul . . . a chance to be something better than Papa was . . . not to spend the rest of my days . . . moulting in hog shit. (*Pause.*) You . . . Judas!

ISEULT. It wasn't like that. I was worried when he found out, but somehow I felt certain he wouldn't . . .

STOFFEL. Like you felt certain about me? (*Pause.*) Why? For God's sake,
why? (*Pause.*) We could've patched her up, fed her, turned her in, a
damn sight more than most whites would've done.

ISEULT. (*Pause.*) She just . . . came.

STOFFEL. (*Sneering laugh.*) That the best you can do? (*Long pause. Begins
undressing.*) So you've begun knitting Hennie's sweater again? A little
late for that, what? (*Enters bathroom.*)

ISEULT. (*Pause. Holds out knitting, examines it. Low.*) It's a . . . belly coat.
(*Pause.*) To keep her womb warm. (*Stares towards shuttered window. Stoffel returns. Pulls down coverlet on bed. Sets clock as he speaks.*)

STOFFEL. (*Dully, speaking to himself.*) Least this works. (*Pause.*) I'll get up
first thing, go and find him. (*Sighs. Brightens a little.*) Still, he's party to
it, too. It'll make it less awkward having to deal with him, least I won't
have to grovel. Ja, I suppose it's a godsend.

ISEULT. He'd help us. I'm sure he would!

STOFFEL. (*Roars.*) Don't even think it! (*Climbs into bed. Checks gun is by
bedside. Pause.*) I'll agree it with him; she turns up here at the crack of
dawn, I report it immediately, he comes and takes her, hands her over
to the police, end of story. (*Pause.*) Even if she could talk, who'd believe
her against us? (*Pause. Lies back, yawns. Stretches. Sleepily.*) A decent
enough fellow, what? Must say I misjudged him . . . turn out the light,
will you? (*Pause. His breathing becomes even, regular.*)

ISEULT. (*Low. Intense, looking towards bed.*) Brute!

*She starts as Stoffel mutters, turns, begins to snore. Rising, she goes to switch out
bedside lamp. The bathroom light illuminates the room softly. She goes quickly to
mKulie's door, raps once, lightly. Instantly mKulie opens it. Iseult enters. Door
closes. Long pause during which radio crackles, Stoffel turns, mutters, snores.
Iseult emerges, finger to her lips as she looks back at mKulie. mKulie can be seen
nodding as Iseult closes the door. She looks at Stoffel, crosses quickly to the kitchen
area, opens fridge. Its light illuminates kitchen area as she takes two cartons of milk
to the sink. She opens and empties them. Repeats the process, glancing occasionally at Stoffel. She goes to pick up knitting from the floor beside the chair, placing it*

on the chair. She strokes it. Slowly she moves to Stoffel's side of the bed. She stares down at the gun. Pause. Bending, she picks it up, flexing as Stoffel turns and mutters. When he settles into sleep again, she moves quickly to kitchen counter and unloads it, glancing at Stoffel as she works. She returns the empty gun to the floor by his side. She returns to kitchen area and places cartridges in one of the emptied milk cartons which she shoves down into the waste bin. She places the other cartons on top. Returning to the bed, she lies down on the outside, as close as she can to the edge. Pause. Rising slightly, she glances at the clock. She lies back down. The fridge snarls quietly into action, startling her upright. She stares across at it.)

ISEULT. (*Whispering.*) A purr . . . in the throat.

Rising, she goes to close it, returns to bed. Long pause during which she rises to glance occasionally at clock while, outside, the sun gradually comes up, accompanied by birdsong, distant animal noises. When it is fully bright outside, she glances at clock, rises, collects car keys from Stoffel's shorts, taps once on mKulie's door. mKulie opens it. Iseult puts a finger to her lips. mKulie nods, steps back inside, closes door. Iseult goes to main door, unbolts it, steps out quietly, closing it behind her. She squints at sun, then hurries around side of hut. Slight pause. Noise of car driving away. Pause. mKulie comes from bedroom, tiptoes to kitchen, collects crockery, takes it outside to patio table, sets it, returns for cutlery, sugar, cereal, etc., brings it outside. Clock alarm rings. mKulie tenses. Stoffel stirs, realises Iseult has already risen. He rises, groans a little, looks about, heads outside.

STOFFEL. Isul? Any coffee? My mouth tastes like . . . (*Pauses in open doorway as he registers mKulie setting table. Looks about. Then back to mKulie.*) Where's my wife?

mKULIE. (*Eyes averted. Carefully enunciating.*) Gone . . . shop.

STOFFEL. Shop?

mKULIE. For . . . milk. No . . . milk. Gone . . . for . . . milk.

STOFFEL. (*Glances at his watch.*) At this hour? Shop won't be open 'til . . . wait up! We've gallons of the bloody stuff! (*Pause. Stares at mKulie.*) What the hell is going on! (*Pause.*)

mKULIE. (*Eyes averted.*) Beck soon. Medem beck soon.

STOFFEL. (*Angry.*) She knew I wanted the car, that I was going to . . .

mKULIE. No . . . milk. Ja . . . baas?

STOFFEL. Don't lie to me, you filthy little weasel! (*Strides out to her, grasps her wrist. She flinches.*) I'll give you no milk! (*Begins to drag her inside. By the time he's finished speaking, he has pulled open door of fridge.*) Fridge is full of the fucking stuff. Just what're you two playing at? (*Stares into fridge, releases mKulie's arm. She steps back a little.*) What the . . . ? (*Turns to her.*) Where's it gone, huh? What've you done with it?

mKULIE. (*Terrified.*) Ja, baas.

STOFFEL. (*Searching kitchen.*) I'll ja baas you! (*Finally looks in bin. Pause. He stares, kicks it, turns to her. She steps back. Low.*) It hardly all went in the soup last night, did it? What've you been doing, drinking it on the sly, fattening yourself? (*Pause as he stares at her breasts.*) Fattening your paps, is that it? (*Steps towards her. mKulie steps back, trembling.*) She betrayed me. Did you know that? Risked everything I have. For you. (*Pause.*) Aren't you going to show a little appreciation? (*Pause.*) After all, you're wearing her dress.

mKULIE. Medem . . . beck . . . soon.

STOFFEL. (*Voice soft.*) Soon? (*Shakes head, smiles.*) Don't think so. Next camp's quite a few kilometers away, you know. (*Pause. He moves towards her again. She steps back, eyes averted as he speaks, tapping his watch.*) Shop doesn't open 'til nine, you see? (*Inclines towards her.*) You can tell me why you drank all the milk. I'm not so bad I'd begrudge you . . . (*Pause.*) 'Course, you can't understand me, can you? That's a bit of a nuisance; that's a bit . . . unfortunate, isn't it now? (*Pause.*) Why don't you just say . . . ja, baas? I'm sure that'll make you feel better. (*Pause.*) Go on, say . . . ja, baas . . . y'know what that means, don't you, huh? You can't say you don't know what that means.

mKULIE. (*Trembling. Eyes averted.*) Ja . . . baas.

STOFFEL. (*The bed has arrested mKulie's backwards progress.*) There now, I knew you could say it if you . . . (*Emphasis, as he gently pulls ribbon from mKulie's hair, drops it on bed.*) wanted.

mKULIE. (*Trembling, pleading as he touches her hair.*) No send . . . no send beck . . . ja, baas?

STOFFEL. No, no send . . . (*He freezes, steps back, rigid, turns away, moves quickly to counter, leans heavily, head in hands, shaking, breathing erratically. Low snarl.*) Christ!

mKULIE. (*Moving a little towards him.*) Please? You no send?

STOFFEL. (*Without turning, sweeping his arm dismissively.*) Just . . . go . . . go! (*Still heaving, eyes averted, he heads quickly for bathroom. Pause as mKulie stares after him before she exits to bedroom.*)

SCENE 3

Patio. Daylight. Stoffel, clean shaven and dressed in khaki shorts and shirt, is standing at the table, sipping coffee. He tenses as he hears car stopping outside. Pause. Iseult walks slowly around side of hut, stops, stares at him, looks about.

ISEULT. Where is she? You haven't . . . ? (*During these exchanges, Stoffel is ill at ease, glancing occasionally towards mKulie's room. Iseult slowly becomes aware of this. Panicked.*) Has he been? Has he taken her?

STOFFEL. (*Gestures towards mKulie's room.*) I told her to pack the bits of clothing you gave . . .

ISEULT. (*Emphasis.*) Told? How . . . told? (*Pause.*)

STOFFEL. So where's the milk? This coffee's putrid.

ISEULT. I went to find de Wit.

STOFFEL. What?

ISEULT. He's out burning a block of veld. They wouldn't tell me where. They said the firebreaks were dangerous . . . (*Pause.*) I was going to ask him to help me get her out. I . . .

STOFFEL. You what! (*Pause.*) After all we talked about last night! (*Pause.*) Christ, I can't take my eyes off you. Sooner it's done, the better. What time do they expect him back? (*She moves past him towards hut. Roars.*) Stay away from her! (*Iseult pauses.*) You, you'll just wind her up, get her going again. Where's the sense in that?

ISEULT. If you think I'm going to let her be taken without telling her. (*Pause.*) Get her going . . . again? (*Pause.*) What've you done?

STOFFEL. (*Nervous.*) What the hell d'you mean, what've I done? (*Pause.*) Look what she was like the first night, a bloody wildcat!

ISEULT. You, you didn't . . . hit her, did you?

STOFFEL. Of course not! What d'you take me for?

ISEULT. But you took it out on her . . . because of the milk, I can smell it!

STOFFEL. I, I ranted a bit, gave her a, a tongue dressing is all.

ISEULT. (*Coldly.*) How could you, Stoffel? You don't speak her language. (*Pause. She moves towards hut.*)

STOFFEL. Where're you going?

ISEULT. I need some coffee. (*Pause. She steps inside.*) But I'm going to tell her, whether you like it or not. (*Pause. She moves to kitchen, begins making coffee. Stoffel moves about nervously on patio. He can't see her, but he watches mKulie's door.*) I'll wait till you're gone, if you like. Save you any . . . inconvenience.

STOFFEL. No you won't. You're coming with me!

Iseult, carrying mug of coffee, crosses and stands near the bed, staring at mKulie's door. Bed is unmade, bedclothes still tossed and turned back from where Stoffel has slept. Noticing the gun on the floor beside the bed, she walks to it, shoves it under with her foot. As she glances down, something catches her eye. She freezes.

STOFFEL. (*Stands, listening, watching mKulie's door.*) You hear me, Isul? You're coming with me. (*As he speaks the following, Iseult reaches into the bed, picks up mKulie's red ribbon, holds it up, her hand trembling.*) I'm not taking my eyes off you until all this is over and done with. (*Pause.*) I'm not leaving you here with her. God knows what the pair of you'd get up to . . . (*Iseult lifts the mug high, tilts it until it pours in a thick black stream into the bed. She drops the mug and ribbon onto the brown stain oozing into the sheets. She wilts.*) I don't want you to say another word to her. I've had it with all your cosy chats, me locked on the outside. (*Iseult moves towards bathroom, enters, pulls shower curtain.*) Isul, you hear me? (*Pause.*) Isul? (*He moves across patio to bush area in front of hut, peers inside. Hesitates, moves forward as though he would step in, then retreats a couple of steps. Stares at mKulie's door. Roars.*) Isul? (*Pause. Roars.*) Isul? (*Pause. Iseult emerges from bathroom, wiping her mouth with the back of her hand. Her eyes are dazed, body slumped as she drags towards front door. Stoffel moves back to patio.*) Where've you left the keys? We'll go in to Skukuza and wait. I want to be certain we don't miss him when he comes in. (*Turns to glance at her.*) You hear? You're coming with me. I'm . . .

ISEULT. (*Now outside, staring at bush. Her tone is dull, heavy during the following dialogue.*) Perhaps it's . . . best, after all.

STOFFEL. (*Keys in hand. Startled.*) What? (*Pause.*)

ISEULT. We'd never've coped with it, would we, really? (*Pause.*) Bound to
. . . fail, from the very beginning. Why couldn't I see it?

STOFFEL. (*Warm, relieved.*) That's my girl! I knew you'd see it my way in
the end. (*Pause.*) She's been pretty lucky, what? Luckier than most.
You've even given her some of your clothes. What more could you do?

ISEULT. (*Soft moan.*) No . . . more.

STOFFEL. C'mon, let's get it over with! (*Searches his pockets.*) You seen
either of the cards for the gate? (*Heads towards hut, hesitates.*) Have a
look, will you? (*Pause.*) Isul, wake up! The key for the gate? We can't
get out unless . . .

ISEULT. Try that. (*Indicates his jacket hanging on back of patio chair. He
searches, finds it, speaking as he does so.*)

STOFFEL. C'mon then! It'll be . . . better . . . when she's gone. (*Pause.*) You
and me and Hennie. Just like old times. (*Pause. Voice almost breaking.*)
The, the same as ever . . . we were.

ISEULT. Old . . . times. (*Pause. Stirs. Looks at him.*) You go, Stoffel. I'll wait
here until you bring him back.

STOFFEL. (*Nervous.*) But you!

ISEULT. I'll just . . . wait.

STOFFEL. No!

ISEULT. I won't talk to her. (*Pause.*) You needn't worry.

STOFFEL. But.

ISEULT. I've nothing to say to her now.

STOFFEL. Iseult, please!

ISEULT. I'm . . . tired, Stoffel. There's a . . . butterfly in my chest. (*Moves to
patio, sits.*) I just want to sit here quietly, wait until it's over. (*Pause.*) I
won't talk to her. (*Pause.*) But I won't leave her, penned up here, waiting for it alone.

STOFFEL. (*Hesitates.*) What if she comes out? I don't want her trying to
persuade . . . she's a . . . bad influence on you, Isul! Look at the mess
she's got us into!

ISEULT. I'm not listening to her any more. The, the words would hurt
my . . . eyes. My ears are . . . blind. Barred. I can't see her pictures any
more. You were right: she has to go away. We, we can't manage if . . .

she has to go away. (*Dismissive gesture.*) Quickly now, and bring him back! (*He hesitates, backs towards side of hut.*)

STOFFEL. Promise me you'll keep away . . .

ISEULT. (*Bitterly.*) Does the hangman chat with his victim?

STOFFEL. Hey, you're stretching it out of all proportion!

ISEULT. Just . . . go. (*Pause.*)

STOFFEL. I'll . . . be back quick's I . . . (*He exits. Sound of car driving off. Pause. mKulie opens door of bedroom, peeps out.*)

ISEULT. A tsetse fly he said. (*Harsh laugh. Pause.*) But I'm the one with sleeping sickness. (*Pause.*) Not a touch. (*Pause.*) A stroke. Stroking her hair. (*Grasps her head between her hands, shakes it violently.*) Out! Out! There's room only for the small lie. Anything else will gorge on the soft layers underneath. (*Pause.*) Crack . . . Mama . . . it . . . crack.

A single, slow, shuddering sob rises in Iseult, bursts from her lips in a long, ago-nised howl. She slams her fists on the table and begins to weep. mKulie, hair loose, hurries from hut, crosses patio, touches her arm. Iseult jerks away. During follow-ing dialogue, Iseult never looks at her. mKulie stands staring at her.

mKULIE. Please, what has happened?

ISEULT. I'm not even sure I cared about you at all. Isn't that a terrible thing to say?

mKULIE. Please, you'll speak in my tongue? Did you find the ranger man? Did he say if he would help us?

ISEULT. Oh, don't say us! The only one here now is Stoffel and I. You're on your own now. They'll be coming for you . . . (*Glances at her watch.*) shortly, I should think. (*Pause.*) Provided the whole park doesn't go up in flames.

mKULIE. Please, please, do not use your other voice. I do not understand!

ISEULT. (*Rising, pacing in circle.*) Imagine! All that rawhide going up in smoke. You'd have nothing to worry about next time you ran across the border, next time the Emmenore came to flush you out!

mKULIE. (*Freezes, backs away. Low.*) Emmenore! (*She backs into the stubble of grass at the edge of the bushveld stage left, crouches down near bushes.*) Vusi, Vusi, help me! Tell me what she is saying! (*She lowers her head, wraps her arms about her knees, rocking her body continuously.*)

ISEULT. (*Staring about.*) Yes, we're living in a laager, but the brute's on the inside! (*Pause. She wilts, sits.*) Oh it's my fault, too. I pushed, I pushed you under his nose . . . I made you kneel before him. It's not the kind of . . . worship . . . he can handle. (*Pause.*) He used to have something beating in his chest. But now it's . . . ticking. (*Pause.*) I wanted him back. (*Pause.*) Gunless. (*Pause.*) Roarless. I thought if I could get him to help you, why then, his eyes would . . . melt . . . again. That was all, really. If it'd happened the way I wanted, I'd've got my son back too; Hennie would've followed the leader . . . (*Very fast.*) on-the-double-left-right-quick-march! (*Pause.*) Straight back into my womb (*Pause.*) I needed you here. I couldn't . . . breathe . . . in his anger. (*Pause.*) Oh, I felt sorry for you—there was that too—but I used you, a, a buffer against the fear in my head. (*Catches breath.*) Haunted, he said. Well, he was right. (*Pause.*) You just . . . came, like Rachel, your hand reaching out. I took it; I tried to save myself, oh yes, I'm . . . ashamed to say it. (*Pause.*) I'm sorry, I'm really sorry it's such a mess. But I can't handle that, you see. (*Jerks her head towards hut while still staring out into the bush. Pause.*) I could smell it . . . a kind of . . . aura . . . about his skin . . . the air . . . thick with its . . . sludge. (*Pause.*) My eyes dipped into it before I could close them. (*Pained.*) Oh! (*Pause.*) I'll have to practice hard at being blind again. I'll have to . . . gouge . . . it out. (*Laughs mirthlessly.*) Take a tsetse to make me sleep. (*Pause.*) If I took that on board, the ship would . . . founder. I'd be end up, deep down . . . (*Terrified.*) in an octopus's garden. (*Pause.*) We can't have any reminders, you see, no honey-brown antennae buzzing on the pillow. (*Pause.*) I'd die from the sting. (*Pause.*) And yet, and yet, (*Broken.*) if I send you back, I'll die from the antidote. (*On a deep breath.*) What'll I do? (*Pause. Weeping.*) These things don't fade when they're out of sight . . . they're . . . cut in the heart. (*Pause.*) Oh the pity is . . . we have to live . . . with the lions.

MKULIE. I will go, Vusi, into the bush. I will not go back to face them. (*Pause. Hands over ears. Intense.*) All night the river weeps . . . in your breath!

mKulie weeps. Long pause. She rises, drags across to Iseult.

MKULIE. I am dead for you now, but you have ears for my tongue. (*Pause.*) I know they come for me; it is painted in your eyes. (*Stretches out her hand.*) For the love of Vusi whose story I have told you, give me the key to the gate. (*Pause.*) I will not go back to the meat cleavers. (*Iseult looks at her.*) I will not take my child back to the birth of its death. (*Long pause. mKulie screams.*) I . . . will . . . not . . . go!

ISEULT. You, you can't go out there. You'd be mauled!

mKULIE. You have done what you can. You have helped me.

ISEULT. Helped?

mKULIE. I had days of hope, they were good days. For these I thank you. But you must release me before they come!

ISEULT. (*Rises.*) Are you mad? There are no protected areas outside the fence!

mKULIE. You must give me the key!

ISEULT. I, I can't!

mKULIE. (*Moving away.*) Then I will climb the fence.

ISEULT. (*Panicked.*) You can't! It's electrified!

mKULIE. I will climb it!

ISEULT. Listen, you can't go out there, I wouldn't be able to live with myself if—(*Pause.*) I won't be . . . able to live . . .

mKULIE. (*Hand out.*) Give me the key to the gate! (*Long pause.*)

ISEULT. (*Shivers.*) You're sure, you're sure that's what you . . . ? (*Pause. mKulie stares at her.*) All right. (*Pause.*) But I'm coming with you.

mKULIE. (*Shocked.*) You?

ISEULT. (*Rushing into the hut. mKulie follows her, stands staring at her as she whizzes about, filling coffee flask, etc.*) Hurry, hurry, there's a survival kit here somewhere (*Searches.*) and a first aid . . .

mKULIE. You cannot do this. (*Pause.*) You cannot!

ISEULT. All he's capable of now is . . . roaring. A, a, self-made roar. It's the same sound in any language, at least for (*Bitter laugh.*) . . . monstera sapiens. (*Pause.*) A deep purr in the throat. (*Pause. Screams.*) Damn you Stoffel, damn your . . . soured . . . heart! (*mKulie steps towards her, stops. Pause. Bitter laugh.*) It's a . . . mystery, isn't it, what we're . . . capable of? Certainly pulls the plug on God, doesn't it? Yes, he's suffered a massive power failure, I'm afraid. Poor dodo. (*Pause.*) It isn't even what he did anymore. (*Pause.*) It's . . . his words. They . . . don't have a meaning . . . no matter which language he speaks. (*Pause. Stares out towards bush.*)

Your Vusi was right . . . all we'll have to contend with out there . . . the . . . logic in a lion's eye. At least that'll be . . . straightforward, won't it? No crooked little maps to addle the heart. (*Pause. Straps survival belt around her waist. Goes to fill the flask with coffee.*) Yes, I'm going with you for the wrong reason, but the going . . . is right. (*Pause.*) Perhaps out there, I'll find it. I'll find it in the fear that we'll share, in the cold and the hunger at night. One thing's certain. We'll need a new alphabet, and, and when we get to "g," when we make the word "God," we'll say "g" is for (*Slight pause.*) get started, and "d" is for departed and "o" is for (*Pause.*) the stranded hours . . . between. Then we'll never forget, will we—? How the word made God, how it . . . coaxed . . . Him to live, so when we blow all His fuses, well, we'll . . . just have to feel our own way. It'll be . . . starless . . . but some (*Transported.*) night, if we keep our eyes open, we'll see Rachel out there, somewhere, a, a moonbeam in her hand. Oh, it'll flicker, it'll waver, but if we keep our eyes fixed to it, why, it'll help us find . . . hot dazzles of wax splashing warm on our skin. (*Pause. mKulie sits, begins to tremble. Iseult goes to her, hunkers down, puts her arms about her.*) Don't, don't! (*Rises, searches, finds a piece of knitting with plaited strings of wool attached, holds it out before mKulie.*) Look, it's a womb bag! Well, only half. I never got to finish it. (*Draws mKulie gently to her feet, ties the knitted piece about her womb.*) There! (*mKulie looks down and laughs through her tears. They embrace. Iseult whispers, voice breaking.*) And when it grows dark . . . we'll sit close . . . we'll sing . . . lullabies . . . in our heads. (*Pause as she picks up card key from the counter. Places the flask, first aid kit, some fruit and a map in a backpack, goes for silver, picks up knives and forks, stares at them.*) Which'd serve us better? Forks, I think. Knives're too rounded. Why, it's rather like we're going on a picnic. D'you think maybe that's why Mama never sold them outright? Maybe she sensed I'd need them someday, I'd find out (*Broken.*) what they were for. (*Pause.*) How they used to dance in the light! (*Pause.*) We'll leave him the spoons. D'you think that's . . . just . . . ? After all, it (*Laughs.*) is . . . banana syllabub. (*Pause.*) All over the world, we eat . . . dessert . . . we eat . . . banana syllabub. (*Agitated as she places knives on counter, holds onto forks.*) I, I even offered it to him one night after dinner, not knowing how he would . . . gorge . . . what d'you think it's blended with? (*Hysterical laugh.*) Who needs gelatin when blood'll do the trick! D'you think if we looked hard enough, we'd find . . . bits of teeth? (*She begins to shake. mKulie hugs her. Pause as she stills, draws away, looks at forks in her hands.*) Three each. D'you suppose that gives us enough chances? (*Stares out at bush. Pause. She packs them in the backpack, swings it on her back. Holds out her hand to mKulie. mKulie takes it. Together they move slowly outside to the edge of the bush, pause. Iseult indicates the way.*) We'll reach the gate more quickly. (*She stares ahead, shuddering.*)

mKULIE. (*Staring ahead.*) And they . . . can't . . . climb? Vusi said it.

ISEULT. (*Pause. Calmer.*) No, no, they can't . . . climb. (*Pause.*) Vusi was wise. (*Pause. Iseult smiles.*) Perhaps we might meet the badger and the honeyguide. Now there's a language that . . . pollinates the heart. Did I tell you? (*mKulie tries to speak, shakes her head. Hand in hand they move slowly into the bush as Iseult speaks, the acacia thorns clutching at their clothing.*) We'll wait 'til we're outside the gate, then I'll tell you. We'll make the story last. We'll tell it and tell it 'til we're out of this place.

They move offstage, left. Long pause. Radio crackles. Lights fade gradually to sunset, night, as crickets fade in, muted at first, becoming louder. Blackout occurs simultaneously with sudden cutting off of sound.

THE END

Notes

1. *In the Talking Dark* has been published in Cathy Leeney's anthology *Seen and Heard: Six New Plays by Irish Women* (Dublin: Carysfort Press, 2001), 227–326.

2. rondawel: Round native African hut.

3. braai: Barbecue grill.

4. savanna: Open plain with long grasses.

5. mopane: A tree native to South Africa.

6. bushveld: Open pasture composed mostly of brush.

7. eland: Elk.

8. *Marie Celeste*: A brigantine, usually called the *Mary Celeste*, which was discovered abandoned between the Azores and Portugal in 1872. No trace of its crew was ever found.

9. knobkerrie: A stick with a rounded head on one end, used by some tribes as a striking or throwing weapon.

10. laager: A temporary camp surrounded by wagons to form a defensive enclosure.

11. kaffir: A member of a South African race belonging to the Bantu family; a disparaging reference to any black South African.

12. syllabub: A light, soft, cold dessert made from cream whipped with brandy, wine or sherry, lemon juice, and a little sugar.

13. Emmenore: Phonetic word made from the acronym MNR (Mozambique National Resistance), that is, the bandits who plundered and raided the villages.

14. Eligama . . . opheli: mKulie laments to herself in her native Xhosa language, expressing her fear of being captured and killed by the MNR and her sense of feeling lost in the dark night without her husband, Vusi.

15. snel: Quickly.

16. limpet mine: An explosive designed to cling to the hull of a ship and detonate on contact or by a signal.

17. Boer: A Dutch colonist in South Africa, generally engaged in agriculture or ranching.

18. olifant: Elephant.

19. dexter: Right.

20. ndiva inxolo enkulu: Inside my head a scream is growing. (Literally, "Inside my head trouble is growing.")

21. baobab (also called monkey bread): A tree with an extremely thick stem.

22. biltong: Strips of sun-dried lean meat.

23. Anna Frank: Anne Frank, a Dutch Jewish girl who, along with her family, hid from the Nazis in Amsterdam.

24. mealie pap: A porridge made of maize and water.

25. NP: National Party.

26. flags: Flagstones.

Patricia Burke Brogan

(1932–)

ℴ Born in County Clare, educated at St. Louis Convent, Balla Country, Mayo, and college in Dublin, the painter and poet Patricia Burke Brogan has lived most of her life in County Galway. Burke Brogan is best known as the playwright of *Eclipsed*, a groundbreaking play that exposed a piece of long-hidden Irish history, the scandal of the Magdalene Laundries. It was this play that led to the numerous documentaries, exposés, books, and films that later followed. Founded in the eighteenth century, the Laundries provided a safe haven where prostitutes could reclaim their lives. Later, however, the Laundries were seen more as a place to hide young Catholic unmarried women who found themselves pregnant. Their babies were taken from them and adopted by Catholic families abroad, often in the United States. Some of the women remained in the Laundries their entire lives. In her younger adult years as a nun, Burke Brogan was assigned to the Magdalene Laundry in Galway. It was an experience she never forgot. Never taking her final vows as a nun, Brogan went on to marry, live, paint, and write in Galway, where she now resides.

The first reading of *Eclipsed* took place in 1988 in Burke Brogan's home in Galway. In 1992 Galway's Punchbag Theatre production of the play went on to win a Fringe First at the Edinburgh Festival. This production toured all over Ireland, and a subsequent tour was mounted in 1998 under the direction of Caroline Fitzgerald. In 1994 the Forum Theatre in Worcester, Massachusetts, premiered the first United States production, which won the Moss Hart Memorial Award for that year. The Theatre Banshee's production in Burbank, California, received the 1995 Critic's Choice and Best of the Weekend recognition from the *Los Angeles Times*. In April 1999, under the direction of Charlotte Headrick, a production from Western Kentucky University toured to the National Endowment for the Humanities seminar "One Hundred Years of Irish Theatre" at Indiana University in Bloomington, Indiana. In December 1999, New York City's respected Irish Repertory Theatre produced the play with the artistic director Charlotte Moore directing; the *New York Times* gave this production a particularly glowing review. Since the time of its initial opening in Galway, *Eclipsed* has received numerous productions throughout the United States and the world, including Ireland, Australia, Japan, Italy, Germany, and Peru.

In 2002 Burke Brogan wrote *Stained Glass at Samhain*, in which she continued to address the Magdalene Laundries. While *Eclipsed* is seen through the eyes of the angry young women, *Stained Glass* is seen through the eyes of the wise, sympathetic Sister Luke, who, on the feast of Samhain, crosses back over from the dead to the land of the living to promote healing, forgiveness, and reconciliation of Laundry atrocities. Directed by Caroline Fitzgerald, the play opened in Galway in 2002. Its 2013 American premiere was directed by Eileen Kearney at the University of Colorado Denver.

Brogan has published volumes of poetry and her artwork has had numerous exhibitions. *Above the Waves Calligraphy* combines her poetry and illustrations. She has written a number of other plays including *Clarenda's Mirror, Yours Truly,* and the verse play *Ladies' Day*. In 2005, *Requiem of Love,* directed by Caroline Fitzgerald, premiered at Galway's Town Hall Theatre. In reference to this dramatic monologue, Patrick Lonergan of the *Irish Times* writes that "Patricia Burke Brogan's plays have always seemed a little ahead of their time."[1] Her latest poetic work, *Décollage New and Selected Poems,* was launched in October 2008 at the Galway City Museum. In 2014 she published *Memoir with Grykes & Turloughs,* which recounts her life and work.

Eclipsed

In memory of the Magdalenes.

CHARACTERS

SISTER VIRGINIA, a white-veiled novice.[2]
MOTHER VICTORIA, a black-veiled Mother Superior.

Juliet, a seventeen-year-old orphan.

Rosa, daughter of Brigit, who has been adopted and raised by a well-to-do American family.

Penitent Women: Unmarried mothers.

Cathy, a penitent woman.

Nellie-Nora, a penitent woman.

Mandy, a penitent woman.

Brigit, a penitent woman.

LOCATION

Interior of Convent Laundry.

TIME

Act 1 Scene 1 and Act 2 Scene 6 are set in 1992. All other scenes are set in 1963.

SCENE

Purple muslin drapes/[3]*cobwebs/washing hang from top of set. Centre hanging drape covers basket downstage, other hanging drapes are spaced at intervals upstage. In Act 1 Scene 2 the drapes are used as background/cloister for Morning Call*[4] *in convent and chapel. At opening of Act 1 Scene 3 the drapes are pulled away energetically by the women to reveal workroom in laundry. Door up centre leads to corridor with convent/cloister on right and washing machine area of laundry on left.*

COSTUME

The nuns are dressed in veil-coif-domino-guimpe (armour-like pre-Vatican 2 clothing with large black rosary beads and long black leather belts.)

The penitents are dressed in shapeless worn-out overalls[5] *with white aprons, black laced-up shoes, and thick black stockings.*

Nellie-Nora to be aged for Act 1 Scene 1 and for Act 2 Scene 6.

SOUND

Orchestral introduction to "He was despised" from Handel's Oratorio "Messiah" and part of the contralto aria "He was despised," sung by Kathleen Ferrier,[6] *are used in Act 1 Scene 1 and in Act 2 Scene 6. Plain Chant. Elvis songs may be recorded.*

ACT 1

SCENE 1 PROLOGUE

Orchestral introduction to "He was despised" continues. In darkness Nellie-Nora and Rosa come down stairs into dusty, cobwebby basement, Nellie-Nora with dragging-slipper-walk[7] carries torch[8] and a bundle of large keys. Large laundry basket covered with torch and suspended drape down centre. Nellie-Nora breaks through cobwebs/drapes. Small cupboard with shelves down left. An old St. Brigit's Cross[9] hangs on cupboard. Old radio on top shelf. Nellie-Nora searches for light switch, puts on light. Music stops. Rosa is dressed in today's fashion.

NELLIE-NORA. You've come such a long distance! From London (Boston, New York, Los Angeles)!

ROSA. It's not so far, Nellie-Nora! It's only an hour (5 hours) on the plane![10]

NELLIE-NORA. I hope you find something to help you. I hope you find what you're looking for.

ROSA. I hope so, Nellie-Nora! When I found her name, Brigit Murphy, and this address in my adoption papers, I had to come!

NELLIE-NORA. Anything that's left from those times is in this basket!

Rosa moves to basket, Nellie-Nora opens basket. Creaks of old basket. Pause. Nellie-Nora opens basket. Creaks of old basket. Nellie-Nora takes out a nun's black habit, holds it up, folds it across her arm. She then takes out Sister Virginia's pinned together white coif-veil-domino, holds it up. Taking habit and veil-coif, she shuffles/fades towards exit, but stays at exit.

ROSA. Thank you, Nellie-Nora!

As Nellie-Nora shuffles towards exit, low lighting shows shadowy shapes of Mandy, Brigit, Sister Virginia, and Cathy behind drapes. Very shadowy scene. Rosa searches in basket and takes out an old apron, a sheet, and mannikin's head. In an old Black Magic[11] chocolate box, she finds black-and-white photographs, examines them, turns one over and reads.

ROSA. "To Mandy Prenderville with all my love. Yours forever and ever and ever. Your Darling, Elvis Aron Garon Presley."

Ghostly women's voices sing one line of Elvis's song "Well, since my baby left me." Rosa smiles. Turns over another photograph and reads.

ROSA. "Rem.[12] the Carnival in Cillnamona,[13] the great craic, Brigit! Yours forever, John-Joe."—Brigit! "To Brigit from John-Joe."—John-Joe! Who is he?

Pause. Takes another photograph. Reads.

ROSA. My baby Rosa. My beautiful baby.

Rosa stares at photograph. Takes a large battered ledger from basket, opens it, flicks through pages, stops, opens other pages, stops. Reads.

ROSA. Killmacha,[14] 1963. Dempsey, Mary Kate—a boy, James. Signed in by her parents, Mr. and Mrs. Dempsey. O' Donnell, Betty Ann—a girl, Agnes. Signed in by her parents. McNamara, Cathy—
VOICE OF CATHY. Twin girls, Michele and Emily. Signed in—
ROSA. Langan, Nellie-Nora—

Rosa turns to Nellie-Nora as Nellie-Nora exits.

ROSA. Nellie-Nora?
WOMEN'S VOICE. A stillborn boy. Signed in by her employer, Mr. Persse.
ROSA. Mannion, Julia—
VOICE OF JULIET. A girl, Juliet. Signed in—
ROSA. Prenderville, Mandy—
VOICE OF MANDY. A boy, premature, stillborn.
ROSA. Murphy, Brigit—
BRIGIT'S VOICE. A girl, Rosa.

Searches and finds baby photograph in chocolate box.

ROSA. (*Puzzled.*) Brigit Murphy—a girl, Rosa? My Mother! Penitent?

Rosa moves to small cupboard down left, searches through shelf, touches St. Brigit's Cross, old radio, and as if following Nellie-Nora, exits through drapes. Straight into Morning Call, Act 1 Scene 2.

SCENE 2   MORNING CALL

Sister Virginia, holding lighted candle, moves between cloister drapes and rings small handbell.

SISTER VIRGINIA. (*Chants.*) Benedicamus Domino![15]
VOICE OF A NUN. (*Chants.*) Deo Gratias![16]

At each "cell[17] door" Sister Virginia repeats Morning Call and a voice answers.
    Four calls.
    Sister Virginia quenches candle and exits through drapes.
    Straight into Act 1 Scene 3, "Cathy's Birthday."

SCENE 3 CATHY'S BIRTHDAY
LIGHTING

Low, Straight from Scene 2 Morning Call. Nellie-Nora, Brigit, and Mandy enter energetically through purple drapes. Mandy and Brigit pull down drapes, fold them rhythmically and put them on shelves up right. Colour of drapes contrasts with darkness of walls. Old shop mannikin wearing Bishop's crimson soutane[18] with white surplice[19] folded across shoulder up left. Energy, light!

SOUND

Women sing "Heartbreak Hotel," Elvis style.

"Well, since my baby left me
I found a new place to dwell.
It's down at the end of lonely street
At Heartbreak Hotel."[20]

Nellie-Nora works at ironing board down left.

MANDY. Any sign of him, Nellie-Nora?

Nellie-Nora runs down centre, and stands on chair, her back to audience. She balances old cracked mirror towards imaginary window as she tries to see the outside world in response to Mandy's query.

MANDY. (*Excitedly.*) Is he here yet?
NELLIE-NORA. Aahk! The window's too high up, Mandy! There's no light! The glass is too thick! It's like the bottom of a jam jar! This mirror's cracked too! Shh! I thought I heard something! Maybe it's himself! No! No! (*Imitating Mother Victoria's voice.*) What are you doing, Nellie-Nora? You're a disgrace! What about His Lordship's linen?[21]

(*Own voice.*) Careful! If you break that mirror, you'll have seven years bad luck! (*Mandy smiles.*) Sure I must have broken a lorry- load[22] of mirrors to end up in this salt mine!

Nellie-Nora blesses herself and manipulates mirror again. Mandy genuflects towards Brigit.

NELLIE-NORA. No sign of him, Mandy! Maybe he got a puncture![23] Ahh! I thought I might see a little sunshine between the iron bars. Mother o' God! Back to penance!

A convent bell rings. Mandy takes mirror and tries to see the outside world.

BRIGIT. Never mind that fella, Mandy! Sure you don't even know his name!

MANDY. He's a smasher,[24] Brigit! Did you never hear him whistling to me?

Nellie-Nora searches her pockets.

NELLIE-NORA. Where did I put that butt? A match, Mandy! A match quick!

MANDY. Here, Nellie-Nora!

Nellie-Nora lights cigarette butt and keeps it between her lips as she speaks.

NELLIE-NORA. Mmn! That's better!

MANDY. Aha! No sign!

NELLIE-NORA. Keep trying, Mandy!

BRIGIT. Shhhh! She's coming!

Brigit and Mandy rush to washboard basins and pretend to work. Nellie-Nora puts out cigarette, hides it in fold of her short stocking and returns to ironing board down left. Mother Victoria enters, nose high in the air and stands down centre.

MOTHER VICTORIA. I hope His Lordship's linen is ready, Brigit! Show me that surplice, Nellie-Nora!

Nellie-Nora comes forward with surplice. Mother Victoria examines it.

MOTHER VICTORIA. Mmn! Careful with this Carrickmacross lace![25] Are His Lordship's shoes cleaned and mended? Buckles shone?

NELLIE-NORA. They're nearly ready, Mother Victoria!

MOTHER VICTORIA. Mmn! His Lordship is leaving for Rome on Tuesday!

BRIGIT. Rome! The lucky beggar!

MOTHER VICTORIA. Did you say something Brigit?

BRIGIT. No, Mother! Yes, Mother! I said "Rome," Mother!

MOTHER VICTORIA. His Lordship'll be talking to His Holiness. Maybe he'll say a prayer for you, Brigit! I'll be back.

Exit Mother Victoria. Women continue to work.

BRIGIT. Rome! Sunshine! Wine! And look at us! That rip[26] Victoria! God, how I hate her! Some day I'll put her through the washing machines! Then I'll smather her with red hot irons! Herself and His Lordship with his buckled shoes!

MANDY. Get her keys first, Brigit!

Brigit moves towards mannikin as she says.

BRIGIT. Himself with His High Falutin' pretence! Dressing up in foll-de-doll lace and flying off to Rome!

NELLIE-NORA. But he's a Prince of the Church, Brigit! Mother Victoria told me!

BRIGIT. So, Brigit here will be Prince of the Church too! Get me my crozier,[27] Mandy! The mop! Quick!

Brigit puts on surplice. Mandy doesn't move.

NELLIE-NORA. Ah, Brigit! Be careful!

BRIGIT. I'll get it myself!

Nellie-Nora and Mandy watch Brigit. Brigit uses upside down mop as crozier.

BRIGIT. Gawd bless you, my scrubbers! Don't squint at me, Nellie-Nora! Stand up straight all of you! Knees together! Say, "Good awfternoon, my lord!"

NELLIE-NORA AND MANDY. "Good afternoon, my Lord!"

BRIGIT. Will you forget your bog accents![28] Say "Good awfternoon, my Lord!"

NELLIE-NORA AND MANDY. "Good awfternoon, my lord!" (*They bow.*)

NELLIE-NORA. What, my lord, are you doing in Purgatory?

BRIGIT. A good question! Here's a tenner,[29] Nellie-Nora, for cigarettes. Your favourite Woodbines! I like a smoke myself—a cigar of course! Say "Thank you," Nellie-Nora!

NELLIE-NORA. You're very generous, my Lord!

MANDY. What about me, Brigit? . . . I mean, Bishop Brigit.

BRIGIT. My dear, Mandy I bless you! You are now head Bottle Washer. And you, Nellie-Nora, the Most Reverend Mother! This big shiny key (*Mop.*) opens the pantry and cellar! You'll find plenty of cream cakes, roast beef, French Wine—and Port!

MANDY. French Wine! Mmn!

NELLIE-NORA. Roast beef!

BRIGIT. Port!

Mandy finds the underpants. Nellie-Nora lights a cigarette butt.

MANDY. My Lord! Your underpants! Freshly starched and trimmed with Carrickmacross lace!

Brigit takes underpants and pulls it over Mandy's head.

BRIGIT. I told you, Mandy, that the handling of my underpants is a mortal sin!

Enter Sister Virginia. Her white veil is pinned back.

SISTER VIRGINIA. Brigit! Stop! Stop immediately!

Brigit takes off surplice. Nellie-Nora places it on shoulder of mannikin.

NELLIE-NORA. Yes, Sister Virginia! Sorry, Sister!

SISTER VIRGINIA. Please, Mandy! Put that away!

MANDY. Sorry Sister Virginia!

SISTER VIRGINIA. Mind that cigarette, Nellie-Nora! You might burn the precious Carrickmacross lace!

The women smile. Keys rattle. Mother Victoria enters with Cathy. Cathy rubs her head and is in tears.

MOTHER VICTORIA. Back to work immediately, Cathy! You've wasted the morning! Hurry with the Athlone[30] baskets! Hurry! To your tub, Mandy and tie back that hair! Mmn! Do I smell cigarettes? Is anyone smoking in here, Sister Virginia? Mmn! This area is in a dreadful mess! It's a disgrace! What would His Lordship say? Have it cleaned immediately, Sister!

SISTER VIRGINIA. Yes, Mother Victoria!

Exit Mother Victoria. Sister Virginia picks up small threads from floor and exits. Brigit grimaces. Mandy and Nellie-Nora approach Cathy, who stands at table up right of centre.

MANDY. What happened, Cathy? You didn't—did you—you didn't try it again?

NELLIE-NORA. Mother o' God, Cathy! You didn't—did you?

CATHY. Mmn! (*Moans.*)

The women resume work. Pause.

CATHY. (*Slowly.*) After Mass, while Mother Victoria was serving Father Durcan's breakfast, I hid in the Confession box! Father Durcan left to collect his car. He never closes the front door. He drove off without closing the main gate either! I hid behind the beech tree! And I got out! Out on the main road!

MANDY. Outside? Oh, Cathy! Outside!

CATHY. Yes! Outside on the road! But I was like this! No coat! As I walked up the hill, I could smell the sea! The sun was shining on me at last! A fella passed on a bike, whistling!

MANDY. A fella whistlin'! Oooh, Cathy what happened? Did you see any smashers when you were out?

CATHY. No smashers, Mandy! No! A few children pointed at me, laughed and called me names. A laundry van passed, turned around and came at me. I fought. I bit them. I screamed. (*Pause.*) But they brought me back. (*Pause.*) Mother Victoria gave me a mug of strong tea and the usual sermon! (*She rubs her head.*) But I'm getting out! I'll keep trying! I'm getting out!

BRIGIT. Bastards! That rip Victoria has her spies everywhere!

Is interrupted by Sister Virginia who returns with clipboard and pen. Pause. Mother Victoria enters with a bundle of letters.

MOTHER VICTORIA. Give these letters out at tea break, Sister! Not until tea break! His Lordship's linens first! Then the Athlone baskets! They mustn't be delayed!

Exit Mother Victoria. Brigit looks at Nellie-Nora.

BRIGIT. It's a gallon o' bleach I need!

MANDY. Today is Cathy's birthday, Sister! The letters, please!

SISTER VIRGINIA. Will you not wait? It's almost tea break, Mandy! (*Looks at watch.*) These tablecloths must be snow white!

MANDY. (*Interrupts.*) Aah, Sister, please!

BRIGIT. Do you hear that, Nellie-Nora? His Lordship's tablecloths must be snow white!

NELLIE-NORA. I washed them by hand, Sister!

BRIGIT. And just the right amount of starch, Nellie-Nora!

SISTER VIRGINIA. Starch, Nellie-Nora?

NELLIE-NORA. I starched them myself, Sister!

SISTER VIRGINIA. Thank you, Nellie-Nora!

BRIGIT. The ironing of His Lordship's tablecloths?

MANDY. The letters, please!

NELLIE-NORA. I ironed them too, Sister!

BRIGIT. Raise up yer hearts, ye washerwomen! The Palace tablecloths are pure perfect! Alleluia! Alleluia!

Sister Virginia checks tablecloths as Mandy tries to peep at letters. Tea bell rings. Sister Virginia gives out letters.

SISTER VIRGINIA. One for you, Mandy. Posted in New York!

BRIGIT. From Elvis himself, I suppose!

SISTER VIRGINIA. One for you, Cathy! Look at the size of it! And one for you, Brigit! Sorry, Nellie-Nora! None for you.

NELLIE-NORA. It's alright, Sister! If I got a letter now, I'd die of shock! I'll get the tea today, Cathy!

Nellie-Nora exits. Brigit tears open letter, sits on basket down right and reads. Cathy and Mandy turn their backs and open letters. Cathy turns to Sister Virginia.

CATHY. Look, Sister! From my twins! A beautiful birthday card! "To Mammy on her birthday. Love, Michele and Emily."
SISTER VIRGINIA. (*Sadly.*) Happy Birthday, Cathy.

Sister Virginia exits. Cathy stares at card and traces the words with her finger.

CATHY. Am I ever going to be a mother to them?

Brigit crumples her letter and stuffs it into her pocket.

MANDY. He's coming! He's coming to visit! Elvis is coming!
BRIGIT. But he was to come last Christmas, Mandy!
MANDY. (*Excitedly.*) This time Elvis is coming for sure!
My cousin Betty-Ann in America says so! Look here in this letter! I'll have to get ready! (*Change of tone.*) I'll have to be beautiful for him!

Nellie-Nora returns with tray on which are old mugs, an old teapot and a plate of bread and jam.

NELLIE-NORA. Come on, girls! We'll have a party!

The women take mugs of tea and bread. They eat hungrily. Brigit sits on basket. Mandy sits on ground. Cathy sits on side of table. Nellie-Nora stands. Pause as they eat. Nellie-Nora gives Cathy a small medal.

NELLIE-NORA. It's only a small Holy Medal, Cathy! Wear it around your neck!
CATHY. Thanks, Nellie-Nora! I'll always wear it!
BRIGIT. A present for you, Cathy! A few love hearts![31]
CATHY. Oh, Brigit, thanks!

Cathy opens paper bag, takes out a sweet and reads, "Forever and ever." Mandy moves towards Cathy.

MANDY. Happy birthday, Cathy! I made it myself! It's a pink lacy hanky! It's only shop lace, Cathy! Nobody ever taught me how to make lace!— I'd love to make a long lacy dress for myself!

Mandy moves around rhythmically.

NELLIE-NORA. A long lacy dress would suit you, Mandy!

Cathy is quiet as she looks at presents.

MANDY. Yes, Nellie-Nora!—Pretend we're in—in Paris! And we're having a huge party for Cathy!

SOUND. *Voice of Elvis "It's Now or Never!" in distance.*

MANDY. The moon is shining on the Seine! People sit outside under the stars, drink wine, and sing. Painters wear big hats and look for beautiful models.

BRIGIT. Elvis drops in! Sees our Mandy in her long lacy dress and falls madly in love with her!

NELLIE-NORA. They dance all the way to the airport and fly off to Hollywood!

Mandy, in fantasy, takes up a shirt and dances downstage. Nellie-Nora and Cathy dance and sing. Brigit dances with upside-down mop.

VOICE OF ELVIS. (*Sound up.*)
"It's now or never!
Come hold me tight!
Kiss me, my darling.
Be mine tonight."

Music stops abruptly. Dancing stops. Mandy is disappointed. Pause.

CATHY. I'd love a slice of homemade cake with sultanas[32] and big juicy cherries!

MANDY. Close your eyes and pretend! It'll be true if you pretend!

The women close their eyes.

BRIGIT. Griskeens[33] and black puddings![34] The smell of turf smoke.

MANDY. Frilly fried eggs and potato cakes!

NELLIE-NORA. A bit of bacon!

CATHY. Almond icing off the Christmas cake!

MANDY. Flaky and crunchy chocolate!

NELLIE-NORA. Loads of big floury potatoes!

BRIGIT. Smothered in butter!

MANDY. No! With nuts!

BRIGIT. Potatoes with nuts?

They laugh.

CATHY. Read my cup, Nellie-Nora. Here, I'll give it another twist!

Nellie Nora takes cup. Pause.

NELLIE-NORA. (*Hesitantly.*) You'll be going on a long journey, Cathy! I see a crowd—a crowd of people! There's a lot of sweetness—lots of letters—and flowers.—Yes—I see sunshine.—Is that alright, Cathy?

CATHY. A long journey? Sweetness, Nellie-Nora? Thanks!

MANDY. Now mine, please! When is he comin'?

Nellie Nora is distressed by what she has seen in Cathy's cup/mug.

NELLIE-NORA. Wait a minute, Mandy!—Now,—Ohhh, lucky stars are shining for you, Mandy!—Mother o' God, I see diamonds! Lucky diamonds!

MANDY. It must be Elvis! Has he blue-blue eyes? Shiny black hair? He's tall and—slim? Elvis? It is my Elvis!

Mandy takes cup/mug and looks into it.

BRIGIT. Stop, Nellie-Nora! stop!

MANDY. Ahh, Brigit! Go on, Nellie-Nora! How is he? My Elvis? Isn't he always thinking of me when he sings?

BRIGIT. Such fools!

NELLIE-NORA. I'll read your cup, Brigit?

BRIGIT. No! Just tell me that I'll find my baby! Never mind that cup o' tea leaves!

MANDY. Do you love your John-Joe, Brigit?

BRIGIT. Love? What's love, Mandy? Love's a trick!

CATHY. Love. Forever and ever.

MANDY. True Love! (*Sings.*)

"And I give to you

And you give to me
Love forever true!"

(*Speaks.*) Richard used to sing that song to me—Every night after the dance he took me home in his shiny red car.—We always folded down the seats in the back!—Lovely, velvety seats. Every Sunday night! But, when I told him about the baby, he never spoke to me again! Ever!—I only saw him once in the distance after that. Before they brought me here. Oooh! I miss that shiny red car!

BRIGIT. Bastard! Didn't I tell you, Mandy! Love is a trick!

NELLIE-NORA. Now you have your own Elvis, Mandy!

MANDY. Yes I have, Nellie-Nora! He's a smasher! Isn't he?—Why don't you read your own cup, Nellie-Nora?

NELLIE-NORA. Aach! I know what's in my cup, Mandy!

Workbell rings. Nellie-Nora collects tray and exits. She returns quickly and goes to ironing board down left. Mandy takes out her scrapbook, kisses photographs, and immediately puts it back in apron pocket, stares at it for a moment, and returns to work at washboard up right.

Machine sound up. Time passing. Lights lower.

Straight into True Love, Act 1 Scene 4.

SCENE 4 TRUE LOVE

Set same as for Act 1 Scene 3. Purple drapes folded on shelves. Brigit, Cathy, Mandy, and Nellie-Nora on stage. Sister Virginia enters with Juliet, a seventeen-year-old girl. Juliet carries a bundle of linen. Sister Virginia takes a white apron from hook and gives it to Juliet.

SISTER VIRGINIA. This is Juliet. She'll be working with you for the next few months.

Women stare at Juliet.

BRIGIT. They're getting' younger all the time! When is it arriving, Juliet?

JULIET. When is what arriving?

NELLIE-NORA. The baby of course!

Nellie-Nora takes bundle of linen from Juliet.

SISTER VIRGINIA. Juliet is from the orphanage! No baby, Nellie-Nora.

CATHY. Hello, Juliet!

MANDY. Juliet!

NELLIE-NORA. Welcome, Juliet!

BRIGIT. Howya!

CATHY. The orphanage? St. Anthony's?

JULIET. Yes!

CATHY. Do you know my Michele and Emily? My twins? They're six years old. Do you know them?

JULIET. Oh! The twins! Blonde curly hair and blue eyes?

CATHY. Tell me about them please!

JULIET. Have you not seen them lately?

CATHY. No! No, Juliet! Are they growing fast? Do they eat enough?

JULIET. Yes! They're growing very fast. They'll be making their first Holy Communion next year!

CATHY. My babies making First Holy Communion! I must see my babies!

SISTER VIRGINIA. (*Gently.*) Will you check the Athlone blankets for me, Cathy? Please?—Now we'll fold the sheets, Juliet. First we find the code. It's in the corner in red thread—see! We fold carefully this way. Corners together so!

They stand down center and fold sheets rhythmically. Women work in background.

SISTER VIRGINIA. You're seventeen now, Juliet. Have you been out at all—outside?

JULIET. No, Sister! I don't want to live out there!

SISTER VIRGINIA. Why, Juliet? Your life's ahead of you!

JULIET. My Mammy lived here until she died. I want to stay in here!

SISTER VIRGINIA. But you can't make a choice until you've been out.

JULIET. I'd hate to live out there! All those men!

SISTER VIRGINIA. What men, Juliet? There are fathers and mothers, brothers and sisters—families!

JULIET. But look what happened to Mammy! No! No babies for me!

SISTER VIRGINIA. Most men are good, Juliet!

JULIET. They're not! Men are oversexed! Mother Joachim said so, when I was working in the convent!

SISTER VIRGINIA. Mother Joachim! Why did she say that?

JULIET. When I answered the side door. When I screamed!

SISTER VIRGINIA. You screamed! But why? Tell me, Juliet!

JULIET. You see, Mick, the vegetable man! He grabbed me here! Pushed me against the wall. Said he'd murder me—break my neck if I moved! Old Mother Benedict was just in time. She hit him a wollop with her big rosary beads, but Mother Joachim wouldn't believe me—that I didn't lead him on!

SISTER VIRGINIA. (*Lifting sheets.*) He was just one man, Juliet! You mustn't stay in here! Take a job outside! Go away and see new places! Read the great books! Earn your own money. We're on an island here!

JULIET. But, Sister, I was never on a bus or a train. I'd be afraid!

SISTER VIRGINIA. Put the sheets on the shelves now, Juliet. Cathy will give you something to sew. I'll—We'll pray for you.

JULIET. Thank you, Sister!

Sister Virginia moves toward Cathy.

SISTER VIRGINIA. Will you give Juliet something to sew, Cathy? (*Lowers her voice.*) See that she eats, that she finishes her meals.

CATHY. Yes, Sister! Can you sew on buttons, Juliet?

JULIET. Yes, Cathy!

NELLIE-NORA. Look, Sister! More shirts from the seminary!

Nellie-Nora gives Sister a bundle of white shirts. Sister Virginia examines them.

SISTER VIRGINIA. Mmn! Buttons missing!

JULIET. Would there be many students in the seminary, Sister?

SISTER VIRGINIA. Yes, Juliet! Nearly every mother west of the Shannon has a son studying for the priesthood. Where I grew up all the fine young men enter a seminary!

JULIET. They never go out in the world?

SISTER VIRGINIA. Some go to Maynooth.[35] Others prepare for the Foreign Missions.

JULIET. I'd like that! Teaching black babies!

MANDY. All those nice young men! What a waste!

SISTER VIRGINIA. They go to the Far East. Others to the States. Some to Africa. My three uncles, my cousin in Galway, and my brother John are priests. Grand Aunt Teresa and Aunt Mary are nuns. The Island of Saints and Scholars is now an island of priests and nuns!

CATHY. My Uncle Jeremiah is a Canon!

BRIGIT. For all the good that'll do you Cathy! Sure my uncle is an Archbishop and look at me!

SISTER VIRGINIA. Will you help sew buttons on the shirts, Brigit?

BRIGIT. Buttons! Yes, Sister! I'll sew on a hundred buttons, if you give me the keys.

SISTER VIRGINIA. You know I can't—

BRIGIT. Ah, Sister! This letter I got from my cousin Katie in Cillnamona says that John-Joe is getting married next week! He doesn't know about Rosa! She's his baby too, Sister! I have to tell him! Please, Sister! The keys!

SISTER VIRGINIA. I can't Brigit! I'm not in charge!—I'm sorry!

Sister Virginia exits.

BRIGIT. Bloody nuns! They don't give a damn! Damn! Damn! Damn His Lordship! Damn the Pope and all the bloody lot o' them!

Juliet moves closer to Cathy.

JULIET. Did you know my Mammy, Julia Mannion?

CATHY. Julia Mannion! Yes, I was with her when—she—got the heart attack.

JULIA. They wouldn't let me see her!

CATHY. We'll look after you, Juliet!

Brigit examines a seminary shirt.

BRIGIT. A hedge tear[36] in a seminary shirt!

MANDY. They play football[37] and hurling,[38] Brigit.

BRIGIT. Hurling's smashin'! I played camogie[39] at school! Got my head opened once! Had to get thirteen stitches!

MANDY. Football's better! All those lads rollin' around in the mud cursin' and swearin'!

NELLIE-NORA. Better than kicking people.

Cathy has a bad attack of coughing.

CATHY. My head! Oh, my head! Oh, God!

Cathy holds head in her hands and sways in pain.

BRIGIT. Take a rest, Cathy!
NELLIE-NORA. Stop the sewing, Cathy!
MANDY. Is it the asthma, Cathy?
CATHY. I'll ask Sister Virginia for an aspirin!

Cathy stumbles to door and exits.

MANDY. She needs more than aspirin!
JULIET. What's wrong with Cathy? She's not dyin' is she?
NELLIE-NORA. She's worn out, Juliet! Her heart's broke!
BRIGIT. Wasn't it a rotten bastard, who left her in the lurch! Cathy never talks about him!
NELLIE-NORA. She keeps quiet about him!
JULIET. Who is he?
BRIGIT. The father of her twins! Told nobody!—Some Big Shot, I suppose.
NELLIE-NORA. Sure, maybe he's married.
BRIGIT. Or a Bishop!
MANDY. Or a film star!
BRIGIT. Seven years without tellin' anyone! Women are fools!
MANDY. Would you like to see my scrapbook, Juliet?

Mandy takes scrapbook from apron pocket.

JULIET. What's in it?—Oh, snaps! I've snaps too! In my prayerbook!
MANDY. Of Elvis?
JULIET. No! Of Audrey Hepburn!
MANDY. Audrey Hepburn?
JULIET. Yes! She's so thin! You see, she doesn't eat bread or potatoes! That's why! Oooh, I'd love to be that thin!
BRIGIT. But you're as thin as a wisp, Juliet!
JULIET. No! I'm not! I'm huge!

Enter Sister Virginia and Cathy. Mandy hides scrapbook.

SISTER VIRGINIA. Take it easy with the mending, Cathy.
NELLIE-NORA. Yes, Cathy! I'll help you in a minute!
CATHY. Thanks!

Mother Victoria enters, walks downstage, beads and keys rattling. She beckons to Sister Virginia.

MOTHER VICTORIA. There's a visitor, a Father McCarthy, to see you, Sister Virginia! Says he's a friend of your brother, Father John! I've told them in the kitchen. Tea in the small parlour. Ten minutes. I'll give you ten minutes. And remember. Custody of the eyes,[40] Sister. I'll see you afterwards in the cloister.
SISTER VIRGINIA. Thank you, Mother Victoria!

Sister brings forward her veil, unhooks her outerskirt,[41] puts on Big Sleeves,[42] and exits.

MOTHER VICTORIA. We'll say the Rosary[43] together for a special intention. "Thou, O Lord wilt open my lips."
BRIGIT. But we said the Rosary while we were ironing the sheets for His Lordship's Palace! Five and a half decades,[44] Mother!
MANDY. And Nellie-Nora offered them up for His Lordship, Mother!
MOTHER VICTORIA. Very good indeed, Nellie-Nora! I'll say my office[45] here. You may sing hymns if you wish. Softly please! Hmmmm . . . (*She intones.*) "The bells of the Angelus[46] are calling to pray: In sweet tones announcing the sacred Ave:
Ave, Ave, Ave Maria.
Ave, Ave, Ave Maria."

Brigit sings in contrast but uses same tune.

"On top of old Smokey
All covered with snow.
I lost my true lover
From courtin' too slow."

MOTHER VICTORIA. Aperi, Domine, os nostrum ad benedicendum nomen sanctum tuum.—Stop that rubbish! Stop, Brigit! You're a disgrace! In front of this innocent young girl too!—How do you like the
laundry, Juliet?

JULIET. 'Tis—alright, Mother Victoria! Thank you!

MOTHER VICTORIA. Very good, Juliet! Is His Lordship's linen ready, Brigit? Tablecloths for the crimson gold dining room? Did you double-
check the mending?

BRIGIT. Aren't we busy with the Athlone scrubbin', Mother Victoria?

MOTHER VICTORIA. His Lordship must be looked after first! Remember
he's a Prince of the Church!

*Brigit and Nellie-Nora exchange smiles. Mother Victoria walks to and fro down-
stage. Slight pause.*

MOTHER VICTORIA. Aperi, Domine, os nostrum ad benedicendum nomen sanctum tumm: numda quoque or nostrum ab omnibus vanis,
perversis et alienis cogitationibus: intellectus illumina.

BRIGIT. Nellie-Nora is knitting crimson combinations[47] to keep His
Lordship comfortable during those chilly evenings in Rome. Isn't that
right, Nellie-Nora?

Nellie-Nora is in shock. Mother Victoria looks at Nellie-Nora. Pause.

NELLIE-NORA. It's not a combinations, Mother! It's a jumper![48]

Mother Victoria continues to walk to and fro as she reads office.

MOTHER VICTORIA.—Ab omnibus vanis, perversis et alienis cogitationibus: intellectus illumina, affectus inflamma, ut digne, attende ac
devote hoc beatae Virginis Mariae valeamus et exaudiri mereamur
ante divinae conspectum Majestatis tuae—

BRIGIT. (*Sings.*)
"On top of old Smokey
All covered with snow,
I lost my true lover
From courtin' too slow."

MOTHER VICTORIA. Per Christum Dominum nostrum! I'm saying my
office, Brigit!

Women continue to wash, iron, and sew.

CATHY. (*Sings softly.*)
    "And I give to you
    And you give to me
    Love forever true."
BRIGIT. Love forever true? Huhh!

*Lights down. Brigit, Cathy, Nellie-Nora, and Mandy freeze. Machine sounds up
for three seconds, then fade as Plain Chant Credo[49] comes up. Mother Victoria
stands for a moment at doorway upstage, inspects women, then exits.*

SCENE 5   CREDO SCENE
SOUND

One soprano voice sings:

    "Credo in unum Deum,
    Patrem omnipotentem
    Factorem coeli et terrae,
    Visibilium omnium et invisibilium.
    Et in unum Dominum, Jesum Christum,
    Filum Dei unigenitum.
    Et ex Patre natum ante omnia saecula.
    Deum de Deo, lumen de lumine.
    Deum verum de Deo vero, genitum non factum,
    Consubstantialem Patri . . ."

*Stage in darkness except highlight on Sister Virginia as she enters "convent cha-
pel." She dips finger in Holy Water Font[50] and makes Sign of the Cross. Glow from
stained-glass windows and sanctuary lamp. Sister Virginia walks downstage and
kneels. She then lies prostrate, arms spread out in shape of cross for five seconds.
She kneels in highlight and prays the Credo.*

SISTER VIRGINIA. I believe in God the Father almighty. Creator of
heaven and earth, and in Jesus Christ His only son our Lord, who

was conceived by the Holy Ghost. I believe in God—God? I believe in God—I try—I believe in God the Father almighty. Creator of heaven and earth, and in Jesus Christ His only son our Lord, who was conceived by the Holy Ghost, born of the Virgin Mary . . .

VOICE OF BRIGIT. Keys, Sister! My John-Joe is getting married next week! He doesn't know about our baby!

SISTER VIRGINIA. Creator of heaven and earth, and in Jesus Christ His only son our Lord who was conceived . . .

VOICE OF BRIGIT. Keys! My baby, Rosa! I have to find my baby!

SISTER VIRGINIA. Born of the Virgin Mary, suffered under Pontius Pilate, was crucified, died, and was buried . . .

Sound of Cathy's breathing during asthma attack.

VOICE OF MANDY. It's Cathy! She's chokin', Sister!

VOICE OF NELLIE-NORA. A kettle! Steam! Hurry, Sister! Hurry!

SISTER VIRGINIA. Was crucified, died, and was buried. He descended into hell.

VOICE OF MOTHER VICTORIA. Mandy thought she could leave if she wasn't pregnant, so she performed an abortion on herself!

SISTER VIRGINIA. He descended into hell. The third day He arose from the dead.

VOICE OF MOTHER VICTORIA. We give them food, shelter, and clothing. We look after their spiritual needs. No one else wants them! No one else wants them!

SISTER VIRGINIA. The third day He arose from the dead . . .

VOICE OF MOTHER VICTORIA. A vow of obedience, Sister! Blind obedience!

SISTER VIRGINIA. Is it just a story from the East—from St. Paul? A story? The women need help from you, the Risen! But, did you rise from the dead?—You're supposed to be a Loving Father! Are you a God of Love?—A God of Justice?—I thought I'd be working for the poor! Am I being brainwashed? Will I become dehumanised too, if I stay here long enough? Locked in by obedience? The Rule? Why are there changes in our Holy Founder's Book? Was early Christian history rewritten too? Woman's witness submerged? Christ crucified! Help them! For a woman bore you, carried you for nine months! Mother of Jesus, do something about Cathy, Mandy, Nellie-Nora, and the others! When you arose from that tomb, women were your first witnesses! Your first miracle was performed at your Mother's request!—Help us!—Help me!

Sister Virginia makes the Sign of the Cross, stands, and exits. Lights up for Act 1 Scene 6.

SCENE 6 EFFIGY

Hum of huge washing machines. Bleach smells. Brigit and Mandy work at wash-tubs with washboards right of centre. Nellie-Nora at ironing board down left. Manikin dressed in Bishop's soutane (surplice folded across shoulders) up left. Cathy and Juliet are mending at work table up centre. Large laundry basket down right. Manikin's head on lower shelf. Cathy has breathing difficulties.

BRIGIT. Spit out your troubles, Cathy! They'll rot in your brain if you don't! 'Tis far from this dirt you were reared!

CATHY. Thanks, Brigit!

NELLIE-NORA. Troubles you can't talk about—they're the bad ones (*Shows Cathy a small mirror.*) I'm tellin' you, Cathy, you're better lookin' than Grace Kelly! Sure if Cary Grant, Bing Crosby, or Frank Sinatra himself saw you, they'd all fall in love with you!

MANDY. But not Elvis! Remember he's mine! He belongs to me!

CATHY. You can keep your Elvis, Mandy! Thanks Nellie-Nora!

MANDY. Elvis! That voice! Just to see him would be heaven!

NELLIE-NORA. We'll all go to heaven when we die!

BRIGIT. Mmnn! What the hell good will that be?

MANDY. I want my heaven now with Elvis!

Mandy takes out her scrapbook and examines snapshots.

MANDY. I'll ask Sister Virginia for snaps of Elvis! And one of Frank Sina-tra for you, Cathy!

CATHY. Sister Virginia is not allowed look at film stars.

BRIGIT. Only at Father Durcan! Some film star that fella! Face like the back of a bus!

NELLIE-NORA. Mother o' God, Brigit! Don't forget he gave us the old radio!

MANDY. I could write to Elvis in Hollywood!
BRIGIT. No! Not again!

Nellie-Nora blesses herself.

MANDY. Juliet! Will you give me a pencil! Quick!
JULIET. You're going to write to a film star in America? Will he get the letter?
MANDY. Of course he will! Elvis gets all my letters!

Juliet gives pencil to Mandy and looks on as Mandy writes.

MANDY. Now! (*Slowly as she writes.*) "My dearest Elvis, Thank you for your beeeautiful wonderful photo! I'll keep it under my pillow! Please send me more photos of yourself for my scrapbook too. You're gorgeous! All my love and—a hundred kisses!"
JULIET. A hundred kisses!

Mandy puts crosses on letter.

MANDY. Yours forever!—No! Yours forever and ever and ever! Your darling Mandy! Kiss! Kiss! Kiss!
NELLIE-NORA. Your sweetheart sounds nicer!
JULIET. Maggie Brennan was writing a letter to a boy and she wrote S.W.A.L.K.—sealed with a loving kiss! Will you put that in too, Mandy?
MANDY. Yes! That's a great idea! (*Mandy writes S.W.A.L.K. She and Juliet giggle. Brigit is scornful.*)
BRIGIT. Yours until hell freezes! And now the address! Your address, Mandy? Your address?

Brigit snaps letter and reads.

BRIGIT. Saint Paul's Home for Penitent Women! Home for the unwanted. The outcasts! Saint Paul's Home for the women nobody wants!
MANDY. No, Brigit! No! Give me my letter!

Brigit and Mandy push one another, Mandy falls to floor.

BRIGIT. How do you think that sounds? What'll he think? Ha? You'd be finished with him! Finished forever and ever!

MANDY. (*Sobbing.*) No, Brigit! No address! Elvis will find me! Elvis will find his Mandy!

BRIGIT. Nobody wants you! Nobody wants any of us!

Brigit throws letter on floor. Cathy stares at Brigit. Nellie-Nora walks towards Brigit.

NELLIE-NORA. Brigit!

Brigit catches Cathy's accusing eye.

NELLIE-NORA. (*Louder.*) Brigit!

Pause.

BRIGIT. I'm sorry, Mandy! (*Pause.*) Sorry! I'm really sorry!

Juliet picks up letter and tries to comfort Mandy. Nellie-Nora lights a cigarette and offers it to Mandy, who is very distressed.

JULIET. I'll write the address for you, Mandy.

Juliet writes.

JULIET. Ireland!

Pause. Brigit moves towards basket.

BRIGIT. I've got a great idea! We'll post Mandy off to Hollywood! Come on, Mandy!
MANDY. No! No! Leave me alone, Brigit!
BRIGIT. Into this basket with you, Mandy! Give us a hand, Nellie-Nora!

Brigit opens basket and moves it down center stage.

NELLIE-NORA. Yes, Mandy! Come on!
BRIGIT. Hop in, Mandy! Now's your chance! Off to Hollywood! Come on, Cathy! We'll pack her off to the USA!

Mandy reluctantly gets into basket.

BRIGIT. Let down your hair!

Mandy unties her long hair.

MANDY. How do I look?

NELLIE-NORA. You look gorgeous! Just like a film star!

BRIGIT. Off you go! First class!

NELLIE-NORA. Watch that door, Juliet!

BRIGIT. Are you ready, Mandy?

Brigit and Nellie-Nora hum as they move the basket to and fro to the tune of "Wooden Heart."

NELLIE-NORA. Are you watching the door, Juliet?

    Juliet is more interested in business with basket.

JULIET. I am, Nellie-Nora!

Mandy twirls in basket.

MANDY. But, Brigit! Where's my Elvis?

BRIGIT. Wait a minute, Mandy! Where's our Wooden Heart Fella?

Brigit rushes upstage to mannikin. She takes off soutane and surplice, throws them on table, stands behind mannikin and walks it towards Mandy in basket.

BRIGIT. (*Elvis Voice.*) Hi there, Mandy! You sure are lookin' pretty today! (*Own voice.*) Help me, Cathy, Nellie-Nora! Help me to dress him up like a "Big Shot Film star"!

They giggle and laugh.

NELLIE-NORA. Hurry! Give us a shirt, Cathy!

MANDY. Yes! A colourdy shirt, Cathy! A gorgeous shirt for my Elvis!

Cathy moves to shelves and finds a multicoloured shirt.

CATHY. Here's a nice cotton shirt, Mandy!

MANDY. A tie! He needs a tie!

Brigit searches shelves and finds a blue tie.

MANDY. A Paris blue tie for my Elvis!

MANDY. Trousers!

Nellie-Nora finds trousers on a lower shelf.

MANDY. Oh no! Not those old trousers!

NELLIE-NORA. These are great trousers, Mandy! Hold him up and we'll put them on!

They pull on trousers and lift manikin into basket as Mandy complains.

MANDY. His head! He has no head! Elvis's head?

CATHY. Get that old head from the press,[51] Nellie-Nora!

As Brigit and Cathy button shirt and zip trousers, Nellie-Nora finds old head and puts it on mannikin.

JULIET. He's like a doll! He is!

NELLIE-NORA. Stay at that door, Juliet!

MANDY. His hair! His black shiny hair!

BRIGIT. Hair? What will we do about hair?

JULIET. Shhh! There's someone comin' down the corridor!

BRIGIT. Take her out! Quick!

CATHY. Out of the basket! Hurry, Mandy!

The women, in a state of panic, close the basket on the Elvis figure. His head protrudes. They return to work. Pause. Brigit exits towards cloister. Pause. She returns.

BRIGIT. False alarm! Come on, girls! Hair for this beautiful bachelor from Hollywood! Hurry. Take him out of the basket.

CATHY. What about a piece of Mother Victoria's winter shawl?

NELLIE-NORA. No! Mother o' God! No! Just pretend, Mandy! Pretend he has beautiful black shiny hair! Now, Mandy, back into the basket!

Mandy steps into basket. She covers her eyes with her hands.

MANDY. Yes, Nellie-Nora! Yes! Now I can see his shiny hair! And look, Cathy! His eyes! His gorgeous come-to-bed eyes!

CATHY. He has long curly eyelashes, Mandy!

They laugh.

MANDY. And lips! Big and wide!

CATHY. Smiling! A dimple in his chin!

NELLIE-NORA. And clean fingernails!

CATHY. A gold pin for his Paris blue tie!

Cathy takes a hairgrip[52] from her hair and fastens his tie.

BRIGIT. Ears! For whisperin' in!
JULIET. He's very nice, Mandy!
NELLIE-NORA. Stay at that door, Juliet!
MANDY. Yes! Isn't he a smasher, girls?
CATHY. He needs a pure silk hanky!
BRIGIT. Where's that purply hanky, Cathy: Wait a minute—here it is!

Cathy fixes silk hanky in shirt pocket.

JULIET. A pure silk hanky?
BRIGIT. Now, Mandy! Here's your Elvis!

Mandy stares at mannikin, kisses it.

MANDY. (*Sings.*)
     "Have I told you lately
     That I love you?
     Could I tell you once again somehow?
     Have I told with all my heart and soul
     That I adore you?
     Well, Darlin', I'm tellin' you now!"

Mandy hugs mannikin as she sings. Women watch her, then they return to work. Lights are rose coloured.

BRIGIT. He's askin' you to marry him, Mandy!
MANDY. I will! Oh, yes! I will!
NELLIE-NORA. I've a great idea! We'll dress Mandy for her weddin'! Hurry! Hurry! Mother o' God! He might change his mind!

Cathy takes Mandy's white apron and fastens it veil-like on her hair, then drapes a long white sheet over her shoulders as a train. Juliet helps.

CATHY. A pure white veil! A long satin train!
JULIET. You're very posh, Mandy!
NELLIE-NORA. You look gorgeous, Mandy!

MANDY. I am! I'm gorgeous!

BRIGIT. Remember! I'm the Bishop! I'll do this important wedding!

Brigit moves table to left centre, jumps on to table, and dresses in crimson soutane. She puts suplice/mitre[53] on her head, while women finish dressing Elvis. They lift Elvis into basket beside Mandy and sing:

> "Daisy, Daisy!
> Give me your answer, Do!
> I'm half crazy, all for the love of you!
> It won't be a stylish marriage.
> We can't afford a carriage
> Won't you look neat upon the seat of a
> Bicycle made for two?"

Brigit deepens her voice as she says.

BRIGIT. Silence!

The women push basket towards Bishop/Brigit. Juliet holds long train.

BRIGIT. Do you, Mandy Prenderville, take this Elvis Presley as your lawful husband to have and to hold in sickness and in health until death do you part?

MANDY. I do! Oh, yes! I do!

BRIGIT. And now, Elvis Presley, do you—

MANDY. (*Interrupts.*) But, Brigit, his real name is Elvis Aron Garon Presley!

BRIGIT. Do you, Elvis Aron Garon Presley, take Mandy Prenderville . . .

NELLIE-NORA. He does! He does!

BRIGIT. Don't interrupt, Nellie-Nora!

The women smile.

BRIGIT. Do you, Elvis Aron Garon Presley, take Mandy Prenderville as your lawful wedded wife to have and to hold in sickness and in health until death do you part?

Nellie-Nora rocks Elvis's head in assent. Cathy is in tears. Sister Virginia stands at doorway in background, but the women do not notice her.

BRIGIT. I now pronounce you man and wife. Bless you!
NELLIE-NORA, BRIGIT, AND CATHY. Congratulations, Mandy!

Mandy begins to kiss Elvis, but Brigit interrupts.

BRIGIT. You—may kiss the bride, Elvis Aron Garon Presley!

Mandy kisses Elvis. The women cheer.

NELLIE-NORA. Have as many babies as you want now, Mandy!

Sister Virginia exits.

NELLIE-NORA. A honeymoon! We'll send them on their honeymoon!
MANDY. (*Sings.*)
   "My heart would break in two
   If I should lose you
   I'm no good
   Without you anyhow!"

Mandy hugs Elvis as she sings. The women push basket in a circular movement and sing with Mandy.

   "Have I told you lately that I love you?
   Could I tell you once again somehow?
   Have I told with all my heart and soul
   How I adore you?
   Well, Darlin', I'm tellin' you now!"

Lights down as Elvis's voice comes up over women singing. Elvis sings.

   "Dear, have I told you lately
   That I love you," etc.

Continue during interval.[54]

ACT 2
SCENE 1   OFFICE 1
SOUND

Plain Chant. "Magnificat."[55] *One soprano voice.*

"Magnificat anima mea Dominum.

Et exultavit Spiritus meus.

In Deo salutary meo.

Quia respexit humilitatem ancillae suae.

Ecce enim ex hoc beatam me dicent omnes generationes.

Quia fecit mihi magna qui potens est et sanctum nomen ejus."

Small office in Convent laundry. Mother Victoria sits on high-backed chair at desk up center. Two Bibles, a telephone, keys, a crucifix, and office book on desk. A stool at right of desk. Photographs of bishops and a pope on walls. If using same set as in laundry workspace, a chair, small table with telephone, and stool will do. Lighting effects change the set. A gentle knock is heard.

MOTHER VICTORIA. Come in!

Sister Virginia enters quietly. Her veil covers her shoulders. Big Sleeves cover her arms and hands. She carries a box of Black Magic chocolates in her Big Sleeves. She kneels on floor. The phone rings. Mother Victoria answers. Plain Chant fades.

MOTHER VICTORIA. Yes!—Yes, Father! I'll hold on!—Oh!—Good morning, my Lord!—Yes!—I'm working on the ledgers now!—I should have them finished by tomorrow, my Lord!—I'll send on the cheque too!—Thank you, my Lord!

She smiles as she puts down phone.

MOTHER VICTORIA. You may sit down, Sister!

Sister Virginia remains on her knees and takes a box of Black Magic chocolates from her Big Sleeves.

SISTER VIRGINIA. Thank you, Mother Victoria! May I keep and dispose of this box of chocolates?

MOTHER VICTORIA. Chocolates? Black Magic chocolates? Mmmn? Did that seminarian give you chocolates, Sister?

SISTER VIRGINIA. Yes, Mother Victoria!

MOTHER VICTORIA. Aaam! Yes! You may dispose of them! Sit down, Sister!

Sister Virginia sits on stool.

MOTHER VICTORIA. How do you like the laundry? A change from Spiritual Year in the Novitiate, I'm sure! Are you happy? Tell me!

SISTER VIRGINIA. The work—the women—I find it difficult, Mother!

MOTHER VICTORIA. Difficult, Sister!

SISTER VIRGINIA. Yes, Mother!—It's very sad!

MOTHER VICTORIA. Sad, Sister? You find them sad?

SISTER VIRGINIA. Yes, Mother! The women need their children!—Is it really necessary to keep them locked away?

MOTHER VICTORIA. Those women can't be trusted! They're weak, Sister! No control! They've broken the sixth[56] and ninth[57] commandments!

SISTER VIRGINIA. But isn't our God a loving Father, a forgiving Father? The men, who made them pregnant, broke the same commandments!

Mother Victoria stands and walks around office.

MOTHER VICTORIA. Men? You don't understand, Sister! No one wants those women! We protect them from their passions! We give them food, shelter, and clothing! We look after their spiritual needs!

SISTER VIRGINIA. They need medicines—vitamins, fresh air, sunshine!—Cathy's asthma! The attacks are more frequent! Brigit mourns the baby she gave up for adoption! She's a bitter woman! The others are . . .

MOTHER VICTORIA. Well, Sister?

SISTER VIRGINIA. Cathy has a constant headache, Mother Victoria.

MOTHER VICTORIA. Headache, Sister?

SISTER VIRGINIA. Cathy told me—you hit her around the head, when the van men brought her back yesterday.

MOTHER VICTORIA. Cathy was hysterical! I had to slap her—to—bring her back to reality!

SISTER VIRGINIA. I'm very worried about her. She needs help. She's very low in spirits.

MOTHER VICTORIA. Custody of the eyes. You forget yourself, Sister! You are preparing to take vows! A vow of obedience! I know Cathy's tricks! She's a bit of an actress! She exaggerates! Give her a tonic! A spoonful three times a day. It'll build her up.

Mother Victoria stands in shadows behind chair.

MOTHER VICTORIA. When I was nineteen, I had the same thoughts! I wanted to free the penitents—mothers of some of the women in the laundry now. You see, this weakness to sins of the flesh stays in the blood for seven generations! When you take vows, Sister, you'll receive grace and understanding. Keep aloof from those fallen women! St. Paul says, "People who do wrong will not inherit the Kingdom of Heaven.—People of immoral lives—fornicators, adulterers."

SISTER VIRGINIA. But St. Paul hated women!—Christ had many women friends!

MOTHER VICTORIA. St. Paul, Sister! St. Paul may have been afraid of women! Women tempt men! Remember the Garden! Eve started it all!

SISTER VIRGINIA. Eve? The Garden, Mother?

MOTHER VICTORIA. Don't interrupt, Sister! Those women can be treacherous! I warn you to be careful in the laundry!

SISTER VIRGINIA. They won't harm me, Mother Victoria!

MOTHER VICTORIA. Just be careful, when Brigit is using bleach! Sister Luke has permanent scars on her face and hands!

SISTER VIRGINIA. If I were Brigit or Cathy and my babies were taken from me, I'd tear down the walls with my nails!

Interrupted.

MOTHER VICTORIA. Calm yourself, Sister! Calm! Wisdom will be given to you! Grace to do God's will. God's ways are not our ways! I'll pray for you!

Mother Victoria sits at desk and faces Sister Virginia.

MOTHER VICTORIA. Have you been meditating properly, Sister?

SISTER VIRGINIA. I try, Mother! But there are dark—dark clouds— doubts, Mother! The women are drudges, are bondwomen! I—I didn't expect this!

MOTHER VICTORIA. Doubts, Sister! We all go through those dark nights!—
Dark nights! Try to remember that we are eclipsed! But that deep inside there is a shining that is immortal—a part of us, which is outside
time. Hold on to that thought! Do not question the system! You want to
change the rule, the Church, the world! You must start with yourself!
Change yourself first! Get rid of pride! Obey the rule, Sister! Remember—we are eclipsed. But blind obedience[58] will carry you through!

SISTER VIRGINIA. But, Mother Victoria!—Thank you, Mother!—I'll—I'll
try!

*Sister Virginia leaves office as lights change. Plain Chant "Magnificat" sung by
one soprano voice. Magnificat continued.*

"Fecit potentiam in bracchio suo:
dispersit superbos mente cordis sui.
Deposuit potentes de sede et exaltavit humiles.
Esurientes implevit bonis: et divites dimisit inanes.
Suscepit Israel puerum suum, recordatus
Misericordiae suae."[59]

Fade to machine sounds.

SCENE 2 FLOOR

*Machine sound up. Enter Cathy, Nellie-Nora, Brigit, Mandy, and Sister Virginia to
set of Office 1. Table up left. Nellie-Nora places large dustbin[60] center stage. Mandy
and Brigit exit with chair and stool. They return immediately with sweeping
brushes, polishing cloths. Sister Virginia pins back her veil and hooks up her skirt.
Cathy brings on old wooden polishing blocks[61] and tin of polish. Mandy washes
floor upstage with mop and bucket of water. Sister Virginia stands and watches.*

BRIGIT. It'd take more than soap and water to clean up this place!

*The women sweep floor rhythmically. Cathy has attack of coughing. Cathy takes
a polishing block.*

CATHY. We need a machine for polishing instead of these old wooden
blocks, Sister!

BRIGIT. We're the machines, Cathy!

SISTER VIRGINIA. I'll speak to Mother Victoria about new equipment, Cathy!

Cathy tries to use heavy polishing block, but continues to cough. Sister Virginia takes block from Cathy and polishes down left beside Brigit. Nellie-Nora sweeps up right.

SISTER VIRGINIA. Take a rest, Cathy!

Cathy sits on table up left. Church bell rings.

BRIGIT. The prayer bell, Sister! Shouldn't you be on your knees in the chapel instead of in here?

SISTER VIRGINIA. To work is to pray, Brigit!

BRIGIT. We'll go straight up so. Won't we?

After prayer bell is heard, the rhythm of sweeping and polishing changes to rhythm of a tune, which Cathy is humming, "The Irish Washerwoman." She uses tabletop or washboard as bodhran[62] (percussion). Lighting changes to warmer tones.

BRIGIT. Work! Work! Work! Work is God here! Washing, scrubbing, washing, scrubbing, scrubbing, labouring! (*Rhythmically as she polishes.*)

NELLIE-NORA. Cigarette! Where did I put the matches?

No answer.

JULIET. Where will I put the dust?

No answer. Nellie-Nora lights cigarette butt. Puffs of smoke. Mandy kneels down center, presses a polishing cloth to her nose.

MANDY. Oomn! I love perfumy wax. Look! It's getting nice and shiny! Like a dance-hall floor! Look!

Mandy begins to waltz-dance as Cathy hums. Others polish and brush to rhythm of Cathy's humming, which now grows slightly faster.

MANDY. Ahh, but no fellas!

BRIGIT. No fellas! No trouble you mean! Do you hear me, Mandy?

MANDY. Still—nice trouble, Brigit!

Brigit takes Mandy's polishing cloth, stands behind dustbin facing audience. Crimson highlight on dustbin.

BRIGIT. Into the bin goes Mandy! (*Throws cloth into bin.*)

Others continue to polish-sweep.

BRIGIT. Bin gobbles her up!

She takes Cathy's cloth and throws it in.

BRIGIT. Bin gobbles up Cathy! Look at the smoke and flames rising from his huge jaws! Bin waits for your white bones, Sister Virginia!

SISTER VIRGINIA. I'm not ready for Purgatory yet, Saint Peter! There are things I must do here first!

NELLIE-NORA. (*Chants.*) Purgatory is a place or state of punishment, where some souls suffer for a time before they can enter heaven!

BRIGIT. (*Looks into bin.*) Richard's in here, Mandy! Come on! Have a look!

MANDY. No No! No, Brigit! I don't want to see him!

Mandy continues to waltz-dance around stage. Rhythm grows faster.

BRIGIT. Hello, Mandy! Hello, Richard! It's gettin' hotter, is it? Did His Lordship arrive yet, Richard? He did! He's in there! Good! In you go, Nellie-Nora!

Brigit takes dust from Juliet and throws it into bin.

BRIGIT. Mandy and Richard are waltzin' away in the red-hot flames!

Rhythm of music grows faster. Brigit takes a brush and bangs it into bin.

BRIGIT. Ha, Mother Victoria! No! Not in here! You've to go to the other place! The hotter place! No, Mother Victoria, I've no keys! No keys for that place! Goodbye! For all eternity! Goodbye, Mother Victoria! Forever and ever!

Brigit throws in more dust and twists brush in a circular fashion. Rhythm of polishing/sweeping, singing, and Mandy's dancing grows still faster.

BRIGIT. Ha! Ha! John-Joe! Is it not hot enough for ya? No? Purgatory isn't hot enough for my John-Joe! Oh! You're thirsty? You're all thirsty down there? All we have here is dirty water! No! We've no porter or whiskey! Look, Cathy, Mandy, Nellie-Nora! They're all thirsty! Richard, John-Joe, His Lordship, your fella, Cathy! And Elvis!

Activity stops suddenly. Pause.

BRIGIT. They're all burnin' with thirst!

Sudden full sound of washing machines as women exit with brushes, polishers, and return to set up for Red Hearts scene.

SCENE 3   RED HEARTS

Brigit and Mandy move large laundry basket to position a little to right of center and at a slight angle. Basket contains bundles of unwashed linens.
    Nellie-Nora sews at table center left. Juliet to right of Nellie-Nora.
    Sewing basket containing pincushion, needles, and threads on table.

MANDY. Where's this basket from, Brigit?

BRIGIT. Athlone—you know—all around there! The middle of Ireland! Come on, Nellie-Nora! Juliet, help us with these filthy yokes! They're even worse than last week!

Juliet moves to right of Brigit and Mandy at basket. Mandy examines label on unseen side of basket.

MANDY. Do you not see the label, Brigit? This basket is not from Athlone! It's from Galway! From the city!

JULIET. From Galway? The city? But, this is a terrible job! Smellier than in the orphanage!

CATHY. Whites in the corner, Juliet! Coloureds over there! Socks in the middle!

NELLIE-NORA. Search for cigarette butts, Juliet! Don't forget trouser pockets! Mother o' God! Where did I put that last butt?—A match, Mandy! Quick!

MANDY. They're on the table, Nellie-Nora!

JULIET. Does Nellie-Nora smoke other people's cigarettes, Mandy?

MANDY. Yes! All the time, Juliet!

Nellie-Nora finds a butt and matches. She lights butt. She keeps butt between her lips as she speaks. The others continue to sort dirty linens.

NELLIE-NORA. Mmn! That's better! Doesn't this lot come from your place, Cathy? Near the sea—?

CATHY. Yes! Near the sea and the river. Though I can't smell salty seaweed!

(Turns her nose away.)

JULIET. Uuuch! Aah!

BRIGIT. Would you look! (*Holds up white underpants covered with red hearts.*) From your place, Cathy? Look! (*Brigit grabs underpants and reads.*) Made in the USA! Wouldn't you know! This fella doesn't wear his heart on his sleeve! He wears it on his Micky![63] (*Throws underpants in the air.*)

JULIET. Oh no, Brigit! No! (*Dodges underpants.*)

NELLIE-NORA. They're all below the waist!

MANDY. A smasher I'd say—a film star or an actor or—what do you think, Cathy?

Mandy throws underpants to Brigit, who throws to Cathy, and so on.

NELLIE-NORA. It's like what the Yanks[64] would wear, Cathy!

CATHY. Yes! They wear funny clothes. Plaids, spots, stripes all mixed up together! I remember when the Yanks came home, when the second cousins from Boston visited! The colours they wore on the street!

JULIET. But—I thought you were off a farm, Cathy!

NELLIE-NORA. No, Juliet! Cathy is from the city!

CATHY. (*Dreamily.*) A small city, Juliet! It's a lovely place—

Cathy takes a man's silk dressing gown from basket, touches it lovingly.

MANDY. A silk coat, Cathy? No! It's a dressing gown.

Mandy touches the silk. Cathy is in a dream.

JULIET. Why did you leave?

NELLIE-NORA. She just couldn't stay, Juliet!

MANDY. The fellas—what were they like, Cathy?

BRIGIT. What're fellas always like? A few quick ones in a pub, then crowded like jackdaws[65] at the door of a dance hall, their minds as dirty as their fingernails!

JULIET. But Sister Virginia says only a few men are like that!

BRIGIT. Sister Virginia says! What does she know about it? Squeezing through the dance-hall door was awful! When you'd be in the crush, some big hand would come out and grab you!

Cathy puts dressing gown aside carefully.

CATHY. I didn't go to dances much!

NELLIE-NORA. They were terrible at the back of the chapel and in the organ gallery! They were all the same!

BRIGIT. And they think we're the dirty ones!

JULIET. A dance! I never went to a dance! I think I'd like to go to one!

BRIGIT. Our Canon[66] stood at the back of the dance hall and watched! On Sundays he'd shout, "Company-keeping is a mortal sin! Hell for all eternity!" When Ellen Moran got pregnant, he walked up and down outside her house in broad daylight saying the rosary!

NELLIE-NORA. A curse will fall on you, Brigit! Talking like that about the Canon!

Mandy and Nellie-Nora bless themselves.[67]

BRIGIT. A curse! Don't be daft! I'm here—isn't that enough? The Canon's housekeeper bossed everyone in the parish! Bossed him too! Listened to all the gossip and gave the orders, pointing at us with her scarlet fingernails!

NELLIE-NORA. I often think about Our Lady the time she got pregnant! Did the neighbours point at her too?

Women smile.

NELLIE-NORA. She must have had a terrible time, when she began to show!

MANDY. But she had Saint Joseph! Didn't he stay with her!

NELLIE-NORA. I wonder did the neighbours whisper and sneer?

BRIGIT. Gossiping neighbours going home from Mass like holy-water hens! Bloody hypocrites! But the missioners were the worst! Hellfire and brimstone every morning and evening!

JULIET. The dances, Mandy! Tell me!

MANDY. Well, Juliet! My second cousin, Jamsie, loved women, but was afraid of courtin'. Halfway through the last dance, he'd say to his partner, "I've to go now! Early start tomorrow! I've to drive my mother to teach in the Tech."[68] He had no car of course! No mother either! All that fella had was an old crock of a bike! Poor Jamsie!

CATHY. In our city we had a glamour boy who did great business with tourists. He arranged with the ballroom porter to announce, "Dr. O'Connell is wanted urgently on the telephone! Dr. O'Connell! Dr. O'Connell," while he was dancing cheek to cheek with some gorgeous blonde! "Excuse me, my love," he'd whisper. "One of my patients is very ill. I must check! I'll be back! Wait for me!" Success! The "doctor" bit never failed! They'd be waiting for him when he came back after his pint in a pub down the road! Believing every word!

BRIGIT. Johnnie in Cillnamona! Mirrors on the tops of his dancing shoes!

JULIET. Mirrors on his dancing shoes? But why, Brigit?

Brigit comes forward, calls Juliet and demonstrates Johnnie's antics.

BRIGIT. You see Juliet! When Johnnie was dancing with a girl, he . . .

Brigit dances and sings.

"Oh Johnnie! Oh, Johnnie!
Heavens above!
Oh, Johnnie! Oh, Johnnie!
How you can love!"
A bell rings. A door bangs.

JULIET. Shh! She's coming!

Nellie-Nora goes to exit and listens to bell. Bn. Bn.—Bn. Bn Bn.

NELLIE-NORA. That's Sister Virginia's bell! Mother Victoria's gone to his Lordship's Palace!

BRIGIT. Virginia! That piece of plaster!

CATHY. Aah, Brigit! I often wonder why Sister Virginia wants to be a nun!

BRIGIT. She's probably afraid of men! Thinks it's easier to hide in here? But watch her! Soon she'll be strutting around like the others, waving her leather belt and treating us like dirt!

NELLIE-NORA. No Brigit! You're too hard on her!

CATHY. But she doesn't have to stay in here! She's not afraid of men, Brigit! Priests and seminarians come to visit her!

NELLIE-NORA. She can leave anytime she wants!

BRIGIT. Sounds daft to me, Cathy! Staying in this dungeon with that cage on her head! How can she think straight?

JULIET. I think I'd like to be a nun!

CATHY. Well, you can't go to dances if you're a nun, Juliet!

NELLIE-NORA. I think you'd make a lovely nun!

BRIGIT. Sure, they wouldn't have Juliet! Her mother was one of us!

Stunned silence, as they continue to sort dirty clothes.

JULIET. Another cigarette butt, Nellie-Nora! Look! Oh no! It's not! Look what I found!

MANDY. Show me! Ooh! It's lipstick! Ooh! Lipstick!

BRIGIT. In a trouser pocket!

MANDY. Look! "Outdoor Girl!"—rose red—Mmmn! Where's the mirror, Nellie-Nora?

NELLIE-NORA. Here, Mandy!

MANDY. Will you get the mirror, Juliet!

Juliet takes mirror, gives it to Mandy. Mandy pouts as she puts on lipstick. Brigit takes lipstick and puts two spots, (rouge) on Mandy. Mandy decorates Brigit. They laugh and joke. Cathy and Juliet crowd around them. Brigit looks in mirror.

BRIGIT. Ach! Look at the cut o' me! You're like an Indian, Mandy! Rub it in! Like this!

Mandy and Brigit rub one another's cheeks. They laugh, but Nellie-Nora remains detached.

MANDY. Mmn! It tastes nice and perfumy!—How do I look?

CATHY. You're gorgeous, Mandy! If only Elvis could see you now!

Mandy prints her lips on hands.

BRIGIT. Now I'll paint you, Cathy.
CATHY. Can I do it myself, Brigit? Please?

Brigit gives Cathy lipstick. Cathy paints her lips.

JULIET. Will you put some on me, Cathy?
CATHY. Of course, Juliet! Stand here!

Cathy paints Juliet's lips.

BRIGIT. It suits your eyes, Juliet!
JULIET. My eyes?
MANDY. Don't heed her, Juliet!

Brigit takes lipstick from Cathy and moves towards Nellie-Nora.

BRIGIT. Come on, Nellie-Nora! A bit o' war paint for you! It'll cheer you
    up!
NELLIE-NORA. No! Oh no!

Brigit insists.

NELLIE-NORA. Noooo! Not lipstick!

Nellie-Nora screams, wipes her lips and backs away. Brigit is upset. The others stare. Nellie-Nora is very agitated. Pause.

NELLIE-NORA. He—he—made me wear lipstick—and perfume. He—
    wanted me to be like a city girl.—No! No! He—he—in the room—No!
    No, Mr. Persse! No!—Before he—he hurt me! He wet me! No! No!

Nellie-Nora takes sewing basket from table and throws it to floor.

NELLIE-NORA. It's all your fault! All your fault!

Nellie-Nora falls to floor. She hugs her knees then starts to rock her body. Sister Virginia enters carrying a box of Black Magic chocolates. She rushes to assist Nellie-Nora.

SISTER VIRGINIA. Now, what have you done, Brigit?

BRIGIT. Nothing, Sister!

JULIET. It's only lipstick, Sister!

MANDY. Rose red lipstick. A bit o' colour, Sister!

BRIGIT. It's this place! This dungeon! This cage! And you, Sister! Locking us up with your two sets o' keys!

SISTER VIRGINIA. I've chocolates here, Nellie-Nora! Take some!

NELLIE-NORA. Get away from me!

SISTER VIRGINIA. Here, Cathy! Mandy! Chocolates! Juliet?

The women refuse chocolates.

BRIGIT. Chocolates! Hhh! Keep your bloody chocolates. The keys, Pasty Face! Give me the keys!

SISTER VIRGINIA. I—I can't! You know I can't give you the keys, Brigit!

BRIGIT. (*Imitating Sister.*) "You know I can't give you the keys. Brigit! I'll pray for you Brigit!"

Brigit blocks escape route.

BRIGIT. Pretending to help! You're just like the rest o' them! You think if you keep us locked up, that we'll forget about living! About being alive! Don't you? That our heads will go soft and mushy from hymns and prayers! You think that we won't see what your crowd is up to! Well, Pasty Face! Brigit Murphy here sees through you! Sees through the whole lot o' you! Mother Superiors, bishops, popes, and all!

Sister Virginia fingers her rosary beads. Brigit approaches her.

BRIGIT. Look at yourself, Pasty Face! You're a woman—aren't you? Did you ever have a lover? Tell us that now, Sister! Ha?—Would you like a bit o' lipstick, Sister?

Brigit holds lipstick menacingly. The women move away. Sister Virginia tries to escape, but Brigit pins her against the wall.

BRIGIT. You don't know anything! Never had a lover! Never had a baby! So you're white and shining, Sister! Not the same as us, are you? Whose side are you on anyways? Why aren't our lover-boys locked

up too? One law for them and another for us? Scab![69] Spy! I'll daub it
on the walls of hell!

Brigit scribbles, "Scab" on wall with lipstick, as she struggles with Sister Virginia. She drags off Sister Virginia's veil and shouts.

BRIGIT. I'll daub it on your baldy skull! Scab! Spy! Informer!

She throws Sister Virginia to the floor. Sister Virginia falls on top of soiled linens. Juliet sits on floor and bites her nails. Mandy hides behind basket. Nellie-Nora sobs and rocks her body.

BRIGIT. (*Change of tone.*) All sweet smiles and "Here's chocolates"! But
you're as bad as the rest! You're young and you keep the keys! Stiff
and starched you go back every night to your nice white bed in your
nice white cell! You say your nice sweet prayers to your nice clean
God! Prayers and hymns and heaven when we die! No! No! NO! Now
is what matters! We're alive now! It's no use when we're dead! We
want to live now!
SISTER VIRGINIA. But I want to help, Brigit! I am on your side!
BRIGIT. No! You're not! I'd kill you, but you're not worth it!

Brigit throws lipstick at Sister Virginia, takes box of chocolates and throws contents on top of Sister Virginia. She moves towards basket. Sister Virginia gets up slowly, tries to smooth her habit, then, with dignity, walks through exit. Her white coif/veil is on floor downstage. Brigit stands at basket.

BRIGIT. Rosa! Rosa! (*Second "Rosa" a keening[70] scream.*)

Pause. Mandy peeps out from behind basket, finds scattered chocolates, eats one and puts some in pocket of her apron.

MANDY. She'll tell Mother Victoria on us!
CATHY. No. She mightn't tell. Sister Virginia mightn't! But we'll have to
clean up the wall. Quick, Mandy! Get a bucket of hot water and a
bottle of bleach. Hurry, Mandy!

Mandy exits. Cathy tries to clean off lipstick from wall. Brigit hurriedly throws some clothes from basket. Visual rhythm of clothes thrown high in the air.

BRIGIT. I'm going out now! In the basket! Come on! Quick! Help me!

Cathy turns as Brigit speaks. Mandy returns with bucket.

MANDY. I put half a bottle of bleach in, Cathy.

Brigit steps into basket and kneels as she tries to cover herself with clothes.

BRIGIT. I'm goin' out now to find my baby, Rosa. Cover me with clothes and push me into despatch![71] Quick! Stop staring at me! Help me!

Cathy moves to Brigit.

CATHY. But, Brigit! I wanted to! Please, Brigit, let me come with you! I'm so long trying!
BRIGIT. No! I'm going to find my Rosa!
CATHY. My twins, Brigit! Please!
BRIGIT. (*Screams.*) No! I'm going alone now!
CATHY. (*Screams.*) My Emily! My Michele!

Brigit tries to close basket. Cathy is hyperventilating. Mother Victoria enters, looks at writing on wall and walks around slowly as she speaks.

MOTHER VICTORIA. What's all this about? Get out of that basket, Brigit! Stand up, Nellie-Nora! Stop that sniveling, Cathy McNamara! Back to work immediately, Mandy! You too, Juliet—Where's Sister Virginia! Why isn't she here? Why?

Brigit steps out of basket. The others obey automatically. As Mother Victoria exits, she sees Sister Virginia's veil/coif on floor. She picks it up. The stiffly starched empty veil/coif held on high by Mother Victoria looks like a head trophy. She turns to Brigit.

MOTHER VICTORIA. What's this, Brigit? This?—To my office immediately, Brigit Murphy! His Lordship will hear about you.
BRIGIT. No! No! I'm not going!
MOTHER VICTORIA. (*Shouts.*) To my office now, Brigit Murphy!

Brigit walks reluctantly in front of Mother Victoria towards exit.

MOTHER VICTORIA. I always knew you were an evil woman!

Cathy gets idea of going out alone in basket. She waits until Mother Victoria has gone.

CATHY. (*Excitedly.*) I can go now! Me! Help me, Mandy! Please, Nellie-Nora!

Cathy steps into basket. Nellie-Nora moves to help her.

CATHY. Cover me! Will you help me, Juliet? Hurry! Hurry!
NELLIE-NORA. Are you sure, Cathy? Are you alright?

They cover Cathy with bundles of clothes. Nellie-Nora places a purple drape on top.

CATHY. Hurry! Please! Hurry! The van will be gone!
MANDY. We'll be thinking of you, Cathy!

They close basket. Nellie-Nora opens basket to say.

NELLIE-NORA. Have you that holy medal I gave you?
CATHY. Hurry! Hurry!

They close basket, fasten metal locks and push it hurriedly through exit. Lights lower. Pause. Mandy, Brigit, and Nellie-Nora return to set up Act 2 Scene 4 Office 2. Sound for Plain Chant "Magnificat" sung by one soprano voice.

SCENE 4   OFFICE 2

Set as in Office 1 may be used, but a small table with telephone a little to the left of centre is sufficient. Lights down except for highlight on Mother Victoria, who is standing centre stage. She taps her office book with crucifix. Plain Chant "Magnificat" sung by one soprano voice as in Act 2 Scene 1. Plain Chant fades as Sister Virginia stands at door of office.

MOTHER VICTORIA. Come in!

Sister Virginia enters, pauses.

MOTHER VICTORIA. What delayed you, Sister?—On your knees!

Sister Virginia hesitates.

MOTHER VICTORIA. On your knees, Sister!

Sister Virginia kneels, head bowed, then looks straight at Mother Victoria.

MOTHER VICTORIA. I told you to keep aloof from those women! I warned you about Brigit Murphy!

SISTER VIRGINIA. But they are our Sisters in Christ, Mother Victoria.

MOTHER VICTORIA. Our Sisters!

SISTER VIRGINIA. Yes, Mother Victoria! Part of His Mystical Body!

MOTHER VICTORIA. You are lucky you are not scarred for life!

SISTER VIRGINIA. We are scarred! We, their jailers!

MOTHER VICTORIA. Scarred! You disobeyed me again, Sister!

Takes open letter from office book and pushes it towards Sister Virginia.

MOTHER VICTORIA. This letter! Sealed without my permission!

Pause.

SISTER VIRGINIA. Yes, Mother Victoria! His Lordship should come to this laundry! He should see things as they really are!

MOTHER VICTORIA. His Lordship, the bishop, in that laundry talking to—those—those—sinful women!

SISTER VIRGINIA. Yes, Mother Victoria!

Sister Virginia stands.

MOTHER VICTORIA. On your knees, Sister!

Sister Virginia kneels.

MOTHER VICTORIA. (*Reads letter.*) "My Lord Bishop, as you are patron of this laundry, I invite you to visit us at our workplace. You should see and speak to the mothers, who are locked in here. Out of the goodness of your heart, you will, I am sure, allow them weekly visits to the orphanage. Their conditions of work and diet need to be improved immediately. Because of the deterioration in the health of a woman called Cathy McNamara, I beg you to come before you leave for Rome. I am, my Lord, your obedient and humble servant, Sister Virginia O'Brien."

Pause.

MOTHER VICTORIA. Why didn't you give me this letter before you sealed it? Why?

Sister stands.

MOTHER VICTORIA. On your knees!

Pause. Sister kneels.

SISTER VIRGINIA. You'd quote rules, Mother Victoria! You'd . . .

MOTHER VICTORIA. (*Interrupts.*) During my thirty years in this community. I've never come across such—such impudence! A white novice takes it on herself to invite that holy man to visit those—those—!

She crumples letter and throws it to floor.

SISTER VIRGINIA. Permission to say more, Mother Victoria?

MOTHER VICTORIA. More to say, Sister Virginia? Is that seminarian putting the ideas into your head?

SISTER VIRGINIA. I can think for myself, Mother Victoria!

Telephone rings. Mother Victoria answers as she points her hand to silence Sister Virginia.

MOTHER VICTORIA. (*Softly.*) Hellooouuu! Yeees! (*Sharper tone.*) Oh, Sister Perpetuo!—Ring the Mass bell now!—And breakfast for that missionary priest in the small parlour! Tea and toast will do him!

Mother Victoria bangs down the telephone.

SISTER VIRGINIA. Maybe I should write to His Holiness!

MOTHER VICTORIA. Did you say something, Sister Virginia?

A Mass bell rings.

SISTER VIRGINIA. I must write to His Holiness! It takes a long time for news of change to reach this island, this laundry!

Pause. Mother Victoria straightens her back.

MOTHER VICTORIA. Now I have something to say to you, Sister Virginia O'Brien! Your brother, Father John, is saying Mass in the side chapel! (*Sister Virginia stands up.*) On your knees, Sister! (*Slowly Sister kneels.*) He has asked for you from the altar! Imagine! From God's holy altar!

SISTER VIRGINIA. Permission, please, to serve my brother's Mass!

MOTHER VICTORIA. No! You may not serve his Mass! No! You may not speak to him afterwards!

SISTER VIRGINIA. But I must see my brother! I must speak to him!

MOTHER VICTORIA. No, sister! You may not see him!

SISTER VIRGINIA. I must speak to him! I must! I must speak!

MOTHER VICTORIA. Back to the laundry! Now! Remember blind obedience, Sister Virginia O'Brien! Blind obedience!

Sister Virginia rises from her knees and leaves office. Pause. Mother Victoria picks up crumpled letter, looks at it and says.

MOTHER VICTORIA. A white novice says she'll write to His Holiness! (*Puzzled and worried.*) My Lord Bishop, what is happening to our Holy Church?

Mother Victoria turns and leaves office. Lights change.
   Sound. Plain Chant "Magnificat" as women set up for Act 2 Scene 5.

SCENE 5   DISCOVERY

Low hum of washing machines. Afternoon of next day. Same workroom set. Nellie-Nora and Mandy sew at table centre left. Laundry basket up right. Brigit scrubs at washboard centre right. Folded sheets and blankets on shelves.

NELLIE-NORA. Such a hullabaloo last night! Aach! Must be a lot o' sore heads this morning!

MANDY. I couldn't sleep!

NELLIE-NORA. One fella kept shoutin', "Goodnight, Reverend Mother! Sweet dreams, Reverend Mother! Sleep tight! Don't let the fleas bite, Reverend Mother!

BRIGIT. I wonder if the fellas from Cillnamona were up! Dark suits over farmer tans! Pioneer pins[72] pushed under lapels, foolin' their mothers!

MANDY. I heard the drums and the saxophones. But why didn't they play Elvis's music?

Mandy breaks down in tears.

NELLIE-NORA. I couldn't sleep either, wonderin' about Cathy! Aach, don't cry, Mandy! What's the use? There's broken hearts out there too! Elvis'll send you another photo! He'll write to you! He will!

Nellie-Nora gives Mandy her Elvis scrapbook.

MANDY. (*Change of tone.*) No! He won't! I know he won't! (*Mandy throws scrapbook onto floor.*) My only chance is to do what Cathy did! Would she be there now?

NELLIE-NORA. She should be! Mother o' God, she should!

Nellie-Nora picks up scrapbook and puts it on table near Mandy. Mandy pushes it away.

BRIGIT. Mother Victoria can't drag her back this time! The Black Viper threatened the Big House[73] on me! She's the one that should be in there! Power mad! Money mad! More-money-for-the-bishop mad!

MANDY. Puttin' poor Juliet back in the orphanage!

BRIGIT. The rip says we're bad company for a young girl!—Ugh! They're all the same! Virginia! Victoria!

NELLIE-NORA. Poor Sister Virginia! She didn't tell!

MANDY. Yes, Brigit! She didn't tell on us!

BRIGIT. Hasn't she two eyes? Two ears? Can't she see what's going on?

Enter Sister Virginia carrying broken sunflowers. Daisy-like flowers if sunflowers not available. She notices Mandy's distress.

SISTER VIRGINIA. Put these in water, Mandy. Please.

BRIGIT. Flowers here? Flowers from the sun? No, Sister! Keys!

Mandy takes flowers and proceeds to pull petals away one by one as she says.

MANDY. "He loves me! He loves me not. He loves me. He loves me not."

Mandy repeats this chant as she tears flowers and stalks into fragments, throws them on floor and stamps on them, picks them up and tears them apart.

SISTER VIRGINIA. Where's Cathy?—Is she in the steamroom?

Sister Virginia looks into side rooms and returns.

SISTER VIRGINIA. Have you seen her, Mandy?
NELLIE-NORA. No, Sister!
SISTER VIRGINIA. Brigit?

No response from Brigit.

NELLIE-NORA. But sure, you were in the kitchen all mornin', Sister! How could we?

Sister Virginia notices blankets on shelf.

SISTER VIRGINIA. Those blankets should have gone in the Athlone basket! Will you parcel them, Brigit? Put a label on them?

No response from Brigit.

SISTER VIRGINIA. I'll do it myself!—Maybe Cathy is sick! Where could she be?—Maybe—I must speak to Mother Victoria!

A bell tolls. Keys rattle. Mother Victoria enters, walks slowly to Sister Virginia and whispers. She offers overall to Sister Virginia, who refuses to take it. The women pretend to work. Mother Victoria turns to women, puts apron on table and moves down centre.

MOTHER VICTORIA. I . . . I . . . We must all pray now. We must pray for Cathy!
BRIGIT. She got to Galway? She did?
NELLIE-NORA. What's wrong, Mother?
MANDY. Did she get the twins? Tell us, Mother!
SISTER VIRGINIA. In the basket! May she rest in peace!
BRIGIT. Rest in peace? Cathy? No! No!
MANDY. Cathy? She got out? She's outside! She got to Galway!
SISTER VIRGINIA. They found her in the basket! Her asthma!
NELLIE-NORA. It's a mistake, Sister! It's not our Cathy! No! No!
MOTHER VICTORIA. We must pray!

Sister Virginia confronts Mother Victoria.

SISTER VIRGINIA. Her asthma, Mother! Cathy suffocated! I told you she needed attention! Her attacks were . . .

MOTHER VICTORIA. It was an accidental death! We must pray for her soul! The first sorrowful mystery.[74] The Agony in the Garden. Our Father who art in heaven. Hallowed be Thy name. Thy Kingdom come. Thy will be done on earth.

Brigit and Nellie-Nora walk around in a confused state. Nellie-Nora calls out Cathy's name. Mandy, kneeling and holding broken flowers, moves from Mother Victoria to Sister Virginia.

BRIGIT. I should have gone! I was goin' first! I wouldn't have suffocated!

NELLIE-NORA. No! No, Brigit! I should've stopped her!—No! It's a mistake! It's somebody else! It's not our Cathy!

MOTHER VICTORIA. Thy will be done on earth as it is in heaven. Give us this day our daily bread and (*Small bell rings.*) forgive us our trespasses as we forgive those who trespass against us. And lead us not into temptation but deliver us from evil. Finish the prayers, Sister Virginia! My bell calls.

NELLIE-NORA. Amen!

SISTER VIRGINIA. Yes, Mother Victoria. Hail Mary full of grace! The Lord is with Thee. Blessed art Thou amongst women and blessed is the fruit of Thy womb, Jesus.

Mandy and Nellie-Nora sob and contradict one another. Brigit moves and stands menacingly behind Sister Virginia.

BRIGIT. The keys, Sister! You'll give us the keys! We'll get out now! Won't we, Sister?

SISTER VIRGINIA. Pray, Brigit! We must pray for Cathy! Hail Mary, full of grace. The Lord is with Thee. Blessed art Thou amongst women and blessed is the fruit of Thy womb, Jesus!

Sister Virginia turns to face Brigit. They stare at one another. Pause. Sister Virginia unclips keys from her belt and praying "Holy Mary, Mother of God," etc., gives keys to Brigit. Brigit grabs them.

BRIGIT. Ye're the ones that are dead, Virginia! Dead inside yer laundry basket hearts!

Shouts as she runs through audience and away.

BRIGIT. Yer laundry basket hearts!

Sister Virginia, praying softly, moves upstage to wall. Mandy prays "Hail Mary" and "Holy Mary Mother of God, pray for us sinners now and at the hour of our death" continuously, distractedly, as she washes clothing in basin. Lights lower.

SOUND. (*Voice of Kathleen Ferrier.*)
>"He was despised.
>Despised and rejected.
>Rejected of men.
>A man of sorrows.
>A man of sorrows.
>And acquainted with grief."

As Nellie-Nora in slow movement takes purple drapes from shelves and covers/ shrouds Mandy, Sister Virginia, and table. She puts Cathy's apron into basket and moves it down left. (Same position as in Act 1 Scene 1.) She slowly looks around laundry space and exits. Sound up of "He was despised."
> *Straight into Act 2 Scene 6.*

SCENE 6 EPILOGUE

Lights low after Act 2, Scene 5. Voice of Kathleen Ferrier.

>"He was despised.
>Despised and rejected.
>Rejected of men.
>A man of sorrows.
>A man of sorrows
>And acquainted with grief."
>*From Handel's "Messiah."*

Set as in Act 1 Scene 1, but drapes are not hanging. Rosa, carrying laundry register and Black Magic box, enters and moves downstage to laundry basket. Mandy and Sister Virginia shrouded-frozen in purple drapes. Highlight comes up on basket. Music fades as Nellie-Nora (aged) shuffles on. (Dragged-slipper sound.)

NELLIE-NORA. Did you find what you were looking for, Rosa?

ROSA. Brigit Murphy and a girl, Rosa? Nellie-Nora? Yes! And this photograph, "My baby, Rosa." Is this me?

Rosa shows photograph to Nellie-Nora. Nellie-Nora examines it.

NELLIE-NORA. Ah Rosa, that's just a photograph she found in an unwashed pocket! Brigit adopted that paper baby.[75] She let on it was you!

ROSA. So—It's not—me. A paper baby? She called me Rosa! Everyone calls me Caroline!—But why, Nellie-Nora, why did she ever come here?

NELLIE-NORA. Brigit was put in here! Her brother signed her in before he got married! When Cathy died, she disappeared. Not a word, not a trace of her since!

ROSA. Where did she go?

NELLIE-NORA. I don't know, Rosa! Maybe she went back to Cillnamona—to try to see John-Joe!

ROSA. John-Joe? Is he my father? Do you know his last name, his address?

NELLIE-NORA. No, Rosa! She only ever called him John-Joe! He must live near Cillnamona!

ROSA. Do you think he's still there? Do you think she's alive?

NELLIE-NORA. I don't know, Rosa.

ROSA. Would you have heard if—

NELLIE-NORA. I don't know! After Saint Paul's closed that time, none of the women ever came back to visit! I suppose they wanted to forget this place.

ROSA. I must go to Cillnamona tomorrow!

Rosa moves nearer to Nellie-Nora.

ROSA. Did Brigit talk about—going—to look for me?

NELLIE-NORA. She always wanted to find you, Rosa! It broke her heart giving you up like that. You can be certain she tried! You can be certain she spent the rest of her life lookin' for you!

ROSA. Can I take these? (*Black Magic box with photographs and ledger.*) Would anybody mind? And the paper baby too?

NELLIE-NORA. Yes, Rosa! I don't think anyone knows they're still here.

Rosa moves closer to Nellie-Nora.

ROSA. Maybe I'll call to see you again,—if that's alright?

NELLIE-NORA. Yes, Rosa! That'd be nice.

ROSA. Would you like to visit us at Shannon, Nellie-Nora? I'll collect you myself in the car?

NELLIE-NORA. (*Shaking.*) No! No, Rosa! I—I—I don't go out much.

Nellie-Nora, head shaking and hand in tremor, turns away and crumples towards basket. Rosa looks at her for a moment, then hurries away into audience. Nellie-Nora suddenly looks out towards Rosa, then takes a long look at the old laundry workspace, as sound of Kathleen Ferrier's voice comes up.

> "Despised, rejected.
> Rejected of men.
> A man of sorrows.
> A man of sorrows.
> And acquainted with grief."

Nellie-Nora shuffles dragged-slipper sound to lightswitch on wall. As she switches off light, fade music, lower lights.

VOICE-OVER. (*Sister Virginia.*) In 1992, to make place for a building development at St. Paul's Home, the remains of Mary Kate Dempsey, Mary Jane O'Sullivan, Kitty O'Hara, Julia Mannion, Betty and Annie Gormley, Ellen McAuley, Cathy McNamera, and three hundred other unnamed penitents were exhumed, cremated, and reburied outside in Killmacha Cemetery. Mandy Prenderville has not left the local mental institution since 1963.

THE END

Notes

1. Patrick Lonergan, rear jacket notes for Patricia Burke Brogan, *Requiem of Love* (Galway: Wordsonthestreet, 2006).

2. novice: A person who has entered a religious order, is under probation before taking final vows, and wears a white veil rather than a black one.

3. purple drapes: In Catholic liturgical tradition, purple material is draped over statues, crucifixes, etc. in a church during times of penance, such as Lent.

4. Morning Call: A nun had charge of calling the community at 6 a.m., knocking at each cell door and calling out, "Benedicamus Domino!" while ringing a small bell. Each nun would then answer "Deo Gratias" from her cell.

5. overalls: Loose-fitting garments worn over ordinary clothes for protection.

6. Kathleen Ferrier (1912–1953): A renowned English concert and operatic contralto who suffered an unfortunately early death from cancer.

7. dragging-slipper walk: The way an older person often walks in floppy old slippers without lifting their feet properly.

8. torch: Flashlight.

9. St. Brigit's Cross: A woven cross with three or four legs, symbol of St. Brigit, one of the three patron saints of Ireland. The St. Brigit's Cross is a symbol of truth and it protects one's home from evil.

10. Burke Brogan wants productions to localize Rosa's origins. Babies of the Magdalene women ended up in England, Ireland, and the United States. For production purposes, Burke Brogan suggests choosing a more local city (e.g., Boston, New York, Los Angeles, etc.) and changing the flight time to an appropriate length.

11. Black Magic: A British-Irish brand of assorted chocolates.

12. Rem.: Abbreviation for "remember," as written on the back of the photo.

13. Cillnamona: Brogan invented this name, since she wanted Brigit's home place to be connected to the country, close to a bog. "Cill" in Irish means church; "na mona" means of the bog where turf was cut for lighting fires. Irish bogs are the source of many treasures; hoards of precious chalices and manuscripts are still being found in bogs.

14. Killmacha: Brogan invented this name; from "cill," which is Irish for church, and "Macha," who was a Celtic warrior goddess.

15. Benedicamus Domino: "Let us bless the Lord."

16. Deo Gratias: "Thanks be to God."

17. cell: A small room in which a nun or monk lives.

18. soutane: A type of cassock worn by Roman Catholic priests.

19. surplice: A loose white linen robe worn over a cassock by clergy.

20. For production purposes, permission rights must be secured in order either to sing any of the Elvis songs and other popular music in this script or to play recordings of them during performance.

21. linen: Tablecloths, sheets, handkerchiefs, shirts, and possibly underwear.

22. lorry-load: Truckload.

23. puncture: Flat tire.

24. smasher: A very attractive or impressive person.

25. Carrickmacross lace: Exceptionally fine, hand-made Irish lace.

26. rip: A term of derision, that is, a nasty woman.

27. crozier: A hooked staff carried by a bishop.

28. bog accents: Country, rustic.

29. tenner: A ten-pound note.

30. Athlone: A town on the River Shannon close to the geographic center of Ireland, bordering both County Westmeath and County Roscommon.

31. love hearts: A piece of candy.

32. sultanas: Raisins.

33. griskeens: Pork fillets.

34. black pudding: Blood sausage, part of a traditional Irish breakfast.

35. Maynooth: Site of one of the famous Irish Roman Catholic seminaries.

36. hedge tear: A tear from some bushes.

37. football: Soccer.

38. hurling: Irish game similar to field hockey.

39. camogie: A popular competitive team sport for Irish girls, played with sticks, a ball, and goalposts; the woman's variant of hurling.

40. custody of the eyes: A practiced regimen in which the nuns train their eyes downward and avoid eye contact with others, lest they become distracted from their meditative state.

41. outerskirt: Long skirt of a nun's black serge habit, pleated, worn over another lighter skirt.

42. Big Sleeves: Detachable wide funnel-shaped sleeves that were worn over a nun's habit sleeves in chapel, when seeing visitors in the parlor, and on public occasions.

43. Rosary: A Roman Catholic prayer devotion in which five or fifteen sets of ten Hail Marys are repeated; a string of beads for keeping count in such a devotion.

44. decade: A group of ten Hail Marys in a rosary.

45. office: The Divine Office, a series of services of prayers and psalms said daily by Roman Catholic priests, nuns, and other clergy.

46. Angelus: A Roman Catholic prayer devotion commemorating the Incarnation of Jesus and including the Hail Mary; a ringing of bells announcing this devotion, typically at 6:00 a.m., noon, and 6:00 p.m.

47. combinations: A single undergarment covering the body and legs.

48. jumper: Sweater.

49. Plain Chant Credo: Chanted Latin version of the Nicene Creed, a formal statement of Christian belief. It begins: "I believe in one God,/ the Father almighty,/ Maker of heaven and earth,/ Of all things visible and invisible./ And in one God, Jesus Christ/ son of god, only begottten,/ and born of the Father before all ages./ Lord and God, Light of Lights/ Very God of Very God, born not made/ And of the same substance of the Father."

50. Holy Water Font: A receptacle (usually by the entrance of a church or room) containing special water blessed by a Catholic priest for use in religious ceremonies such as Baptism.

51. press: Closet or wardrobe for clothing.

52. hairgrip: A flat hairpin with the ends close together.

53. mitre: A tall headdress that tapers to a point front and back, worn by bishops.

54. interval: Intermission in a theatrical performance.

55. Magnificat (also known as Mary's Song): A canticle used in Christian liturgy, especially at Vespers and Evensong, the text being the hymn of the Virgin Mary (Luke 1:46–55). "My soul doth magnify the Lord. And my spirit hath rejoiced in God my Saviour. Because he hath regarded the humility of his handmaid; for behold from henceforth all generations shall call me blessed. Because he that is mighty, hath done great things to me; and holy is his name. And his mercy is from generation unto generations, to them that fear him."

56. sixth commandment: Thou shalt not commit adultery.

57. ninth commandment: Thou shalt not covet thy neighbor's wife.

58. Blind obedience: Unconditional submission to a superior's authority without question, as seen in traditional religious orders.

59. A continuation of the Magnificat, which translates: He hath shewed might in his arm: he hath scattered the proud in the conceit of their heart. He hath put down the mighty from their seat, and hath exalted the humble. He hath filled the hungry with good things; and the rich he hath sent empty away. He hath received Israel his servant, being mindful of his mercy: As he spoke to our fathers, to Abraham and to his seed for ever.

60. dustbin: Trash can.

61. polishing-blocks: Heavy wooden blocks with long handles. A polishing cloth was usually attached to the block and the block was used to polish the waxed corridors.

62. bodhran: A shallow, one-sided drum used to play traditional Irish music.

63. Micky: Slang term for penis.

64. Yanks: Informal, often derogatory term for "Americans."

65. jackdaws: A term of derision. Black birds like crows; scavengers. In the 1960s Irish men wore dark suits to church and to dances.

66. Canon: A senior parish priest in the Roman Catholic Church.

67. bless themselves: Make the Sign of the Cross in order to call on God to protect or treat one favorably.

68. Tech: Technical School. A second-level school where technical subjects such as crafts and carpentry, as well as languages, were taught.

69. scab: A person or thing regarded with contempt. "Scab" also has the connotations of strikebreaker (a worker who betrays their fellow workers).

70. keening: Wailing in grief for a dead person; an Irish funeral song accompanied with wailing in lamentation for the dead.

71. despatch: The act of sending something off to its destination (e.g., laundry).

72. Pioneer pin: A brooch or clasp-style badge denoting membership in the Pioneer Total Abstinence Association of the Sacred Heart, an Irish Catholic movement. A Pioneer makes a commitment to abstain from alcohol for life, to wear the pin, and to recite the Pioneer Prayer twice a day: "For Thy greater glory and consolation, O Sacred Heart of Jesus, for Thy sake to give good example, to practice self-denial, to make reparation to Thee for

the sins of intemperance, and for the conversion of excessive drinkers, I will abstain for life from all intoxicating drinks. Amen."

73. Big House: Prison or penitentiary.

74. the first sorrowful mystery: A meditation on a decade of the rosary that focuses on Jesus Christ's Agony in the Garden of Gethsemane, where He foresaw his upcoming suffering and inspired sinners to pray for true repentance from their sins.

75. paper baby: A paper photograph of a baby. Brogan is pointing to the tragedy of Brigit's substitution of a piece of paper for a real flesh-and-blood baby.

Jennifer Johnston

(1930–)

   Jennifer Johnston was born into a theatrical family in Dublin in 1930; her parents were the novelist, playwright, and war correspondent Denis Johnston, and the actress and theatre director Shelah Richards. She grew up in Dublin and was educated at Trinity College Dublin. Johnston is married, has four children, and now resides in Derry, Northern Ireland, where she continues to write.

Since 1972 Johnston has produced an impressive succession of highly acclaimed novels, two of which have been shortlisted for the Booker Prize for Fiction. Her fictional works include *The Captains and the Kings* (1972), *The Gates* (1973), *How Many Miles to Babylon?* (1974), *Shadows on Our Skin* (1977), *The Old Jest* (1979), *The Christmas Tree* (1981), *The Railway Station Man* (1984), *Fool's Sanctuary* (1988), *The Invisible Worm* (1992), *The Illusionist* (1995), *Two Moons* (1998), *The Gingerbread Woman* (2000), *This Is Not a Novel* (2002), *Grace and Truth* (2005), *Foolish Mortals* (2007), and *Truth or Fiction* (2009). In 2004, the award-winning novelist Roddy Doyle pronounced that Jennifer Johnston was "Ireland's best novelist."[1] For her contributions to Irish literature, Johnston has won both the Irish PEN Award (2006) and the Bob Hughes Lifetime Achievement Award (2012).

Johnston has written several noteworthy plays that demonstrate her sharp humor and insights into characterization. All of them have been produced in various theatres in Ireland. Garry Hynes directed a production of Johnston's one-act play *The Nightingale and Not the Lark* at both the Abbey's Peacock Theatre and Galway's Druid Theatre in 1982. In 1983

Robert Cooper directed a production of *Indian Summer* at the Lyric Theatre in Belfast. *The Porch*, a one-act play, was produced at the Gaiety Theatre Bar in 1985 under the direction of Caroline Fitzgerald. Fitzgerald also directed productions of the one-act play *The Invisible Man* (1987) and the full-length play *Triptych* (1989) at the Abbey's Peacock Theatre. *The Nightingale and Not the Lark*, *The Porch*, and *The Invisible Man* were published in one volume in 1988. Her play *The Desert Lullaby* was produced by the Lyric Theatre, Belfast, in 1996.

In 1995 Lagan Press published three of Johnston's one-act plays under the title *Three Monologues*. Two of the monologues first written in 1990, *Christine* and *Billy* (which later she retitled *Mustn't Forget High Noon*), were designed to be performed together. The pieces portray a couple destroyed by the turmoil in the North. Under the direction of Caroline Fitzgerald, *Christine and Billy*, as the monologues were titled then, premiered at the Peacock Theatre in 1988. They have subsequently been produced and repeated twice on BBC Radio 4. *Christine* also has been published under the title *O Ananias, Azarias and Misael* in *Selected Short Plays* (2003), which also includes *Moonlight and Music* (first produced in 2000 by the Fishamble Theatre Company at Dublin's Civic Theatre). The third monologue in the series is *Twinkletoes*.

Twinkletoes was first performed in 1993 by the Project Theatre at Bewley's, Grafton Street, Dublin. The role of Karen was played by Carol Moore (also known as Carol Scanlan) and was directed by Caroline Fitzgerald. *Twinkletoes* had its American premiere in 2000 in a student-directed production at Oregon State University. Under the direction of Charlotte Headrick, in 2001 the university staged a new production of the play that toured to the American Conference for Irish Studies Western Regional meeting in Tacoma, Washington, in that same year. In 2011, under the composite title *Reflections: An Evening of Women's Voices from Northern Ireland*, the British National Theatre of America presented *Twinkletoes* in the First Irish Festival in New York City; it shared the bill with Bernard McMullen's *Forgotten Milk*. *Twinkletoes* centers on the lonely life of Karen, an IRA prisoner's wife. Having just returned from her pregnant daughter's wedding, with humor and some bitterness, Karen shares with the audience the highs and lows of her life.

Twinkletoes

It is quite late at night. The empty living room of a small terrace house. Light shines in from the street outside. A car draws up, the headlights shining on the walls. A door slams and the car drives off. There is the fumbling of a key in the door. The door opens and Karen comes in. She switches on the light. She is dressed in finery; a hat in her hand, flowers pinned to her coat, very high-heeled shoes, a shiny bag. She is in her midthirties, a bit the worse for wear. She flings her hat across the room.

KAREN. That hat cost me.

I never before bought anything that cost me like that hat.

She picks it up and puts it on the table. She unpins the flowers from her coat and puts them beside the hat. She giggles.

Tell me something, hat, I might need to wear you to the christening, so I might. On the other hand . . .

She hokes[2] off her shoes and sighs with relief.

Tell you something else for nothing, I'll not be wearing them again.
They have my feet tortured.
Our Mary always says that plastic shoes draw your feet. Well, plastic or not, my feet'll never be the same again.
Never.
I'd of stayed on a bit and had a bit of crack,[3] danced.
Yeah.
Danced.
If it hadn't been for the pain of my feet.

She wriggles out of her tights[4] and throws them across the room.

Freedom!

She does a few quickstep twirls around the table.

I like a bit of a dance.
My daddy taught me to dance when I was wee.
Quickstep.

Foxtrot.

Tangooooo.

Twinkletoes, he used to call me.

He told me about this little kid who used to dance on the pictures.

Shirley Temple.

All curls, he said, and twinkletoes.

I never saw her. Only heard the name from my dad.

Some people think you're over the hill at thirty, past it. Past everything, but I have news for them.

I can rock and roll, jive, strut.

Given the chance.

A lot of other things I could do too, given the chance.

God, my head's going round and round.

Cup of tea.

I'm spinning.

Where's the kettle?

Everything's spinning.

Ya dee da da.

There it is.

God bless us.

Isn't it well tomorrow's Sunday.

Ya dee da da.

I can spend all day in bed, curtains pulled.

Tight, real tight.

Just lie there.

Let the feet recover.

Let the head stop jiving.

Cigarette. Poison.

Who the fuck cares?

A short life and a merry one.

What's merry?

I could die in my bed tonight and no one would know.

Till Thursday.[5]

Someone would be sure to know on Thursday.

I was sure I had matches in my bag.

On Thursday, someone would wonder.

Nothing but tissues in here. A million tissues; my bloody eyes all over them.

Bin[6] for them.

I never thought I'd cry.

Matches.

Thank you, God. At least you recognise the need for poison.

I said to our Mary[7] this morning or yesterday or whenever it was. Why should I cry? Amn't[8] I only too glad to be getting that problem off my back?

If I'da had sense, I'da brought another pair of shoes with me and stayed on.

Danced.

Takes your mind off things.

Yip.

That's what I'da done.

Never had sense.

That's what my daddy always said.

He never said that about our Mary, only me.

Right enough, Danny McCartney was coming on a bit strong, but I could have handled that.

I could have . . .

Just dance, I could have said and stop messing about.

I could have said that if I'd wanted to.

I called him Twinkletoes once.

One night I was out with our Mary and the girls and he asked me onto the floor.

Right enough, he was a great dancer. So I said it. I gave him that name.

There's other bits of him twinkle too.

Keep your twinkling hands off me or I'll deck you.

He laughed.

He didn't mind, not like some of the others I won't mention who won't take no for an answer.

Dirty buggers.

Only one thing on their minds.

If they had minds.

Danny's not like that.

Danny's a gentleman.

His wife's inside in the hospital.

Stuck on tablets.[9]

Four, five years now, she's been going in and out.

Ever since her brother was shot by the army.

She just sits there, Danny says, staring at the wall.

Well, that's what he says anyway.

Lucky they've no kids.

You've no time to sit and look at the wall if you've kids.

It's her nerves is shot to hell.

She was always nervous. I remember her at school, if the teacher looked crooked at her she'd burst into tears.

We used to pull her leg.

Waterworks we called her.

I never thought I'd cry.

Tea bags.

But I did.

She looked so young.

She is so young.

And the baby showing. Maybe not to everyone, but if you knew you could see.

My daddy was affronted having to walk to the altar with her.

He said no when I asked him. Nothing on earth would make me, he said, but I said just get on and do it. Isn't she your own flesh and blood. Don't you love her no matter. I said if you don't say you'll do it, I'll have to get Declan's da down from Belfast to do it and you won't like that one little bit. That did the trick. But wild horses wouldn't drag him to the party.

He never liked Declan.

My Declan.

Not our Noreen's Declan.[10]

He's a harmless young fella.

I thought it was an odd thing she took up with a fella of the same name.

Coincidence like.

Milk in the fridge.

Light goes on, always the light goes on. One of life's miracles. Oh Holy God! No milk in the fridge.

Isn't that just my luck.

Black tea turns my stomach.

He never liked Declan from the moment he laid eyes on him.

He wouldn't open his mouth to him when he came to the house.

Eighteen years ago.

That's the waste of a tea bag anyway.

Bin.

Last week there were mice in this bin.

I got Noreen's Declan to set a trap.

Two he caught.

It's not a very nice way to kill an animal, but who wants mice in their bins.

He'd just sit there and read the paper, or a book.

Here's Declan, I'd say, and he wouldn't lift his eyes from the page.

Never you mind, my mammy said, he'll come round.

But he never did.

Wouldn't speak Declan's name when things got really bad.

He was in the navy during the war and he worked at the base here till the government closed it down.

You can't beat the navy, he used to say.

That's where he learnt to dance, when he was in the navy.

"Joined the navy to see the world and what did I see, I saw the sea."[11]

He'd sing that.

He doesn't sing songs any longer now.

No one to sing them to, he says now.

Who'd want to hear my songs now.

All the nice girls love a sailor. Look at your mother. She was the nicest girl of the lot. She'd go red when he said things like that.

She'd pretend to be cross, but she loved it. My Jack Tar[12] she called him.
Do you take this man . . . That's when I cried. I couldn't help it. I knew
I was ruining my eyes, but I cried and cried. Quite quietly you under-
stand, but I used a lot of tissues.

For Declan.

I'll tell him about it on Thursday.

Not all.

I'll tell how pretty she looked and how young.

I'll tell him my daddy gave her away.

Straight and frail standing up there beside her.

Remembering, I'm sure he was remembering.

I won't tell him that I cried.

I won't tell that the baby showed.

No.

I cried for Danny McCartney too.

Though I shouldn't.

We both been alone such a long time.

What with her being in and out staring at the wall.

Not alive really.

I shouldn't think about him.

I won't mention his name to Declan.

Or anyone else.

I cried for my daddy.

He's alone too, now.

So many people alone.

I wonder if there's a drop of vodka.

Might as well be hanged for a sheep as a lamb.[13]

He'd have come to the party if my mammy'd still been alive.

She'da made him.

You're a big baby, Sean, she'd have said.

She could have coaxed him. Wind him round her little finger.

Jack Tar.

We could have asked the band to play a slow foxtrot and he and I
could have dazzled them all. Big solo performance.

Only perhaps they wouldn't have known how to play a slow foxtrot.

What's that when it's at home? A slow fucking foxtrot.

There are pictures of him and her all round their house.

Together.

Him in his uniform.

Them being married. Very old fashioned.

Do you take this man?

And then pictures of us all, our Mary and me.

I was the baby.

He loved me.

I was always surrounded by love.

I asked him if he'd come and live here after my mammy died.

There was just Noreen and me.

She could have slept in the room with me.

He could have been a father to her.

Your Declan's friends might shoot me, he said to me.

I didn't speak to him for six months after that.

I told Declan one Thursday.

He laughed.

Ay, he said, the old bugger, they might and all. But he didn't mean it.

He always told me not to mind the way my daddy carried on. It's just the way he is, he said.

Declan's a good man.

I sometimes wonder if he'd been here how things would have worked out.

Would Noreen have stayed at school?

I wanted her to stay at school.

Education is the only way, I said.

Way out.

My daddy said it too, and our Mary.

And her teachers.

Maybe too many people said it.

She wouldn't listen.

She wanted to live, she said. She wanted a few pounds in her pocket.

She wanted freedom.

She was growing up, she said, and she wanted.

I knew there was vodka somewhere.

She finds a bottle of vodka.

A glass. Freedom.

She had her wee job in Dunnes[14], so what could I say to her?

Fair dues[15] to her, she gave me a few pounds every week. Left it on the table there every Friday evening. I couldn't fault her for that.

When we were young my daddy had us in by ten o'clock.

A minute late and you were in trouble.

Maybe that's why I married Declan, so that I could stay out after ten at night.

I loved him.

Excuse me, I love him. Yes.

I think.

He's a hero.

It's hard being married to a hero.

It's a bit like being in prison too.

Don't get me wrong. I mean no harm when I say a thing like that.

Nine years he's been in there.

It was Noreen's eighth birthday when they picked him up.

At a checkpoint in County Tyrone.[16]

I'd said to him that morning as he was going out, don't you be late for the wee party. It wouldn't do to disappoint the child.

Would I be late? He said, just like that, real cool. Would I be?

We heard it on the six o'clock news. BBC.

Three men lifted.[17]

In possession.

They showed us the car on the screen.

Jesus God, I said to our Mary, that's Paddy Breen's car.

I think they've got Declan.

Don't cross your bridges until you come to them, our Mary said.

He never turned up for the party.

I had a cake with pink icing and eight wee red candles.

What'll I say to my daddy, I said to our Mary.

Nothing, she said, keep your lip buttoned.

I knew it would happen one day.

I used to get those shaking fits.

All I could do was sit there with my hands locked between my knees and wait for the shaking to stop.

I didn't tell Declan.

I didn't want to put those sort of worries on him.

The doctor wanted to put me on tablets, but I wouldn't take them.

I'd seen what the tablets did to other women.

Like Danny McCartney's wife.

I'd rather feel.

I don't think he knew what I meant, the doctor, when I said that to him.

He just shrugged his shoulders up and down. Suit yourself he said.

I had terrible dreams when Declan was out at night. Sometimes I'd sit up half the night just so I wouldn't have those dreams.

Our Mary said I should have taken the tablets.

She's always full of sense.

That doesn't mean she's right though.

I was too young to be a mother.

That's what I think about Noreen too.

She's too young.

What about her freedom now?

I haven't told Declan.

My Declan.

He'd be shocked, like my daddy.

Angry with me.

Why didn't you keep an eye on her?

That's what he'll say.

God knows, I tried.

He couldn't understand.

Things are so different now.

Young ones want freedom.

Nine years of changing.

He wanted freedom too.

Words are such silly things.

I'll say nothing yet awhile.

Stay mum.

I think I'll have another drop of vodka.

Someone once told me that the Russians just throw it down their throats. Like that. Oh Jesus!

It must have been my daddy.

He was on the Russian convoys during the war.

He said it kept the cold out, drinking it down like that.

He said he couldn't describe the cold. Your breath froze, he said, tears froze on your cheeks.

He said they used to hug you, put their arms around you and hug you. Russian men did that. Maybe it was because of the cold.

If I'd stayed on a while, maybe Danny McCartney would have come home with me.

I shouldn't be thinking things like that.

God forgive me.

But I do.

Maybe he would have come home with me.

Maybe . . . oh god, maybe . . .

It's the drink in me talking.

No.

It's not.

I'm not a bad woman.

This house is empty now. ·

Full of shadows.

Noreen took all her things out of her room. Her wee bits and pieces. She left the window open and it rained and I came home and found the floor all wet and the blue rug Declan and I bought on our honeymoon in Galway. Soaking wet.

I sat on the bed and cried and she came in and put her arms around me and she cried a bit too.

We'll only be down the road, she said.

It's not that, I said. It's my blue rug.

Is that all, she said. It'll dry, she said.

So it will, I said.

It was raining the day we bought the rug and we brought it back to the caravan.[18]

Our Mary's husband he said we could have their caravan for our honeymoon.

And it rained.

It rained like I had never seen it before.

Maybe that was just Galway.[19]

I didn't know.

I'd never been down to Galway before.

Or since, if it comes to that.

What does it matter on your honeymoon if it rains or not was what everyone said. Nudge, nudge, wink, wink.

I'd never seen the west before.

I'd never seen the ocean.

Next town America, Declan said.

It was all white waves and seagulls.

Like kittens crying they were.

Our clothes never got dry.

Mind you the air was good. Wild air. Not like you get here.

He laid the rug down on the bed and said, ever heard of a magic carpet?

Heard of one, I said, but never come across one.

Not too many magic carpets in Derry.[20]

Come here to me and I'll show you just how magic a carpet can be.

He was so sweet.

We didn't get to America, but we forgot about the rain for awhile.

Magic carpets.

Happy ever after.

Fairy tales.

Shit, all shit.

But we tell them to our children just the same.

My daddy used to tell me about the Russian convoys and the high crashing seas and the torpedoes and the rum ration and how to drink vodka, and how the ack-ack guns sounded when the bombers came over.

He used to tell Noreen too, but she didn't want to listen.

Everything changes.

The things we want to listen to; the things we want to be.

Is she happy now with her Declan and the baby just starting to show.

She laughs. She dances.

I laugh.

I could dance.

Twinkletoes.

Do you take this woman . . .

Do you take this child just starting to . . .

Oh, sweet fucking shit!

I told her she had a choice, but she didn't believe me.

She didn't want me to tell her daddy.

She didn't want to tell her daddy herself one Thursday.

I hate empty bottles.

Empty.

I'd like to drown in drink.

Float away and then just slowly drown in vodka.

Russian convoys.

I had the choice.

No.

I was wild for Declan.

Even my daddy couldn't stop me loving Declan.

He's a terrorist, my daddy said.

I went out of the house and slammed the door.

The house shook.

A freedom fighter, said Declan. Tell him that. And I'm fighting for his freedom as well as my own. Tell him that.

Of course I didn't.

Tell him up the RA.[21]

I didn't tell him that either.

I had more sense.

The people I love most all go on and on about freedom.

I don't know what it means.

I don't see it around.

Maybe you could find freedom with a magic carpet? If you could find a magic carpet.

I made her come up with me the Thursday before last.

I'm passing no messages to your daddy, I said.

If you're getting married, you're going to tell him yourself.

You owe him that.

Since she left school, she's hardly come at all.

I can't be taking time off work to go up and see him, she said.

Excuses, excuses.

Anyway, I don't want them to know.

Anyway, I hate that bus and all those women with their plastic bags full of oranges and new jeans and the talk about our boys. And they're all so old.

And I hate the prison and the screws staring at you. And I hate . . .

Don't say another word, I said.

Fuck, she said.

And don't use language like that.

You do.

I'm old, I said.

Thirty-five last May.

Coming on seventy.

Anyway the long and short of it was that I made her take the day off and she came up in the bus with me.

He was so glad to see her.

He looked great, all dressed up and his face excited with his big smile.

I kept my fingers crossed.

He held her hand so tight, like he thought she might fly away. You're so pretty, just like your mammy.

I sat watching them, quietly, thinking my own thoughts.

And the time flew in and she never said what she'd come to say.

So, out of my silence, I said, Haven't you something to tell your Daddy?

She stopped talking and looked at the table.

She gave a little nervous clear to her throat.

I'm getting married on Saturday week.

He didn't seem to take it in.

So I repeated what she'd said.

But you're only a kid, he said.

I'm seventeen.

You've only left school. You're too young.

You and mammy were going out when she was only seventeen, she told me that.

He glared at me.

Karen . . . he said.

I shook my head.

She won't listen, I said.

She'll listen to me. Won't you listen, love? You're only young.

You've all your life in front of you.

I'm getting married on Saturday week no matter what you say and that's all there is to it.

She stood up, ready to go.

At least tell your daddy what his name is.

Declan. Isn't that funny. Same as you. O'Hare.

He looked like someone had hit him.

Why didn't you tell me before, Karen?

I could only shake my head.

He's a nice lad, I whispered.

He looked like he'd looked in the court the day the judge had said he was going away.

I'd like to meet him, he said.

Sentences to run concurrently the judge said.

After the wedding. I'll bring him up some Thursday after the wedding.

Three life sentences to run concurrently.

If you gave a cat three life sentences, it would still have six lives left.

Or eight if they ran concurrently.

And they don't run, believe you me.

They crawl.

You might have waited till I came out, he said.

Thanks, she said. We've better things to do with our lives than wait for miracles to happen.

She turned and walked out.

She didn't kiss him or nothing.

Young people can be . . . can be . . .

I've done my best, I said. Honest to God, Declan . . . very hard sometimes, yes.

I know, love.

He smiled at me.

My dad's helping out with the wedding. We'll do it well. You know, the hotel, a meal, a few drinks . . .

Have a band, he said.

Yes.

Tell me Karen . . . is she . . . is she . . .

No, I lied.

He believed me. I could see him believing me.

I'm quite good at lying.

Thirty-five.

I want to dance.

Jive.

Jitterbug.

Tango.

Rock.

I really want to rock.

I want to have more kids.

I want to love.

Not just on Thursdays.

Aye, Declan, I love you.

I lie well.

You've fucking well ruined my life, Declan. That's what I want to say.

And your own.

You're a hero.

Wear it well, I say.

I'm just a woman whose plastic shoes hurt.

She laughs suddenly.

I saw these shoes in a book the other day.
Pale cream-coloured leather. Soft. With tiny little straps around the
ankles. Not too high. Just perfect for dancing all night.
A hundred and thirty quid.[22]
Just this little pair of soft leather shoes.
You wouldn't want to wear them in the rain.
I could do the slow foxtrot with Danny McCartney, forever.
Or someone.
He has a good job with Ulsterbus.[23]
An office job.
Pensionable.
He's not a messer.
He doesn't look at anyone else, only me.
Twinkletoes.
I wonder if Declan knows all the things I don't tell him?
I don't want him to be upset.
I loved him.
He did what he had to do.
Even after nine years I haven't worked out what to say to him on
Thursdays.
I practise going up in the bus. In my head, you know.
All the little things I'm going to say.
The jokes.
Keeping some sort of door open for him.
I often wonder if the other women are doing the same.
If Danny McCartney came over one night, would anyone tell him?
I bet they would.
Does it matter any longer?
I can't answer that question.
Not when I'm full of drink.
I don't think I could answer it when I'm stone cold sober either.
My daddy would be angry.
You've made your bed and you must lie in it, he'd say.

Perhaps we could both be a bit happy.

Laugh a bit.

Care.

Ever heard of a magic carpet, I might say to him.

I wonder what he'd say to me.

Declan sent the flowers . . . and some for Noreen too. Pink roses.

Hold them over your tummy, I said, and no one will notice the way you are.

Wasn't it good of your daddy to think, I said.

She didn't answer, but she carried the roses.

Over her tummy.

She looked lovely.

My daddy thought so too.

You look lovely pet, he said and kissed her. I only hope this young lanky isn't in the same kind of business as your daddy.

I could have killed him, there and then.

She just laughed.

Of course he isn't grand-dad. Things have changed.

Amen, said my daddy.

Amen, I said, inside my head. Nothing changes and everything changes.

On Thursday I'll tell him . . . everything and nothing.

I'll smile and talk about the band.

And the roses.

And the way my daddy walked up the aisle.

And about my hat and how my shoes hurt me.

Everything and nothing.

THE END

Notes

1. Angelique Chrisafis, "Overlong, Overrated, and Unmoving: Roddy Doyle's Verdict on James Joyce's *Ulysses*," *The Guardian*, February 10, 2004.

2. hokes: Flings.

3. crack: Has the same connotation as the word "craic," Irish for good times, great fun.

4. tights: Irish and British term for panty hose.

5. Thursday: Visiting day at the prison where Karen's husband is imprisoned.

6. bin: Trash can.

7. Mary: Karen's sister.

8. amn't: Contraction of "am I not."

9. tablets: Pills, medications.

10. Noreen's Declan: Karen's daughter Noreen has married a man named Declan; Karen's husband's name is also Declan.

11. "Joined the navy to see the world and what did I see, I saw the sea." Lyrics from the Fred Astaire film *Follow the Fleet*.

12. Jack Tar: A sailor, particularly a British sailor.

13. Might as well be hanged for a sheep as a lamb: Expression meaning that the result is still the same no matter what the crime. In Karen's case, she is drunk, and she might as well be even drunker.

14. Dunnes: A store that carries clothes, household appliances, and groceries in Northern Ireland.

15. fair dues: An expression meaning to give credit for something.

16. Tyrone: The border country between Northern Ireland and the Republic of Ireland.

17. lifted: Arrested.

18. caravan: A camper.

19. Galway: A city on the West Coast of Ireland on the Atlantic Ocean.

20. Derry: In the United Kingdom and on British maps of Northern Ireland, the city is listed as Londonderry. In modern usage, in order to avoid the political implications of the name, it is often printed as "Derry/Londonderry."

21. RA: Slang for the IRA, the Irish Republican Army.

22. hundred and thirty quid: Pounds sterling. Depending on the fluctuation of the pound, around 225 to 260 dollars.

23. Ulsterbus: Public transportation in Northern Ireland.

Nicola McCartney
(1972–)

❧ Originally from Belfast, Nicola McCartney was educated at the University of Glasgow. Her diverse theatrical and writing talents have won her an impressive array of artistic awards. She first trained as a theatre director with Charabanc, the Northern Irish women's theatre company, and at Glasgow's Citizens Theatre. Although known best as a prolific playwright, her career reflects additional expertise in other theatrical areas. She directed the 1996 national touring version of the award-winning *Trainspotting* (Harry Gibson, G & J Productions). She has served as a dramaturg for several companies, including Vanishing Point, TAG, Theatre Hebrides, Theatre Cryptic, Stellar Quines, and the Edinburgh International Festival 2005. Her writing talents have also ventured into radio, television, and film. In television she has written for numerous programs (including *The Bill* and *River City*) and has developed new projects for BBC Scotland, STV and Channel 4, Tiger Aspect, and Ideal World. In the film world, she has established projects for Freeway Films/Scottish Screen and is currently writing the screen version of *Heritage* for Brockenspectre, funded by Scottish Screen.

McCartney has been honored with several academic and community-based residencies. She served as the artistic director of the Glasgow-based new writing theatre company lookOUT from 1992 to 2002. Before being a writer-in-residence at the University of Edinburgh in 2005, she was an associate playwright at the Playwrights Studio Scotland. She is currently the director of the playwriting program at the University of Edinburgh.

McCartney specializes in working with children and young people from diverse backgrounds, both in the United Kingdom and internationally. Her ongoing commitment to theatre for youth is evidenced in her play *The Millies* (Replay Productions, Belfast), which had an international tour in 2006. *Lifeboat*, written for the Catherine Wheels Theatre Company in Edinburgh, received several awards, including a Theatrical Management Association Award (Barclays Stage Award) in 2002. *Lifeboat* played in New York in the spring of 2007 and also toured to the highly acclaimed Pacific Conservatory of Performing Arts in Solvang, California. It continues to be widely produced.

McCartney's interest in social justice issues is reflected in two of her dramas. *Jury Room* was part of *Convictions, the Crumlin Road Project* produced by Belfast's Tinderbox Theatre Company. McCartney was one of seven impressive Northern Irish dramatists including Damian Gorman, Marie Jones, Gary Mitchell, and Martin Lynch who wrote site-specific plays for locations within the historic Belfast jail and courthouse. *Convictions* won the Best New Play in the Irish Theatre Awards for 2001. McCartney's crafted her newest play, *Rachel's House* (2014), from a month of interviews with women transitioning out of the prison system and the people who support them at Rachel's House, a community recovery program in Columbus, Ohio. Presented by Ten Fifty Theatre Project, the play opened at the Wild Goose Creative and toured to other urban venues in May 2014.

As a playwright, McCartney's work has been seen at a number of theatres: *Cave Dwellers* (7:84 Theatre Company, Glasgow); *Underworld* (Frantic Assembly, London); *Home, Easy,* and *Laundry* (lookOUT Theatre Company, Stafford, England); *For What We Are About to Receive* (Brunton Theatre); *Standing Wave: Delia Derbyshire in the 60s* (Tron Theatre/Reeling & Writhing); *The Hero Show* (EGYT, East Glasgow Youth Theatre); *A Sheep Called Skye* (National Theatre of Scotland); and *Bog People* (Big Telly Theatre Company). Other plays include *Entertaining Angels, The Hanging Tree, Transatlantic,* and *Heritage* . . .

Heritage has had two productions by the Traverse Theatre in Edinburgh (1998 and 2001), and a production at the Royal Scottish Academy of Music and Drama in Glasgow (2006). Under the direction of Charlotte Headrick, the American premiere of *Heritage* took place at the University of Central Oklahoma in September 2006. Later that year, it traveled to Lawton University in Creighton, Oklahoma, for the state's Kennedy Center/American College Theater Festival, where it received a standing ovation and won numerous awards.

Heritage

CHARACTERS

SARAH, a young emigrant from County Antrim, Ireland.

MICHAEL, Sarah's lover.

HUGH McCREA, Sarah's father. About forty years.

RUTH McCREA, Sarah's mother.

PETER DONAGHUE, Michael's father. A farmer. Canadian.

EMER DONAGHUE, Irish. About eighty years.

SCENE

Farmlands surrounding the fictional township of Stanley, Saskatchewan, Canada.

TIME

The action spans six years, from 1914 to 1920.

ACT 1
SCENE 1

Fire. A boy dances, slowly at first, to the beat of a drum. The dance grows more frenzied as the beat quickens. Fire consumes the boy dancer.
    Silence.

SCENE 2

Early morning. The open fields of Saskatchewan.
    Sarah enters. Her clothes are spattered with an ashen dust and her face and hands are dirty with the same. Music.

SARAH. Nearly day.
    Sun bleeds morning over pigs and sheep and hens and goats
    Over the Land of the Shining Waters
    Over Canada

Where we have come
To reap the Wheat Boom.[1]
    I will tell you the story:
In the Wheat Country
Winter comes hard
And Spring comes harder
Walking along river valley to home
Pulling top coat chill-proof tight
It is bitter
No shelter
Trees felled mercilessly
But still more trees than I remember from home
Ice twists on strange boughs of
Kentucky coffee
Tulip tree
Sassafras
Sycamore
Spruce
Jack pine
Red pine
White pine
Black walnut
Blue ash
Balsam fir
Basswood
Chinquapin oak
Sugar maple
Left in the rush of clearance
Sharp bite of the axe
Signal of settlement.
Boots heavy sludge through
Heavy clay soil each step a job of work
Panting
To the top of the rise

Breathless.

Below me

Vastness of the plain

Dotted with matchbox houses

Fields sleepin under white snow meltin

Spattered little brown patches where the plow went in late

Criss-cross sewn together with snake-rail fences

Muddy grey below stretches wide under muddy grey above

Forever.

Springtime 1914. The pasture by the water. Michael appears, carving a piece of wood.

SARAH. I will tell you the story:

By the big river I met him

My boy

Mine

All mine

Top of the tallest tree and jump off boy

Fight boys twice his age and still win boy

Boy acted like he could take on the world with one arm tied behind his back.

Fearless, they called him.

Not cruel.

Never.

No sir, not he.

I will tell you the story.

Listen I will tell the story to you

As I have been told it.

I met him by the big river

In early springtime

When the freeze of winter was on the turn

And they said that war was coming.

One day when she was out roaming the hills and fields round about,

Deirdre[2] spied the young warrior.

SARAH AND MICHAEL. (*In unison.*) "Take me away from this place,"

MICHAEL. Said Deirdre. "For you know that Conor the King has sworn to take me as his bride. I have no desire to spend the rest of my days wedded to an old man."

"It is my geis,[3] my solemn word of honor to rescue you," said Naiose. "With the help of my brothers, the sons of Usnach, I have got a boat. But we must go quickly. We will leave this place tonight, my love, and never return."

So, in the middle of the night they fled and set sail off the northern coast. And Naiose wept as he left, for it was the land of his father. Across the sea he sailed to Scotland. There the Scottish king welcomed the warrior . . .

SARAH. Hey boy! What're you doin?

MICHAEL. Nothing.

SARAH. I heard you talkin to yourself.

MICHAEL. Not me.

SARAH. Only idiots and mad people talk to themselves . . . What were you sayin?

MICHAEL. Nothing.

SARAH. What's that in your hand?

MICHAEL. Nothing.

SARAH. You are one big nothing! Let me see.

MICHAEL. It's a boat.

SARAH. 'S more the shape of a coffin than a boat. I bet it sinks like a stone . . . This is our land. You have no right to be playin in it.

MICHAEL. This land belongs to the Carews who've gone up to Vancouver. It's not sold yet.

SARAH. It's as good as. My father has gone to the land agent today to bid for it.

MICHAEL. So has mine.

SARAH. My father has one hundred acres this side of the water.

MICHAEL. My father has two hundred this side.

SARAH. Get out of our river!

MICHAEL. No one owns the water. Except God. This is no river anyways. It's a stream.

SARAH. It's a river. See, it reaches all the way into the distance.

MICHAEL. It doesn't matter how long it is but how wide. This cannot be a river because I can jump its width.

SARAH. Go on then. Jump.

MICHAEL. No.

SARAH. Do it—or I say you're a liar.

MICHAEL. I am no liar.

SARAH. Well, I say you are one and I say that this here is a river.

MICHAEL. It's a stream.

SARAH. If you can't jump it, then you're a liar and must tell me the story.

MICHAEL. What story?

SARAH. The one you were tellin to yourself just now.

MICHAEL. And if I can jump?

SARAH. Then you're not a liar.

MICHAEL. But what do I get?

SARAH. Your good name back.

MICHAEL. My name is good anyway. I want something else.

SARAH. What?

MICHAEL. A kiss.

SARAH. Get away! You'll have no such thing!

MICHAEL. Run home to your mama little crybaby!

SARAH. I am no crybaby.

MICHAEL. Well, I say you are one. And a scaredy too!

SARAH. And sure what's there to be scared of? (*A beat.*) Only if you jump the river.

Michael attempts the jump and falls into the water.

SARAH. Tryin to walk on water now?

MICHAEL. Will you give me a hand?

Sarah helps him.

MICHAEL. You're right. It must be a river. Now we're on the same side.

SARAH. Let go of my hand . . .

MICHAEL. I'll wait for my kiss then?

SARAH. A kiss is a thing you'll never have from me. A cuff on the lug, maybe.

MICHAEL. So, you fight, girl?

SARAH. Better than you.

Sarah takes a swing at him. They tussle and she falls in the dirt.

MICHAEL. That's fancy footwork! I don't blame you for mistaking this here for a river. I thought so too when I was a child.

SARAH. I am thirteen years old and five months.

MICHAEL. Near as old as the century. That must make you very wise indeed.

SARAH. Wise enough not to fall in a river.

MICHAEL. Just to fall on your ass in the dirt instead? . . . I am Michael Donaghue of Quebec, now of Stanley township, Saskatchewan.

SARAH. Well, I can't say I'm pleased to meet you, Michael Donaghue.

MICHAEL. What do they call you?

SARAH. Sarah McCrea, of County Antrim, Ireland, now of Saskatchewan.

MICHAEL. You're John McCrea's younger sister.

SARAH. How d'you know my brother?

MICHAEL. I fought him once.

SARAH. What for?

MICHAEL. He called me a Papist bastard.

SARAH. Are you?

MICHAEL. I'm a Papist—but no bastard.

SARAH. Who won?

MICHAEL. He did. He broke my nose.

SARAH. Good.

MICHAEL. But I cut his lip. So, Sarah McCrea of County Antrim, now of Saskatchewan, what drove you here?

SARAH. What?

MICHAEL. How come you to Saskatchewan?

SARAH. All's I know is my father said he'd seen an advertisement offerin settlin on farms and the next thing I know, we're on a steamship out of Belfast.

MICHAEL. My grandmother came out of Derry[4] on a sailing ship.

SARAH. We sailed on the Cunard Line—passenger class. It took us near two weeks.

MICHAEL. My grandmother says the ocean is very big, bigger even than Lake Ontario.

SARAH. Much, much bigger!

MICHAEL. Maybe the ocean gets smaller as you get bigger—just like the river?

SARAH. I think the ocean will always be very big, for my mother says you can only cross it the once and then it's for a lifetime.

MICHAEL. Is Ireland very green?

SARAH. In summer it is. Why do you not go to the school?

MICHAEL. I'm too old.

SARAH. The Martins are Catholics and they go.

MICHAEL. I didn't want to go and my father said I didn't have to if I didn't want.

SARAH. I wish my father'd say that.

MICHAEL. What is Derry like?

SARAH. I don't know. It's only on the other side of the country, as far as we are from Regina, maybe. Isn't that funny? Here I am in Canada, but I've never been to Londonderry.[5] I've been to Belfast, though.

MICHAEL. I know nothing of Belfast except through the newspapers.

SARAH. I was only there the once, on the way to the ship. We came in from the north of the city, down from the mountains, and there it was all spread out in front of us—the Lough, the linen mills, and the factories. I thought it was the biggest, grandest place there was on earth until we passed through Toronto.

MICHAEL. I will go to Ireland one day.

SARAH. Sure what'd you want to go there for?

MICHAEL. To see where I come from.

SARAH. Canada is a far better country than Ireland.

MICHAEL. Do you think?

SARAH. Yes, I do.

MICHAEL. Why's that?

SARAH. Because . . . Because lots of reasons. Because you can grow peaches here. Tell me the story now.

MICHAEL. Why do you want to hear it?

SARAH. I like stories.

MICHAEL. I will tell you the story as I have been told it. One night, Conor mac Nessa,[6] King of Ulster, and his knights . . .

SARAH. Ulster's not a kingdom.

MICHAEL. It used to be.

SARAH. When?

MICHAEL. A long tome ago. Shall I tell you or not?

SARAH. Go on and tell it.

MICHAEL. Without interruption? . . . Okay . . . One night Conor mac Nessa, King of Ulster, and his knights were feasting at the house of his chief poet, Felimidh. They ate and drank their fill and the great hall was full of the sounds of merrymaking. Felimidh's wife dutifully prepared the feast and played the hostess the whole night long, even though she was heavily pregnant. At last, filled with good food and ale, the guests began to fall asleep. Quietly, Felimidh's wife made her way through the sleeping company to her own chamber, for the day had been a great strain for her . . .

Ruth appears. Music.

RUTH. I will incline mine ear to a parable: I will open my dark saying upon the harp.

MICHAEL. And great pain warned her that her child would soon be born.

RUTH. Wherefore should I fear in the days of evil, when the iniquity at my heels should compass me about?

MICHAEL. But passing through the great hall, the child in her womb gave out a cry . . .

RUTH. That they trust in their wealth . . .

MICHAEL. A shriek so loud, that it roused the sleeping warriors . . .

RUTH. And boast themselves in the multitude of their riches . . .

MICHAEL. Who seized their arms and rushed to see what it was that had made such a terrible sound.

SCENE 3

Michael disappears. Night of the same day. The McCrea farmstead. Sarah listens to Ruth reading from the family bible.

RUTH. . . . None of them can by any means redeem his brother, nor give God a ransom for him: for the redemption of their soul is precious, and it ceaseth forever—that he should continue to live eternally and not see the pit. For he sees that wise men die . . . What's that?

Sarah looks to see.

SARAH. It's not them.

RUTH. Yorkton's not so far away that it should take them this long.

SARAH. I wonder if they stopped off at the Millings'?

RUTH. Why would they do that?

SARAH. Maybe I should go and see.

RUTH. Maybe you should be in your bed . . . For he sees that wise men die; likewise the fool and senseless person perish, and leave their wealth to others. Their inner thought is that their houses will continue forever, and their dwelling places to all generations . . . I worry for them, out and about this country so late and the roads in such a state.

SARAH. Maybe they were ambushed?

RUTH. What?

SARAH. By Indians.

RUTH. Oh, for pity's sake!

SARAH. Mary Trimble was attacked by Indians.

RUTH. No she wasn't. The Indians are all on reservations now.

SARAH. Well, six of them come . . .

RUTH. Came. Six of them came.

SARAH. Yes, while her father was away over to Yorkton to get the doctor for her mother who was sick in bed and near dyin.

RUTH. I don't want to hear about it.

SARAH. Mary and her two sisters had to hide under the bed while her brother stood guard with her father's hunting rifle. They thought they would all have their throats cut.

RUTH. Sarah . . .

SARAH. One of them was all painted and he came right up to the window and pressed his face against it with his eyes staring all wide and bloodthirsty—just like that!

RUTH. Get away out of it! I let you sit up with me for company and this is what you do.

Sarah picks up the bible.

SARAH. I was only sayin . . . Shall I read on?

RUTH. Put it away.

SARAH. How old is this?

RUTH. You know how old it is.

SARAH. Your mother's mother's.

RUTH. It's raining now. The roads'll all be washed away.

Sarah reads the inscription in the front of the bible.

SARAH. "Ruth Milling m. Hugh Henry McCrea, November 1898 . . ." This isn't your writing.

RUTH. It's my mother's.

SARAH. John Hugh, Sarah Elizabeth . . .

RUTH. She wrote in all your names too. She had a beautiful hand.

Hugh enters, carrying packages.

HUGH. By Jings, I'm knackered this night!

RUTH. Hugh! Where've you been 'til this hour?

HUGH. The roads is all churned up with the thaw. 'Twas heavy goin for the oul mare.

RUTH. I told you not to be going away up there in this weather.

HUGH. Were you worryin about me, my darling? (*He embraces Ruth.*)

RUTH. Get away out of this you old goat! . . . And take your boots off.

HUGH. Yes, ma'am. (*To Sarah.*) And how's my other girl?

SARAH. I was watchin out for you.

HUGH. I'm glad you was, for I have plenty of news to tell ye. Oh yes, indeed I have.

SARAH. Tell me!

HUGH. The wee boys all in bed?

RUTH. Long ago. Which is where this one's going now.

SARAH. Ach, Mammy!

HUGH. Sure, let her sit up a while and have a yarn.

RUTH. Never let it be said I was the one that spoiled her. Where's John?

HUGH. He's takin the order back over to Samuel's.

RUTH. At this hour? Could he not have waited til the morning?

HUGH. I think he's got sweet on young Miss Rebecca Milling.

RUTH. He's only a boy.

HUGH. Fifteen years makes him near a man. He'd some sort of present he wished to deliver to the young lady. He wouldnae tell me what.

RUTH. Wasting money he's no call wasting.

HUGH. He even washed before he went out this mornin and I could hae sworn all these years he was feart o' water!

SARAH. John's got a sweetheart!

RUTH. Don't you be teasin him now.

HUGH. And sure why would she be teasin him when she's got an admirer herself—young Master Robert Milling.

SARAH. I can't marry him. He's my cousin.

RUTH. He's fine looking.

SARAH. He's too old.

RUTH. He's not nineteen yet.

SARAH. And he smells like a chimney with all that tobacco he smokes.

RUTH. I never knew he smoked tobacco.

SARAH. Sometimes he chews it up and spits it out.

HUGH. Jays! That's desperate.

RUTH. Hugh!

HUGH. A vile habit.

SARAH. I don't want him.

HUGH. Good on ye.

RUTH. She might be glad of somebody to take her, for she'll make no housewife.

SARAH. Are you hungry, Daddy?

HUGH. Starvin! My stomach feels like my throat's been cut.

Sarah gets the food ready.

RUTH. Well, if you would come in for your meal at the proper time and not leave it spoiling . . .

HUGH. And if I come in at the proper time you'd be complainin aboot all the work I hadnae done.

RUTH. Wash your hands! (*To Sarah.*) Be careful with that plate. Don't drop it!

SARAH. I won't. (*Sarah sets plate before Hugh.*)

HUGH. Would you look at that! Ham!

RUTH. You've seen ham before.

HUGH. I'm only sayin we're a damn sight better off . . .

RUTH. HUGH! Mind your talk. (*To Sarah.*) Don't let me hear you repeatin that.

HUGH. . . . Better off where we are than where we were. (*He hands a package to Sarah.*) Here. This is for you.

RUTH. Not more of those books.

HUGH. Books is a good present.

Sarah unwraps the gift.

SARAH. Western Girl's Companion!

RUTH. Filling her head with a load of old nonsense.

HUGH. It's just stories.

RUTH. She's bad enough as it is. She had you and our John attacked by Indians tonight.

HUGH. No Indians is goin to attack your da—don't you worry!

SARAH. Thank you, Daddy!

HUGH. You can read to us ootay that later.

SARAH. How was Yorkton?

HUGH. Big and busy.

RUTH. Did you get the cloth I asked for?

HUGH. Aye.

RUTH. And the lamp oil. (*He embraces Ruth again.*)

HUGH. Give yourself peace, missus. I got all on your list.

RUTH. What is all this cuddlin and getting on? Have you been at the drink?

HUGH. I might ae had a wee nip tae celebrate.

RUTH. Celebrate what?

HUGH. Wait and hear. Sarah, where's my pen and writin paper?

SARAH. Are we going to write to Uncle William, Daddy?

HUGH. We are. For we have news to tell and you shall write it, Sarah.

Sarah finds the pen and paper.

RUTH. What's happened?

HUGH. Wait and hear. (*To Sarah.*) Set down the date first.

SARAH. (*Writing.*) May 14th, 1914 . . .

HUGH. Dearest brother William . . . (*A beat.*) There's a start. Let me look . . . Aye that's good. That's very good now. (*To Ruth.*) The chile has a fair hand.

RUTH. Aye, she can write, but she's slow with her other learning.

SARAH. I do my best.

RUTH. Aye, at sitting daydreaming! It's a wonder you've hand left on you at all with the number of slaps they've had for wandering attention.

HUGH. Who's been baitin my chile?

SARAH. That schoolteacher, Mister Rutherford, did the day.

HUGH. For what?

SARAH. I lost my place at the reading.

HUGH. I thought you liked the reading?

SARAH. I do.

RUTH. Dreaming!

SARAH. I wasn't dreaming. I was thinking.

HUGH. Isn't that desperate? Thinkin's what school's for, is it no? Well, you tell oul Rutherford that the next time he takes after ye with that strap your oul da will be down to that schoolhouse to knock him ontae his Scotch . . .

RUTH. Hugh!

HUGH. I was gonnae say "back."

RUTH. You'll do no such thing. (*To Sarah.*) And better still, the next time I hear you've had correction I'll give you the same myself when you get home, do you hear me?

HUGH. Give the child peace, missus. She'll be ootay school in six months and not need much figurin or letterin to keep a hoose.

SARAH. What will I write to Uncle William, Daddy?

HUGH. Now, let's see . . . I suppose we should tell him about the hoose . . . The new hoose is builded last summer, a wooden frame hoose of two storeys. Ruth has it all fitted out lovely.

RUTH. Tell him I still favour the old-fashioned stone cottage above timber. I fear of fire in these houses.

HUGH. I tell you what, Missus, I'll build ye a double-fronted hoose, a stoan hoose like the Millings' one day. Would that please ye?

RUTH. It would.

HUGH. Then I'll do it. And it will be twice as big and as tall as the Milling hoose and oor farm will be three times as big as their farm and Hugh McCrea will be four times as rich!

RUTH. It's you she gets the dreaming from, indeed.

HUGH. Is it now? (*To Sarah.*) Set this down . . . Brother, I come back from the agent in Yorkton today havin bought myself another thirty acres of good land.

SARAH. You got it!

HUGH. I did so!

RUTH. You did what?

HUGH. I've bought part of the old Carew place. That makes one hunder'd and ninety acres of good fertile soil . . . What's that face for? You're not angered?

RUTH. You would talk it over with a child before your wife?

HUGH. I wanted to surprise you with it, Ruth.

RUTH. How much did you pay for it?

HUGH. Only eighteen dollars an acre.

RUTH. Five hundred and forty dollars?!

HUGH. It's good pasture land. The best for grazin cattle and the stream thereby.

RUTH. We've only two milk cows, for pity's sake!

HUGH. Aye, at the moment. But I reckon to buy another head and a bull with this year's harvest money.

RUTH. If you can get a price for the wheat. How are you to afford it?

HUGH. I went to see Hector Smyth at the bank.

RUTH. Lord!

HUGH. He's one of the brethren.[7] He'll give me a good rate.

RUTH. We're mortgaged up to our necks and still you're takin on more debt?

HUGH. That's my affair. Never worry, missus.

RUTH. How can you tell me not to worry, Hugh McCrea, when you go and do such things without asking me first?

HUGH. And since when did a man have to seek permission from his wife to wipe his nose, eh?

RUTH. He does when he's about to take the family into wreck and ruin.

SARAH. Ma!

RUTH. Keep your nose out!

HUGH. Wreck and ruin?

SARAH. Mammy . . .

RUTH. Go to bed!

HUGH. Stay where you are! (*To Ruth.*) Wreck and ruin? . . . Jays, Missus, can you never be happy but you allus have to see the dark side of a thing? Look at these hands . . . Look! . . . These are the hands that signed the deed to this land. These are the hands that did the plantin and the buildin. These are the hands that the money passes intil and ootay again.

Silence.

RUTH. Go to bed, Sarah.

HUGH. I would have her sit up and finish the letter.

A beat.

Sarah stays put. Hugh continues his dictation. Music.

HUGH. God, Willy, I never knew I was alive until I got ootay Ireland and woke up! What a country this British North America is! Good land with the finest soil and all your own to do with as you see fit, with no older brother Henry at your back givin orders and no landlord to come and take his share of your toil at the month's end. There's been a small depression here of late but it has not hit us too hard as we huvnae got enough yet to lose. It was a right thing I done in comin here. If I had stayed home as you are doin, I would still be in rags workin the dirt and the mud with nothing to show for it. If only you would pluck up the courage and come too. I wonder would you send me some seeds of Balm of Gilead and also some of the lily? I have it in mind to sow a flower garden oot in frontay the hoose, a memory walk, so that Ruth can have all the colours and scents of home aboot her. You will wrap them in a piece of oiled paper, then fold your letter up, then paste them into the crease to hide them well. We will walk on the Twelfth[8] this year again. Young John will play the flute—he is comin on well at it. The Orange Order is strong out here. Remember me to all the brethren. Write soon and send us news of home.

SARAH. Will you mention Peggy, Daddy?

HUGH. Surely we must mention her . . . As I'm sure you heard from Lizzie Milling, our youngest child, Margaret, died from the pneumonia, aged two years, this Christmas last. The winters is very severe here. Remember me also to brother Henry and family.

RUTH. Don't sign my name to it, if you're writing to that one.[9] (*Ruth exits.*)

HUGH. Would you rather be back in Ireland, Sarah?

SARAH. I like it here.

HUGH. Good girl! Let's see now. (*He examines the letter.*) That's fine! Isn't that fine, Ruth? . . . (*To Sarah.*) You're a clever one, aren't ye? I must sign my name to it now.

Hugh writes.

HUGH. Yours . . . with . . . affectation . . .

SARAH. Affection, Daddy.

HUGH. Aye . . . Your brother, Hugh . . . That's good. (*To Sarah.*) Now write on the envelope—to Master William McCrea, McCrea's Farm, Ballinderry Road, near Ballymoney, County Antrim, Ireland.

SCENE 4

Late September 1914. Sarah walking through the pasture, by the water. Michael jumps out at her.

MICHAEL. Heah!

He throws her a stick.

SARAH. Who goes there?

MICHAEL. I am Naoise, Red Hand Knight of Ulster.[10]

SARAH. You cannot step upon this shore.

MICHAEL. Me and my bride seek refuge here with the Scottish king.

SARAH. Stay and prove yourself!

They sword fight.

SARAH. You waited.

MICHAEL. I had nearly given you up. What kept you?

SARAH. Oul Rutherford made me stay behind.

MICHAEL. On your last day? What for?

SARAH. Knocking over a pile of books.

MICHAEL. Clumsy!

SARAH. Got you!

MICHAEL. Mercy

SARAH. Die!

MICHAEL. It's not in the story that you kill me.

SARAH. I will spare you and your bride. Stay here and live as my brother.

MICHAEL. In return for this I pledge my allegiance and skills as a warrior to your service. Say who has offended the honour of our Protector?

SARAH. Mister Rutherford.

MICHAEL. Death to Mister Rutherford!

SARAH. No more Mister Rutherford!

They flay away at an imaginary Mister Rutherford with their sticks.

MICHAEL. What did you learn?

SARAH. Countries and their capitals. I got them all right and oul Rutherford says, "It's a wonder, Miss McCrea, for though you have now reached the age of fourteen I had doubts you could count to that number."

MICHAEL. I'll test you.

SARAH. I'm done with school.

MICHAEL. Turkey?

SARAH. That's a hard one.

MICHAEL. Istanbul . . . Great Britain?

SARAH. Too easy.

MICHAEL. Canada?

SARAH. I'm not stupid.

MICHAEL. France.

SARAH. Paris.

MICHAEL. Italy?

SARAH. Rome. Harder!

MICHAEL. Egypt?

SARAH. I don't know that one.

MICHAEL. It's Cairo, stupid!

SARAH. I am not stupid! Another!

MICHAEL. Bosnia?

SARAH. Sarajevo, where the Duke got shot and the war started.

MICHAEL. Very good. The master was right—you're not as stupid as you look.

SARAH. Mister Rutherford said that it is Canada's duty to give whatever help she can to the efforts of the Allies on the Western Front.

MICHAEL. Russia?

SARAH. You can volunteer.

MICHAEL. I don't want to.

SARAH. Why not? You're old enough. Our John will go as soon as he is sixteen.

MICHAEL. Of course he will. He'd enjoy killing people.

SARAH. That's a terrible thing to say.

MICHAEL. Running Huns through the ribs with his bayonet.

SARAH. He's a damn sight braver than you.

MICHAEL. I won't fight. For it's not our war.

SARAH. It's a threat to the British Empire.

MICHAEL. This is Canada. (*He gives her a present—handkerchief.*)

MICHAEL. Happy Birthday!

SARAH. You've no call givin me presents.

MICHAEL. D'you like it?

SARAH. It's pretty. Did you sew it yourself?

MICHAEL. I found it. In my grandmother's linen chest.

SARAH. Will she not miss it?

MICHAEL. It belonged to my mother, I think. See the little flowers?

SARAH. Lilies. Thank you.

MICHAEL. It's okay.

She kisses him.

MICHAEL. I am Conor mac Nessa, King of Ulster. Where is Felimidh my chief bard?

SARAH. Here I am, sire!

MICHAEL. You have pleased us, Felimidh, with this feast and these revels. We will now retire to our chamber for the night.

SARAH. I will be Felimidh's wife. The feast is over and she is very tired.

MICHAEL. Passing through the great hall . . .

SARAH. What's her name?

MICHAEL. She doesn't have one.

SARAH. She must have a name.

MICHAEL. She is called Felimidh's wife.

SARAH. That's not a proper name.

MICHAEL. All right! Ethne . . . Passing through the great hall, the child in her womb . . .

SARAH. Ethne's womb.

MICHAEL. . . . gave out a cry, a shriek so loud, that it roused the sleeping warriors. Felimidh feared the men at arms. (*He plays Felimidh now.*) "It was the scream of my wife's unborn child that has wakened you," Felimidh said. (*A Warrior.*) "Call your wife before us," said the chief warrior. Trembling with fear . . .

SARAH. This is my part.

MICHAEL. She was so frightened that she could only answer . . .

SARAH. No mother knows what sleeps in her womb.

MICHAEL. That's right! But, later that night, she gave birth to a child, a girl child with shining eyes and fair hair. Cathbad the Druid prophesied over her. "You, O Deirdre of the Sorrows" . . .

SARAH. You can't be all the parts.

MICHAEL. You are Felimidh's wife. That's the only girl in this bit of the story.

SARAH. I want to be the Druid.

MICHAEL. You don't know how to be the Druid. You don't even know what a Druid is.

SARAH. I do too . . . It's a sort of a magician.

MICHAEL. No. A Druid is a seer.

SARAH. Like a fortune-teller or a tinker?

MICHAEL. Sort of, but grander.

SARAH. That's easy.

MICHAEL. Okay, you be Cathbad . . . The Druid took the baby—gently in his arms and prophesied over her.

A beat.

SARAH. What do I say?

MICHAEL. How can you be Cathbad if you don't know the words?

SARAH. Because you will tell me. Come on!

MICHAEL. You, O Deirdre of the Sorrows.

SARAH. You, O Deirdre of the Sorrows.

MICHAEL. Will grow up into a beautiful young woman.

SARAH. Will grow up into a beautiful young woman.

MICHAEL. Vivid as a flame.

SARAH. Vivid as a flame.

Peter enters, unseen by them, and listens.

MICHAEL. So beautiful, that you will bring great sorrow to the province of Ulster.

SARAH. So beautiful, that you will bring great sorrow to the province of Ulster . . . How was that? Did I make a good Druid?

MICHAEL. You were okay. A bit too fairground perhaps. The warriors, alarmed by such a dream prophecy, immediately demanded the child's death that Ulster would be spared this fate.

SARAH. But then, Conor the King spoke forth.

PETER. "I decree that the child be sent far away from Emain Macha, to be reared by a nurse until marriageable age. Then I will take her as my queen," he declared. And he sent her out of harm's way to a lovely place to be raised by a nurse, the poet Levercham, who taught her many things, and a poor herdsman was her foster father.

SARAH. It's a good story.

PETER. It is.

SARAH. I had never heard it before Mike told it to me.

PETER. I'm sure you hadn't. (*To Michael.*) Where've you been? You've been gone since dinner. You know there's baling to be done yet.

MICHAEL. I lost track of time.

PETER. It's nearly supper. Who's your friend?

SARAH. Sarah McCrea.

MICHAEL. Sarah, this is my father, Peter Donaghue.

SARAH. Hello.

PETER. Pleased to meet you, Miss McCrea. So you're the one my son neglects his work for. He's been keeping you a secret.

SARAH. Are you ashamed of me?

MICHAEL. No.

SARAH. I'm sorry to keep him from his work. He came to meet me after school, but I was late.

PETER. It's not your fault that he's work-shy.

SARAH. I just finished at the school today, you see.

MICHAEL. It's her birthday.

SARAH. I wanted Mike to come celebrate with me.

PETER. Well, I hope you take to whatever occupation you choose better than my son has took to farming.

MICHAEL. I'm sorry about the baling.

PETER. No matter. Plenty more work tomorrow. Come on! I'd rather fight in the trenches any day than face your grandmother when late for supper.

MICHAEL. Can Sarah come to supper with us?

PETER. I expect she has a home of her own to go to.

SCENE 5

Music. Ruth plants seeds in the memory walk.

SCENE 6

Later: the Donaghue farmstead.

EMER. It come on so sudden

Morning

Mist rises up out of the lough

Hovers over.

Day before, potatoes good

Now leaves all black

Crumble into ashes

Palm-stain dark

Air hanging heavy

Smell of sickness

Smell of death.

Fields all weepin-wailin women and children

My daddy, poor cottier

Lost foot on the land.

The British!

Not even a crust of bread to chew upon they give us

Ship off cattle and grain we've raised to serve up on English dinner tables

While our children

Perish.

Protestant ministers! They dishin out bowls of free soup

But you must recant

Must throw away soul.

So we live on—

EMER AND MICHAEL. Grass, seaweed, and shellfish.

Michael and Sarah listen to Emer. Peter working away at his ledger.

EMER. That was the beginning of the great disease that destroyed Ireland, Mihal.[11]

SARAH. What's recant?

MICHAEL. To turncoat on our Catholic faith.

EMER. That's right, son.

MICHAEL. They say some ate human corpses.

SARAH. They ate the dead people?

PETER. God in heaven!

EMER. I never saw that now. But they say some turned cannibal. No one can know what we suffered. I pray to God that you and yours may never know.

PETER. Mike! You were walking the top fifty acres this morning?

MICHAEL. Yes.

SARAH. (*To Emer.*) And then you came to Canada?

EMER. For five pounds passage each we sailed on the ship Superior out of Derry on the thirteenth of July, eighteen forty-nine.[12]

PETER. (*To Michael.*) Notice any damage?

MICHAEL. Don't think so.

PETER. You sure?

MICHAEL. Sure, I'm sure.

EMER. We sailed into Quebec City on the fourth of November. I was eleven years old.

SARAH. That's the age I was when I came here. We sailed on the Cunard Line.

EMER. Coffin ships,[13] they called them.

PETER. Good.

EMER. But all my family survived it.

PETER. So, one hundred and ten acres at forty bushels an acre, that makes . . .

EMER. Peadar! We are talking.

PETER. Excuse me.

EMER. My father really wanted to go to Philadelphia.

PETER. Four-four-oh at ninety-three cents a bushel . . .

SARAH. Why?

PETER. The great Republic.

EMER. But it was too expensive.

PETER. Makes two thousand and twenty-eight dollars with tax and a bit more off. (*To Michael.*) That's good isn't it?

MICHAEL. Yeah.

PETER. Better than last year. How's your father's harvest, Sarah?

SARAH. Not as big as that, I think.

EMER. Ah, we should have gone to America at last.

PETER. Liberty and justice for all.

EMER. Thousands were driven out by the Great Hunger.[14]

PETER. They leaving in their droves long before that, mother. Opportunity forced them out long before a bit of potato blight.

EMER. You remember all this, Mihal. It is where you come from.

PETER. He was born in Canada. He was raised in Canada. He will work to pay his taxes to the Canadian government. He is Canadian.

EMER. Cuimhnigh ar sin, a mhicil.[15]

MICHAEL. Cuimhneoidh mé a mhamó.[16]

PETER. Don't start on that.

MICHAEL. Tell about the uprising.

EMER. The Young Irelanders?[17]

MICHAEL. This is a good one.

PETER. Oh yes! Tell us about the Young Irelanders. That was a great and glorious uprising, Sarah. Somebody's gun went off by mistake and another paddy lost his shovel in a County Tipperary cabbage patch.

EMER. Your father was in the Movement.

PETER. The sins of my father are not mine to be judged for.

EMER. Holy God! Your father was no sinner. There was never a finer man

. . .

PETER. Here we go!

EMER. Never a finer man than him. And I'll not sit here and listen to this, you, you—traitor!

PETER. Then go to bed.

EMER. No respect! He has none.

PETER. I have respect for facts and truth.

EMER. We should have stayed in Quebec beside our friends.

PETER. On the good British land granted you by the good British government? You and my father were happy to take that, weren't you? Be careful of history, Sarah.

EMER. Bringing us away out here to be surrounded by Puritans.

PETER. History's more dangerous a friend than an enemy.

EMER. You always were a lover of the British.

PETER. Don't.

EMER. She was no good. No good.

PETER. Nothing but a load of lies and bitterness.

EMER. Ní fédir faic insint duitse.[18]

MICHAEL. Céard faoi a bhfuil tu ag caint?[19]

EMER. Is cuma, a mhic.[20]

PETER. We have company.

MICHAEL. You're talking about my mother aren't you?

PETER. She hardly knew your mother.

MICHAEL. Ba mbaith liom fios a bheith agam.[21]

EMER. Bhí sí posta cheanna.[22]

PETER. She was a widow.

MICHAEL. An raibh? [23]

EMER. Niorbh fhéidir caint leis; thug mé rabhadh dhó. Thug a athair rabhadh dhó.[24]

PETER. Michael, it's time for Sarah to be going home.

MICHAEL. It's not late yet.

PETER. I think it is.

MICHAEL. Céard atá i gceist agat? Abair liom, a mhamó![25]

EMER. Iarr ar d'athair.[26]

MICHAEL. Ni insionn sé faic domsa.[27]

PETER. In English, the pair of you! (*To Michael.*) There's nothing I haven't told you.

EMER. Where is she now, eh?

PETER. Wherever she is, she's getting peace and rest.

EMER. Better than she deserves.

MICHAEL. Céard atá i gceist agat?[28]

PETER. Will you stop!

SARAH. I'd best go, Mike.

PETER. I'm sorry, Sarah. Michael will take you home in the wagon.

MICHAEL. I want to know what she means.

PETER. She's confused.

EMER. My mind's as sharp as a razor.

PETER. Your tongue is. (*To Michael.*) Take your friend home. It's late.

SARAH. Thank you for supper.

EMER. No trouble.

SARAH. Can I come again?

EMER. B'fhearr e mura dtiocfadh se' anseo aris coiche.[29]

MICHAEL. Cén fath?[30]

EMER. Bí curamach a mchicil, maidir le céard atá a dhéabamh agat.[31]

PETER. Sarah is always welcome here.

SARAH. Thank you. Good night.

MICHAEL. I want to know what she means.

PETER. Another time. Good night. And don't be late home. You'll have to rise early to make up the work from today.

MICHAEL. Okay, okay! Slán a mhamó.[32]

Michael and Sarah exit.

EMER. Slán a mhic . . . A Dhía dhilis![33] Goin the same way as you. Every bit of him.

SCENE 7

Summer 1915. The Twelfth of July parade. Yorkton. Music.

SARAH. Dubadum[34] dubadubadum
    Dubadum dubadubadum
    Big lambeg beats
    Boom boom
    Boom boom
    One head made of ass's skin could shatter a window
    And boom and boom and boom boom boom!
    Shudders and shakes you to the liver
    High G on the D flute
    Thrill of pain it gives you in the heart
    Brother John marchin, puffin, whistling
    Isn't he doing well?
    Go on, John!
    It is old but it is beautiful and its colours they are fine . . . [35]
    Banners unfurl under trees green
    Sons of William, Orange
    Loyal Sons of Canada, gold
    Fluttering by

Dubadum dubadubadum
Boom boom
Dubadum dubadubadum
Boom boom
For heh-ho!
The lily-o!
The royal orange lily-o![36]
King Billy on a white charger leading Sunday Best parade[37]
Sashes, all fire-colour marching
Past women in hats
And girls in frocks
And wee boys in long trousers
Waving
And singin our songs
Man with lance
Man with bible
Our bible
Man with white gloves and a big sword
With ting and toot and crash and boom we'll guard old Derry's walls![38]
Marching
To the field.[39]
Our field
Of cake and ginger beer
And aniseed drops
And candy sticks
And kick the can
And hide and seek
And sing on a rope
And red, white, and blue
Our day out
Of tea and sandwiches
And cold meats and currant buns
And summer salad
And little nips of whiskey while the women's backs are turned.
And let us pray.

Our Father which art in heaven
And the Lord's my Shepherd
And God bless Sir Edward Carson[40]
And God save our gracious King
And Ireland shall never submit to Home Rule[41]
And Ulster will fight and Ulster will be right
And God bless our forces on the Western Front
And keep the Empire Protestant.
Oh God, our help in ages past[42]
Our hope in years to come
Our day.

SCENE 8

Night. McCrea farmstead. Twelfth of July, summer 1915. Ruth and Sarah sewing. Hugh raises his glass of whiskey in a toast.

HUGH. To the glorious and immortal memory of King William of Orange who saved Ireland from Popes and Popery and from brass money and wooden shoes. And to any man who denies this toast, may he be rammed, slammed, and jammed into the Great Gun of Athlone and fired into the Pope's belly and the Pope into the Devil's belly and the Devil into Hell and the door locked and the key thrown away forever!

RUTH. Will you mind your talk? (*To Sarah.*) Have you not that finished yet?

SARAH. It's near done.

RUTH. Can you manage?

SARAH. It's only a few oul socks, Ma.

RUTH. Let me see . . . What's this?

SARAH. What's wrong with it?

RUTH. (*To Hugh.*) Will you look at that?

HUGH. Don't ask me now. Nothin at all to do with me.

RUTH. (*To Sarah.*) How many times do I have to tell you? Small stitches. Even stitches.

HUGH. Sure, big or small makes no difference as long as it all holds together.

RUTH. You want holes in your clothes, do you? (*To Sarah.*) Give it to me.

SARAH. I can fix it.

RUTH. Just let it be.

SARAH. I'll start over.

RUTH. Leave it alone, I tell you! Leave it alone . . . It's a disgrace you are
to me. A disgrace.

A beat.

HUGH. Who d'ye think was askin after ye today at the Field, Sarah?

SARAH. I don't know.

HUGH. Robert Milling.

SARAH. Sure, what was he askin you for? He saw me himself.

HUGH. He was askin me if you was walkin out with anybody. I said,
"No." That's right, isn't it?

SARAH. It is.

RUTH. Of course it is.

HUGH. And then he asked me if he could coort ye.

SARAH. And what did you say?

HUGH. I told him ye were too young yet. "Come back when she's forty,"
says I. "That'll be time enough for her to be thinking of coortin."

He takes another drink.

RUTH. (*To Sarah.*) Well, you needn't think you're sitting here 'til you're
forty. No help to me at all. (*To Hugh.*) No more now.

HUGH. Missus, I'm on my holidays.

RUTH. You've had enough to drown the fish.

HUGH. Ah, sure, there's one or two of them no deid yet!

SARAH. It was a big parade the day, Daddy.

HUGH. It was.

RUTH. Our John did well.

HUGH. He did; though I think he hit a few notes wrong in Lilly Bolero.
Jays, my ears was ringin!

RUTH. He did not!

HUGH. I'm telling ye. Aye . . . It was a grand day.

SARAH. How d'ye join the Orange, Daddy?

RUTH. Don't be stupid! You know women cannot join.

SARAH. Why not?

RUTH. Because it's only for the men.

HUGH. In case we have to fight.

SARAH. For what?

HUGH. For the Empire.

SARAH. I don't see the need for it away out here.

RUTH. Who's been filling you head with talk like that?

SARAH. It's my own opinion.

HUGH. She's havin opinions now!

RUTH. That's what comes from too much talk.

HUGH. Well, here's an opinion for you: this here is British North America.
We're no republic yet.

SARAH. I'm sorry.

HUGH. It hurts me to hear you speak like that . . . (*A beat.*) Come here and
tell us one of your stories.

SARAH. Which one shall I tell you?

HUGH. Any one you like.

SARAH. I've a new one. It's about Ulster. I haven't heard it until I came
here. Isn't that strange? . . . It happened many years ago. One storm
night, after a fierce battle, Conor the King was feasting at the house of
his poet, Felimidh. A child was born to Felimidh's wife and . . .

RUTH. What story's this?

SARAH. The story of Deirdre of the Sorrows. Do you know it?

RUTH. I do not. Where did you hear that?

SARAH. At school once.

RUTH. I don't think so.

SARAH. It's about Ulster.

RUTH. I don't want to hear it.

SARAH. Why not, Ma?

RUTH. Because it's not in our heritage, Sarah.

SARAH. But we're Irish.

RUTH. Our ancestors were Scottish. We are Irish—but we're British too.

SARAH. And now we're living in Canada. So what does that make us?

HUGH. We're Scots Irish Canadian British subjects, Sarah. That's what we
are.

SCENE 9

Sarah alone. Music. Sound of war.

SARAH. Heritage
  A brand burned deep through skin of centuries
  Scarring forever
  The soul
  The land
  The memory
  The future
  Carried across deathbeds
  Across oceans to faraway lands
  Burning deep into the soil
  Blood in the veins
  And fire in the blood
  What fire!
  Sixty thousand miles from here
  Big guns go
  Boom boom
  Boom boom
  At Ypres[43]
  Canadians
  French
  British
  Irish
  All
  Defending the Empire
  Boom boom
  Sixty thousand miles away
  They harvesting and reaping and planting the dead
  Sixty thousand miles away
  From planting and harvesting and profit.

SCENE 10

Late summer 1915. The McCrea farmstead. Hugh is building a new barn.

SARAH. Ten cows now
    Twenty sheep
    And one hundred and ninety acres
    Planted
    Corn, oats, and wheat
    Farm laid out in a strict rectangle
    Wooden-frame house at one end
    Stable here
    Outhouse on this side
    Here—orchard
    That will grow apples, plums, cherries, and
    Peaches.
    There—vegetable garden
    Leeks, beets, carrots, potatoes, cabbages, grapes, melons, squash
    In front
    orange lilies in the memory walk
    sown from crease of the letter seeds from home.
    And now
    The barn.
HUGH. Here we go! One, two, three—lift!
SARAH. Progress.

Hugh shouts to his men (offstage).

HUGH. I need two more men on the back walk. Two, I said! You! And you!
    Come on, let's go.
SARAH. Men from Italy
    Doukhobours[44] and Ruthenians[45]
    Irish men
    Orange men
    To build the new barn
    Log on log
    Plank on plank
    Up and up
    Tower of Babel.
HUGH. You! Get me two ropes!

SARAH. Ready for harvest
    Ready to hold the wheat of
    Boom boom
    Wheat boom.

HUGH. No! Ropes, man! Ropes! Does anybody speak English here?

SARAH. Tap tap tap
    Whistle of saw through wood
    Rhythm of the future.

HUGH. All hands to the pump! Sarah! You know how to drive a nail home, don't ye?

SARAH. Yes, Daddy.

HUGH. Well, get to it. John! Reach me my claw hammer. Hurry up! I'm telling ye, no one's raised a barn so quick as this.

SARAH. My nail goes in
    Bang!
    South wall facing
    America.

Ruth enters.

RUTH. Sarah!

HUGH. She's helpin me.

RUTH. Indeed she's not. (*To Sarah.*) I thought I asked you to lift beets for the dinner.

SARAH. I'll do it now.

RUTH. Hurry up! There's eight hungry men to feed.

HUGH. D'ye know what I'll do when I've finished the barn? I'll dig out foundations for the stoan hoose. Would that please you?

RUTH. If we could afford to pay for it.

HUGH. We'll pay for it twice over with the way things is goin. Wheat prices is over one dollar a bushel. I reckon on near thirty bushels an acre. That makes near . . .

RUTH. A thousand dollars.

HUGH. Aye. Wi' taxes and all considered. That'll pay the note on the land and a bit besides.

SARAH. There's somebody comin up the road!

HUGH. Who is it?

SARAH. Mister Donaghue . . . And Michael!

RUTH. What're they doing here?

HUGH. Now! We have to be neighbourly. Donaghue's a polite, quiet sort of a fella. The Catholics here is of a differ'nt nature to the Irish ones.

RUTH. They're just as sleekit[46] here as anywhere.

Peter and Michael enter.

HUGH. Good day.

PETER. Good day to you. Are you well?

HUGH. Couldn't be better. Yerself?

PETER. Well enough. It's a scorcher.

HUGH. 'Tis that. You remember my wife, Ruth?

PETER. Missus McCrea.

RUTH. Mister Donaghue. How is Missus Donaghue?

PETER. Oh, fighting fit.

RUTH. Give her my regards, won't you?

PETER. She'll be pleased to receive them. This is my son, Michael.

MICHAEL. Hello, sir. Missus.

HUGH. We know him.

RUTH. Sarah, away and get those beets for me.

SARAH. Yes, Ma.

RUTH. Now!

Sarah moves a safe distance off, keeping eye contact with Michael.

PETER. Hard to work in this.

RUTH. The heat would kill you, so it would.

PETER. Looks like it (*The barn.*) is going to be a skyscraper.

HUGH. Biggest I know of in the township.

PETER. You must be expecting a good harvest.

HUGH. I've busted my back getting every acre I have broken and planted. I have hope.

PETER. Yes. 'S a fine place you have here.

HUGH. Three years of hard work.

PETER. Have you enough men?

HUGH. There's myself and young John, and Lightbody and Trimble there from the Lodge, and a couple of Russian fellas. The two Italians is bloody useless. (*Shouting offstage.*) No! Not that way! Turn it round! God's sake . . .

PETER. If you need any more pairs of hands, Mike and myself are willing. Aren't we, Mike? . . . Mike!

MICHAEL. What?

PETER. I said; we're willing to help.

MICHAEL. Yeah.

HUGH. That's very daicent of ye.

PETER. Ah well. We're all in the same boat out here, aren't we?

HUGH. We are indeed.

RUTH. I must away and get the dinner on.

HUGH. Will ye stay with us and have a bite?

PETER. If we're welcome.

RUTH. Of course you're welcome . . . Sarah!

SARAH. I'm doin it.

Ruth exits.

PETER. Where shall we start?

HUGH. Well, I could use another big man like yerself on the back wall and the boy here can help our John with the door frame.

PETER. You're the boss man. Got enough tools?

HUGH. Another hammer wouldn't go amiss.

PETER. There's one in the wagon. (*To Michael.*) Well, go on. Go and help John.

Michael exits.

HUGH. I think they've had disagreements.

PETER. That one disagrees with everybody—even himself.

The two men begin work.

SARAH. Tap tap tap
Noonday sun overhead
High

One wall raised
Another begins
I
Fingers scrabble through dirt
Pulling up from earth

Michael enters.

MICHAEL. Your brother's driving me crazy!

SARAH. What's he doin?

MICHAEL. He keeps whispering at me.

SARAH. What's he whisperin?

MICHAEL. Papist! Papist!

SARAH. Is that all? He's only teasin you.

MICHAEL. He's a fool. Twice he's belched in my face.

SARAH. I'll get him for you later if you like. I always get him back when he's sleepin.

MICHAEL. I can defend myself. If I could just take a swing at him, I'd crack that idiot grin of his.

SARAH. Then do it and stop talkin about it.

MICHAEL. Come away!

SARAH. I have to do this.

MICHAEL. Come on! Up to the river. We'll go swimming.

SARAH. It's all dried up.

MICHAEL. Come for a walk then.

SARAH. I have to do this.

MICHAEL. I can't work in this heat.

SARAH. D'you want to land me in trouble?

MICHAEL. Don't talk to me then, if you don't want to.

SARAH. I want to.

MICHAEL. Why is your barn so big?

SARAH. Because my father wants it to be.

MICHAEL. It's four times the size of your house.

SARAH. He's goin to build a bigger house. Out of stone.

MICHAEL. No one builds their houses out of stone here.

SARAH. It's what she wants. And what she wants she gets.

Michael exits.
The men working.

SARAH. Tap tap tap
  Build it up higher
  Passing hand to hand.

Hugh sips a mug of water.

PETER. It's a piece of work.
HUGH. We'll have filled it to the brim in no time.
PETER. That door frame's crooked.
HUGH. What?
PETER. That joint there. The upright is cut at a steeper angle than the crosspiece. See? The edges don't sit smooth together.
HUGH. I wouldn't have noticed that.
PETER. Until you tried to hang the doors. Then the whole frame would twist and leave a gap for the wind to come and blow away your wheat.
HUGH. Honest to God . . . Young ones allus does things in a hurry. (*Shouting offstage.*) John!
PETER. No use asking them to do it. May as well do it ourselves and do it proper.
HUGH. Aye.
PETER. The heat is surely blazing.
HUGH. Here. (*He hands Peter the mug of water.*) It's very good of you to help us out like this. You're good woodworker.
PETER. It was my trade before farming—one of them, anyway.
HUGH. How many trades have you had?
PETER. Carpenter, cooper,[47] railroad digger. And prospector.
HUGH. You were at Dawson City?[48]
PETER. Not for long.
HUGH. I wish I'd been there to see that. You find anything?
PETER. Not much gold. I was too late. Got a wife though.
HUGH. I've allus been a farmer. And my father and his father before him. Don't know nothing else.
PETER. My father had a small holding in Quebec.

HUGH. You give it up?

PETER. I've had enough of the place. It didn't exactly bless me with fortune.

HUGH. It's good to have a man of your experience around. If there's anything I can do for ye all's ye have to do is ask.

Peter hands the mug back to Hugh.
The meal.

SARAH. Broil, bake, and boil
    Midday heat
    Sit men table round
    Women dance attendance
    Bow heads
    Father says

HUGH. Let each man give his own thanks in his own way to his own God, whatsoever that may be.

SARAH. Then
    Feed them
    Fill them all up
    With meat and potatoes
    Spread before them
    Best china
    Clink

They each raise their glasses. The picture breaks.
Outside the house.
Emer enters and Ruth receives her.

RUTH. Sit down, Missus Donaghue and catch your breath.

EMER. Thank you.

RUTH. How did you get away over here?

EMER. I walked.

RUTH. You must be done out.

EMER. Not at all.

RUTH. Why don't you step into the house?

EMER. I will sit here.

RUTH. You'd be better off in the shade.

EMER. I will not go in. Thank you.

RUTH. Will you take a cup of tea?

EMER. I have no thirst for tea. How is Sarah?

SARAH. I'm helping too.

EMER. Good for you. The men shouldn't be allowed to think that they do all the work.

RUTH. Can I not even get you a wee drink of water?

EMER. All right. I'll take a cup of water.

RUTH. Right you be . . . Sarah.

Sarah goes to fetch the water.
Silence.

RUTH. So . . . How are you keeping Missus Donaghue?

EMER. Well enough.

RUTH. Your son and grandson have been very good til us today.

EMER. It's a modest wee house, isn't it?

RUTH. It does us.

EMER. I lived in a shanty much the same myself when first married.

RUTH. My husband is talking of a new house.

EMER. Men are always starting on one thing before another is finished.

Peter enters.

PETER. What are you doing here?

Emer holds out a food parcel and a bottle.

EMER. I brung you this—a bit of bread and cheese and a sup of milk to keep you going.

PETER. We have already eaten, Mother.

RUTH. Beef and potatoes.

PETER. Missus McCrea gave us a good dinner.

RUTH. Surely you didn't think I'd let them starve, Missus Donaghue?

EMER. (*To Peter.*) Take it—in case the boy gets hungry later.

PETER. You'll kill yourself walking about in this heat.

EMER. I will walk where I want to walk, when I want to walk it.

PETER. So you will. I'll not be concerned for you more.

EMER. Nothing to be concerned about.

PETER. How will you get home?

EMER. I will sit here and wait till you are done.

PETER. We'll be a while yet.

Peter returns to work.
The building continues.

SARAH. Rafter by rafter roof goes up
  Bang bang goes the hammer
  Each nail
  A hope
  A reason to stay
  Sun begins to settle
  Meeting land.

HUGH. It is finished.

SARAH. My father says,
  And starts his climb
  Sure-footed on shaky ladder
  To the top
  The very top
  Of the barn.

HUGH. Hello, Sarah!

SARAH. Hello!

HUGH. What a view!

SARAH. What can you see?

HUGH. The whole world! I believe I can see the whole world all the way
  back to Antrim. (*He waves.*) Afternoon, brother Henry! How ye doin?
  . . . I'm glad to hear it . . . Me? Oh, I'm just dandy now. Can't complain
  . . . The farm? Four times the size of your holdin and my barn's ten
  times the size of your'n!

Ruth enters, her hands cupped as if she is holding a jug.

RUTH. Get down from there before you fall and kill yourself, you old fool!

HUGH. What d'ye think, wife?

RUTH. That you'll fall and kill yourself.

HUGH. The barn?! The barn?!

RUTH. As good as any I've seen.

HUGH. Better, I think.

EMER. It's still only firewood—not a treasure house yet.

PETER. Mother!

RUTH. Are you thirsty?

HUGH. I could drink a river.

RUTH. Lemonade's all I have.

HUGH. That'll do.

RUTH. Come down and get it then. There's enough refreshment here for you and the men. Sarah will pour it out for you. (*She hands the "jug" to Sarah.*) Don't spill it now. There's just enough.

SARAH. Yes, Ma.

RUTH. Bring it back when you are done.

Ruth exits. Michael and Sarah alone.

MICHAEL. Look at you! A proper little Felimidh's wife. Dance with me, Ethne! (*He begins to dance with her.*)

SARAH. Michael, mind!

MICHAEL. Passing through the great hall, Ethne danced with each of the warriors . . .

The jug falls and shatters.

SARAH. Oh God! Oh my God! It's broke.

MICHAEL. It's only an old jug.

SARAH. Did anybody see?

MICHAEL. I dunno.

SARAH. So stupid! What am I goin to do?

MICHAEL. You can make more lemonade.

SARAH. No! . . . Quick! Pick the pieces up.

MICHAEL. Sarah, it's only a jug.

Sarah, distressed, tries to pick up the pieces.
Ruth enters.

Silence.

SARAH. I'm sorry.
RUTH. I told you to be careful . . .
SARAH. I know my granny gave it to you.
MICHAEL. It was my fault, Missus McCrea . . .
SARAH. It just fell out of my hand.
MICHAEL. I was messing about and I knocked into her . . .
SARAH. I'm really sorry, Ma.
MICHAEL. I'll pay for it.
RUTH. (*To Michael.*) Have you no work to do?

Michael exits.

SARAH. I'm really, really sorry.
RUTH. All right. Don't make a song and a dance out of it.
SARAH. Maybe my granny'll send you a new one if you ask her.
RUTH. I carried it with me the whole way here.
SARAH. Maybe we can stick it back together?
RUTH. It won't be fixed now.
SARAH. I can try.
RUTH. No. It's broken . . . Let it alone.

SCENE 11

Hugh sowing seeds. Music.

SARAH. Spring
     Year of our Lord
     Nineteen hundred and sixteen
     Arctic blast cold chill from the north
     The ploughing begins
     And
     Father scatters seeds in the big pasture
     Good grass sown from the seeds of home
     And it grows
     Letter from home tells

More warriors in battle
Red Hand defending Ulster
Green Hand defending Ireland.
Rise up all
Defending
Heritage.

SCENE 12

June 1916. The pasture by the water. Michael reads from a copy of "The Worker's Republic"[49] *newspaper. Sarah enters.*

SARAH. Hey boy! What're you doin?

MICHAEL. I thought you were my father.

SARAH. Skivin[50] are ye?

MICHAEL. Taking a break.

SARAH. I went up to the house. Your granny says to give you this.

She hands him a bottle of milk from which he drinks.

MICHAEL. Thanks.

SARAH. What're you doin out digging on a Sunday?

MICHAEL. Peter says we're behind on the sowing.

SARAH. Remember the Sabbath day to sanctify it.

MICHAEL. Honour thy father and thy mother that thy days may be long upon the earth which the Lord thy God giveth thee. I know my commandments as well as you.

SARAH. You might make a priest, but you'll never make a farmer.

MICHAEL. Good! If I have to stay here the rest of my life I'll go mad.

SARAH. Where else would you go?

MICHAEL. Toronto or maybe St. John. They're building three factories a day in the East.

SARAH. You can go only if you promise to take me with you.

MICHAEL. It is my geis.

SARAH. For I have no desire to marry Robert Milling and spend the rest of my days wedded to my cousin.

MICHAEL. I hate him.

SARAH. You hardly even know him . . . He's asked my da to start courting me as soon as I'm sixteen.

MICHAEL. What do you say?

SARAH. I say no.

MICHAEL. He's a good catch for a girl like you.

SARAH. What do you mean, "a girl like me"?

MICHAEL. He's gonna be a lawyer. You could live in a big house in the city, have fancy clothes and a motor car.

SARAH. I don't want a motor car.

MICHAEL. Don't have one then.

SARAH. And I don't want Robert Milling.

MICHAEL. Then don't have him either.

Silence. Sarah picks up the newspaper and begins to read.

SARAH. "We must accustom ourselves to the notion of arms, to the use of arms. Bloodshed is a cleansing and sanctifying thing, and the nation which regards it as the final horror has lost its manhood."

MICHAEL. Isn't it marvelous?

SARAH. Isn't it marvelous? No. It's a load of old horse manure if ever I heard one.

MICHAEL. You can't say that!

SARAH. I'll say it again if you like. Patrick Pearse[51] is talking a load of old horse . . .

MICHAEL. Give it back!

SARAH. No.

MICHAEL. It's mine.

SARAH. It should be torn up into squares for the outhouse.

MICHAEL. Give it back now!

SARAH. Come and get it.

MICHAEL. You're being a child, Sarah.

SARAH. Oh, who's the big man now? Have it back. I don't want it.

MICHAEL. Thank you.

SARAH. Thank you.

MICHAEL. Stop it!

SARAH. Stop it!

A beat.

MICHAEL. This is about freedom. You wouldn't understand.

SARAH. Then don't talk to me any more.

MICHAEL. I'm an Irishman.

SARAH. You're as Irish as the grass in the big pasture—the seed may have come from Ireland but the soil it grows in and the rain that waters it is Canadian.

MICHAEL. I know more of Irish history than you do.

SARAH. I was born there.

MICHAEL. I speak Irish.

SARAH. I was born there.

MICHAEL. You don't have to be born in a country to belong to it.

SARAH. You're father says you're a Canadian and he should know.

MICHAEL. Each generation for the past three hundred years has risen up to free our land of the British. It's tradition.

SARAH. It's murder. Another commandment broken.

MICHAEL. Your lot started it all, bringing guns in and killing Catholics in their beds at night.

SARAH. My lot?

MICHAEL. I'm sorry.

SARAH. Leave me alone.

MICHAEL. Come on.

SARAH. Get away from me, you . . . you . . . Fenian![52]

MICHAEL. It's only play.

SARAH. You can't call it play when you get so worked up about it.

MICHAEL. Deirdre was raised as Conor commanded. Every day she grew more beautiful as Cathbad has foretold.

SARAH. I'm not an idiot.

MICHAEL. One day when it was snowing and cold as cold, Deirdre was watching her foster father preparing a young calf for the table. As he flayed the skin from its carcass, blood flowed out across the frozen snow and a raven circled overhead, ready to drink from the stream.

SARAH. "I could love a man like that," said Deirdre, "With hair raven black and skin as white as snow and cheeks as red as blood."

SCENE 13

November 1916. The Donaghue farmstead.
Emer ushers Sarah in from the cold.

EMER. Mihal's not here. He's gone to a meeting of the parish men with
   his father.
SARAH. May I wait for him?

A beat.

EMER. Step in and keep the cold out.

Emer returns to her sewing. Sarah offers her a cake.

SARAH. I brought you this. It's butter-pound.
EMER. Thank you. We are not big cake eaters in this house. I'm surprised
   your mother let you out on a night like this.
SARAH. I'm on my way back from an errand to the Trimbles.
EMER. She doesn't know that you have come here?
SARAH. No.
EMER. Sit by the fire and warm yourself.
SARAH. Thank you.
EMER. You shouldn't walk the roads in such snow.
SARAH. I told Mike I would come. He said he'd teach me the set dancing.[53]
EMER. What would you be wanting to learn all that for?
SARAH. He thinks I should know it. What do you make?
EMER. Nothing in particular. I sew for its own sake.
SARAH. It's beautiful.
EMER. It's a pretty pattern.
SARAH. I'm a terrible needle-worker. My mother says I've a hand like a
   foot.
EMER. It's the eye that's important. A long as you can see, you can sew.
SARAH. Then I must be blind too.
EMER. Here. (*She hands Sarah the cloth.*)
SARAH. I'll ruin it.
EMER. No matter, it's only cotton. It can be ripped out and started over
   again.

SARAH. What do I do?

EMER. Hold the needle like so.

SARAH. That's not the proper way. Only what's comfortable . . . Is that better? Follow this line here . . . That's it . . . Now, turn the stitch like so . . . Ah! . . . (*She demonstrates.*) A little too big. See? Like this.

SARAH. I'm no good at all.

EMER. All it takes is a bit of practice. Keep on with it. (*She hands Sarah back the needle.*)

EMER. How is your mother?

SARAH. Well, thank you. Though she always gets sick for home comin into the winter.

EMER. I've been here twenty years and I still sicken for it.

SARAH. Why did you not go back?

EMER. I met my husband—a good Irishman—and he wanted to stay. We cleared our land, raised our children. There was nothing left to go back for.

SARAH. Except to see it again.

EMER. Here. Give me your hand. The one on which you will wear your wedding ring . . . We used to do this when I was a girl. It tells your fortune. Put your hand out flat.

Emer rubs the needle three times against the side of Sarah's hand then lets it dangle over the center of her palm.

SARAH. It circles.

EMER. That means you will have a boy. And again. (*She repeats the process.*)

SARAH. Another boy.

EMER. Two sons is a good start. (*And a third time.*) It swings. That's a girl. It's good to have one girl. (*This time the needle is still.*) No. No more. Oh well, two boys and a girl is not bad at all.

Peter and Michael enter.

SARAH. Good evening.

PETER. What are you doin out on a night like this?

SARAH. I came to have my dancing lesson.

MICHAEL. Sorry we're late.

PETER. Dancing is it?

MICHAEL. I'm gonna teach Sarah the set dancing.

EMER. I don't see what she needs to know all that for.

PETER. No better way to keep warm. (*To Sarah.*) Have you been made welcome?

EMER. Of course she has. Do you think me unmannerly? I will make the tea.

SARAH. I brought you a cake.

MICHAEL. Thank you. May I eat it now?

EMER. There's plenty here for you to eat.

SARAH. Your granny was telling my fortune with the sewin needle. I'll have two boys and a girl, she says.

MICHAEL. They will be well provided for with a lawyer for a father.

EMER. What's the news?

MICHAEL. Conscription![54] All the talk is of conscription. If it comes to it, I'll not go.

PETER. Easy. It hasn't happened yet. But you should've heard them flapping and quacking away like ducks as usual!

MICHAEL. Better to be quacking now than shot in the head later.

PETER. Better a clear and reasoned head, Michael. (*To Sarah.*) What do you think?

SARAH. Of conscription?

PETER. That's what I asked you.

SARAH. They need soldiers.

PETER. Would you go?

SARAH. I can't.

MICHAEL. Dad . . .

PETER. Imagine.

SARAH. I wouldn't.

PETER. Why not?

SARAH. Well, I don't understand it all, but . . .

PETER. Good answer.

MICHAEL. Give me your coat.

Peter moves Emer's chair.

PETER. We'd better clear the floor if we are to have dancing.

EMER. I don't see the call for all this fuss.

PETER. If he is to teach her then he must teach her properly.

MICHAEL. Right. I'll show you. Pretend we're standing in a circle. You're opposite me like this. Now, I'll show you the basic steps. (*Slowly.*) And one and two and three and cut and back and back and one, two, three, four . . . See? . . . Now you dance to me.

Sarah makes an attempt.

MICHAEL. No. Come down on your heel at the last like this.

SARAH. I'm no good at all.

MICHAEL. It's easy once you practice. I'll do it with you.

He guides and they dance.

PETER. And one and two and three and cut . . .

EMER. I'll show her. It's better a woman shows a woman how to do a woman's steps.

MICHAEL. No! (*To Sarah.*) Now I dance round you . . . And you dance round me.

SARAH. How am I doing?

PETER. You've got the spirit of it.

Music fades it.
Michael and Sarah take each other's hands.
Slowly, they start turning each other.
The dance quickens.

EMER. What're you doin, Mihal? . . . Careful!

PETER. Give them space!

Breathlessly, they stop.

MICHAEL. What do you think? Am I a good teacher?

SARAH. You are.

PETER. It was fine, wasn't it, Mother?

EMER. Those weren't the right steps.

PETER. It's only a start. Only a start.

Music.
Sarah and Michael dance, beautifully, fluidly together.
Blackout.

ACT 2
SCENE 1

December 1916.

SARAH. First nip of winter in the air
    Down to the city we go
    To bring in the supplies
    To take John to war
    Quiet under starlight
    We creep
    Out of the house
    Children curled up in arms
    And into the wagon
    Horses clip-clop on heavy earth
    Passing by
    Sod huts of the Doukhobours
    Passing through
    At six road ends
    Township of Stanley
    Lot 42
    Grist mill
    Saw mill
    Merchant shop
    Two churches
    Schoolhouse
    Orange Hall
    Passing through
    Passing along
    Long deserted roads that will soon be flowing rivers of mud
    Then frozen under snow.

Knife wind cuts through on the plains
Stretching out on all sides
Ocean of land
Morning wakes up
Before us lies
City on the horizon
Queen of the Plains
Regina
Capital of our province.
Slowly we haul into
Huge and heaving mess
Of mills
Factories
Shop fronts just opening up.
Big engine belching steam
Green carriage new and shiny
Not to carry our cheap wheat
But our men.
Whistle blasts
One two
One two
And he is gone
My brother John
Not yet seventeen years
Off to fight the enemy
Sixty thousand miles away.

SCENE 2

December 1916. Department store, Regina. Ruth and Sarah are buying cloth. Above, a sign reads "No Ruthenians employed here."

SARAH. He'll be all right, Ma.

RUTH. Do you think so?

SARAH. Look how happy he was getting on the train—he was dead proud of himself.

RUTH. Pride'll be no shield to him. I wonder at your father letting him go like that.

SARAH. Ma, he wanted to go.

RUTH. Thousands of them dead already.

SARAH. Our John'll not let anybody kill him. He told me he was comin back with a German's helmet as a souvenir.

RUTH. Have you all the bags?

SARAH. Aye.

RUTH. Shoes . . . shirts . . .

SARAH. What does that sign mean?

RUTH. It's to discourage the immigrants seeking work. How many boxes of that liquorice did you lift?

SARAH. Two.

RUTH. I said three. We'll have to go back to the confectioner's.

SARAH. Why don't they want them?

RUTH. Because there's too many of them and they've no English. Now, material for the winter dresses.

SARAH. How many do we need?

RUTH. Let's see. You and I are of a size. I'd say that's twenty yards. Mind now, we only have fifteen dollars to spend.

SARAH. But Daddy give you near sixty dollars.

RUTH. Shh! Do you want everybody to hear?

SARAH. How about this one?

RUTH. Too gaudy.

SARAH. This one?

Emer enters, unnoticed by Ruth.

RUTH. Too expensive. This one here is good, but not so warm. Oh, well. We'll just have to wear extra layers. If only you were able to help me, but you're like a spider weaving its web with a needle in your hand.

EMER. Hello, Sarah.

RUTH. Missus Donaghue.

EMER. Missus McCrea. I see we all have the same idea today.

RUTH. It's that time of year.

EMER. Now that is a pretty fabric.

RUTH. I was just saying that.

EMER. Poor quality though. But sure, when you haven't much you must make it go further.

RUTH. Isn't that so. Sarah. We'll take the velveteen.

SARAH. I thought it was too expensive.

RUTH. Not at all! It'll be far warmer to wear. This one's more of a spring fabric—I told you that. We'll take that one.

EMER. 'Tis a lovely job of work, dressmaking. I had no daughters to sew pretty dresses for. No granddaughters neither. Only big strapping boys in our stock. Ye have no sons yourself?

RUTH. Four, as you know. The oldest, John, is just left for the war.

EMER. That must distress you sorely.

RUTH. He goes to his duty. So we must be proud of him. I wonder at your grandson's not going.

EMER. I do not . . . Now this here is a fine material. Good heavy winter cloth. Only two dollars a yard. I think I shall have myself twenty yards of it. Good day to you, Missus McCrea.

RUTH. Good day.

EMER. Good day, Sarah. I'll be seeing you again soon, no doubt. (*To Ruth.*) Your daughter and my grandson, Mihal, are friendly, you know.

RUTH. They are acquainted, I believe.

EMER. Oh, not just acquainted, but thick—very thick. We can't keep them apart. Good day again.

Emer exits.

A beat.

RUTH. You go up to that woman's house?

SARAH. I've been there.

RUTH. Often?

SARAH. Several times.

RUTH. What would your father say if he knew?

SARAH. What's the harm in it?

RUTH. Harm? (*More quietly.*) Making love to a . . .

A beat.

SARAH. I'm making love to nobody.

RUTH. Your father a leading member of the Order.

SARAH. I know that.

RUTH. With a . . . for a son-in-law! What are you thinking of?

SARAH. Mother, people will hear you.

RUTH. Don't tell me to be quiet!

SARAH. I didn't.

RUTH. This would never happen at home. Your grandfather wouldn't let the like of this go on, I'm telling you.

SARAH. Are we takin that there material or this one?

RUTH. You would know all about it if your grandfather were here.

SARAH. For God's sake, Ma . . .

RUTH. You thank heaven we are in a public place . . . Never swear at me!

SARAH. All right.

RUTH. And never—ever—go there again. Do you hear me? There's an end to it.

SCENE 3

June 1918. The pasture.

SARAH. Spring nineteen hundred and eighteen
    Awakens us out of frozen sleep.
    America turns its hand
    To a different plough
    War machine
    To dig it up
    Churn it up
    Europe
    More guns
    More mines
    More dead
    All along the Western Front
    Boom boom
    Boom boom

Wheat fields on the boundary between the Donaghue and McCrea farmstead. Peter and Hugh enter.

PETER. It was a hard frost last night.

HUGH. Very hard for June.

PETER. You're planted early.

HUGH. At Easter.

PETER. I wait until these few trees are in full leaf. The spring warmth is deceptive.

HUGH. There's some damage done, I think.

PETER. It usually comes now. Think you've got a good crop and then it's gone.

HUGH. The weather here is surely differ'nt to home.

PETER. May I take a look. (*Peter examines a head of grain.*)

PETER. Red Fife.

HUGH. I suppose you planted Marquis?[55]

PETER. It withstands the frost better. Gives a better yield.

HUGH. Everybody's all Marquis wheat these days.

PETER. It's hard to keep up.

HUGH. Oh, I keep up all right. I bought me a new plough and two horses there a month or so back.

PETER. On loan?

HUGH. Aye, but I have doubled my acreage this year.

PETER. I got a new seeder.

HUGH. On loan?

PETER. No, bought it outright. The head's glassy, that's a tell-tale sign, and see, there's the white ring circling the stalk.

HUGH. It's ruined then?

PETER. Maybe. Maybe not.

HUGH. We'll pay the note back. We will. If wheat prices continue to hold at the two dollars.

PETER. You must strip the heads and quick about it.

HUGH. Where do I cut?

PETER. At the first joint below the head. See? I'll give you a hand.

HUGH. You can spare the time?

PETER. I won't finish this today. I seem to have lost my helper again.

HUGH. It's hard when they don't take after you.

PETER. They must go their own way. You're shorthanded yourself.

HUGH. I hired me a few men. One from the Ukraine and a Doukhobour boy. I get twice as much work done myself in a day than the two of them together.

PETER. They will not play the servant here.

HUGH. Bolsheviks—the lot of them! And argue over pay terrible. I miss my John. But we will have him back for harvest if God spares him.

PETER. You'd word from him, I hear.

HUGH. Yesterday.

PETER. Good news that he is safe.

HUGH. We thought we had lost him. He was wounded at Vimy.

PETER. That's—honourable.

HUGH. Aye. He's a brave lad. How is it that your boy doesn't go?

PETER. He just has his own mind.

HUGH. His own?

The pasture. Sarah and Michael lie together.

MICHAEL. Naiose and his brothers undertook brave missions for the Scottish king.

SARAH. Deirdre kept a veil over her face at all times, lest the king see how beautiful she was.

MICHAEL. And the king wondered what lay behind the veil.

SARAH. One morning, before the day had woken up, the king's steward stole into the brother's encampment. Coming upon the lovers asleep in an embrace . . .

MICHAEL. His eyes fell upon the face of Deirdre and he wept, so beautiful was she. "Most beautiful lady, the King of Scotland loves you. He asks you to leave this warrior and come to be his wife."

SARAH. "I will not go with you," she said. "For I am promised to another."

MICHAEL. Close your eyes.

SARAH. Why?

MICHAEL. Just do it.

He presses a strawberry to her lips. She bites into it.

SARAH. Strawberries!
MICHAEL. I grew them myself.
SARAH. I thought the frost had killed them all.
MICHAEL. Not these ones. Are they sweet?
SARAH. No. But not bitter neither. Taste.

Michael kisses her.
Wheat fields on the boundary between the Donaghue and McCrea farmstead.
Peter and Hugh working.

PETER. How much is rotted?
HUGH. About half.
PETER. I'm sorry.

A beat.

HUGH. Those boys over in Winnipeg have it all sewn up.
PETER. We must stick together. I wonder that you don't join the League of Farmers.[56]
HUGH. We never had such things in Antrim. Sure we had meetings, but not organized demonstrations.
PETER. And that's why you're farming wheat in Canada now instead of flax back home.
HUGH. It smacks of socialism to me.
PETER. What else are we to do? The government's sympathy lies not in people, but in profit.
HUGH. We must all get behind the war effort. That's what I told our John.
PETER. If the new settlers want to go, let them go. They are still wedded to the old country.
HUGH. You don't back the war.
PETER. Oh, it's not just the war that bothers me. Let them fight it—it's a just enough war. It's this conscription business I don't like.
HUGH. You Catholics is all opposed to it.

Silence.

PETER. Nothing to do with being Catholic. Canada's a nation on her own, free to fight her own wars, not the rest of the world's.

HUGH. That's Fenian talk where I come from.

PETER. Where you come from, maybe. Here, it's just progress . . .

The pasture. Sarah and Michael lie together.

MICHAEL. "You must leave Naoise and come willingly to the king as his bride or be taken away by force and your lover and his brothers slain."

SARAH. "I will not go with you," she said. D'you know what would go beautiful with these just now?

MICHAEL. What?

SARAH. Silverwoods'[57] ice cream. You ever had it?

MICHAEL. Not Silverwoods'.

SARAH. When we first came to Toronto we ate Silverwoods' ice cream.

MICHAEL. When Naoise returned that night she told him of the King of Scotland's treachery.

SARAH. "We must leave Scotland."

MICHAEL. So away they fled, fugitives adrift on the sea once more . . . I've never been to Toronto.

SARAH. Never?

MICHAEL. Never.

SARAH. Look at me! I'm covered.

They kiss.

SARAH. Little seeds pop pop popping
   Sweet like sugar cane
   Sugar sweet little strawberry kiss
   Flutter-belly
   Like jumpin off high tree into stream.
   Hands grapple my hands.
   Arms holdin him
   Fingertips pressing into my shoulder
   Hands on my hands, my legs
   Hands up and under my skirt to my
   Belly.

So close
Skin on skin
His touch
Feather soft
Oh, he is beautiful!
Scent of his hair all meadow-perfume
Eyelash tickle on my cheek
This is not a bad thing.
I bury myself
I rise and fall on him
Like the big ship on the ocean.
Bad?
Not bad,
Not me. Never.
Between my legs he rests
And his hair is soft as hay
Like good hay sown from the grass seed
Scent in the crease of the letter from home.
No.
Not home.
This is home.

SCENE 4

June 1918. The McCrea farmstead.
Sarah, Hugh, and Ruth.

RUTH. What's lost?

HUGH. All—except forty acres.

RUTH. What's to be done?

HUGH. The oats will be all right. We'll have to make oor money ootay those. The building of the new hoose will hae to wait a while. (*To Sarah.*) You've been goin up to the Donaghue house.

SARAH. So I have.

HUGH. Often?

SARAH. Only once or twice.

RUTH. Didn't I tell you not to go up there?

SARAH. You did.

RUTH. I warned you.

HUGH. Hush, Ruth. (*To Sarah.*) I don't like it that you see Michael Donaghue so much.

SARAH. I don't see him often.

RUTH. Yes, you do.

SARAH. He's a neighbour.

HUGH. No one's telling ye not to be neighbourly. Just break the habit of seein him alone.

SARAH. Why?

RUTH. Sarah!

HUGH. No . . . It's a straightforward enough question. (*To Sarah.*) I dinnae like his father's politics.

SARAH. His father never talks about Ireland.

HUGH. Whatever he thinks about Ireland is his own concern.

SARAH. Then what is it?

HUGH. They're republicans, through and through.

SARAH. They're Canadians.

HUGH. That's the same thing in my book.

SARAH. No it's not.

HUGH. Are you contradictin me? . . . I'll have nae truck with republicans.

A beat.

SARAH. All I'm sayin is, Da, this here's a new country. You're always tellin us that.

HUGH. There's some things that shouldnae be forgot.

SARAH. More that shouldnae be remembered.

HUGH. Where does she get these notions from?

RUTH. Where do you think?

SARAH. I get them from myself.

RUTH. (*To Hugh.*) You've brought it on yourself.

HUGH. (*To Sarah.*) It turns me to think of you with him.

SARAH. He's my friend.

RUTH. I hope friends is all it is.

HUGH. Ruth . . .

RUTH. Well, is it?

SARAH. Friends is all.

RUTH. I've never made friends with a Catholic in my life. Their bigotry is too much.

SARAH. Michael's people are good, kind people, Ma.

HUGH. Better see him no more in future.

SARAH. I can't just stop speakin to him, Daddy!

RUTH. You'll do as you're told to do.

SARAH. He's my friend.

HUGH. All right. Ye've done nae wrong. He's only your friend and that was fine while youse were children, but youse are near grown now. Things are differ'nt when you're grown.

SARAH. I don't see how.

HUGH. Because people is all differ'nt! . . . D'ye understand?

SARAH. I understand.

HUGH. There now. Ye willnae see him again, sure ye won't?

SARAH. No.

HUGH. D'ye promise me?

Silence.

HUGH. See him again and I'll be hard on you. D'ye hear me?

SARAH. I hear.

HUGH. Come on! There's plenty more young men to take your fancy, eh? There's young Robert Milling, soon to be a lawyer like his father and his grandfather before him. He still pays you attention.

SARAH. I thought it was unnatural to marry a cousin.

RUTH. It could be worse.

SCENE 5

Autumn 1918.

SARAH. Fall
    Leaves on gold fields
    War no more

Germany
Turkey
Austria
All fall down
Bow to righteous Empire
No more
Boom boom
Armistice
End.

Ruth enters, with a sheet in her arms. She rocks her son, John, to sleep.

SARAH. Half come home of those who went
    And some of them are only half of what they were
    Brother John returns
    But not to harvest
    Hollow as reed
    Pale as milk
    All a-tremble
    Screamin terror
    Sweat-lashin
    She rock-a-byeing him in her arms
    Sayin—
RUTH. There, there, my son. You're all right now. You're home.

SCENE 6

November 1918.
The pasture by the water.

SARAH. He saw men lyin dead.
MICHAEL. And killed too.
SARAH. I expect so. He won't say more about it.
MICHAEL. Things can start moving in Ireland again. There'll be elections for the new parliament next month. We'll be a republic before Christmas.

SARAH. Don't talk to me about that. It's all anyone can speak of now—
you, my father . . .

MICHAEL. Where'd you say you'd gone?

SARAH. Into Stanley for cotton.

MICHAEL. That's not a good lie.

SARAH. They'd never think I'd lie to them so one lie's as good as another.

MICHAEL. I don't like sneaking about like a criminal.

SARAH. Then don't come and meet me any more.

MICHAEL. Take your hair down. I like the look of it that way.

SARAH. . . . Look above. What a sight!

MICHAEL. Sharp shins[58] going south. All the way down to Florida.

SARAH. There's thousands of them.

MICHAEL. They're flying high.

SARAH. Means a hard winter.

MICHAEL. Wouldn't you just love to be away up there with them?

SARAH. Why don't we go?

MICHAEL. Where?

SARAH. Toronto—like you said.

MICHAEL. I'd go to the United States. There's farms to be had out west.

SARAH. Think again. You're no farmer.

MICHAEL. Toronto it is, then.

SARAH. When'll we go?

MICHAEL. In the springtime, after the planting.

SARAH. Why not today?

MICHAEL. Today it is then.

SARAH. What'll we do there?

MICHAEL. Go to the Silverwoods' dairy.

SARAH. We could get married.

MICHAEL. What do you mean?

SARAH. What I said.

MICHAEL. We can't do that.

SARAH. Who says?

MICHAEL. If we don't pray in the same church together we can't marry.

SARAH. I think we've done worse than pray together, Mike.

MICHAEL. I know that.

SARAH. So I'm to give you all this for nothing?

MICHAEL. It's not for nothing, I hope.

SARAH. You tell me. All's I know is I have given you all of me . . . Do you love me?

MICHAEL. Sarah . . .

SARAH. Tell me.

MICHAEL. Yes.

SARAH. Say it. (*A beat.*) What's the matter? I can say it. I love you. Michael Donaghue! I'd tell anybody.

MICHAEL. Taím i ngrá leat.[59]

SARAH. In English.

MICHAEL. I love you. Now you say it in Irish.

SARAH. Taím i ngrá leat.

MICHAEL. That's terrible!

SARAH. To hell with the Pope!

MICHAEL. Shh! Sarah, don't say that.

SARAH. Why not? He can't hear me.

MICHAEL. You're a rebel, d'you know that? You're a hardened revolutionary, Sarah McCrea.

SCENE 7

Spring 1919. The McCrea farmstead. Hugh and Ruth wait. Sarah enters.

HUGH. So, you're returned.

SARAH. I am.

HUGH. Where'd ye go?

SARAH. Out walking across the fields.

HUGH. On your own?

SARAH. You know I wasn't. She saw me.

RUTH. Who do you call "she"?

HUGH. Ah Sarah, Sarah . . . What did I tell ye?

RUTH. Remember what you said, Hugh.

HUGH. (*To Sarah.*) What possessed you? After all we talked about?

RUTH. Hugh . . .

HUGH. I know what I said. (*To Sarah.*) What did I say til ye?

SARAH. That I was to walk out with Michael Donaghue no more.

HUGH. But you did so?

SARAH. I did.

HUGH. Sarah . . .

RUTH. Headstrong, she is!

HUGH. All right! I'm tryin to talk til her.

RUTH. Talk til her?! How many times have you talked til her?

HUGH. Will ye leave it in my hands?

RUTH. She cannae carry on like this. You're the one said it . . . Soft!

HUGH. Soft am I, now?

RUTH. No. Weak. Do you hear me? Weak! You backed up arguing with Henry over your share of the land being willed away to Henry . . .

HUGH. Don't start on that again, Missus! My father was dyin.

RUTH. No matter. You backed up and let the land go, making yourself no better than a hired hand.

HUGH. Christ, ye have to go back years!

RUTH. Don't curse!

HUGH. Ye allus have to go back years, every bloody difference we have!

RUTH. Bringing us away out here to make a something out of nothing.

HUGH. To make us a fortune.

RUTH. To live in a sod hut, break our backs and lose a child! And not a word have I ever spoken . . .

HUGH. You say plenty. In words and in looks—always downin me.

RUTH. I only ever worked to raise you up.

HUGH. Shut your mouth now!

RUTH. I tell you this and I tell you no more: you give in to this one here tonight and you'll surely have a Fenian for a son-in-law. Now either you do what you said you would or I'll do it myself.

Silence.
Hugh undoes his belt.
Music.

HUGH. (*To Sarah.*) Come here to me, you.

SARAH. He says.

But it is he who moves toward me.

And I look into my father's eyes

I want to say,

"No, Daddy. Don't beat me and I will never see him again."

But the words do not come

They cannot.

A draft creeps in under the door, around my ankles and up under my skirt.

I say to myself

It is his touch

In the big pasture

When I ate strawberries and kissed him

My mouth full of the sweet taste.

He grasps the belt

I hear her draw breath.

RUTH. Now you'll listen.

Sarah. She says.

First crack of pain

Flying forwards

Left arm across my chest

Winded

Flying backwards

Slam onto table

I close my eyes

I make no sound

He is breathing hard

Second, third, fourth crack come down across my spine

He stops

After each blow

Waiting

For a tear, a plea, a cry

I give him nothing.

RUTH. Enough now.

SARAH. I hear buckle clunk on floor

He grabs me by shoulders
Throws me backwards
We are dancing
And one and two and three and cut
Hitting me now with hand open
Bang on this side of the head
Bang on the other
Round and round we go

RUTH. Enough now. Hugh!

SARAH. Against the wall
Against the door
Against the floor
Under table
Tumbling on back
Feet chase me to the other side
Hands drag me up again
And bang on this side of the head
And bang on the other
And bang in the face
Mouth fills with thick salt taste.
She is screaming now

RUTH. Stop! Stop!

SARAH. And back and back and fall to the floor . . .
It is cold
Soothing
The little ones are at the doorway
I can hear them
Cryin.

Ruth shouts to the children offstage.

RUTH. Go up to bed now, the lot of you. Upstairs this minute or I'll give youse all something to cry about. (*She crosses to Sarah.*) Sit up.

HUGH. You don't see him no more.

Silence.

RUTH. Sarah?

HUGH. D'ye hear me?!

RUTH. She hears you. She hears you.

Sarah remains lying on the floor.

SCENE 8

Spring 1919. Donaghue farmstead.

PETER. A man maybe he goes exploring. He comes across something good, rich—a big diamond ring, say. "I'll have that for myself," he says. Now what do we call that?

MICHAEL. I'm late already.

PETER. Then be late. When it comes to a good piece of land, we call that pioneering. Now this pioneer gets caught red-handed by the man was there before him—the owner. But our pioneer y'see, he doesn't want to back off, so he fights the owner, beats him back or kills him.

EMER. How's Sarah?

MICHAEL. I don't know.

PETER. Finally, our pioneer, he looks at this beautiful gold ring and he thinks to himself, "What use is the ring to me like this?" So he melts it down, breaks the big stone into little pieces, sells it off and makes a profit.

EMER. (*To Michael.*) Have you had a falling out?

MICHAEL. No.

PETER. Now the previous owner might see that as destruction . . .

EMER. (*To Michael.*) That's good.

PETER. . . . But to the settler that's progress.

MICHAEL. And that's what happened in Ireland.

PETER. And what are we doing here except farming land that never belonged to us?

EMER. It's not the same thing at all, Peadar.

MICHAEL. This country belonged to land agents.

PETER. And before them?

MICHAEL. You didn't fight the Indians for the farm, Peter.

PETER. No. The French took the land from the Indians and then the English took it from the French. There were a few Dutch mixed up in it somewhere, too. Whichever way you look at it, I bought a little piece of the diamond. So what do you want to do, Mike? After I'm dead, you want to trek up north to the reservation, find the chief, and give him the deed to the farm?

MICHAEL. No.

PETER. No?

MICHAEL. All right then, yes! Yes I do.

PETER. Good for you! That's integrity. But which one of the Plains owns it? The Metis,[60] or is it the Cree or the Alongquipin?[61]

MICHAEL. I'll give it to them that originally owned it.

PETER. They all owned it one time or another.

EMER. It's only meetings. (*To Michael.*) Go on now.

PETER. I've heard whispers that there's more planned than talk.

MICHAEL. What've you heard?

PETER. That they've been burning barns over near Hamilton.

EMER. He'd never get mixed up in all that.

MICHAEL. That was in retaliation for—

PETER. If you're going to fight, do it out in the open.

MICHAEL. For an attack on a Catholic farmer's livestock by a group of Loyalists.[62]

PETER. None of this jumping about in shadows.

MICHAEL. You're sounding like McCrea.

PETER. We don't disagree on everything.

MICHAEL. He beats her.

EMER. For friendship with you?

MICHAEL. He tells her that if I go there, she will suffer for it.

PETER. That's hard.

MICHAEL. What do I do about that then, father?

EMER. Just what you are doing—let it go.

MICHAEL. Tell me, honest.

PETER. Is she a good girl, Michael?

MICHAEL. I believe it.

PETER. Does she believe the same of you?

MICHAEL. More than I believe of myself.

PETER. Then if you want her, take her to you and let no one come between.

Michael crosses to where Sarah lies on the floor, picks her up and holds her.

SCENE 9

Autumn 1919.

SARAH. Day to day
    Small army marches farm to farm
    Harvesting
    They come
    Bagging-hook[63] and basket armed
    Under blue so big
    Hazy heat broods over
    Red wheat splashed white with barley
    All hands to
    Reap and bind and bale
    Scalded green lies the plain
    Fruits of the earth in their season
    Gathered in
    Safe in the big barn it lies
    And thank we all our God
    But we do not live by bread alone
    Not us

The Harvest Fair, township of Stanley.
Sarah joins Ruth at the McCrea Barrow.

SARAH. For now comes
    The fair
    Cold sunshine
    Sweet breeze
    Apples pears plums
    Taties carrots cabbages

> Barrow by barrow
> All in a row
> Our barrow
> Butter and eggs.

RUTH. Twelve dollars and forty-eight cents.

SARAH. Is that all?

RUTH. Enough to buy a few bits of groceries for the winter.

SARAH. Swarm

> Stanley
> Six road ends
> Do I hear
> Trading
> Twelve dollars
> Twelve
> Fourteen dollars
> Do I hear
> Fourteen
> Clydesdales
> Apaloosians
> Fourteen
> Ponies
> Steers
> Stallions
> Street running
> Up and down
> Sixteen dollars
> Eighteen dollars
> Eighteen
> Do I hear
> Twenty
> Twenty dollars
> Black stallion
> Eighteen hands high
> Rearing.

Hugh enters.

RUTH. Well?

HUGH. They're sold.

RUTH. How much?

HUGH. Twelve dollars each.

RUTH. That'll not pay even interest on the note.

HUGH. Look, missus I know that, but the two animals was near done out. Donaghue has offered me for the pasture land—six hundred dollars.

RUTH. We must sell the machinery.

HUGH. Who'll buy it? Samuel says that he'll make us a loan if we need it.

RUTH. We cannot take it.

HUGH. What would you do? Starve.

RUTH. You've accepted, then? (*To Sarah.*) Go and give two pennies each to the boys for spending. Tell them not to be wasting it.

HUGH. I've told Robert Milling that you'll dance wi' him the night.

SARAH. Why?

HUGH. What d'ye mean, why? Because he asked me and I said yes.

SARAH. I don't want to go to the dance.

HUGH. Aye, ye do! Girls love the dancing.

SARAH. Ma?

RUTH. She's tired, Hugh. We've been working all day.

HUGH. After all the Millings have done for us?

RUTH. That doesn't make a match.

HUGH. (*To Sarah.*) In the name of God, just dance wi' the fella.

RUTH. Let her alone, Hugh.

HUGH. I've told him now.

SARAH. So I walk with him
    My cousin
    Heavy arm on my shoulders
    Organ grinding rusty tune
    Round roll-a penny booth
    Round merry-go-round
    Up and down
    Swing boats

Pull on a rope[64]
And up we go
And down down
Sick I am
His chimney breath
Choking me
I will not dance with you
Says I
You will, says he
And lifts me up
And so it begins
Turning me
Burling me
Round and round
'Til I can hardly stand
Never mind
Place one foot in front of the other

Michael enters.

MICHAEL. Enjoying yourself?

SARAH. Do I look like I'm enjoyin myself?

MICHAEL. That's a handsome young man you've got there.

SARAH. He looks like a pig.

MICHAEL. Now you must have him if Daddy says you must.

SARAH. I will not have him.

MICHAEL. I think you will.

SARAH. Dance with me.

MICHAEL. No . . . Here?

SARAH. Yes, here. Why not here?

MICHAEL. No.

SARAH. Why not?

MICHAEL. All right then. When Conor the King heard of the lovers' flight, he said . . .

SARAH. "Let them return to Emain Macha."

MICHAEL. He sent Fergus, a warrior of honour, and his own son, Cormac, to meet them.

SARAH. But on the way he laid a trap for them. What's that smell on you?

MICHAEL. Nothing.

SARAH. Smoke.

MICHAEL. We were burning up the chaff yesterday is all.

SARAH. James Lightbody's hay rick was burned last night.

MICHAEL. Was it? Conor the King ambushed the lovers and a bloody battle raged.

SARAH. Naiose was slain but not before he had slit Cormac's throat and killed him.

Hugh breaks them apart and dances Sarah off.

HUGH. Isn't he some dancer now? Shift you! (*To Sarah.*) What're you doin? Heh? What?

SARAH. I'm only dancing.

HUGH. D'ye know what he is?

SARAH. No. What is he, Daddy?

HUGH. Don't try an' make a fool out of me.

SARAH. I'm not the one doin that.

HUGH. You will dance with Robert Milling.

SARAH. I won't.

HUGH. By Christ, I'll kill ye.

MICHAEL. Mister McCrea!

HUGH. Get away from me. Get away and stay away.

SARAH. Mike . . .

HUGH. Shut up!

MICHAEL. I'm telling you, Mister McCrea.

HUGH. Somebody better go quick and get this wee bastard's da.

RUTH. Now Hugh, there's people looking.

MICHAEL. I'm no bastard.

HUGH. Aren't ye? That's no' what I heard. I heard your mammy was a travellin stage hoor who'd been tossed by every man up the Klondike.

Michael goes for Hugh. Peter rushes in and stops him.

PETER. Mike!

MICHAEL. Did you hear what he said?

PETER. Let him have his opinions. It makes no difference to me.

HUGH. Right, big man, get this wee fella of yours to hell's gates or I'll send him there myself.

PETER. Let's go, son.

HUGH. And keep him away from me and mine.

PETER. He goes where he wants. I put no rein on him.

HUGH. Well you tether him or I'll leather him! You, thinking so much of yerself. So right about all things.

MICHAEL. Did you hear what he said? Do something!

PETER. What would you have me do, Mike?

MICHAEL. Defend us.

PETER. Against what? Ignorance?

HUGH. D'ye think? I know all about you. And I'm telling you, I'll not have my line soiled with that.

MICHAEL. Damn you!

RUTH. Sarah, come here.

EMER. Hugh McCrea! Hugh McCrea, take your hands off my grandson . . . There'll be no more of this. (*To Michael.*) Get over here now and stand beside me. Sarah, go to your mother.

HUGH. Keep out of this!

EMER. I will not.

HUGH. I do not want to lay eyes on this young Fenian near my daughter in the future.

EMER. If you would listen a moment.

HUGH. Tell the oul woman to shut up!

EMER. I'm no oul woman . . .

HUGH. Look, Missus. This isn't an argument for you.

EMER. Oh be quiet man, I'm agreeing with ye. I certainly want no more of my blood mixed in with your sort. One of your lot was enough.

PETER. If you shame me in public, mother . . .

EMER. You can do that with no help from me, standing there letting this Puritan talk to you like a child. It's the two of you that's at fault. You let it run on too long. Do you see what happens? If I thought a marriage would come out of this . . . Mharaodh se me. An glsoiseann tú méa, Mhicil?[65]

PETER. Don't blackmail him.

EMER. Do you understand me? I want an end to this business. Here's what will happen. Michael will keep away from Sarah. I will see to it if I have to chain him to my wrist, I'll see to it.

MICHAEL. Mamo.

EMER. I didn't ask you to speak. What a carry on this is! And if he doesn't keep to it, then we will send him away to work.

PETER. Am I allowed to speak?

EMER. Indeed not. Sure what have you ever said that's any use at all? (*To Hugh and Ruth.*) The rest is your concern. There will be no more lending of tools or helping hands or even a word spoke between us from this day on. Fair enough?

HUGH. Fair enough.

EMER. Good. (*To Sarah.*) Now you, go home with your mother and father and do as they tell you.

Sarah exits and Ruth follows her. Emer brandishes her walking stick at Hugh.

EMER. That girl you have's a fine, clever, honest, young woman. And if I hear you've been less than good til her, I'll come after you and rattle your skull for you, Hugh McCrea.

SCENE 10

Spring 1920. Night.
Sarah waits, hidden.
Michael enters.

SARAH. Hey! Donaghue!

MICHAEL. Sarah? Where are you?

SARAH. Over here . . . You're getting warmer . . . Warmer . . . Hot . . . Hot . . . Hot!

MICHAEL. What are you doin here?

SARAH. Aren't you pleased to see me?

MICHAEL. Your father'll give you the gears.

SARAH. He'll be home late and he'll be full. There's a lodge meeting tonight.

MICHAEL. My grandmother'll kill the both of us.

SARAH. I had to come . . . What's happened to you?

MICHAEL. Nothing.

SARAH. Don't give me nothing Mike, you're hurt.

MICHAEL. I got into a fight.

SARAH. Who with?

MICHAEL. Your sweetheart, Robert Milling.

SARAH. He's no love of mine.

MICHAEL. And John.

SARAH. John?

MICHAEL. Them and a few others. They sort of bumped into me coming out of the meeting.

SARAH. Meeting? Ah, Michael!

MICHAEL. Just a meeting. Only a meeting.

SARAH. Were they drunk?

MICHAEL. Stone, cold sober. "What sort of meeting's this?" Johnny boy says. So I told him. "Youse are raisin money to buy guns for murderers," he says. Then they laid into me—feet and all.

SARAH. I'll gut him! I told you nothing good would come of all this Deval, Davel, De Van—

MICHAEL. De Valera.[66]

SARAH. Aye, whatever his name is.

MICHAEL. You should've seen it, Sarah! One of De Valera's right-hand men. He fought right beside James Connolly[67] in the Uprising. He reloaded his gun for him. The room was packed wall to wall. I had to pull myself up onto a table to stop myself from getting crushed. You should've heard him! "Ireland has tirelessly struggled for her freedom since the hour she was first put in chains. Now . . . our day has come at last! A parliament has been set up, the true government of the free nation of Ireland. The organisation of which you are member has set up a committee to arm the Defenders of Ireland. I see young men in the room and it fires my blood. Young exiled sons of Ireland, do not despise your youth. Young comrades in Canada, join us in our struggle . . ." You're not listening to me.

SARAH. I am.

MICHAEL. Sarah, he was right there in the room with me.

SARAH. He's just a man, Mike, like any other . . . I'm listening.

MICHAEL. And we all stood up and waved our fists in the air and someone stared singing, "A nation once again, a nation once again! And
Ireland long a province be a nation once again."[68]

SARAH. My father says the Bolsheviks are taking over the whole world.

MICHAEL. Loyalist bastard!

SARAH. Don't call him that.

MICHAEL. You're defending him?

A beat.

SARAH. Will you come tomorrow to the stream?

MICHAEL. Sarah . . .

SARAH. Will you come?

MICHAEL. Yes . . . Go home.

SCENE 11

The same night. Outside the Donaghue farmstead. Emer waiting. Peter enters.

PETER. Mother, come inside. It's too cold to be standing about.

EMER. I'm warm enough,

PETER. The doctor said . . .

EMER. A Dhía dhilis! Only a cough and a splutter.

PETER. Mother . . .

EMER. There's nothing to worry about, Peadar.

A beat.

PETER. I told him to be back here before midnight.

EMER. He's of age. He can do as he wishes.

PETER. Where did he go?

EMER. Into Stanley for a . . .

PETER. A meeting! Another meeting. I told him!

EMER. It's good for him to be interested.

PETER. In what? Getting himself killed? . . . Joseph Trimble's bull was found lying in a ditch with its throat slit last night.

EMER. Who'd do a thing like that?

PETER. And what about these fire-settings?

EMER. Families feuding . . .

PETER. It frightens me.

EMER. It's only meetings.

A silence.

Michael enters.

MICHAEL. Mamo. You should be in bed.

EMER. And so should you. Where have you been until this hour of the night?

MICHAEL. I told you. Into Stanley.

EMER. You were told to be back before midnight.

PETER. To do what?

MICHAEL. To meet with friends. Mamo, I'm a man.

PETER. We're calling them friends now?

EMER. You're not so grown yet.

PETER. I thought we agreed no more meetings?

MICHAEL. You may have done so.

EMER. Go to your bed!

PETER. You know what kind of a district we live in?

MICHAEL. I won't be ordered to bed, Mamo.

EMER. Now you listen to me, Mihal . . .

PETER. Mother, let me talk to him.

EMER. What's happened to you?

MICHAEL. I got in a fight coming out of the meeting is all.

EMER. God in heaven!

PETER. Who with?

MICHAEL. Some of the lodge men . . . John McCrea.

PETER. For God's sake, Michael!

MICHAEL. I gave back as good as I got.

PETER. And that's what worries me, Michael. That's what worries me.

MICHAEL. It's only meetings.

EMER. (*To Peter.*) It's only meetings.

PETER. He doesn't tell me where he goes when he leaves the house any more. He doesn't even lower himself to lie about it. Now . . . Now, this!

EMER. That's what happens when you let them run free.

PETER. I know the fault lies with me: leaving him to you for all these years to go filling his head with romantic nonsense about the Old Country and coffin ships and martyred rebels. Now he's going to get himself . . .

MICHAEL. She only told me my history.

PETER. That's not history!

EMER. What more should I expect from a man who hasn't been to mass this past twenty years?

PETER. I will not attend the church that refused to recognize my marriage.

EMER. How could it? With all that she was? How could it?

PETER. Well, I recognize it and to hell with you and the Pope and anyone else who doesn't!

MICHAEL. Leave her alone!

EMER. Godless! That's what you are . . .

PETER. You want him to get himself killed? That's what you want?

MICHAEL. I won't get myself killed, Peter. Don't you worry about me.

PETER. Be quiet, boy! Be quiet!

EMER. Mihal, it is only meetings?

PETER. Only meetings? (*He pulls Michael by the coat, toward Emer.*) Smell! Smell it?

Emer smells the coat.

EMER. Smoke.

MICHAEL. I wasn't smoking, Mamo. Honest.

PETER. You want him to kill himself?

Emer's coughing fit returns.

PETER. Mother . . . I'm sorry . . . Come inside, will you? Come.

EMER. (*To Michael.*) You will not go any more.

MICHAEL. Mamo . . .

EMER. You will not go.

MICHAEL. You can't tell me that.

Michael exits.

EMER. Mihal! I haven't finished yet. Michael! Don't walk away from me.
Mharaodh se me. An glsoiseann tú méa, Mhicil?

SCENE 12

Spring 1920. Day. A graveyard. Michael and Peter stand at Emer's graveside.
Sarah enters.

SARAH. Lord, have mercy.[69]

MICHAEL. Christ, have mercy.

SARAH. Lord, have mercy.
Ding dong
Snaky procession black through stones grey
Open earth
To swallow it up
Seed of life
Departed
Will not grow again.

PETER AND MICHAEL. Lord Jesus Christ
Deliver souls of all faithful
From pains of hell and deep pit

SARAH. Mumble word jumble
This is the sign of the cross.

SARAH, PETER, AND MICHAEL. Amen.

SARAH. Silent staring stands he
Through fingers running memory dust

PETER. May hell not swallow up
Nor may they fall into darkness

SARAH. Shovel it all in
Dirt

PETER. Eternal light shine upon her

Holy light once promised to Abraham and his seed

SARAH. Slap backslap

shake handshake

MICHAEL. Eternal rest grant her

With your saints

Forever.

For you are Merciful, O Lord.

SARAH. Bye.

Goodbye.

Peter exits. Sarah approaches Michael.

SARAH. Is it all right that I came? . . . Where's your father gone?

MICHAEL. To start the planting . . . Someone will see you.

SARAH. . . . For a full year, Deirdre did not smile or speak or lift her head to look upon the faces of those who had killed her beloved. Her heart was broken and nothing would mend it . . .

MICHAEL. We killed her.

SARAH. It was the influenza, Mike.[70]

MICHAEL. Go home.

SARAH. Conor the King sent Deirdre away to dwell with the evil . . .

MICHAEL. Stop!

SARAH. On the way she hurled her body from the chariot into the way of a huge boulder and was slain . . . Finish it.

MICHAEL. You know the ending.

Silence.

MICHAEL. The true friends of Deirdre and Naoise claimed her body and gently laid it in the earth next to her lover. In time . . . In time . . .

SARAH. I can't stay here . . . Come away with me, Michael.

MICHAEL. I have work to do here.

SARAH. What work? . . . It's finished, Michael . . . In time two yew trees grew up from out of their graves and did not cease to grow until their branches entwined.

MICHAEL. You can't go without me.

SARAH. Then I will go with you.

Silence.

MICHAEL. I love you.

SARAH. Where?

MICHAEL. Toronto . . . When?

SARAH. Tonight.

MICHAEL. Not tonight.

SARAH. Why not? When?

MICHAEL. I will come for you. Tonight. I will come for you tonight. I promise.

SCENE 13

Spring 1920. Night. The McCrea farmstead.

SARAH. I lay sleep-drifting, dreaming of
Toronto-we-will-go
And calico
And Silverwoods' ice cream.
He comes calling up at my window.

MICHAEL. I have come, true to my geis.

SARAH. He says.
We strawberry kiss and I says, he says . . .
Strange scent
Oven bread
Who would be baking bread this time of night?
Sleep
Silverwoods' dairy . . .

MICHAEL. Sarah!

SARAH. I am sure
Calling
Under my window

MICHAEL. Come!

SARAH. Crystal clear.

    I come . . .

    Quiet.

    Too quiet.

    No dog-bark.

    Through night eyes

    I see

    Shadows moving in shadows

    Men of the night: masked men

    Light at the window

    Bright not moonlight

    Orange

    It is old but it is beautiful

    Crash of glass smash on wood.

HUGH. Jaysus!

SARAH. Rattle, rattle, rattle, bedsprings

    Thud trip bang bang

RUTH. What's there?! Who?!

SARAH. Smell of

    Bread burning

    Smell of

HUGH. Fire! Fire in the barn! Fire!

SARAH. Awake I am and

    Running

    Out into the nightmen night

    Frozen I

    Eyes on fire

    I see

    Our barn roaring flames

    Doorposts of my brother's burning

    Rafters of the lodgemen snapping

    Little shingle where my nail went in

    Crashing down into

    Burning, popping grain.

I see

Mother father oh mammydaddy water dancing

PETER. And one and two and three.

Michael appears, dancing to the beat of a drum.

SARAH. And splash

And back and back

And one, two, three, four

I hear

Singing

A man singing.

Is he?

No screaming.

I see

In the fire

Man

Orange man

Leaping

Flinging arms updown

Crackle crackle crackle jig

I know who he

Can't be

Smell of smoke on topcoat

Can't be

Sweet strawberry juice on my lips

Toronto and Silverwoods' ice cream

Splash him down

Oh mammydaddy

No

Please God

No

Hands grasp shoulders hurling me back

No

I will go forward

Break through hands
To see
I see
Black burning skin like potato leaves
Crumble into ashes

EMER. That destroyed Ireland—
SARAH. His granny said.

Hands white
Waxy white mash melting
Under red burned blood
Charred all through to the bone
Feet still jig-dancing
Muscle blackened meat, all spoiled.
His hair
Sour
Sour smoke rising
His no lips gasping fear-wide eyes.

Hugh tries to douse the flames with a blanket.

HUGH. Come on boy, breathe!
SARAH. No.
HUGH. Don't look at him.
RUTH. Sarah, come away with me into the house.
SARAH. Come back to me.

Dance! D'ye hear me?
Get up to your feet and dance!

SCENE 14

After the fire. The McCrea farmstead.
Ruth tries to comfort Sarah.

HUGH. (*To Sarah.*) He wasn't on his own. I saw two or three more runnin
away. D'ye know who it was?
RUTH. How's she going to know that?

HUGH. Well, she knew him didn't she? She knew him. (*To Sarah.*) Will you answer me?

RUTH. Leave her in peace, Hugh.

HUGH. No one ever razed a barn so quick as that.

RUTH. We can build another barn.

HUGH. With what? Ashes?

RUTH. (*To Sarah.*) You'll be all right.

HUGH. Everything I have. My whole. And she sits there and will not speak to me.

RUTH. Leave her alone. (*To Sarah.*) What're you crying for?

HUGH. She's cryin for him.

Ruth faces Hugh.

RUTH. Leave her alone now, I tell you. (*To Sarah.*) There now. You'll be all right . . . I know . . . The Lord is my shepherd, I shall not want. He maketh me to lie down in green pastures . . . [71]

SARAH. No more.

RUTH. He leadeth me beside the still waters . . .

SARAH. Mine

Black ashes

All mine

Shouldn't be forgotten

None can redeem

RUTH. I know.

SARAH. Dubadum

No more

RUTH. He restoreth my soul . . .

SARAH. Boom boom.

RUTH. He leadeth me in the paths of righteousness . . .

SARAH. Kentucky coffee

Sassafras

Sugar maple

Twisting strange boughs

RUTH. I will fear no evil . . .

SARAH. Entwined
>   Knife wind
>   Cuts through
>   It is cold

RUTH. My cup runneth over . . .

SCENE 15

Early morning. The open fields of Saskatchewan. Music.

SARAH. Bitter
>   Not me
>   It is old
>   Old
>   So old
>   Not beautiful
>   Sharp shins wheeling
>   Turning
>   Will I
>   Home
>   Not home
>   Not beautiful
>   No more
>   Shouldnae be remembered
>   Boots heavy sludge through
>   Heavy clay soil
>   Sun bleeds
>   Awake
>   Township of Stanley
>   Six road ends
>   Which
>   Nearly day

THE END

Notes

1. Wheat Boom: Associated with the early settlement of the Canadian plains; during the period 1896 to the outbreak of World War I, wheat became central to the Canadian economy.

2. Deirdre: The story of Deirdre and Naoise in Irish mythology is the equivalent of the Romeo and Juliet story. These two star-crossed lovers die tragically. This story weaves its way throughout *Heritage*.

3. geis: One's fate.

4. Derry: Michael uses the Catholic Republican name of the city.

5. Londonderry: Sarah uses the Protestant Nationalist world for the city.

6. Conor mac Nessa: This is a continuation of the Deirdre and Naoise myth.

7. Brethren: A reference to the Protestant Orange Order that was strong in Canada at this time.

8. Twelfth: The Twelfth of July commemorates the triumph of the Protestant King William III of Orange over the Catholic James II in the Battle of the Boyne in 1690. In Northern Ireland, this anniversary is celebrated yearly.

9. to that one: Hugh is a younger son and his father's estate has gone to his elder brother. Ruth resents this.

10. Red Hand Knight of Ulster: The Red Hand is the symbol of Ulster based on Irish mythology.

11. Mihal: Emer uses the Irish name for Michael.

12. eighteen forty-nine: This is the famine time in Ireland.

13. coffin ships: During the Potato Famine, so many people died on board Atlantic crossings from Ireland that the ships became known as coffin ships.

14. The Great Hunger: The time during the Potato Famine from 1845 to 1852 became known as the time of the Great Hunger.

15. Translated from the Irish: You remember all this, Michael. (In the continuing conversations between Emer and Michael, there are references to Michael's absent mother, who was probably British and Protestant. Emer also warns Michael about becoming too close to Sarah.)

16. trans.: I will remember, Grandma.

17. Young Irelanders: The Young Ireland Movement of the 1830s was a political, cultural, and social movement that sought to change the perception of Irish nationalism. The activist Daniel O'Connoll sought to repeal the 1800 Irish Act of Union with Great Britain.

18. trans.: You couldn't tell him anything.

19. trans.: What are you talking about?

20. trans.: No matter, son.

21. trans.: I want to know.

22. trans.: She was married before.

23. trans.: Was she?

24. trans.: There was no talking to him either; but I warned him. His father warned him.

25. trans.: What do you mean? Tell me, Grandma!

26. trans.: Ask your father.

27. trans.: He never tells me anything.

28. trans.: What do you mean?

29. trans.: It's better she doesn't come here again.

30. trans.: Why?

31. trans.: Be careful of what you are doing, Michael.

32. trans.: Goodbye, Grandma.

33. trans.: Goodbye, son . . . God in Heaven!

34. Dubadum: Sarah is imitating the sound of a lambeg drum, a very large drum used in Orange Parades celebrating the Twelfth of July.

35. It is old . . . they are fine: This is a lyric from a traditional Orange Order song; it is from "The Sash My Father Wore."

36. The royal orange lily-o!: Another Orange Order song.

37. King Billy . . . parade: The Orange tradition has a man portraying King William/King Billy riding on a white horse.

38. With ting and toot and crash . . . old Derry's walls: Another Orange song that refers to the Protestant apprentices of Derry protecting the city from the invading forces of James II.

39. the field: After the celebrations and parades of the Twelfth, families would go to a large field for picnics and patriotic speeches.

40. Sir Edward Carson: The leader of the Ulster Unionist Party, Lord Carson (1854–1935) was the champion of Ulster Protestants and the anti-Home Rule Campaign that sought to preserve the union with Great Britain.

41. Home Rule: The movement that sought an independently governed Ireland, separate from Great Britain.

42. Oh God, . . . ages past: Among the Protestants of Northern Ireland, this is a dearly beloved, patriotic hymn.

43. Ypres: The Second Battle of Ypres in World War I, 1915, established the Canadians as a great fighting force.

44. Doukhobours: An immigrant religious group who rejected many traditional church orthodoxies. Pacifists, they chiefly came from Russian territories of Eastern Europe.

45. Ruthenians: Another group of immigrants to Canada, the Catholic Ruthenians came from an area of Eastern Europe populated by Slavs.

46. sleekit: Sly, deeply untrustworthy.

47. cooper: Someone who makes or repairs casks or barrels.

48. Dawson City: In the Canadian province of the Yukon, Dawson City was a central site of the Klondike Gold Rush.

49. The Worker's Republic newspaper: This newspaper was a vehicle for the Irish Republican cause; it ran articles by James Connolly on guerilla warfare and also articles that attacked the Irish Volunteers for their inactivity.

50. skivin: Avoiding work.

51. Patrick Pearse: A poet-patriot, Pearse was one of the leaders of the Easter Rising of 1916.

52. Fenian: A person dedicated to the establishment of an independent Irish Republic. Sometimes used negatively to denote an Irish Catholic.

53. set dancing: A popular form of Irish folk dancing based on quadrilles.

54. conscription: Compulsory enlistment for active duty in the armed services of a country.

55. Red Fife and Marquis: Red Fife is a type of winter wheat. Marquis is a sturdy hybrid wheat developed in Canada.

56. League of Farmers: Saskatchewan was a largely agrarian province in early Canadian history. The Farmer's Union of Canada, founded in 1921 by former members of One Big Union, a radical union founded in 1919, sought to better farm conditions in Canada. The reference is McCartney's nod to this labor movement in Canada.

57. Silverwoods: This famous dairy in Toronto, Ontario, Canada operated in the early twentieth century.

58. sharp shins: A variety of hawk.

59. trans.: I love you.

60. Metis: Descendants of marriages of Cree and other indigenous peoples to Europeans. They are officially recognized as one of the three aboriginal peoples of Canada.

61. Cree or the Algonquipin: First Nation and native tribes of Canada.

62. Loyalists: People in Northern Ireland who are loyal to the British Crown.

63. bagging-hook: A large sickle or reaping hook used to harvest grain.

64. round roll-a penny booth . . . pull on a rope: These are early carnival and fairground amusements.

65. trans.: It would kill me. Do you hear me, Michael?

66. De Valera: Ěamon De Valera was the American-born first president of the Republic of Ireland.

67. James Connolly: Union organizer and Irish patriot, a leading Marxist theorist of his day, shot by a British firing squad for his involvement in the Easter Rising (the Uprising) of 1916.

68. "A nation once again . . .": An early Irish nationalist song.

69. Lord, have mercy: The translation of the Kyrie. During this scene, parts of the Roman Catholic funeral mass are heard.

70. It was the influenza, Mike: In 1918, the flu pandemic swept the world, killing approximately fifty million people. It lasted from September 1918 to June 1919.

71. The Lord is my shepherd . . . : The twenty-third Psalm.

Courtesy of the author

Eileen Kearney, PhD, has been a leading Irish theatre scholar and director since the 1980s, when her rediscovery of the playwright Teresa Deevy prompted years of publishing and lecturing about bringing Irish women playwrights into the limelight. Currently an instructor of theatre at the University of Colorado Denver, she also taught at Pomona College, the University of Texas at Austin, and Texas A & M University. She has been cited by the Kennedy Center/American College Theater Festival for excellence in directing. Before her academic career, she acted in New York and Los Angeles. She is also an award-winning knitter and weaver of fiber arts in the Irish tradition.

Photo by Ashna Graves, 2012

Charlotte Headrick, PhD, is a professor of theatre at Oregon State University. She has directed numerous Irish plays and premieres of Irish plays nationwide, including several in this volume, as well as the Turkish premiere of *My Name Is Rachel Corrie.* She has published widely on Irish drama, focusing on plays by women. She is the recipient of the Kennedy Center Medallion for outstanding service to the Kennedy Center/American College Theater Festival. A member of Actors Equity, she continues to act as well as direct.